Skip·Beat!

Skip·Beat!

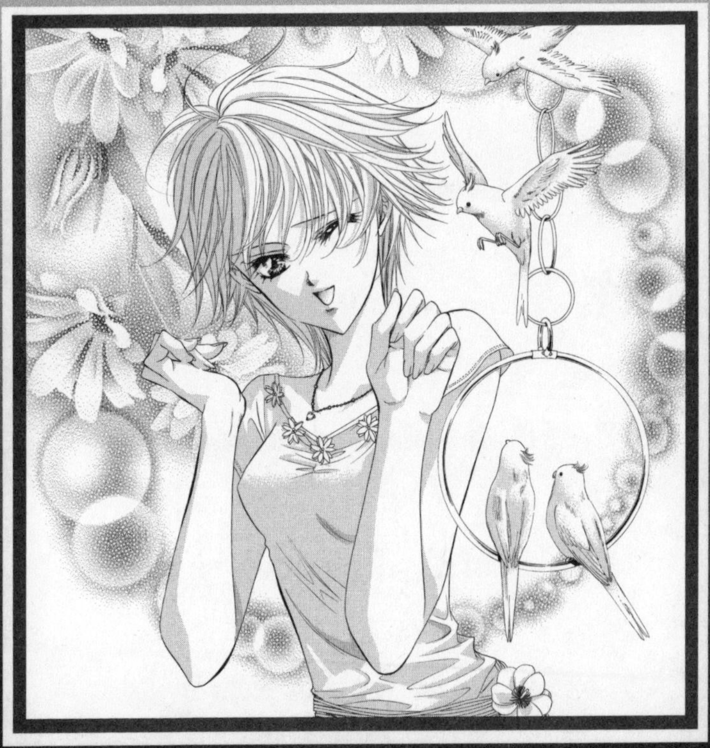

4

Story & Art by Yoshiki Nakamura

Shojo Beat

Skip·Beat!

Volume 4

CONTENTS

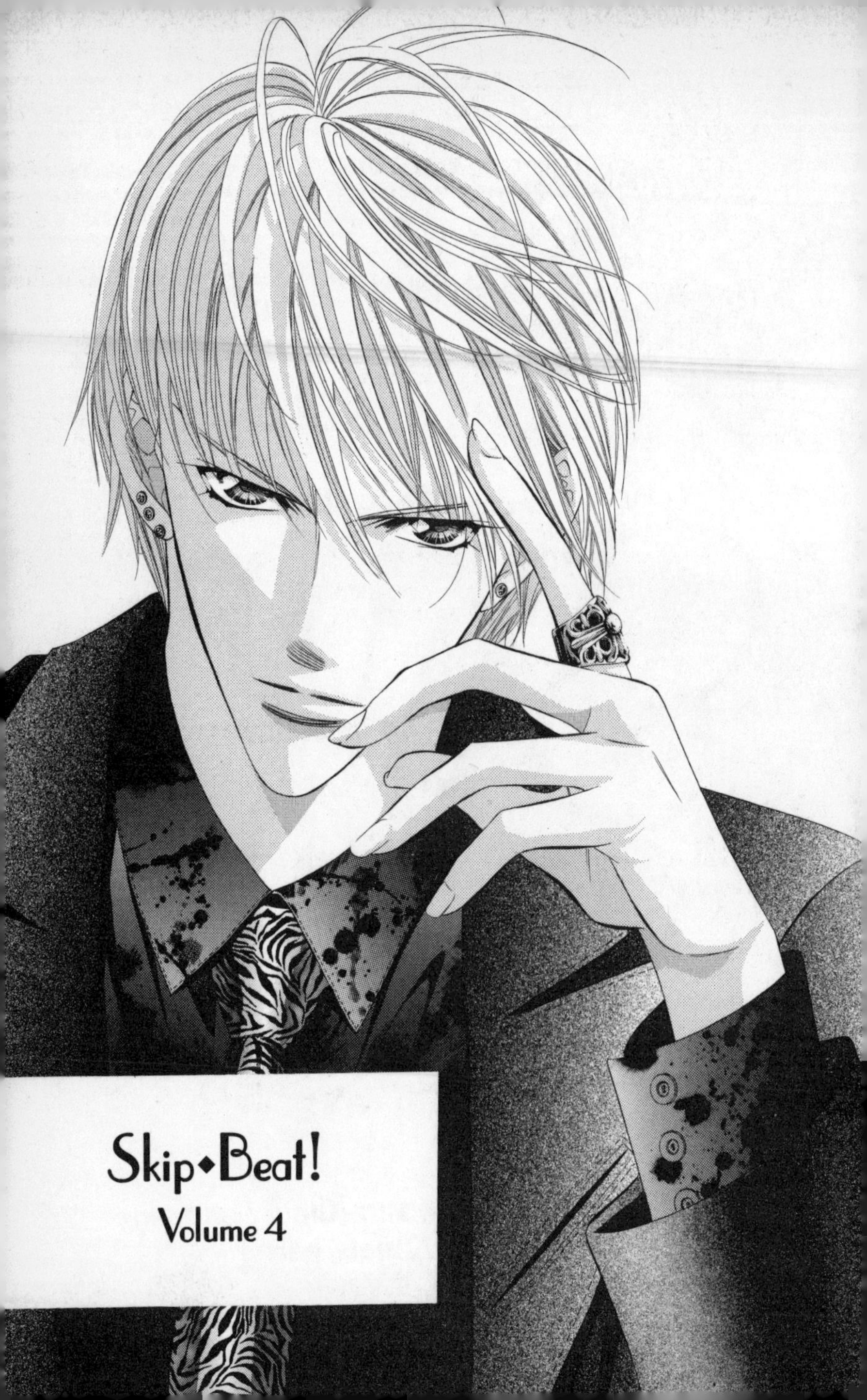
Skip•Beat!
Volume 4

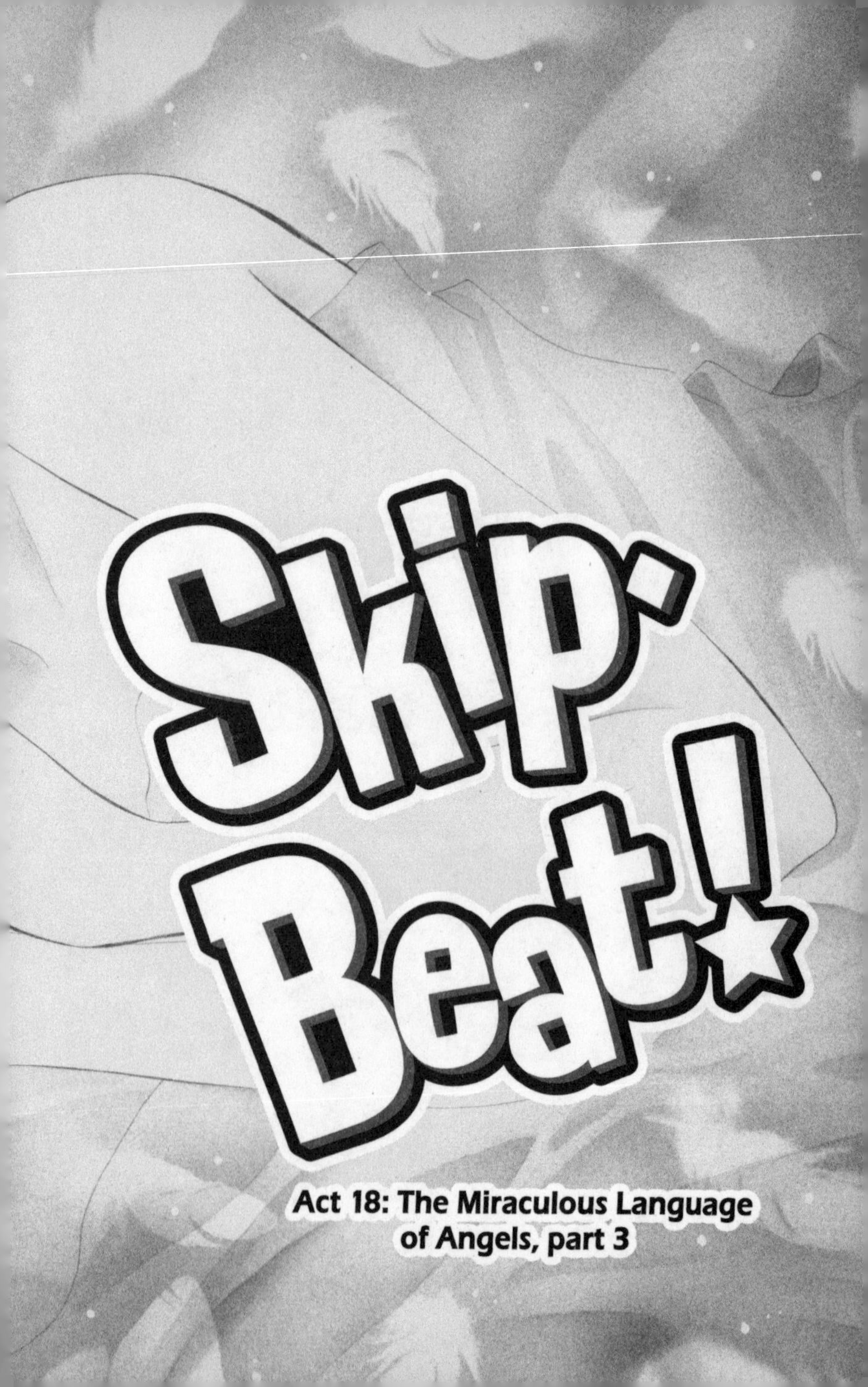
Skip Beat!

Act 18: The Miraculous Language of Angels, part 3

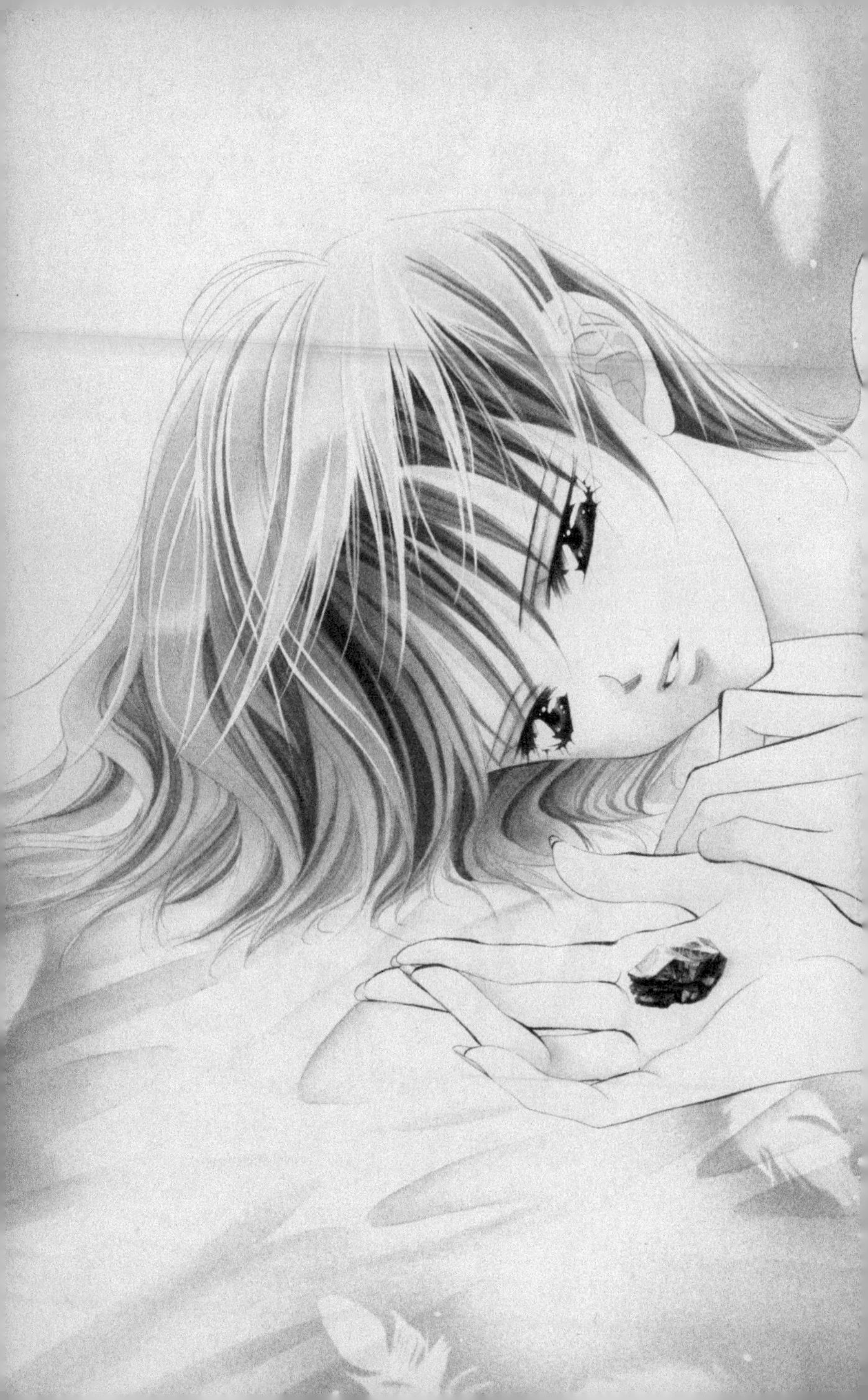

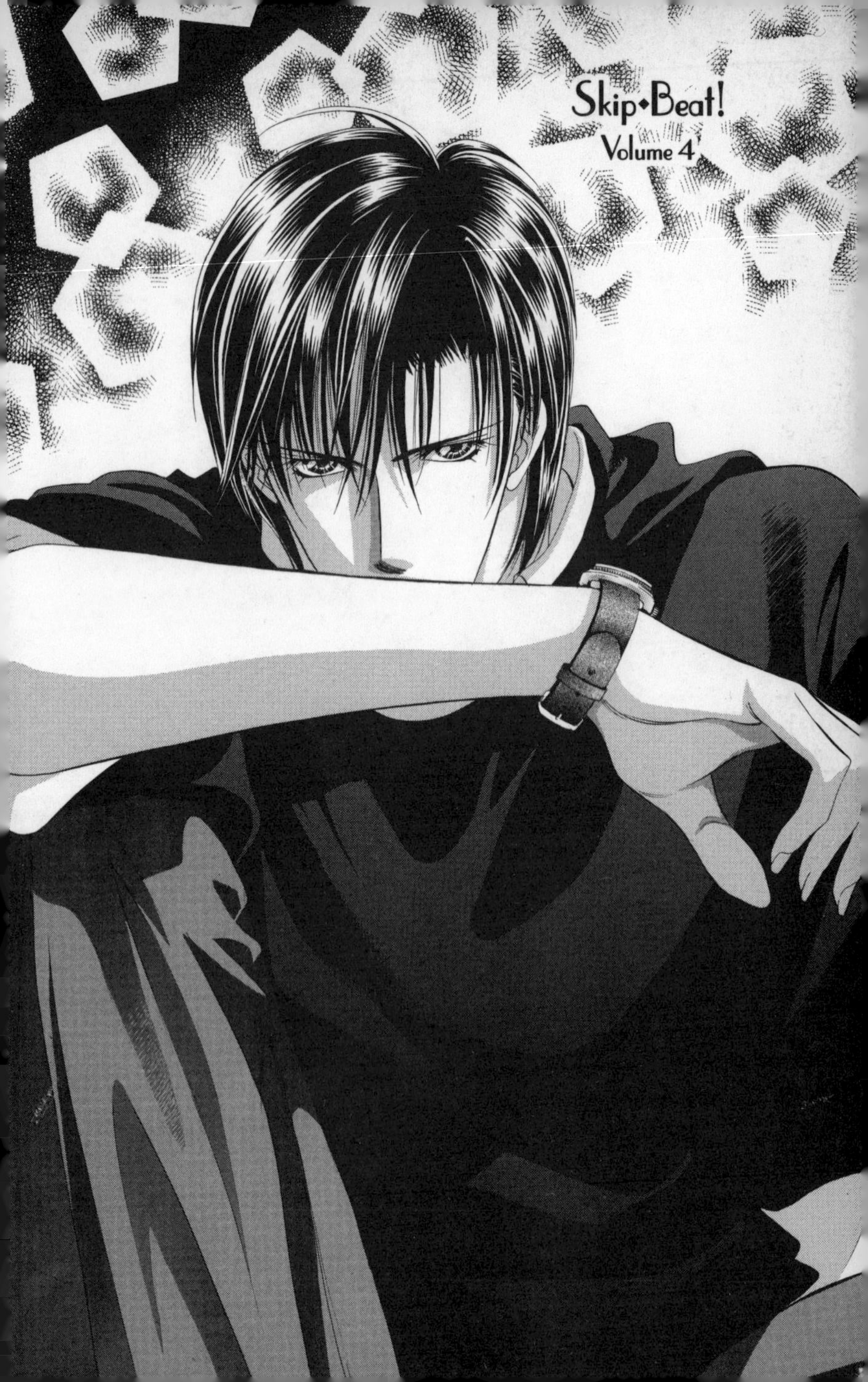
Skip•Beat!
Volume 4

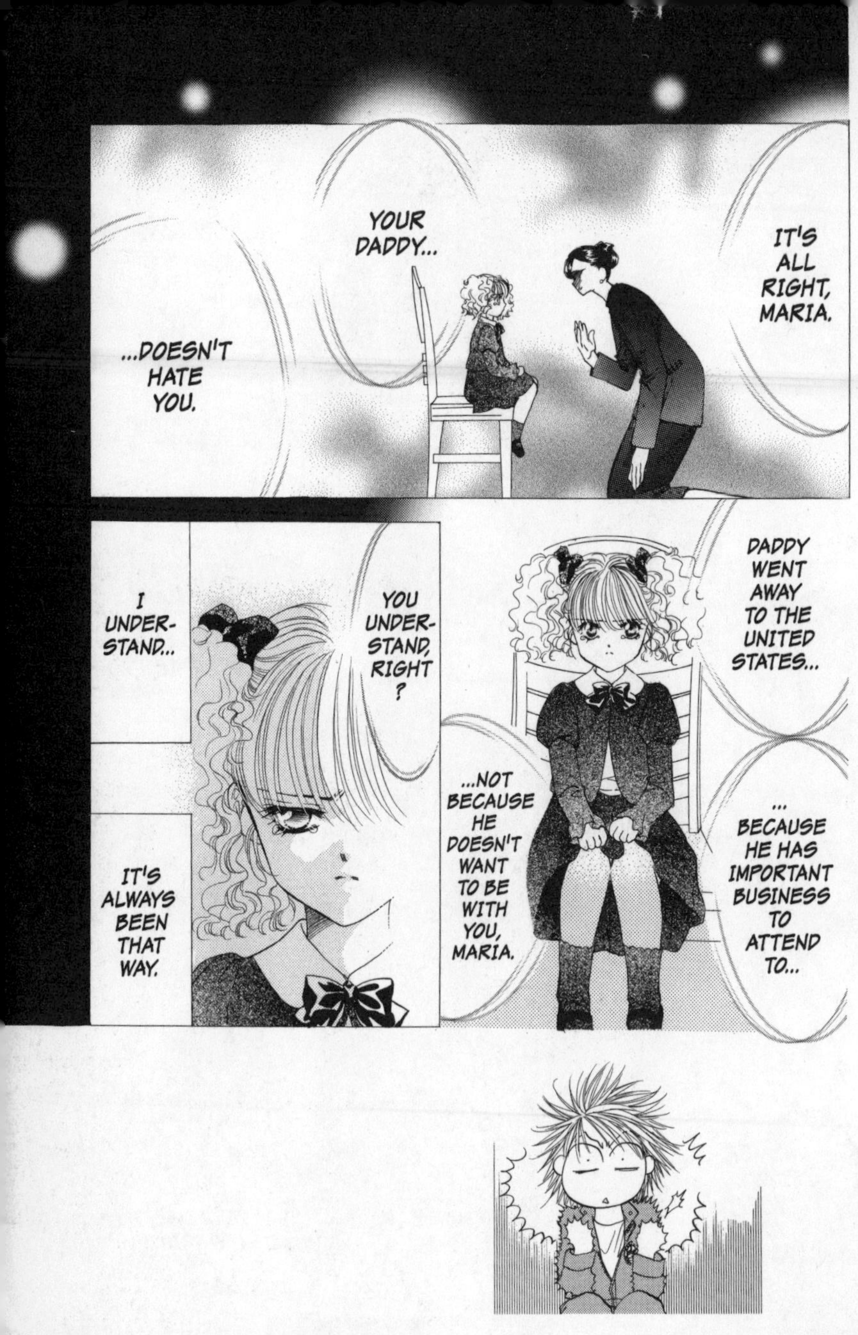
IT'S ALL RIGHT, MARIA.
YOUR DADDY...
...DOESN'T HATE YOU.
DADDY WENT AWAY TO THE UNITED STATES...
...BECAUSE HE HAS IMPORTANT BUSINESS TO ATTEND TO...
...NOT BECAUSE HE DOESN'T WANT TO BE WITH YOU, MARIA.
YOU UNDER-STAND, RIGHT?
I UNDER-STAND...
IT'S ALWAYS BEEN THAT WAY.

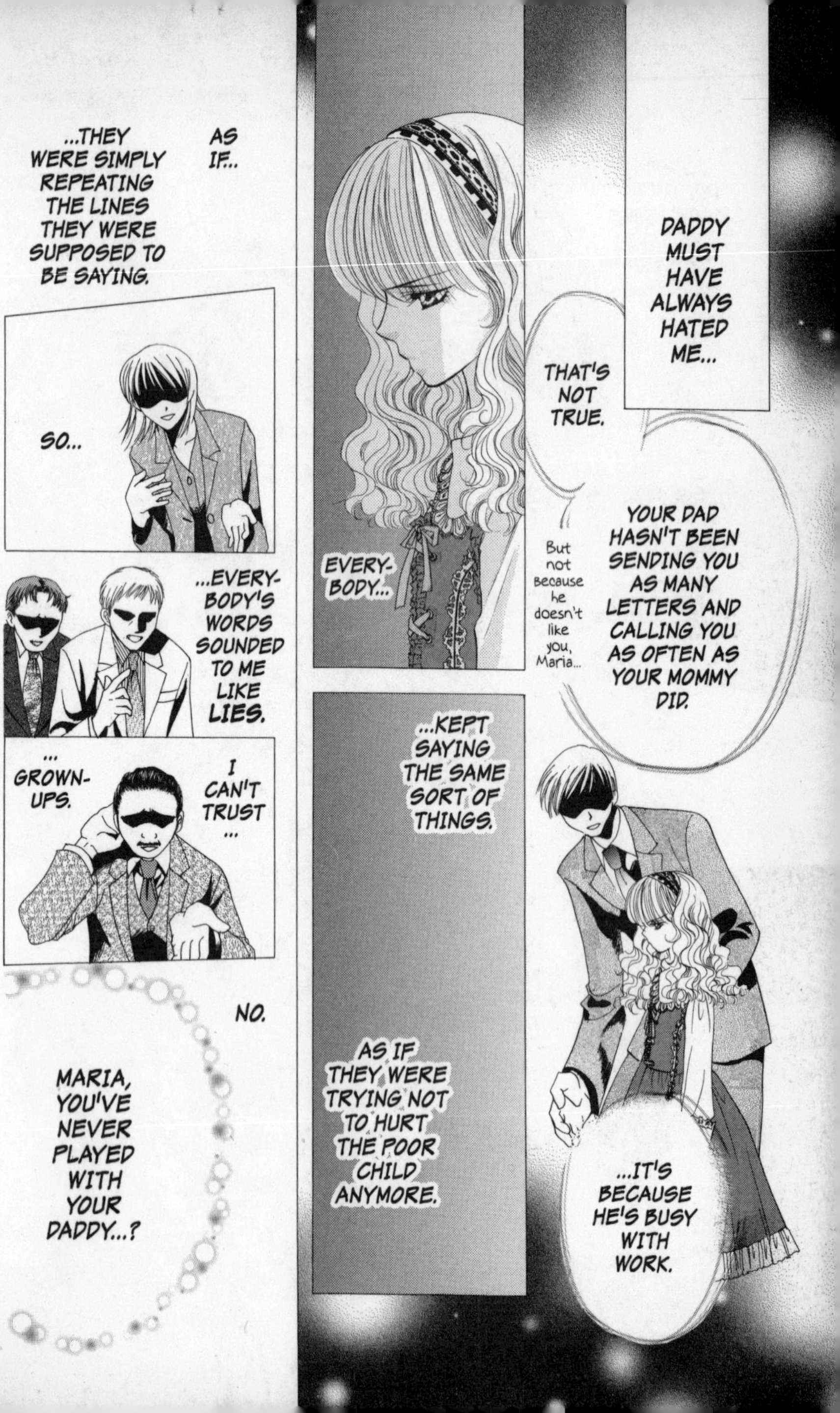
DADDY MUST HAVE ALWAYS HATED ME...
THAT'S NOT TRUE.
YOUR DAD HASN'T BEEN SENDING YOU AS MANY LETTERS AND CALLING YOU AS OFTEN AS YOUR MOMMY DID.
But not because he doesn't like you, Maria...
...IT'S BECAUSE HE'S BUSY WITH WORK.
EVERY-BODY...
...KEPT SAYING THE SAME SORT OF THINGS.
AS IF THEY WERE TRYING NOT TO HURT THE POOR CHILD ANYMORE.
AS IF...
...THEY WERE SIMPLY REPEATING THE LINES THEY WERE SUPPOSED TO BE SAYING.
SO...
...EVERY-BODY'S WORDS SOUNDED TO ME LIKE LIES.
I CAN'T TRUST...
...GROWN-UPS.
NO.
MARIA, YOU'VE NEVER PLAYED WITH YOUR DADDY...?

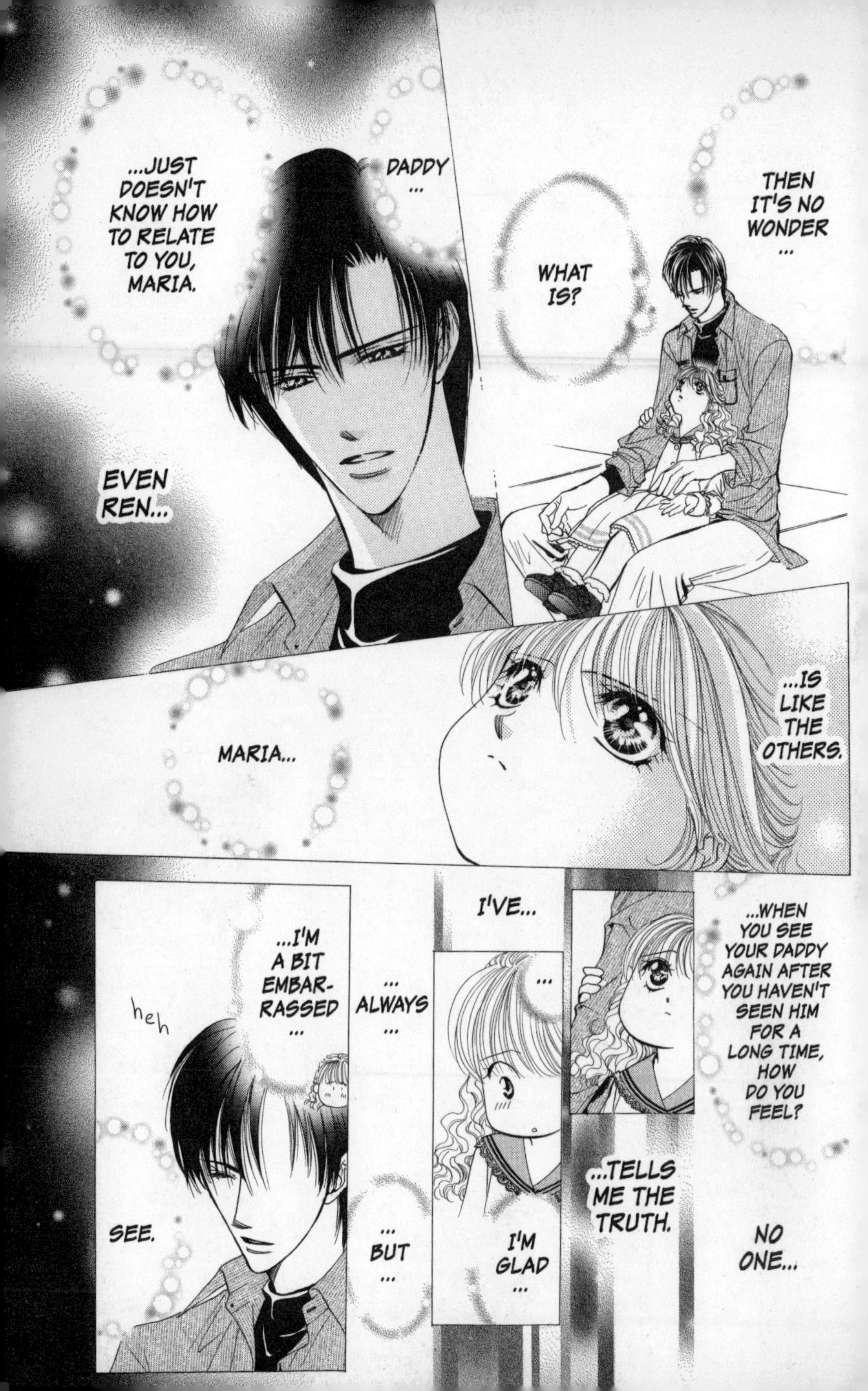
THEN IT'S NO WONDER ...
WHAT IS?
DADDY ...
...JUST DOESN'T KNOW HOW TO RELATE TO YOU, MARIA.
EVEN REN...
...IS LIKE THE OTHERS.
MARIA...
...WHEN YOU SEE YOUR DADDY AGAIN AFTER YOU HAVEN'T SEEN HIM FOR A LONG TIME, HOW DO YOU FEEL?
NO ONE...
...TELLS ME THE TRUTH.
I'VE...
...
... ALWAYS ...
I'M GLAD ...
... BUT ...
...I'M A BIT EMBARRASSED ...
heh
SEE.

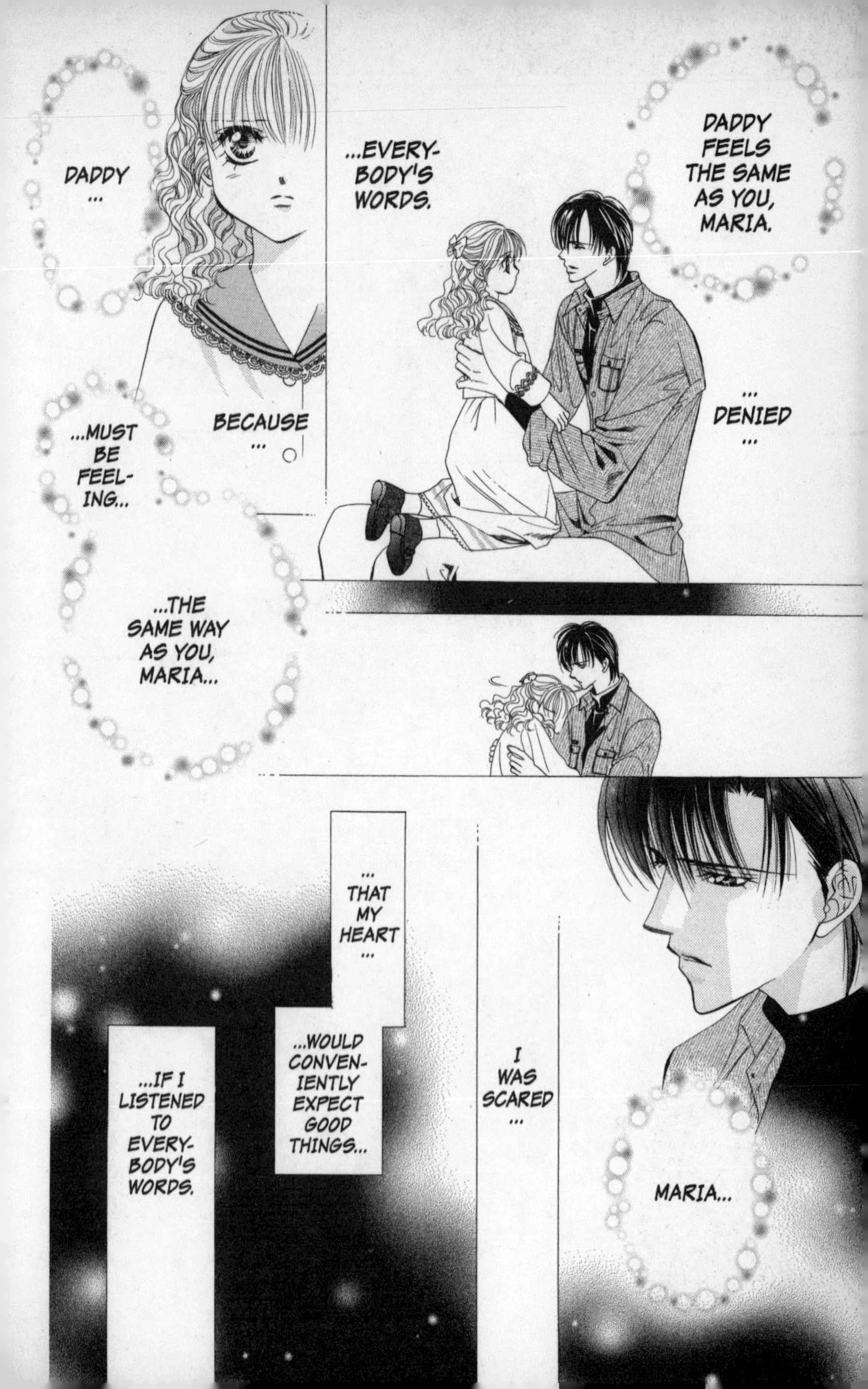
DADDY FEELS THE SAME AS YOU, MARIA.
... DENIED ...
...EVERY-BODY'S WORDS.
DADDY ...
BECAUSE ...
...MUST BE FEEL-ING...
...THE SAME WAY AS YOU, MARIA...
MARIA...
I WAS SCARED ...
... THAT MY HEART ...
...WOULD CONVEN-IENTLY EXPECT GOOD THINGS...
...IF I LISTENED TO EVERY-BODY'S WORDS.

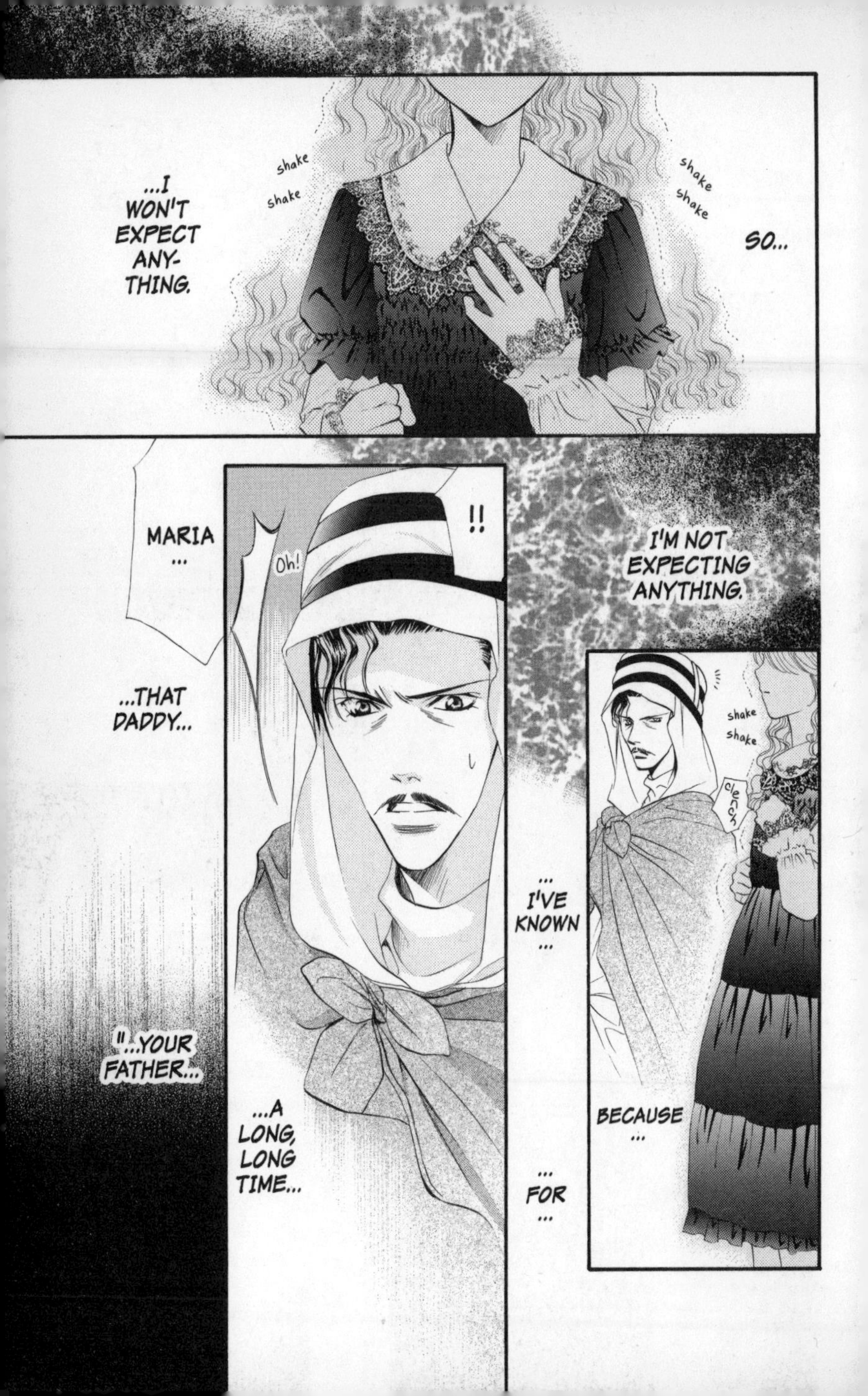
SO...
shake shake
shake shake
...I WON'T EXPECT ANYTHING.
I'M NOT EXPECTING ANYTHING.
shake shake
clench
BECAUSE...
...I'VE KNOWN...
...FOR...
!!
Oh!
MARIA...
...A LONG, LONG TIME...
...THAT DADDY...
"...YOUR FATHER...

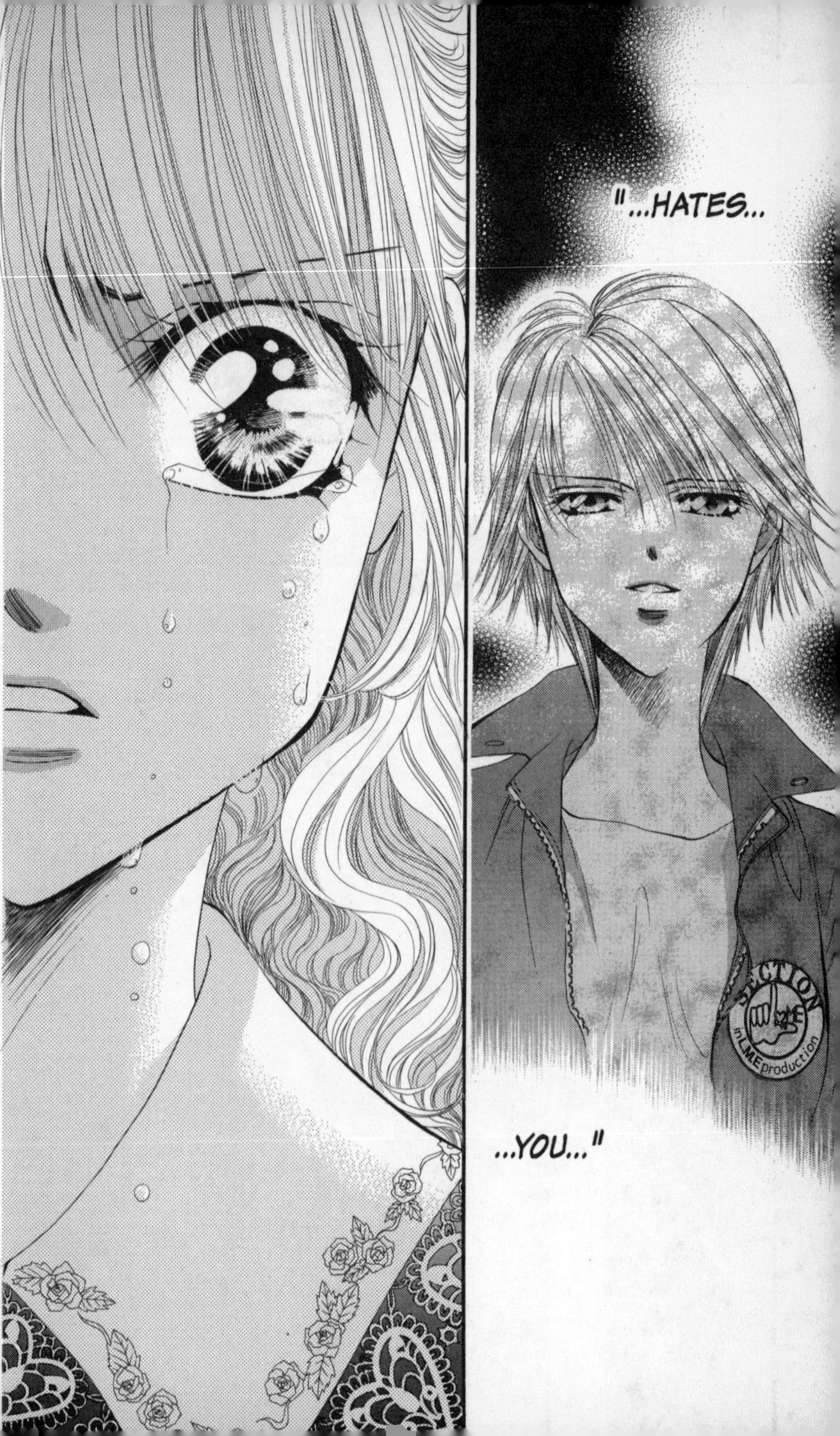
"...HATES...
SECTION
in LME production
...YOU..."

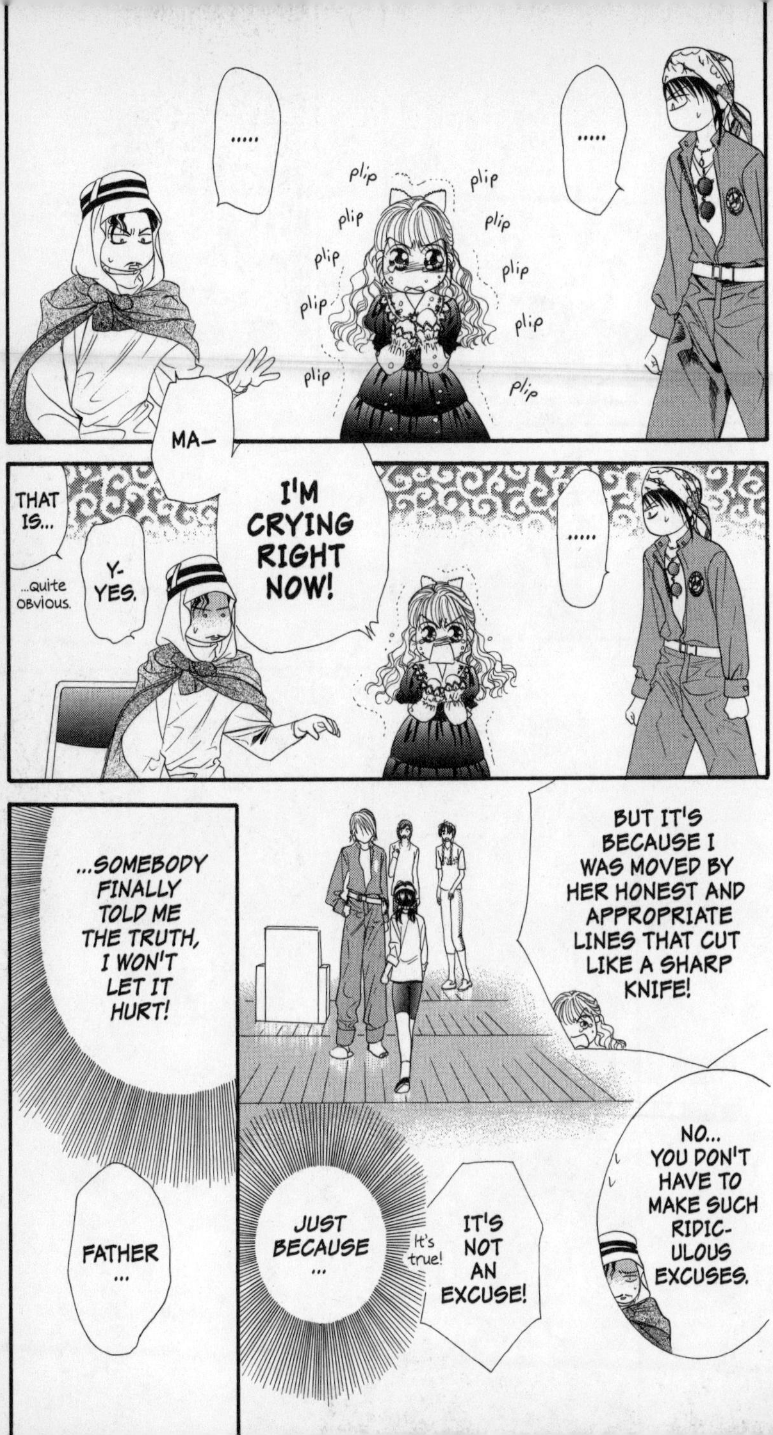
.....
plip plip plip plip plip plip plip plip plip plip
.....
MA—
.....
I'M CRYING RIGHT NOW!
Y-YES.
THAT IS...
...quite obvious.
BUT IT'S BECAUSE I WAS MOVED BY HER HONEST AND APPROPRIATE LINES THAT CUT LIKE A SHARP KNIFE!
NO... YOU DON'T HAVE TO MAKE SUCH RIDIC-ULOUS EXCUSES.
IT'S NOT AN EXCUSE!
It's true!
JUST BECAUSE ...
...SOMEBODY FINALLY TOLD ME THE TRUTH, I WON'T LET IT HURT!
FATHER ...

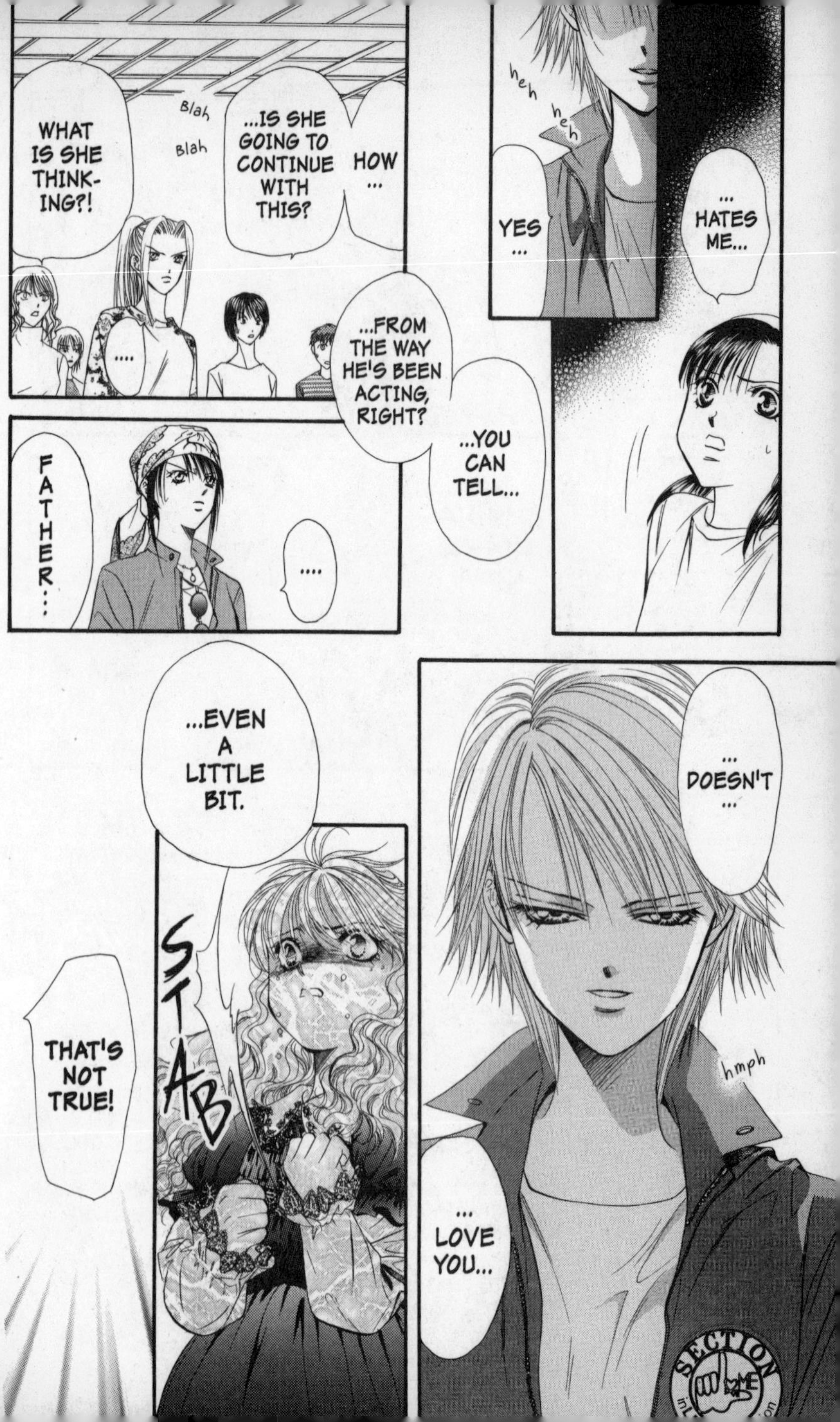
heh heh
YES ...
... HATES ME...
...YOU CAN TELL...
...FROM THE WAY HE'S BEEN ACTING, RIGHT?
HOW ...
...IS SHE GOING TO CONTINUE WITH THIS?
Blah
Blah
WHAT IS SHE THINKING?!
....
....
FATHER...
... DOESN'T ...
hmph
... LOVE YOU...
SECTION
...EVEN A LITTLE BIT.
STAB
THAT'S NOT TRUE!

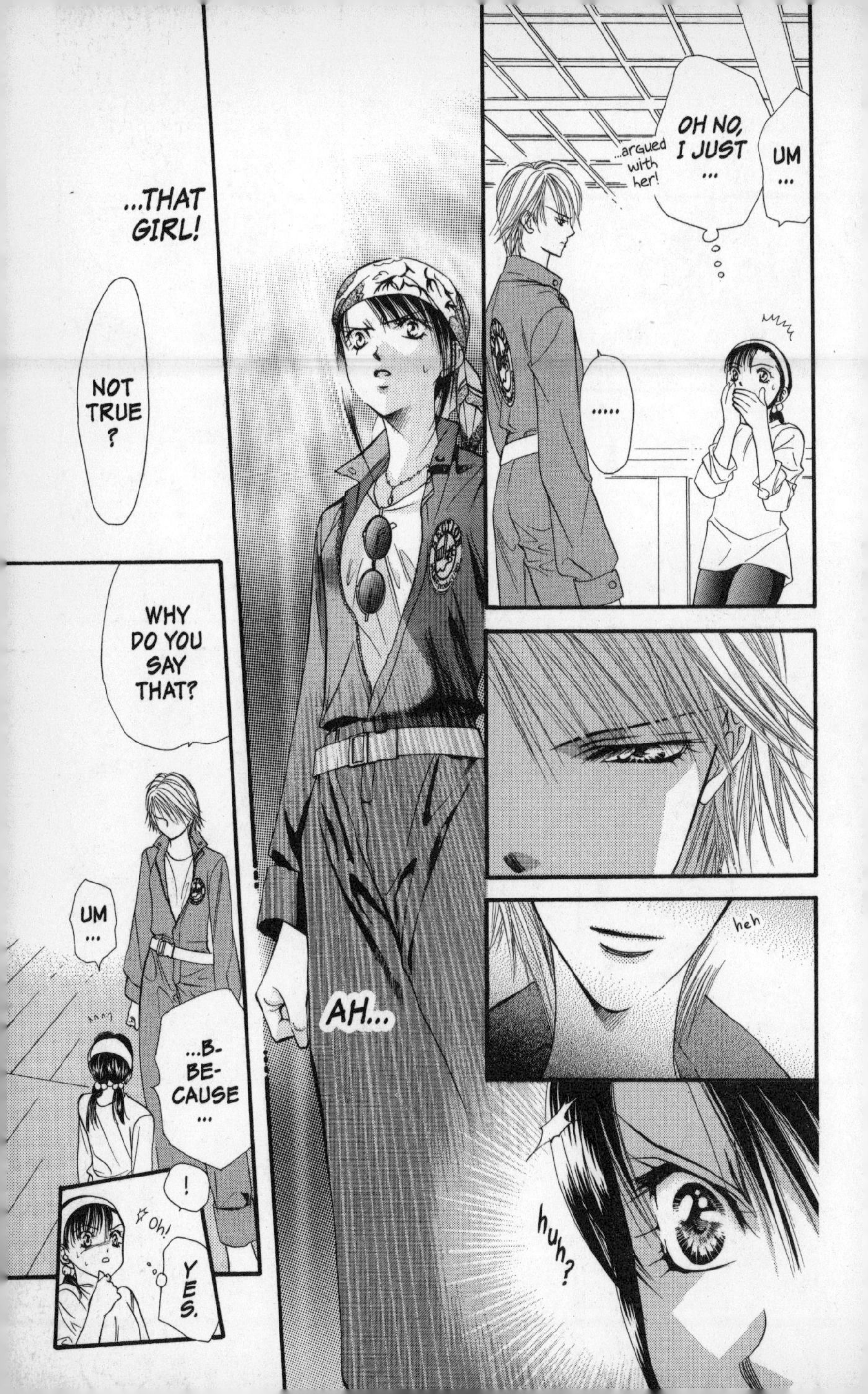
UM ...
OH NO, I JUST ...
...argued with her!
.....
heh
huh?
AH...
...THAT GIRL!
NOT TRUE?
WHY DO YOU SAY THAT?
UM ...
...B-BE-CAUSE ...
!
Oh!
YES.

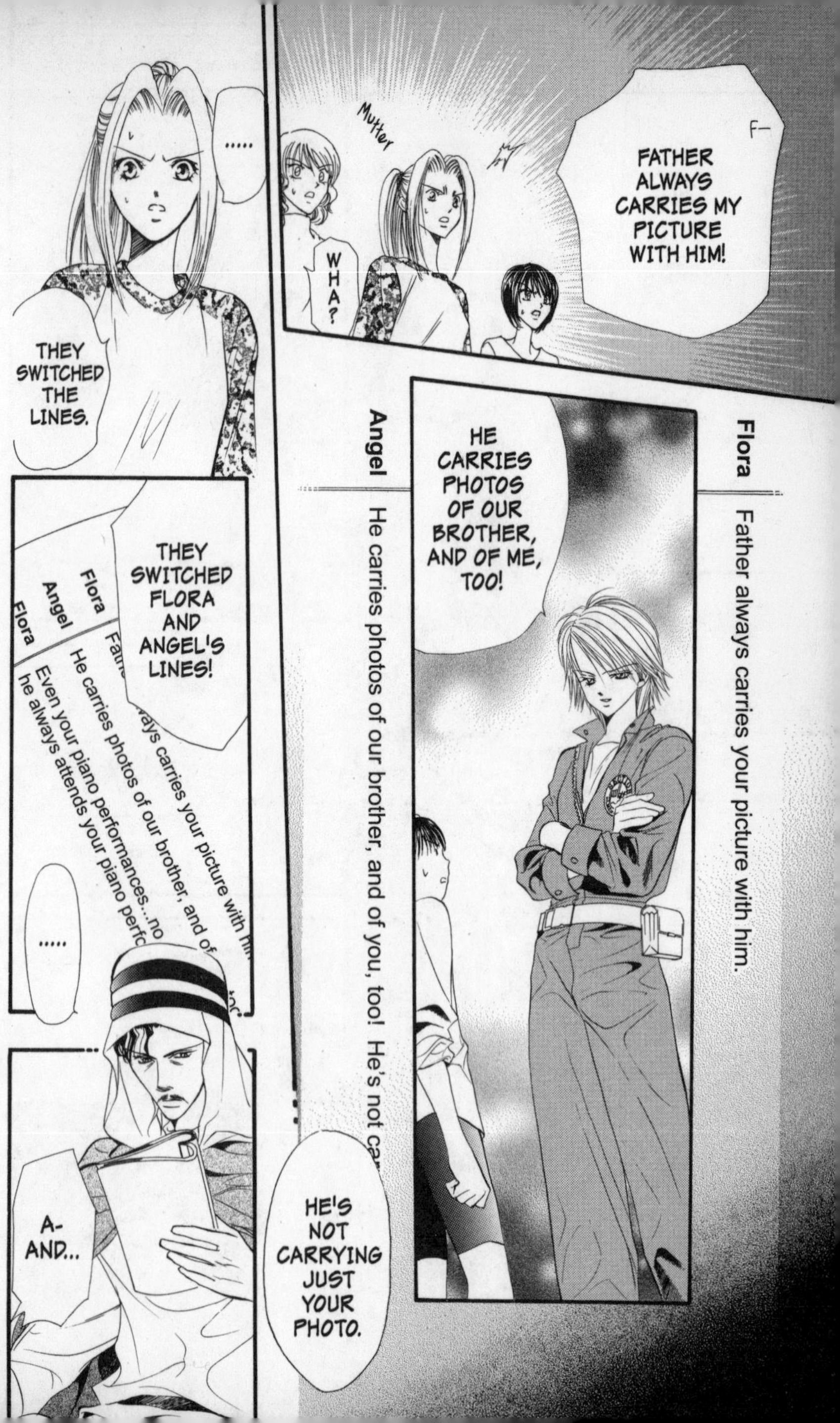
F—
FATHER ALWAYS CARRIES MY PICTURE WITH HIM!
Mutter
WHA?
.....
THEY SWITCHED THE LINES.
Flora
Father always carries your picture with him.
Angel
He carries photos of our brother, and of you, too! He's not ca
HE CARRIES PHOTOS OF OUR BROTHER, AND OF ME, TOO!
HE'S NOT CARRYING JUST YOUR PHOTO.
THEY SWITCHED FLORA AND ANGEL'S LINES!
Flora
Angel
Flora
He carries photos of our brother, and of
Even your piano performances...no
he always attends your piano perfo
.....
A- AND...

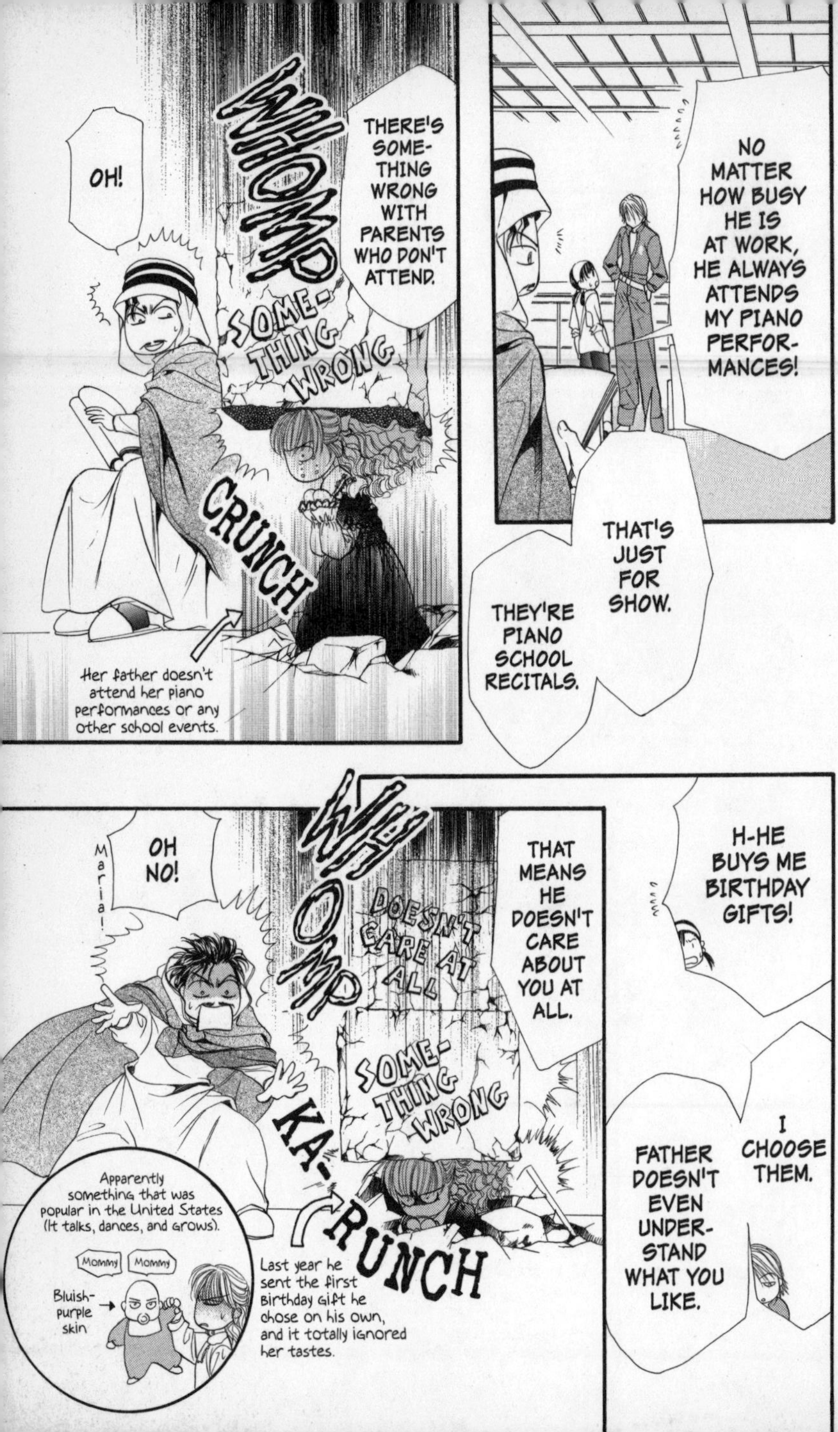
NO MATTER HOW BUSY HE IS AT WORK, HE ALWAYS ATTENDS MY PIANO PERFORMANCES!
THAT'S JUST FOR SHOW.
THEY'RE PIANO SCHOOL RECITALS.
THERE'S SOMETHING WRONG WITH PARENTS WHO DON'T ATTEND.
WHOMP
SOMETHING WRONG
OH!
CRUNCH
Her father doesn't attend her piano performances or any other school events.
H-HE BUYS ME BIRTHDAY GIFTS!
I CHOOSE THEM.
FATHER DOESN'T EVEN UNDERSTAND WHAT YOU LIKE.
THAT MEANS HE DOESN'T CARE ABOUT YOU AT ALL.
WHOMP
DOESN'T CARE AT ALL
SOMETHING WRONG
KA-RUNCH
OH NO!
Maria!
Last year he sent the first birthday gift he chose on his own, and it totally ignored her tastes.
Apparently something that was popular in the United States (It talks, dances, and grows).
Mommy
Mommy
Bluish-purple skin

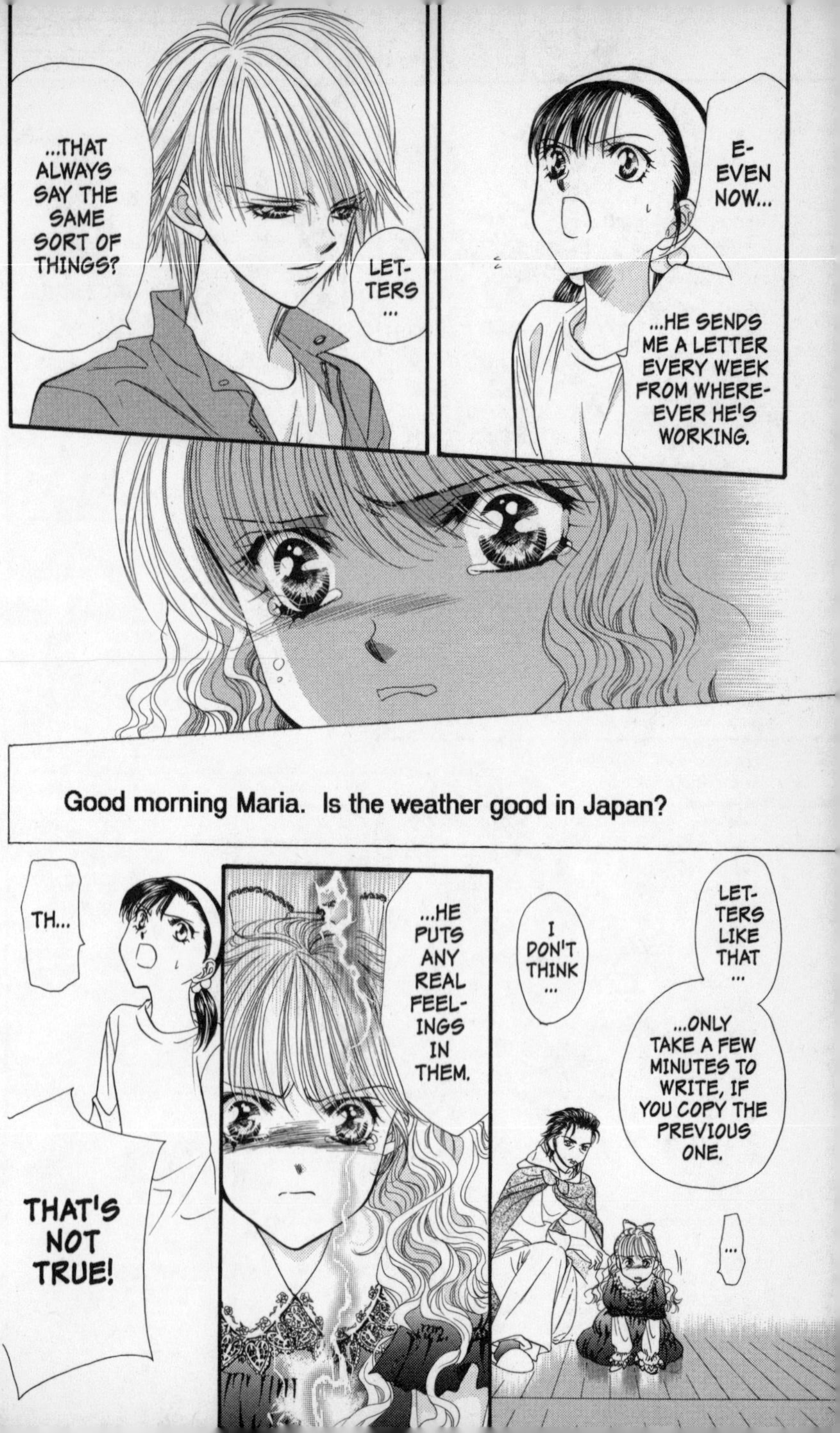
E-EVEN NOW...
...HE SENDS ME A LETTER EVERY WEEK FROM WHEREEVER HE'S WORKING.
LETTERS...
...THAT ALWAYS SAY THE SAME SORT OF THINGS?
Good morning Maria. Is the weather good in Japan?
LETTERS LIKE THAT...
...ONLY TAKE A FEW MINUTES TO WRITE, IF YOU COPY THE PREVIOUS ONE.
I DON'T THINK...
...HE PUTS ANY REAL FEELINGS IN THEM.
...
TH...
THAT'S NOT TRUE!

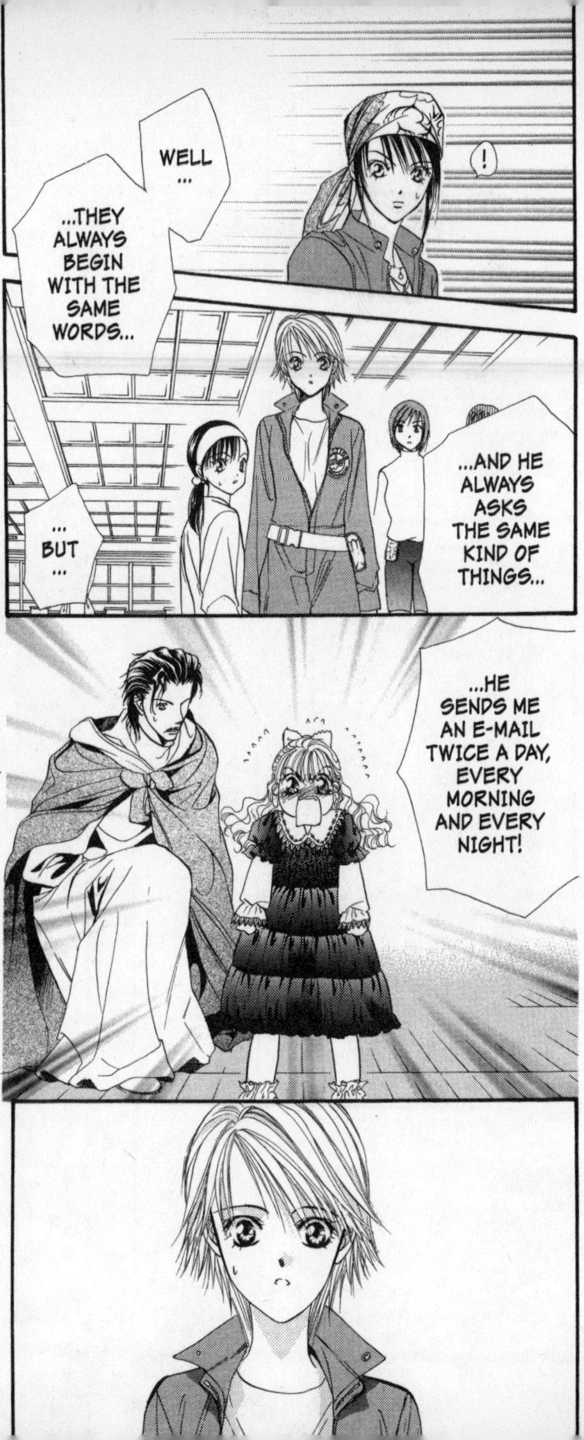
!
WELL ...
...THEY ALWAYS BEGIN WITH THE SAME WORDS...
...AND HE ALWAYS ASKS THE SAME KIND OF THINGS...
... BUT ...
...HE SENDS ME AN E-MAIL TWICE A DAY, EVERY MORNING AND EVERY NIGHT!

Greetings

Hello. I'm Nakamura. Thank you for reading *Skip Beat!* Vol. 4. This time I was finally able to have Shotaro (who doesn't appear often) and Kyoko interact in the show-biz world. Since Kyoko is just starting out, a super-newcomer, she has no contact with Shotaro, so it's tough... To tell the truth, he hadn't appeared for so long, when I drew him at the end of Act 20, his looks had changed... He looked young, and almost like a girl...

My editor put in "Even if I become a bird, I will not forget that face!" for the copy on that last page. But the moment I read that, I added the snarky comment, "...Yes...even if Kyoko hasn't forgotten, I have..." I'm sorry Haorin...

↑ My editor's nickname

This time I once again redrew lots of stuff, and I suddenly messed up my work schedule... I apologize for not being able to do my work as planned.

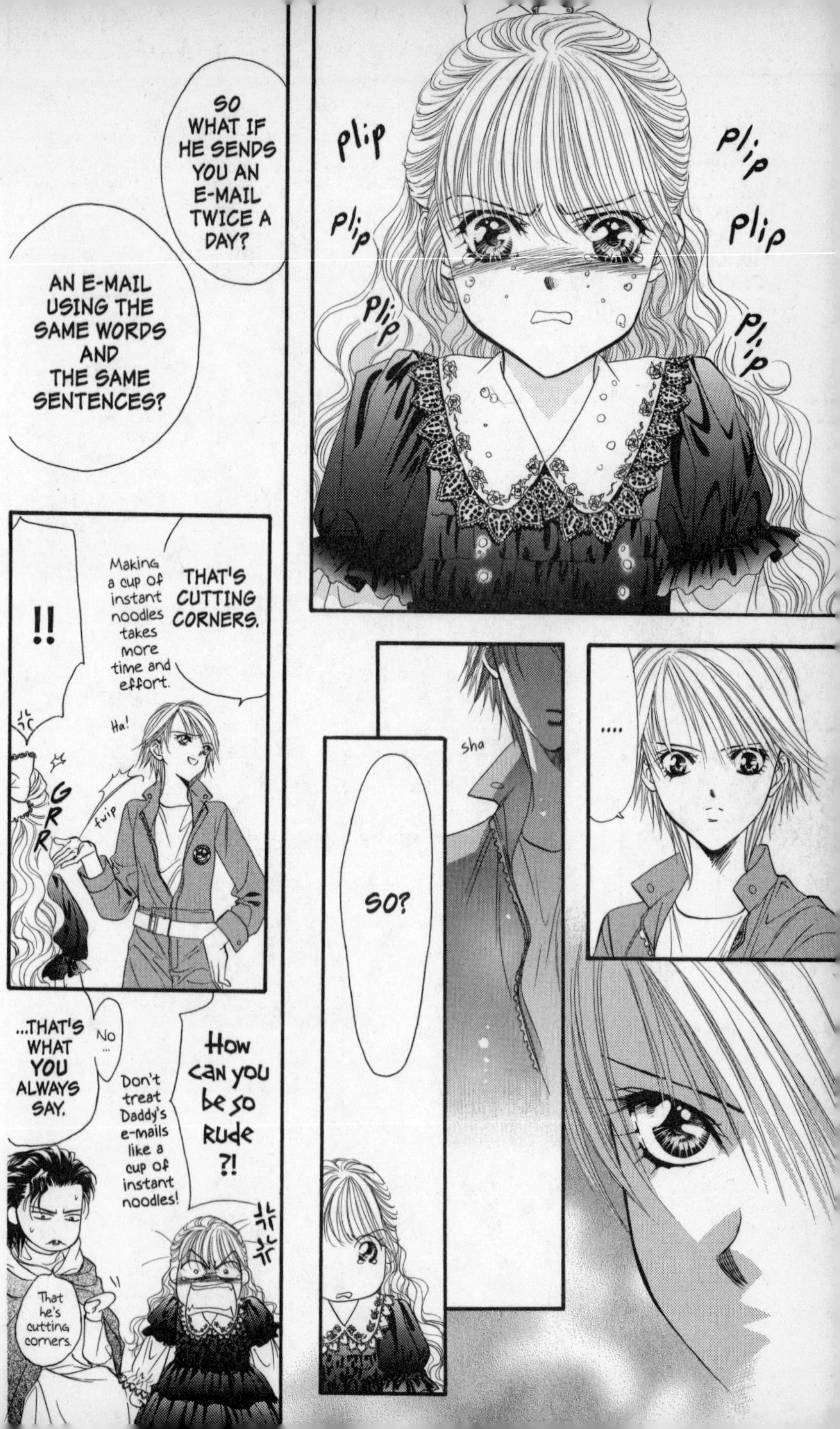
plip
plip
plip
plip
plip
plip
....
sha
SO?
SO WHAT IF HE SENDS YOU AN E-MAIL TWICE A DAY?
AN E-MAIL USING THE SAME WORDS AND THE SAME SENTENCES?
THAT'S CUTTING CORNERS.
Making a cup of instant noodles takes more time and effort.
!!
Ha!
GRR
fwip
How can you be so rude?!
Don't treat Daddy's e-mails like a cup of instant noodles!
No...
...THAT'S WHAT YOU ALWAYS SAY.
That he's cutting corners.

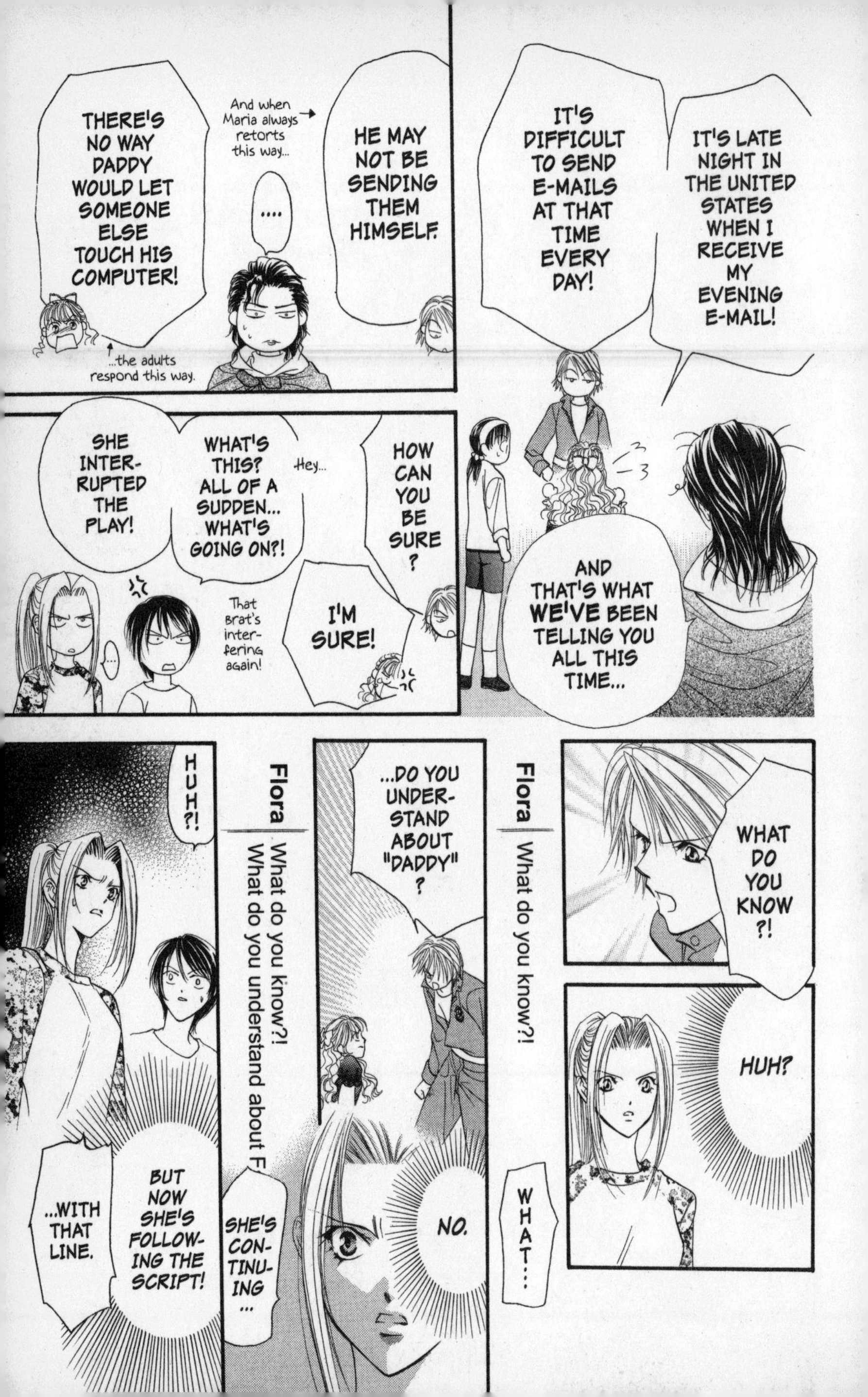
IT'S LATE NIGHT IN THE UNITED STATES WHEN I RECEIVE MY EVENING E-MAIL!
IT'S DIFFICULT TO SEND E-MAILS AT THAT TIME EVERY DAY!
AND THAT'S WHAT WE'VE BEEN TELLING YOU ALL THIS TIME...
HE MAY NOT BE SENDING THEM HIMSELF.
And when Maria always retorts this way...
....
THERE'S NO WAY DADDY WOULD LET SOMEONE ELSE TOUCH HIS COMPUTER!
...the adults respond this way.
HOW CAN YOU BE SURE?
I'M SURE!
Hey...
WHAT'S THIS? ALL OF A SUDDEN... WHAT'S GOING ON?!
SHE INTER-RUPTED THE PLAY!
That Brat's inter-fering again!
...
WHAT DO YOU KNOW?!
Flora What do you know?!
HUH?
WHAT...
...DO YOU UNDER-STAND ABOUT "DADDY"?
Flora What do you know?! What do you understand about F
NO.
SHE'S CON-TINU-ING...
HUH?!
BUT NOW SHE'S FOLLOW-ING THE SCRIPT!
...WITH THAT LINE.

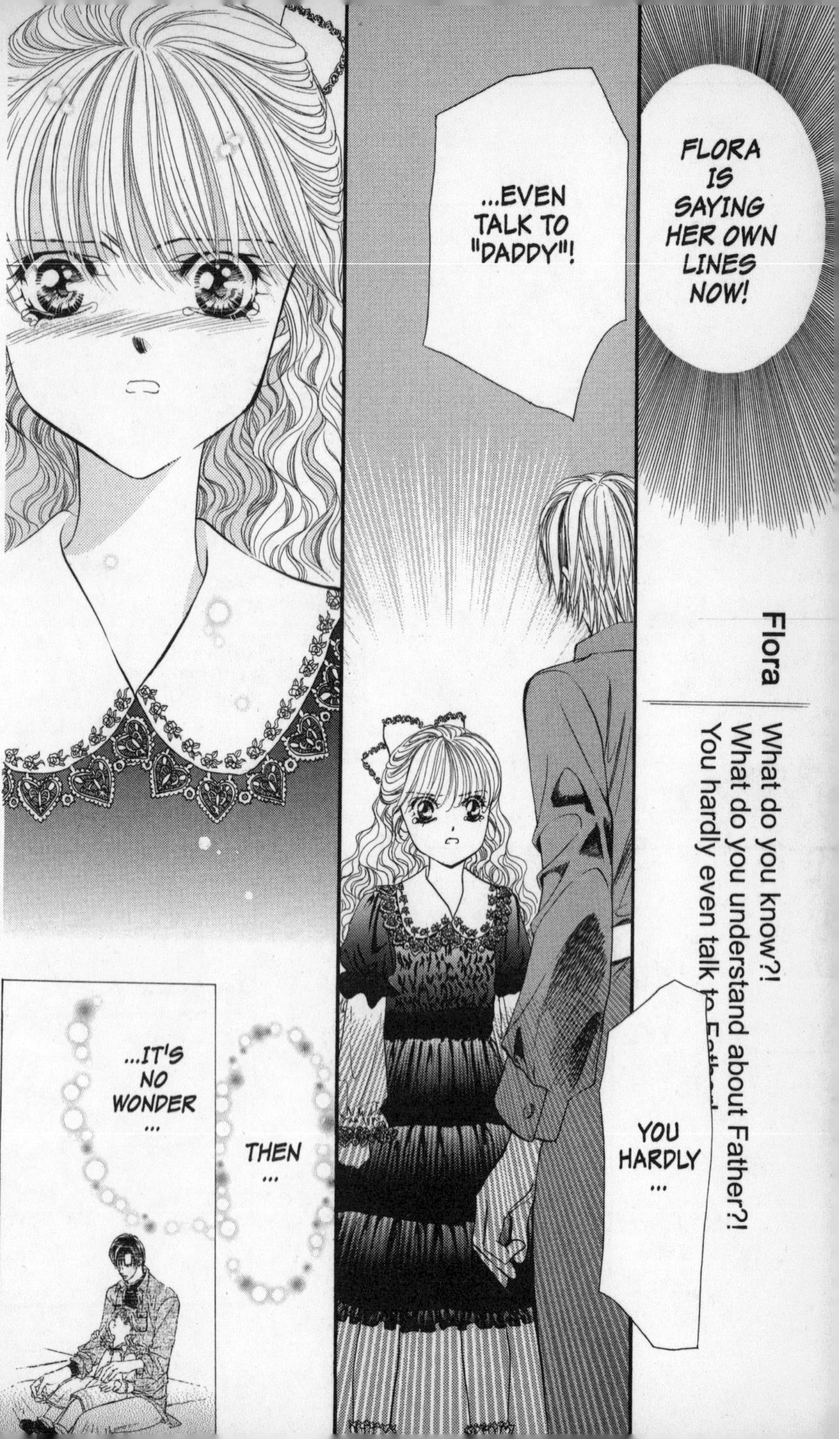

FLORA IS SAYING HER OWN LINES NOW!
Flora
What do you know?!
What do you understand about Father?!
You hardly even talk to
YOU HARDLY ...
...EVEN TALK TO "DADDY"!
THEN ...
...IT'S NO WONDER ...

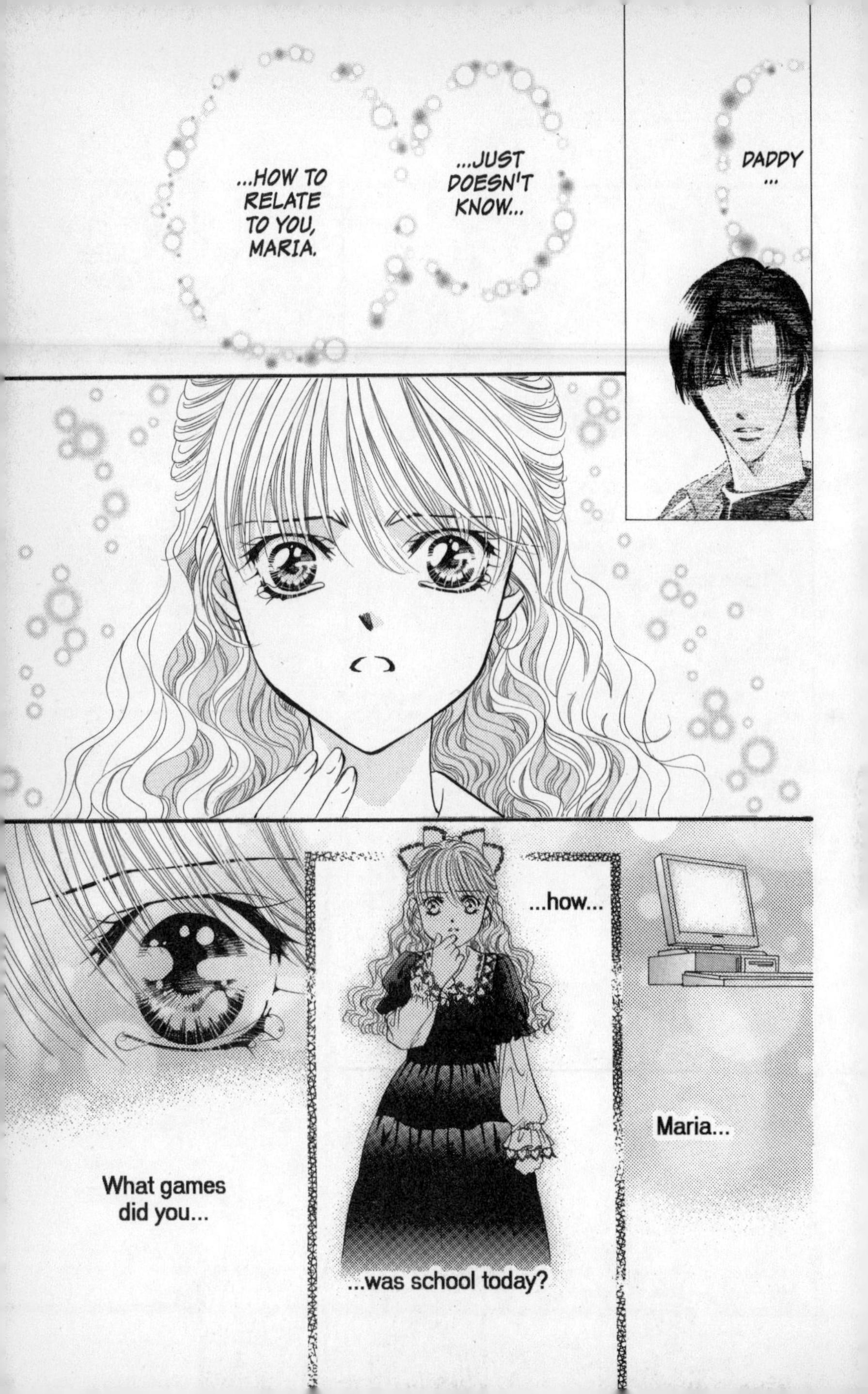
DADDY ...
...JUST DOESN'T KNOW...
...HOW TO RELATE TO YOU, MARIA.
Maria...
...how...
...was school today?
What games did you...

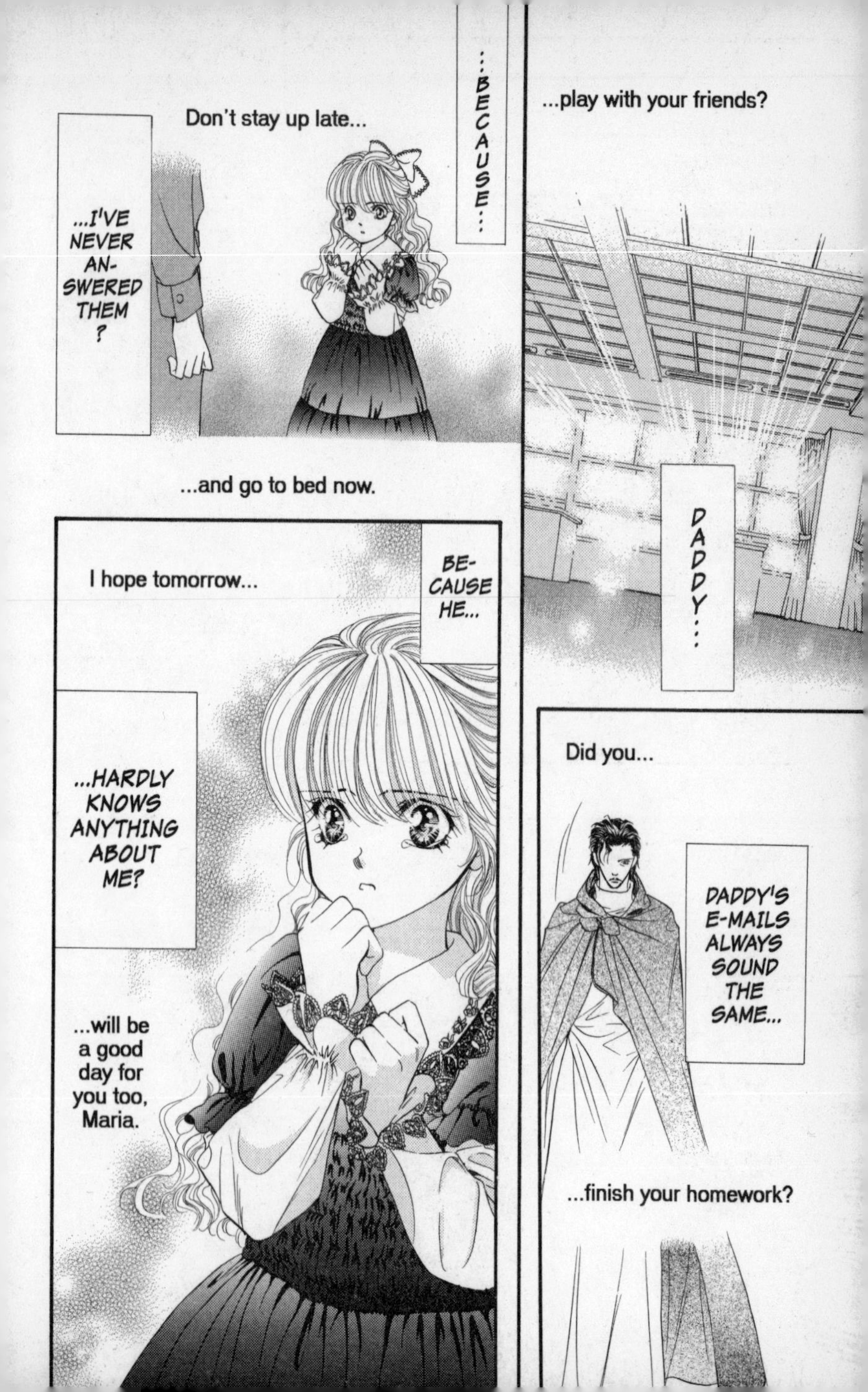
...play with your friends?
DADDY...
Did you...
DADDY'S E-MAILS ALWAYS SOUND THE SAME...
...finish your homework?
...BECAUSE...
Don't stay up late...
...I'VE NEVER AN-SWERED THEM?
...and go to bed now.
BE-CAUSE HE...
I hope tomorrow...
...HARDLY KNOWS ANYTHING ABOUT ME?
...will be a good day for you too, Maria.

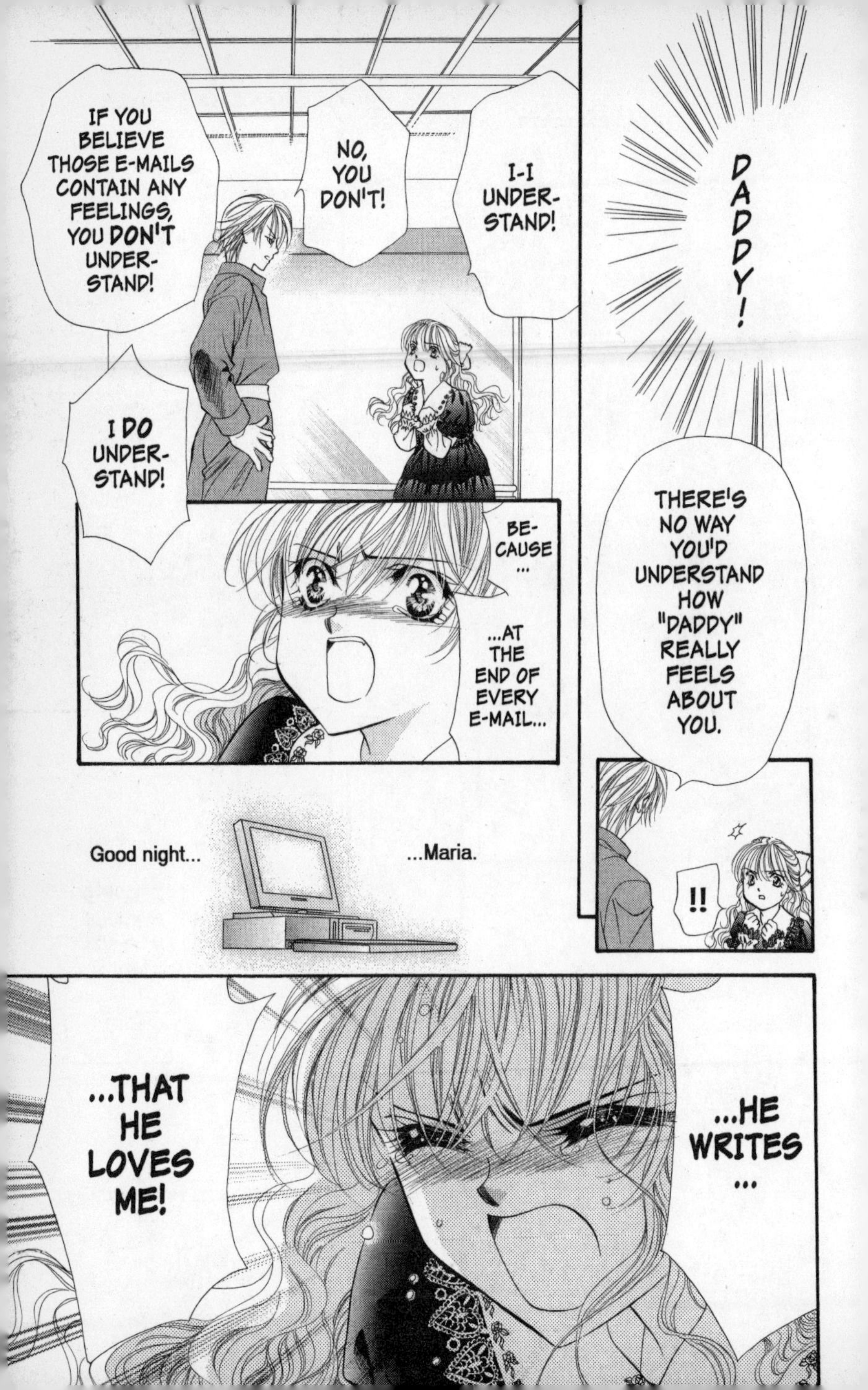
DADDY!
THERE'S NO WAY YOU'D UNDERSTAND HOW "DADDY" REALLY FEELS ABOUT YOU.
!!
I-I UNDER-STAND!
NO, YOU DON'T!
IF YOU BELIEVE THOSE E-MAILS CONTAIN ANY FEELINGS, YOU DON'T UNDER-STAND!
I DO UNDER-STAND!
BE-CAUSE ...
...AT THE END OF EVERY E-MAIL...
Good night...
...Maria.
...HE WRITES ...
...THAT HE LOVES ME!

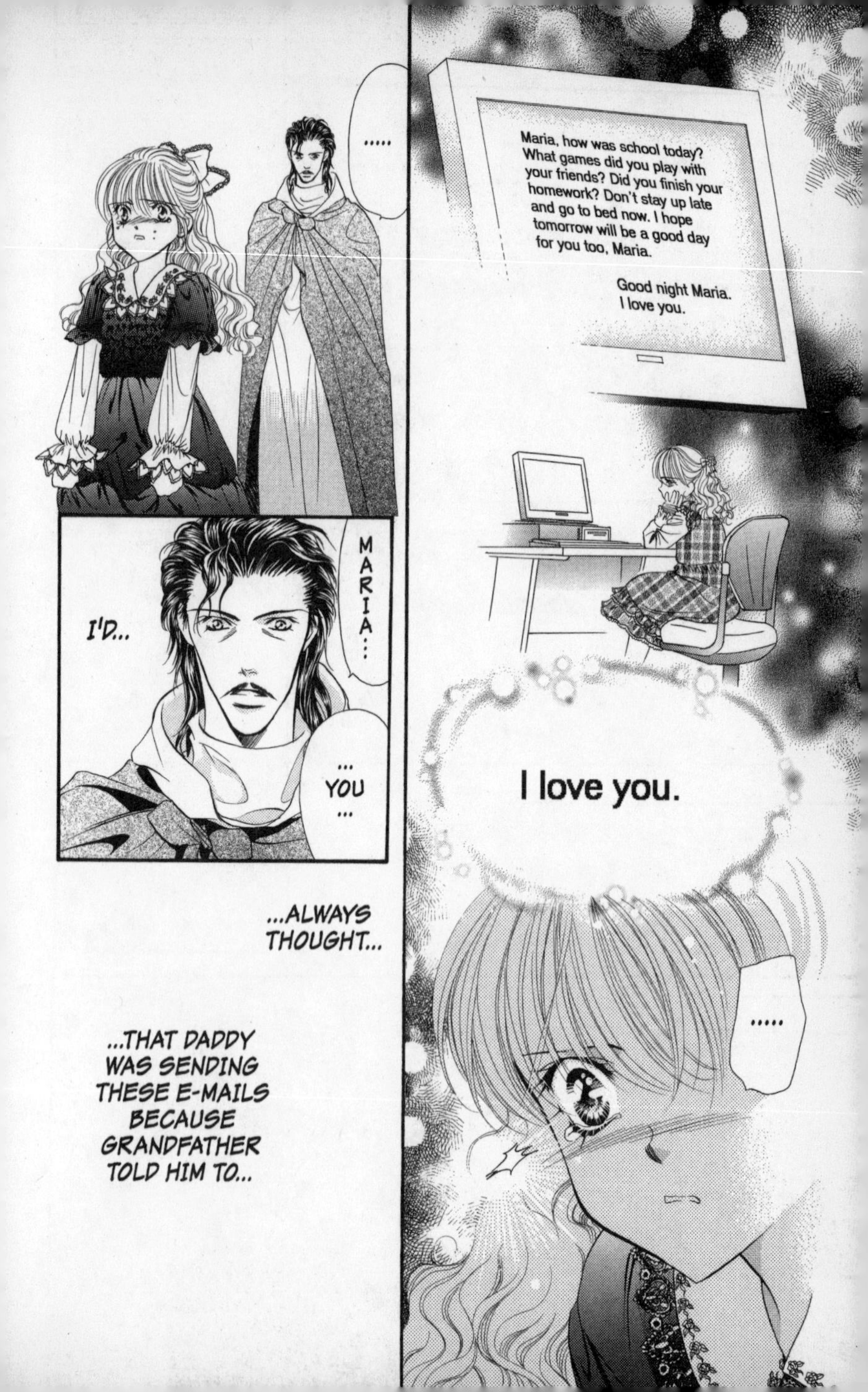
Maria, how was school today? What games did you play with your friends? Did you finish your homework? Don't stay up late and go to bed now. I hope tomorrow will be a good day for you too, Maria.
Good night Maria. I love you.
I love you.
.....
.....
MARIA...
I'D...
...YOU...
...ALWAYS THOUGHT...
...THAT DADDY WAS SENDING THESE E-MAILS BECAUSE GRANDFATHER TOLD HIM TO...

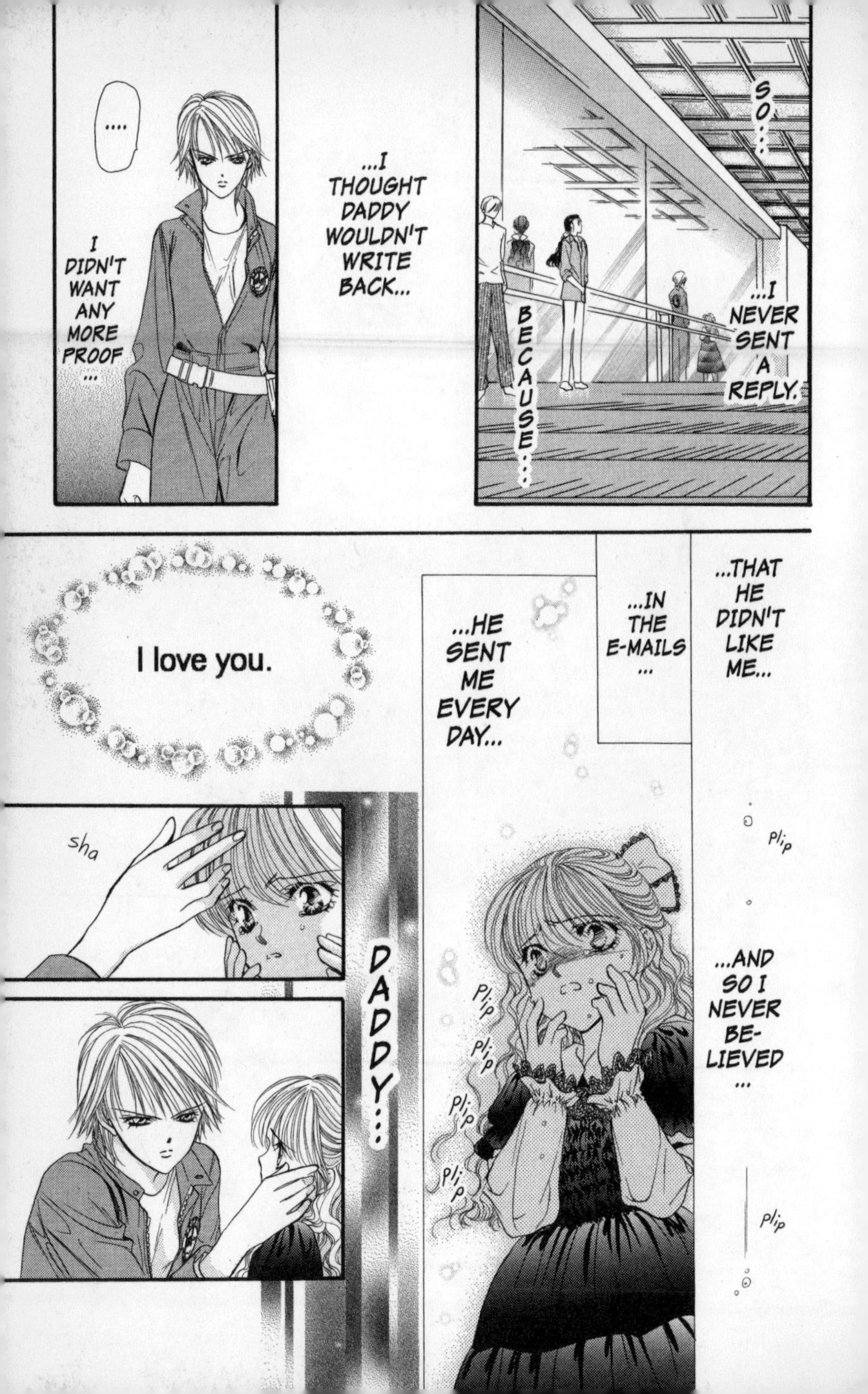
SO...
...I NEVER SENT A REPLY.
BECAUSE...
...I THOUGHT DADDY WOULDN'T WRITE BACK...
....
I DIDN'T WANT ANY MORE PROOF...
...THAT HE DIDN'T LIKE ME...
...AND SO I NEVER BE-LIEVED...
plip
plip
...IN THE E-MAILS...
...HE SENT ME EVERY DAY...
plip
plip
plip
plip
I love you.
sha
DADDY...

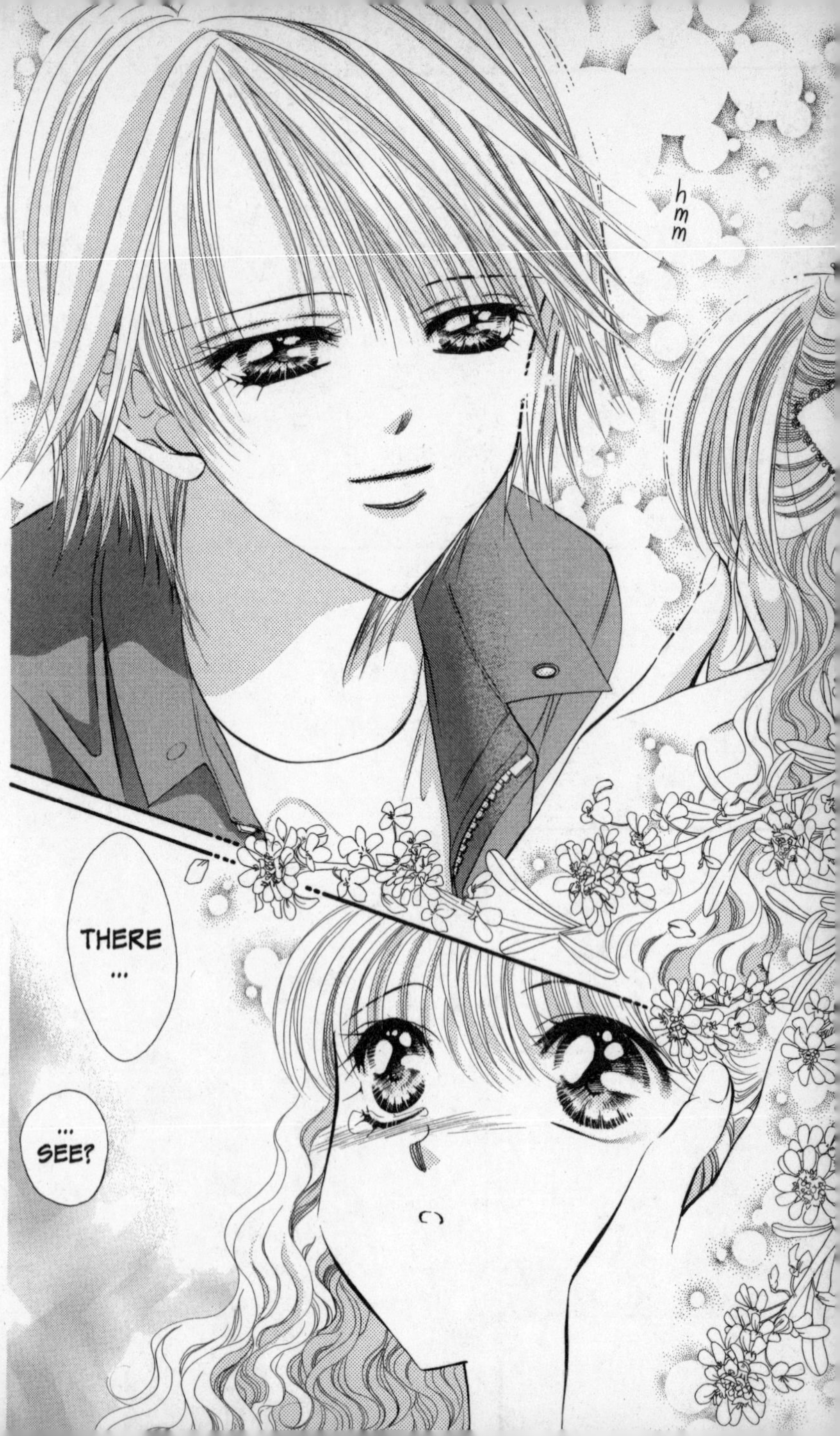
hmm
THERE ...
... SEE?

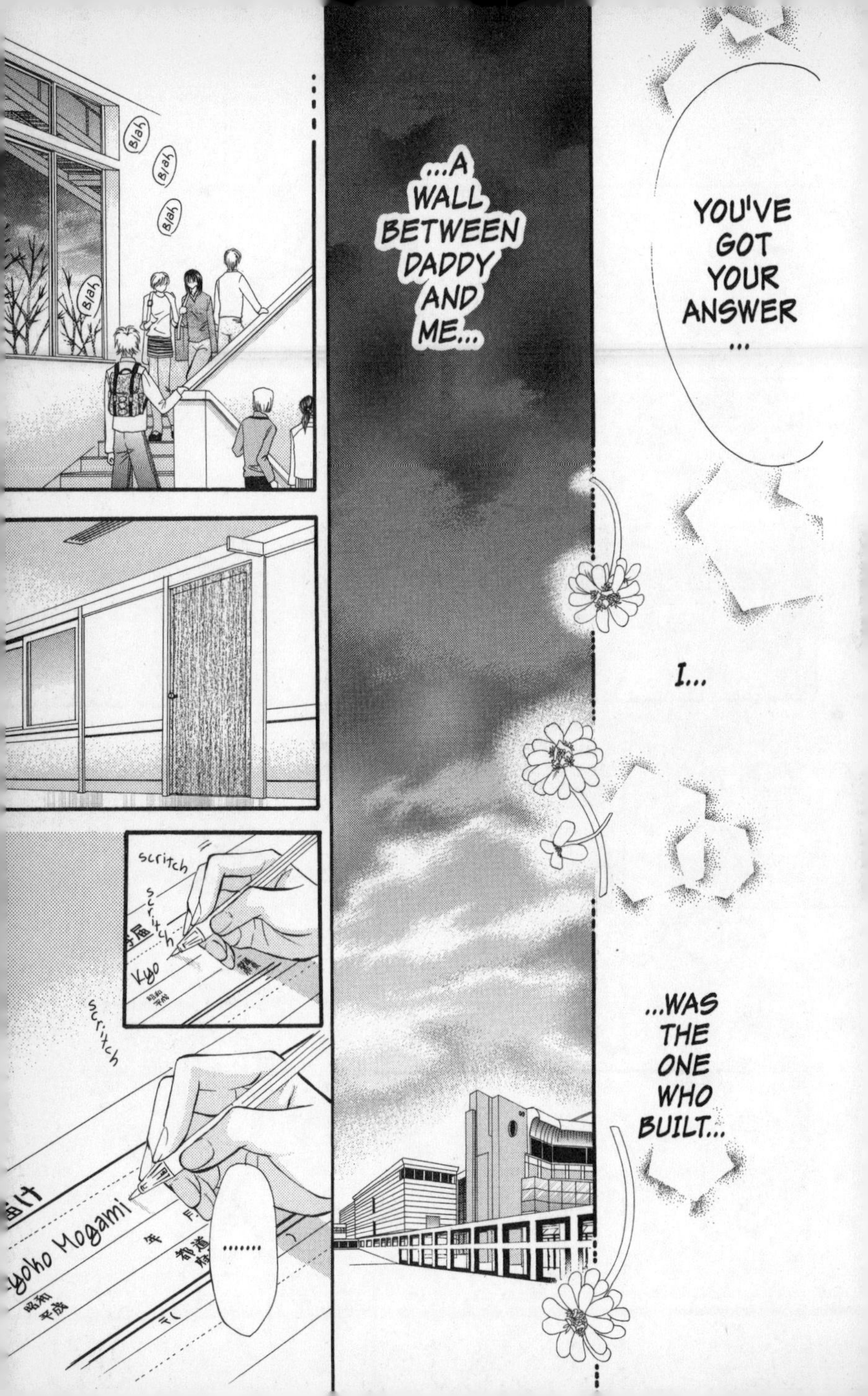
YOU'VE GOT YOUR ANSWER...
I...
...WAS THE ONE WHO BUILT...
...A WALL BETWEEN DADDY AND ME...
Blah
Blah
Blah
Blah
scritch
scritch
Kyo
scritch
......
yoko Mogami

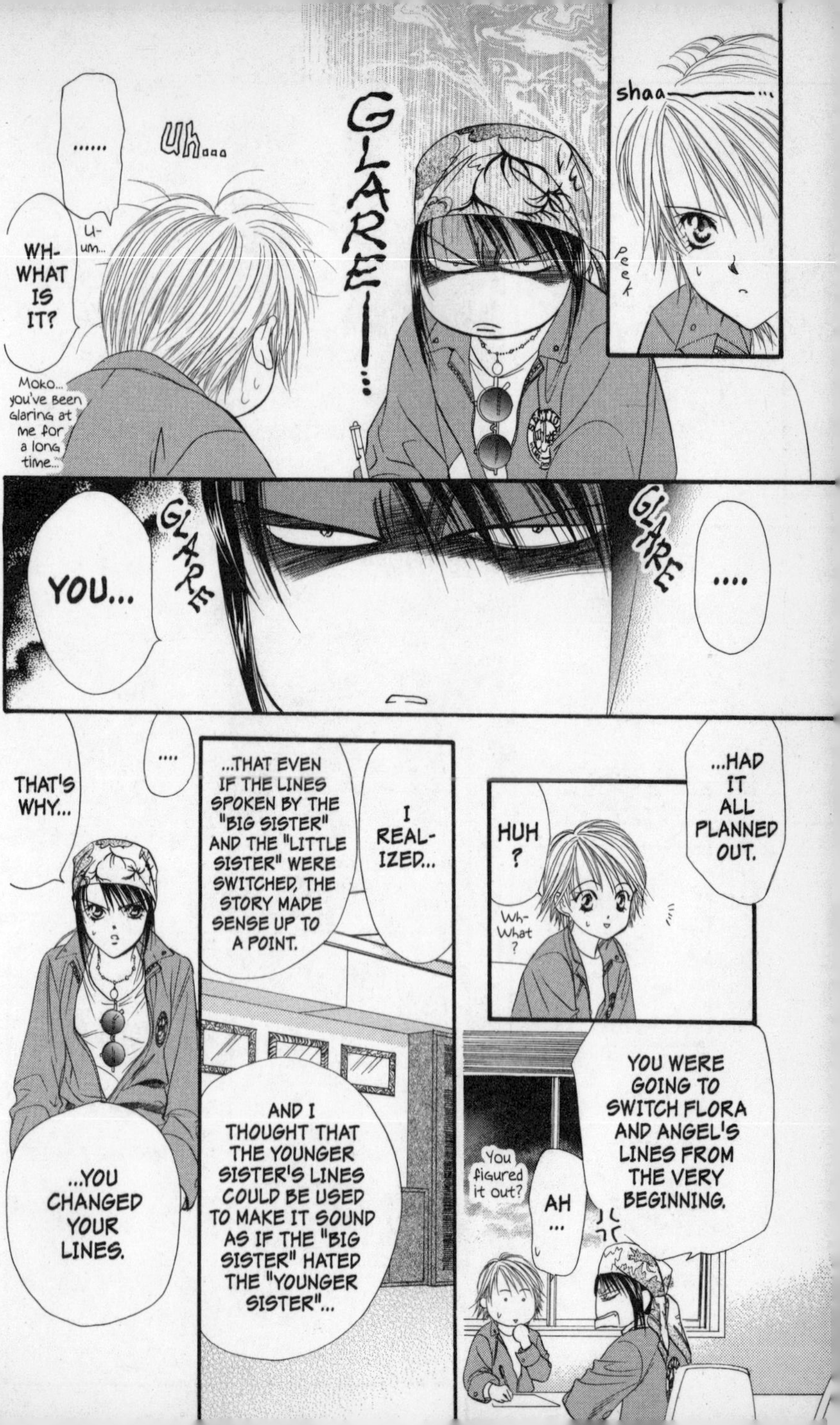
shaa———...
Peek
GLARE!!
......
Uh...
WH-WHAT IS IT?
U-um...
Moko... you've been glaring at me for a long time...
....
GLARE
GLARE
YOU...
...HAD IT ALL PLANNED OUT.
HUH?
Wh-What?
YOU WERE GOING TO SWITCH FLORA AND ANGEL'S LINES FROM THE VERY BEGINNING.
AH...
You figured it out?
I REALIZED...
...THAT EVEN IF THE LINES SPOKEN BY THE "BIG SISTER" AND THE "LITTLE SISTER" WERE SWITCHED, THE STORY MADE SENSE UP TO A POINT.
AND I THOUGHT THAT THE YOUNGER SISTER'S LINES COULD BE USED TO MAKE IT SOUND AS IF THE "BIG SISTER" HATED THE "YOUNGER SISTER"...
....
THAT'S WHY...
...YOU CHANGED YOUR LINES.

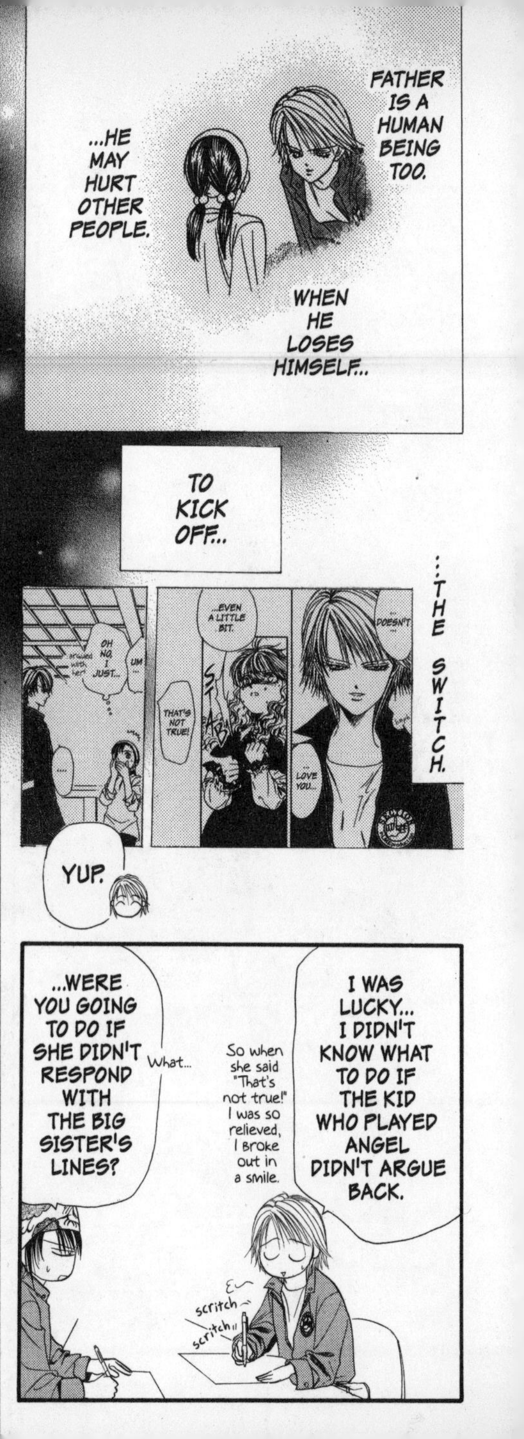
FATHER IS A HUMAN BEING TOO.
...HE MAY HURT OTHER PEOPLE.
WHEN HE LOSES HIMSELF...
TO KICK OFF...
...THE SWITCH.
...DOESN'T...
...LOVE YOU...
...EVEN A LITTLE BIT.
THAT'S NOT TRUE!
UM...
OH NO, I JUST...
argued with her!
....
YUP.
I WAS LUCKY... I DIDN'T KNOW WHAT TO DO IF THE KID WHO PLAYED ANGEL DIDN'T ARGUE BACK.
So when she said "That's not true!" I was so relieved, I broke out in a smile.
What...
...WERE YOU GOING TO DO IF SHE DIDN'T RESPOND WITH THE BIG SISTER'S LINES?
scritch
scritch
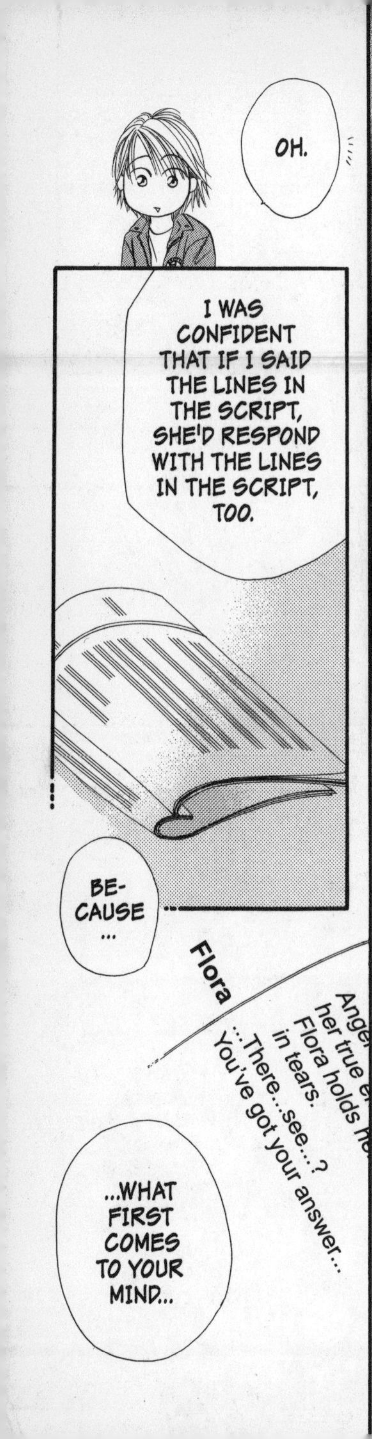
OH.
I WAS CONFIDENT THAT IF I SAID THE LINES IN THE SCRIPT, SHE'D RESPOND WITH THE LINES IN THE SCRIPT, TOO.
BE-CAUSE...
Flora
Angel
her true e
Flora holds h
in tears.
...There...see...?
You've got your answer...
...WHAT FIRST COMES TO YOUR MIND...

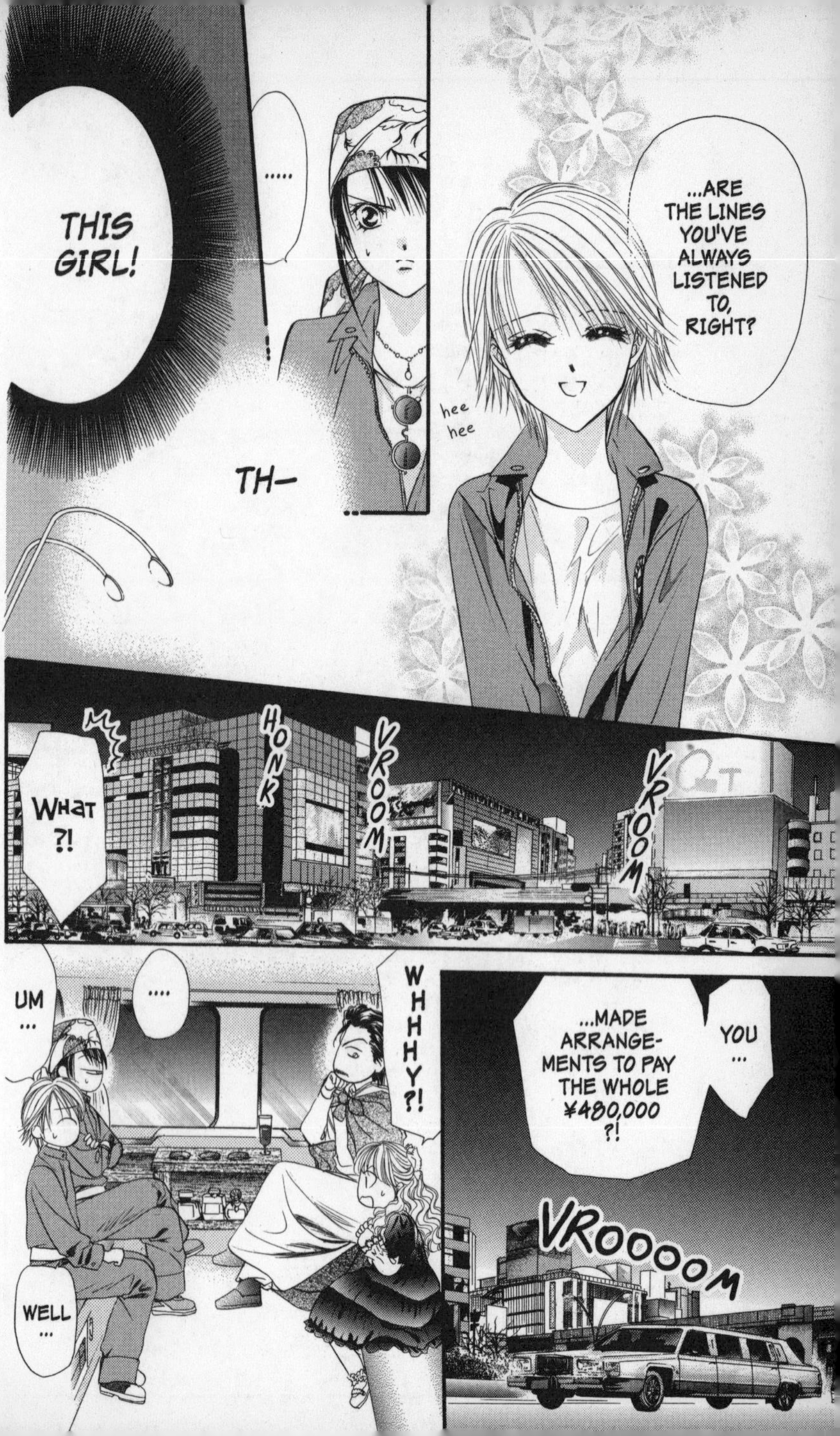
...ARE THE LINES YOU'VE ALWAYS LISTENED TO, RIGHT?
hee hee
.....
TH-
THIS GIRL!
VROOM
VROOM
HONK
What ?!
YOU ...
...MADE ARRANGE-MENTS TO PAY THE WHOLE ¥480,000 ?!
VROOOOOM
WHHHY?!
....
UM ...
WELL ...

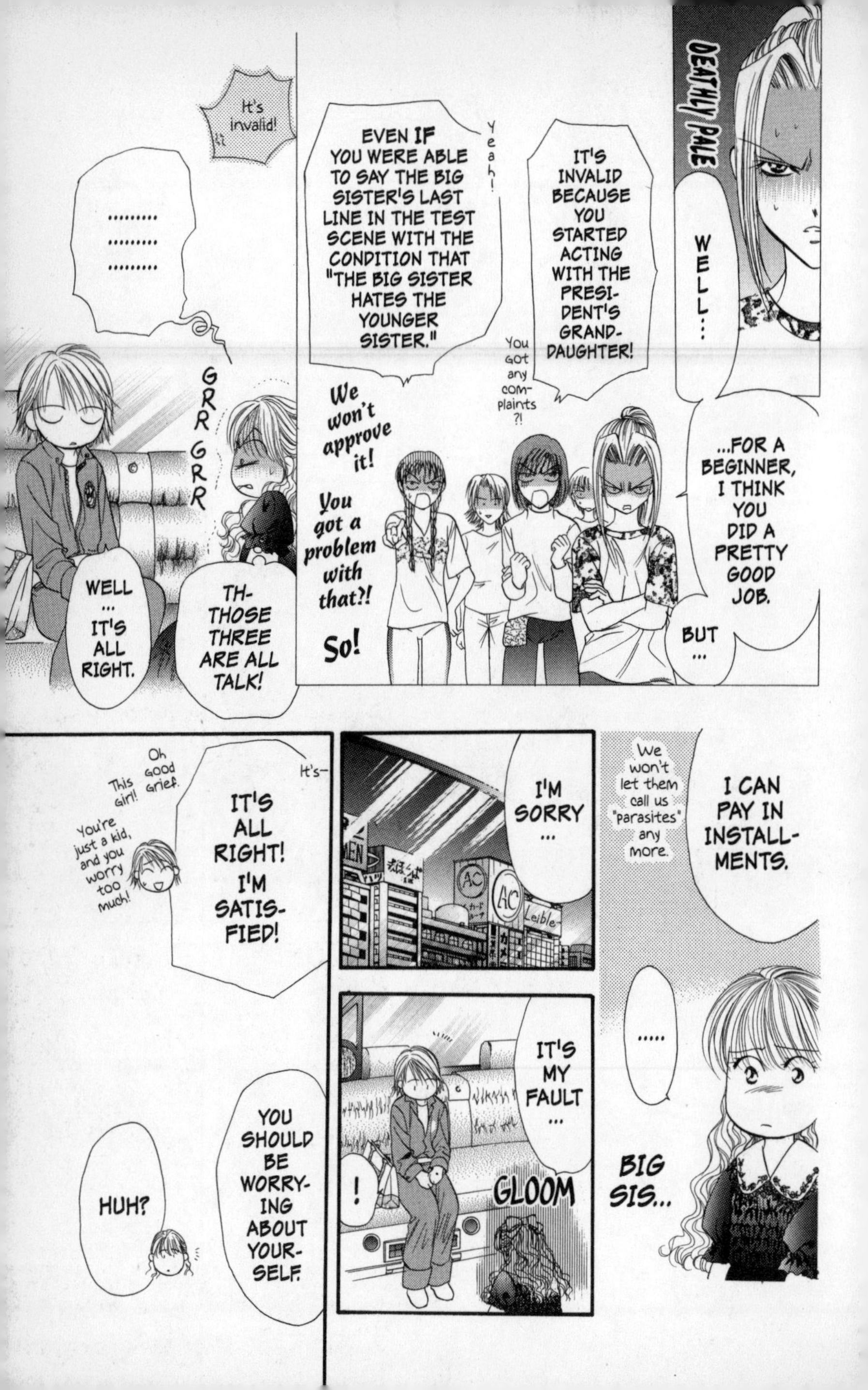
DEATHLY PALE
WELL...
...FOR A BEGINNER, I THINK YOU DID A PRETTY GOOD JOB.
BUT ...
IT'S INVALID BECAUSE YOU STARTED ACTING WITH THE PRESIDENT'S GRANDDAUGHTER!
You got any complaints?!
Yeah!
EVEN IF YOU WERE ABLE TO SAY THE BIG SISTER'S LAST LINE IN THE TEST SCENE WITH THE CONDITION THAT "THE BIG SISTER HATES THE YOUNGER SISTER."
We won't approve it!
You got a problem with that?!
So!
It's invalid!
It
....
....
....
GRR GRR
TH-THOSE THREE ARE ALL TALK!
WELL ... IT'S ALL RIGHT.
I CAN PAY IN INSTALLMENTS.
We won't let them call us "parasites" any more.
.....
BIG SIS...
I'M SORRY ...
IT'S MY FAULT ...
GLOOM
!
It's—
IT'S ALL RIGHT! I'M SATISFIED!
Oh good grief.
This girl!
You're just a kid, and you worry too much!
YOU SHOULD BE WORRYING ABOUT YOURSELF.
HUH?

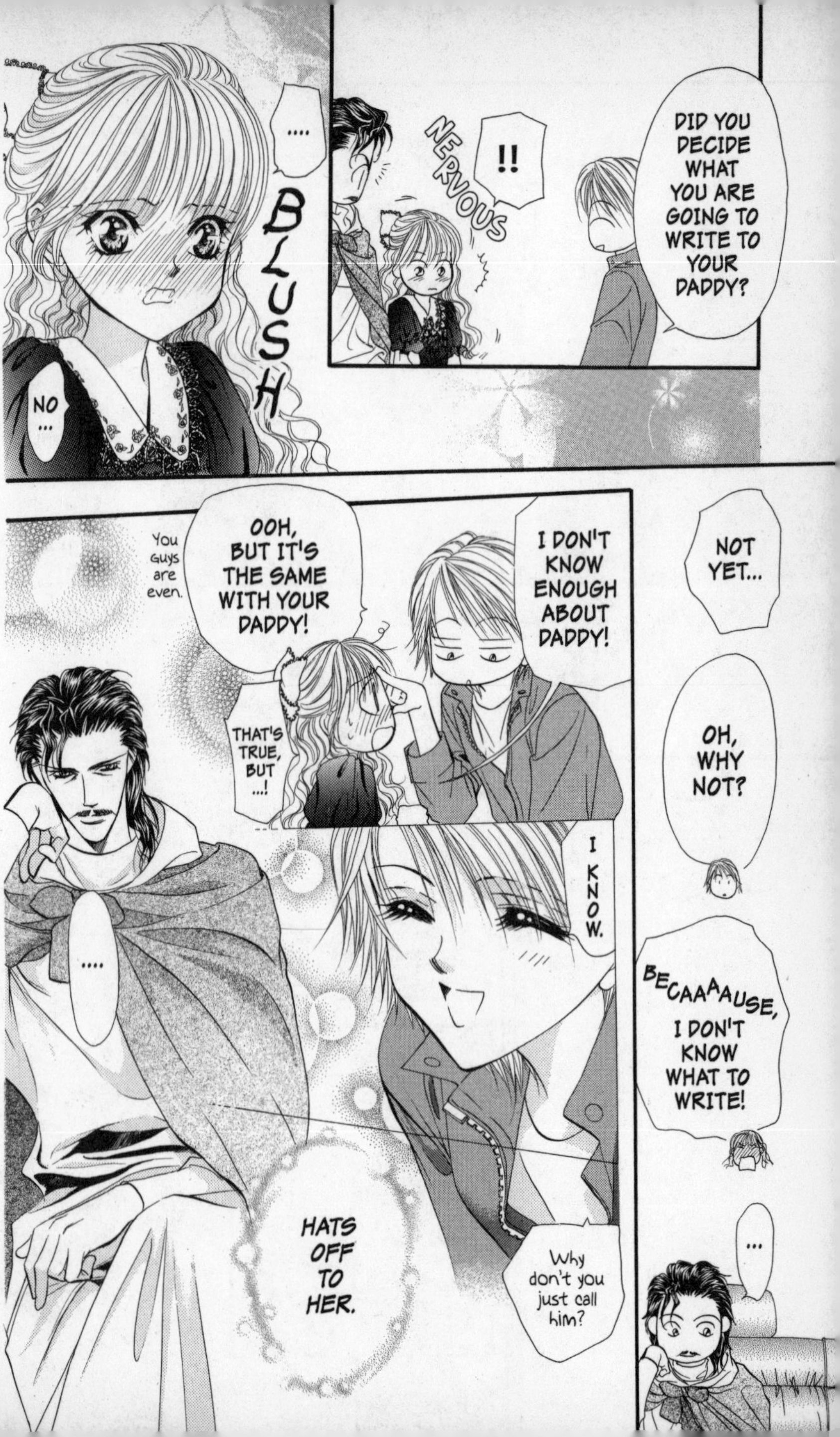
DID YOU DECIDE WHAT YOU ARE GOING TO WRITE TO YOUR DADDY?
!!
NERVOUS
....
BLUSH
NO ...
NOT YET...
OH, WHY NOT?
BECAAAAUSE, I DON'T KNOW WHAT TO WRITE!
...
I DON'T KNOW ENOUGH ABOUT DADDY!
OOH, BUT IT'S THE SAME WITH YOUR DADDY!
You Guys are even.
THAT'S TRUE, BUT ...!
I KNOW.
Why don't you just call him?
HATS OFF TO HER.
....

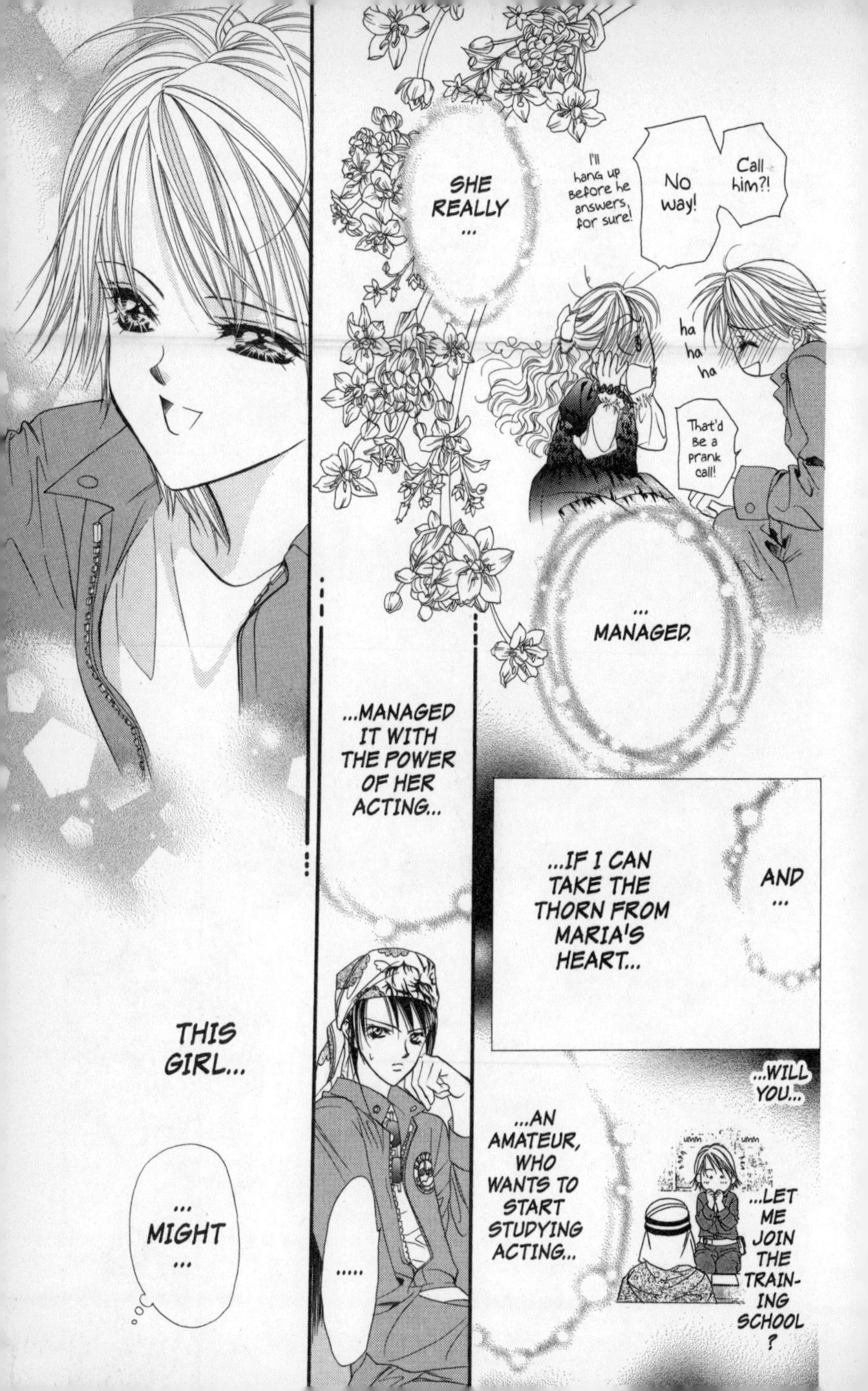

Call him?!
No way!
I'll hang up before he answers, for sure!
ha ha ha
That'd be a prank call!
SHE REALLY ...
... MANAGED.
...MANAGED IT WITH THE POWER OF HER ACTING...
AND ...
...IF I CAN TAKE THE THORN FROM MARIA'S HEART...
...WILL YOU...
umm umm
...AN AMATEUR, WHO WANTS TO START STUDYING ACTING...
...LET ME JOIN THE TRAINING SCHOOL?
.....
THIS GIRL...
... MIGHT ...

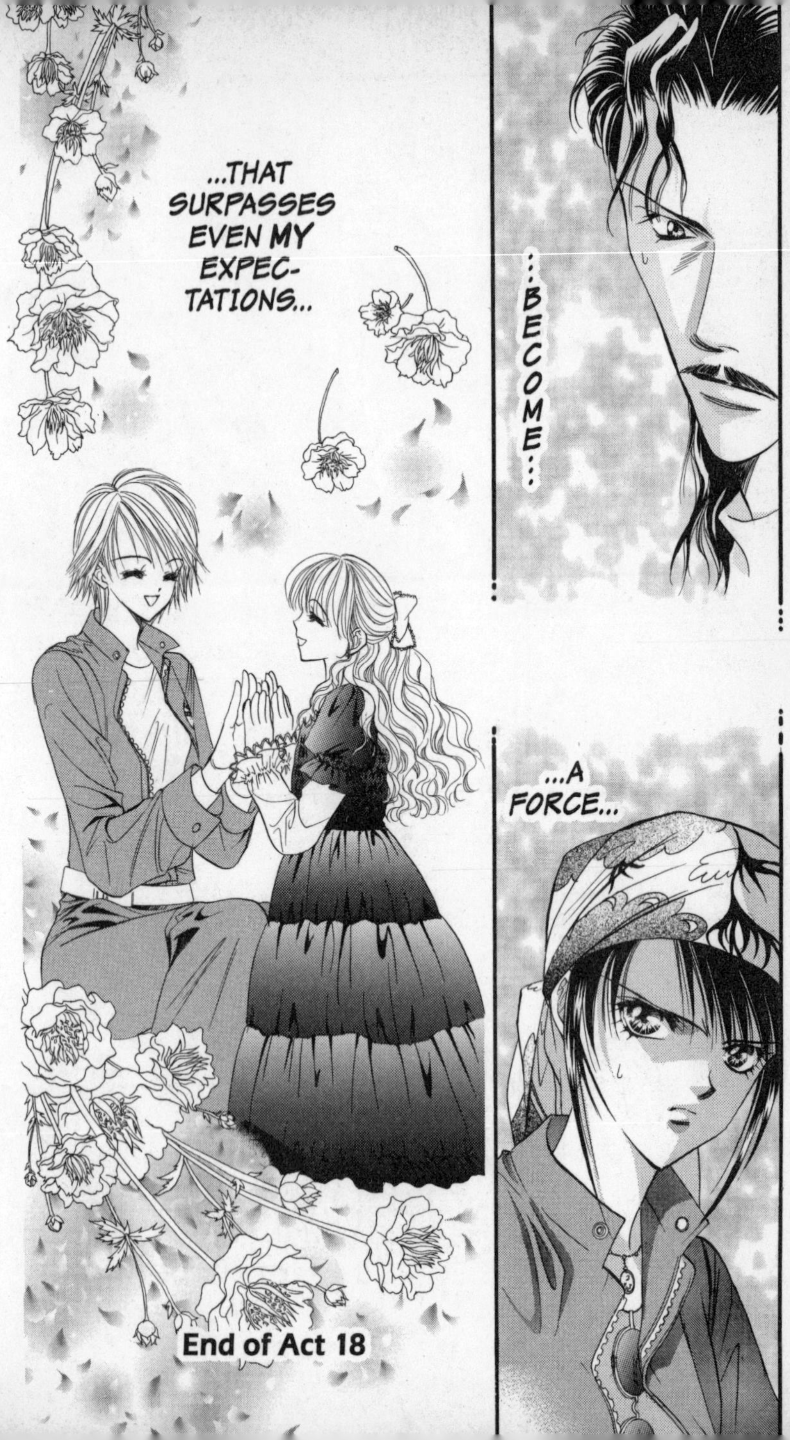
...BECOME...
...A FORCE...
...THAT SURPASSES EVEN MY EXPEC-TATIONS...
End of Act 18

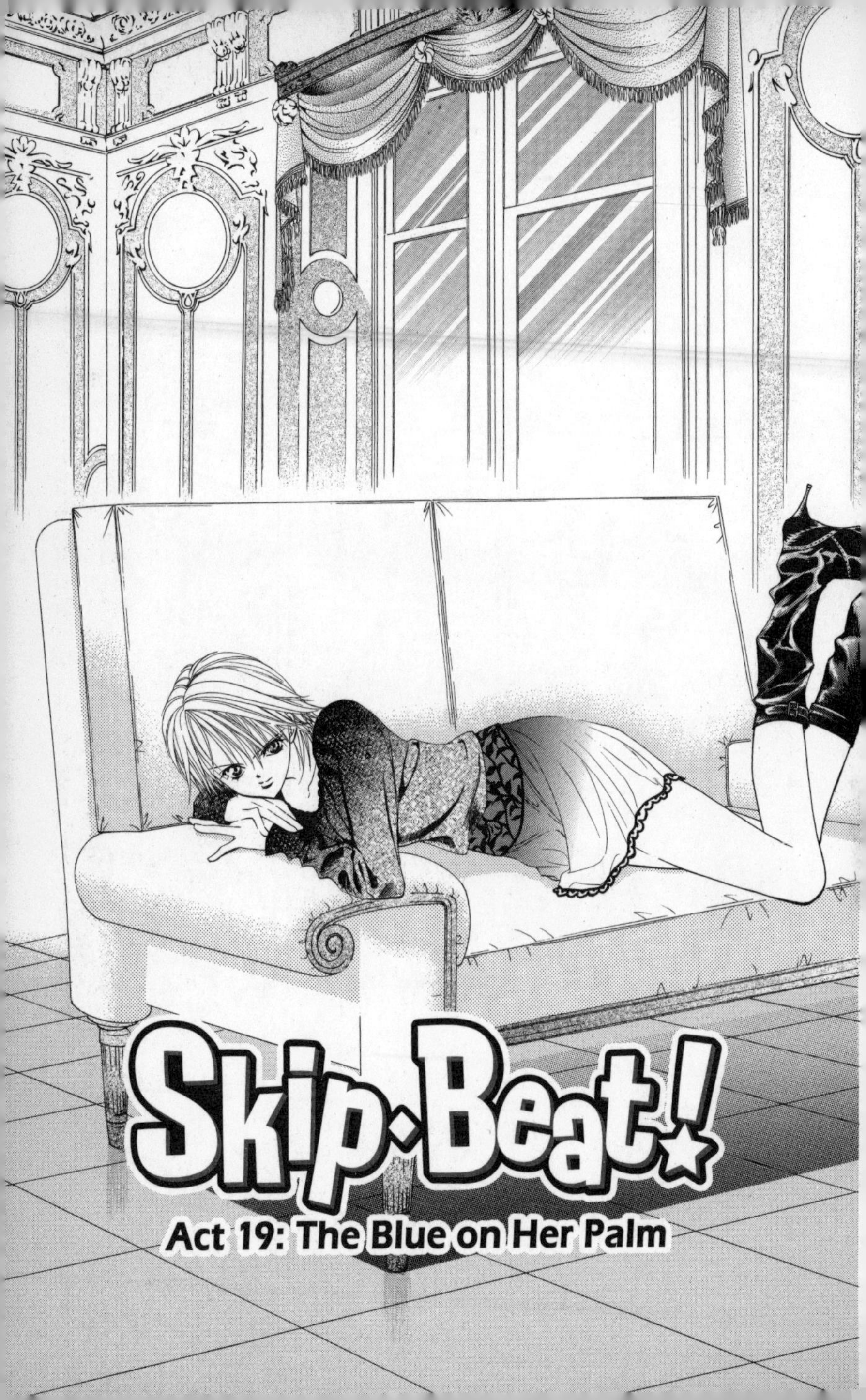
Skip·Beat!
Act 19: The Blue on Her Palm

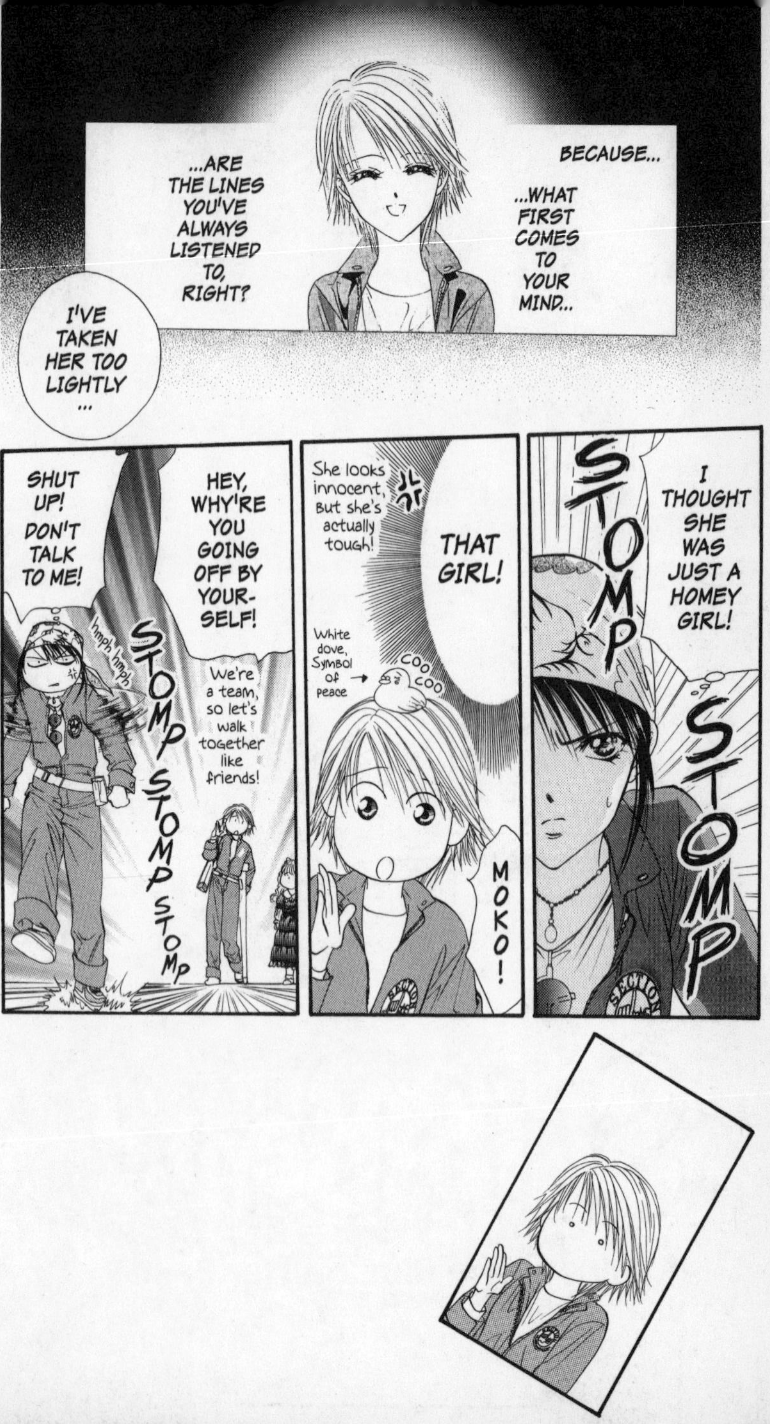
BECAUSE...
...WHAT FIRST COMES TO YOUR MIND...
...ARE THE LINES YOU'VE ALWAYS LISTENED TO, RIGHT?
I'VE TAKEN HER TOO LIGHTLY...
STOMP
I THOUGHT SHE WAS JUST A HOMEY GIRL!
STOMP
THAT GIRL!
She looks innocent, but she's actually tough!
MOKO!
White dove, Symbol of peace
COO COO
HEY, WHY'RE YOU GOING OFF BY YOURSELF!
SHUT UP! DON'T TALK TO ME!
hmph hmph
We're a team, so let's walk together like friends!
STOMP STOMP STOMP

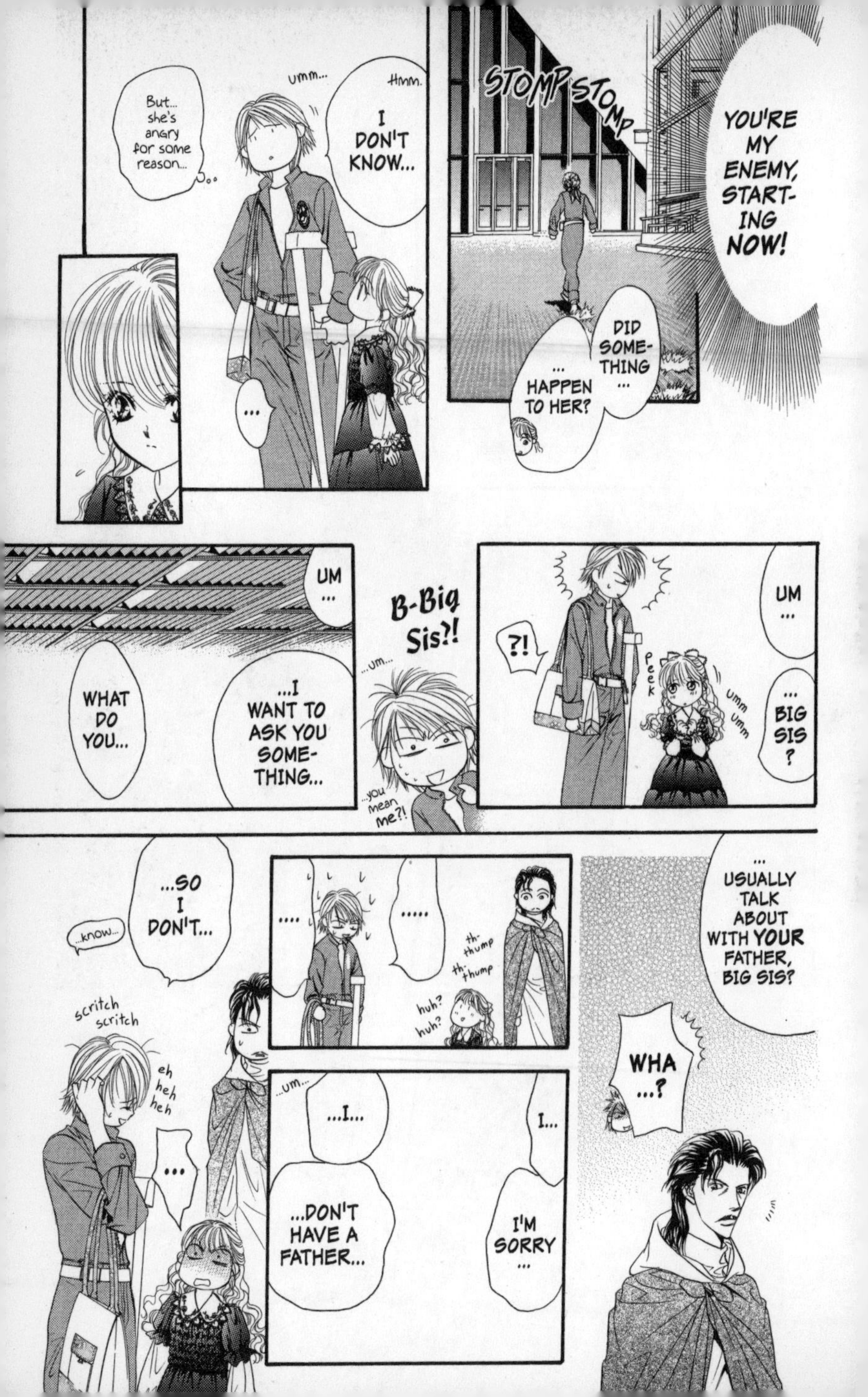
STOMP STOMP
YOU'RE MY ENEMY, STARTING NOW!
DID SOMETHING...
...HAPPEN TO HER?
Hmm.
I DON'T KNOW...
umm...
But... she's angry for some reason...
...
UM...
...BIG SIS?
?!
Peek
umm umm
B-Big Sis?!
...um...
...you mean me?!
UM...
...I WANT TO ASK YOU SOMETHING...
WHAT DO YOU...
...USUALLY TALK ABOUT WITH YOUR FATHER, BIG SIS?
WHA...?
.....
....
th-thump th-thump
huh? huh?
I...
...I...
...um...
I'M SORRY...
...DON'T HAVE A FATHER...
...SO I DON'T...
...know...
scritch scritch
eh heh heh
...

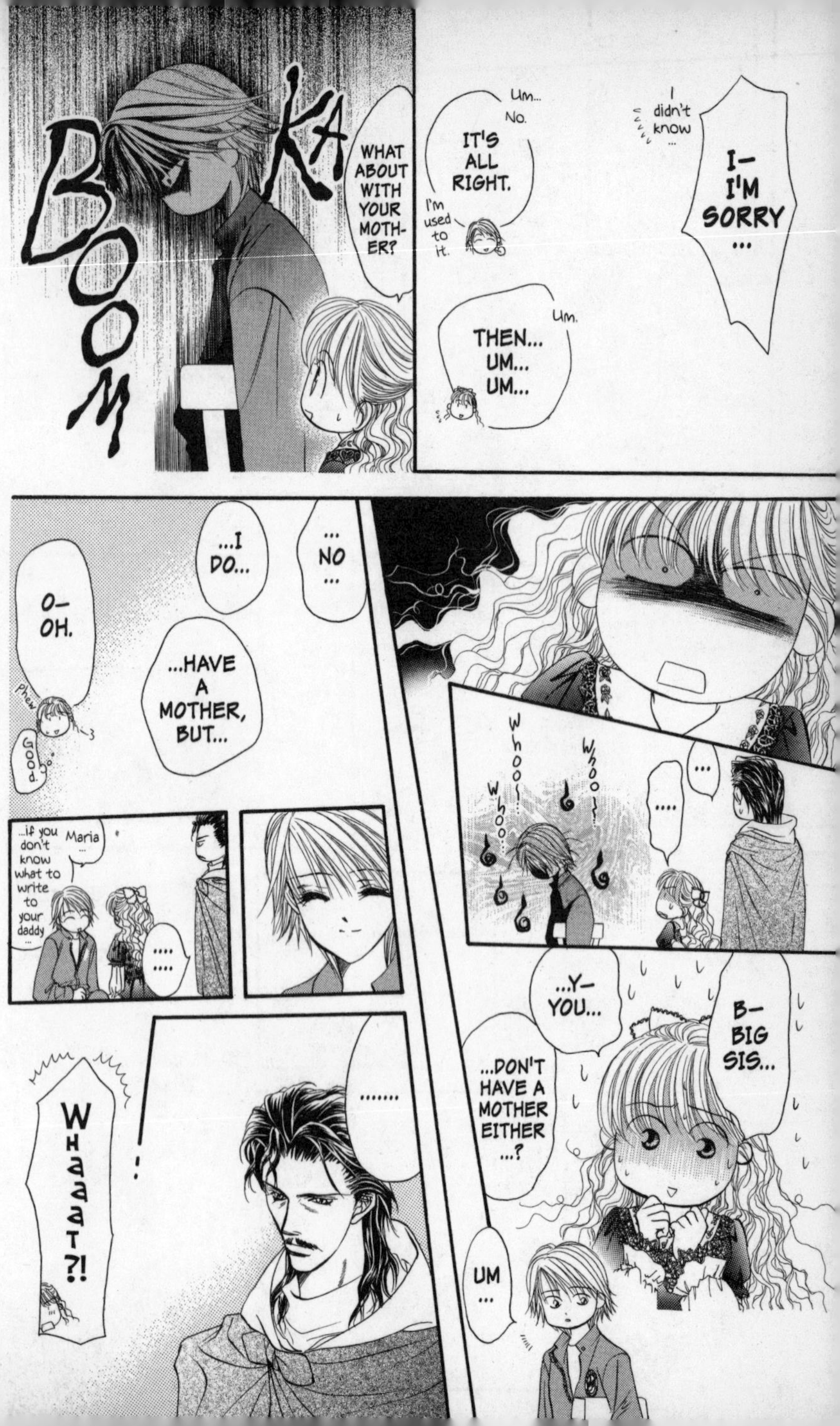
I didn't know...
I— I'M SORRY...
Um... No.
IT'S ALL RIGHT.
I'm used to it.
Um.
THEN... UM... UM...
KA BOOM
WHAT ABOUT WITH YOUR MOTHER?
Whoo~... Whoo~... Whoo~...
...
....
B— BIG SIS...
...Y— YOU...
...DON'T HAVE A MOTHER EITHER...?
UM...
... NO ...
...I DO...
...HAVE A MOTHER, BUT...
O— OH.
Phew
Good.
Maria...
...if you don't know what to write to your daddy...
....
....
!
Whaaat?!

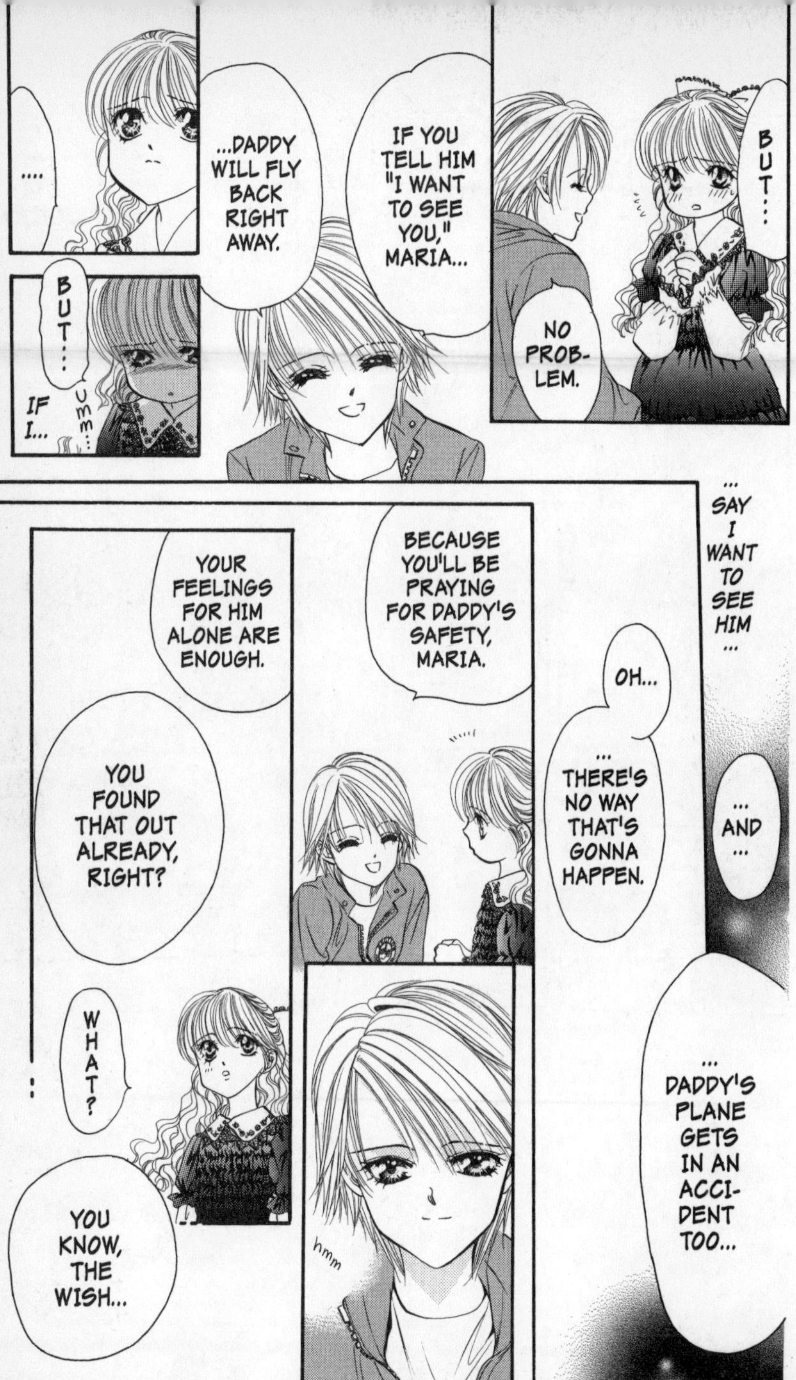
BUT...
NO PROBLEM.
IF YOU TELL HIM "I WANT TO SEE YOU," MARIA...
...DADDY WILL FLY BACK RIGHT AWAY.
....
BUT...
UMM...
IF I...
... SAY I WANT TO SEE HIM ...
... AND ...
... DADDY'S PLANE GETS IN AN ACCIDENT TOO...
OH...
... THERE'S NO WAY THAT'S GONNA HAPPEN.
BECAUSE YOU'LL BE PRAYING FOR DADDY'S SAFETY, MARIA.
YOUR FEELINGS FOR HIM ALONE ARE ENOUGH.
YOU FOUND THAT OUT ALREADY, RIGHT?
hmm
WHAT?
..
YOU KNOW, THE WISH...

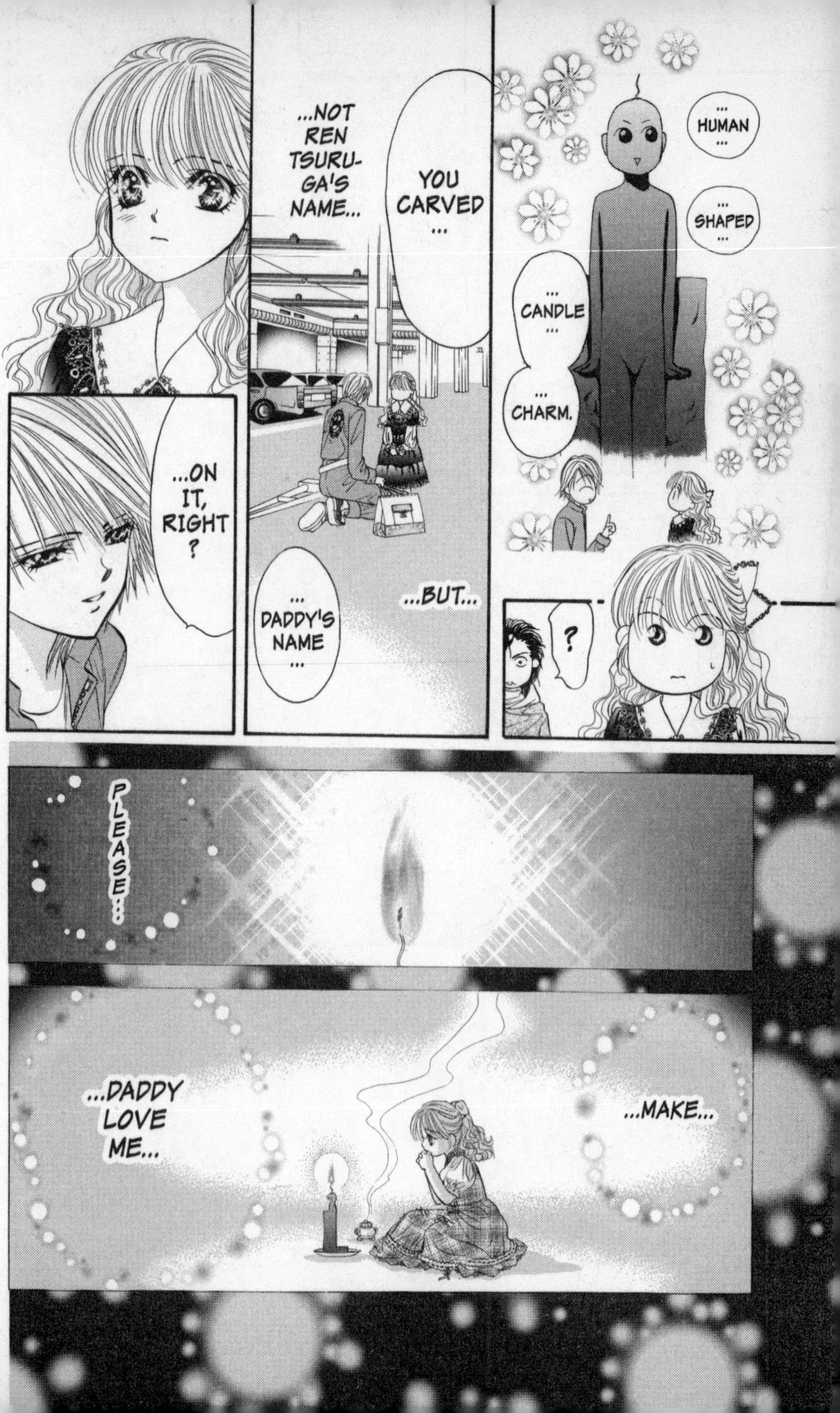
...HUMAN...
...SHAPED...
...CANDLE...
...CHARM.
?
YOU CARVED...
...NOT REN TSURUGA'S NAME...
...BUT...
...DADDY'S NAME...
...ON IT, RIGHT?
PLEASE...
...MAKE...
...DADDY LOVE ME...

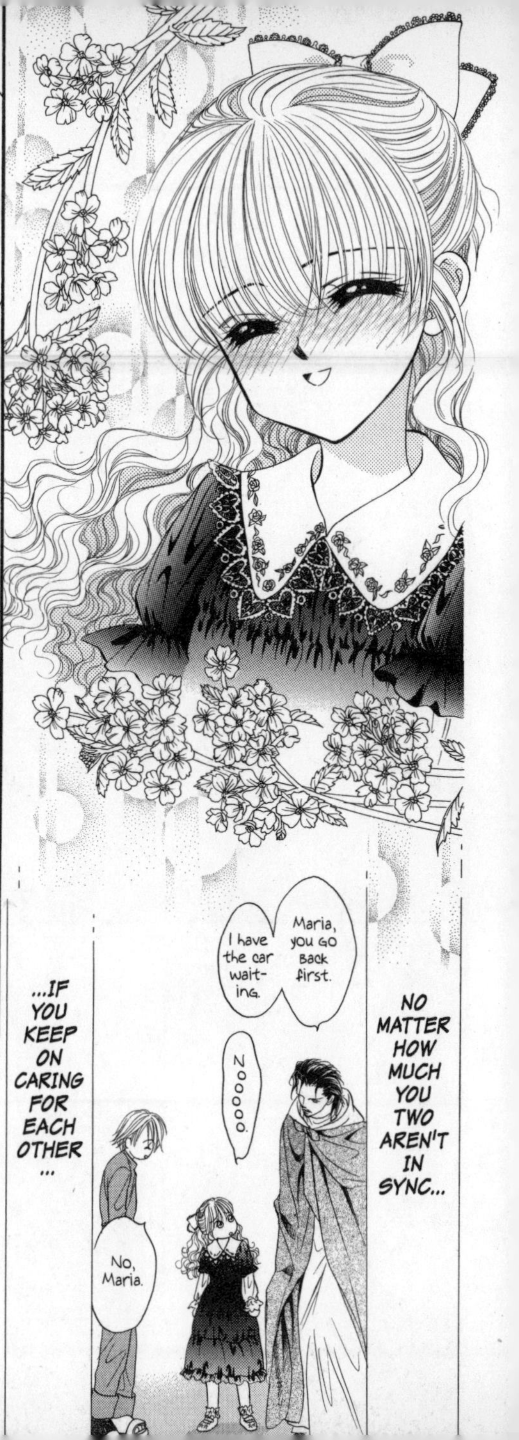
NO MATTER HOW MUCH YOU TWO AREN'T IN SYNC...
Maria, you GO Back first.
I have the car wait-ing.
Noooo.
No, Maria.
...IF YOU KEEP ON CARING FOR EACH OTHER ...

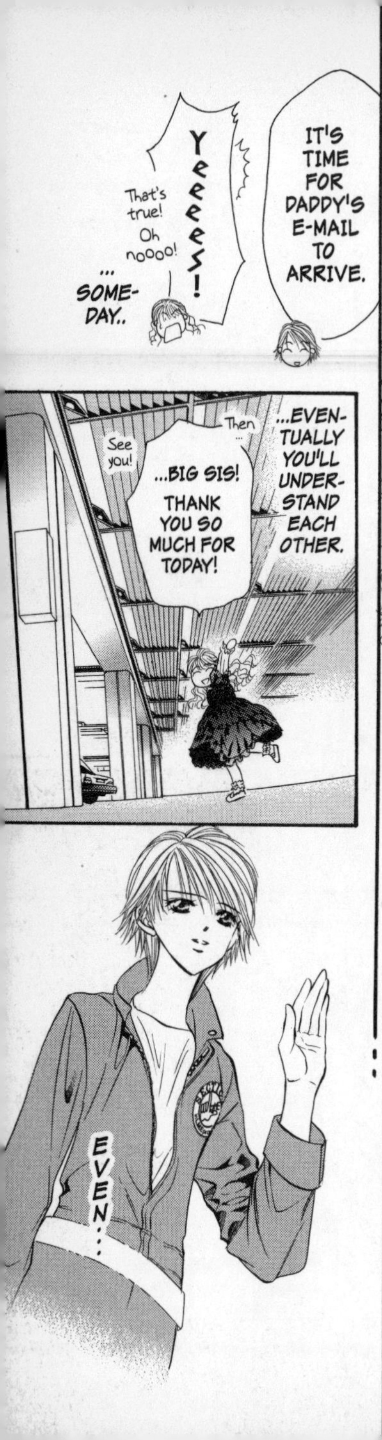
IT'S TIME FOR DADDY'S E-MAIL TO ARRIVE.
Yeeees!
That's true! Oh noooo!
... SOME-DAY..
...EVEN-TUALLY YOU'LL UNDER-STAND EACH OTHER.
Then ...
...BIG SIS! THANK YOU SO MUCH FOR TODAY!
See you!
EVEN...

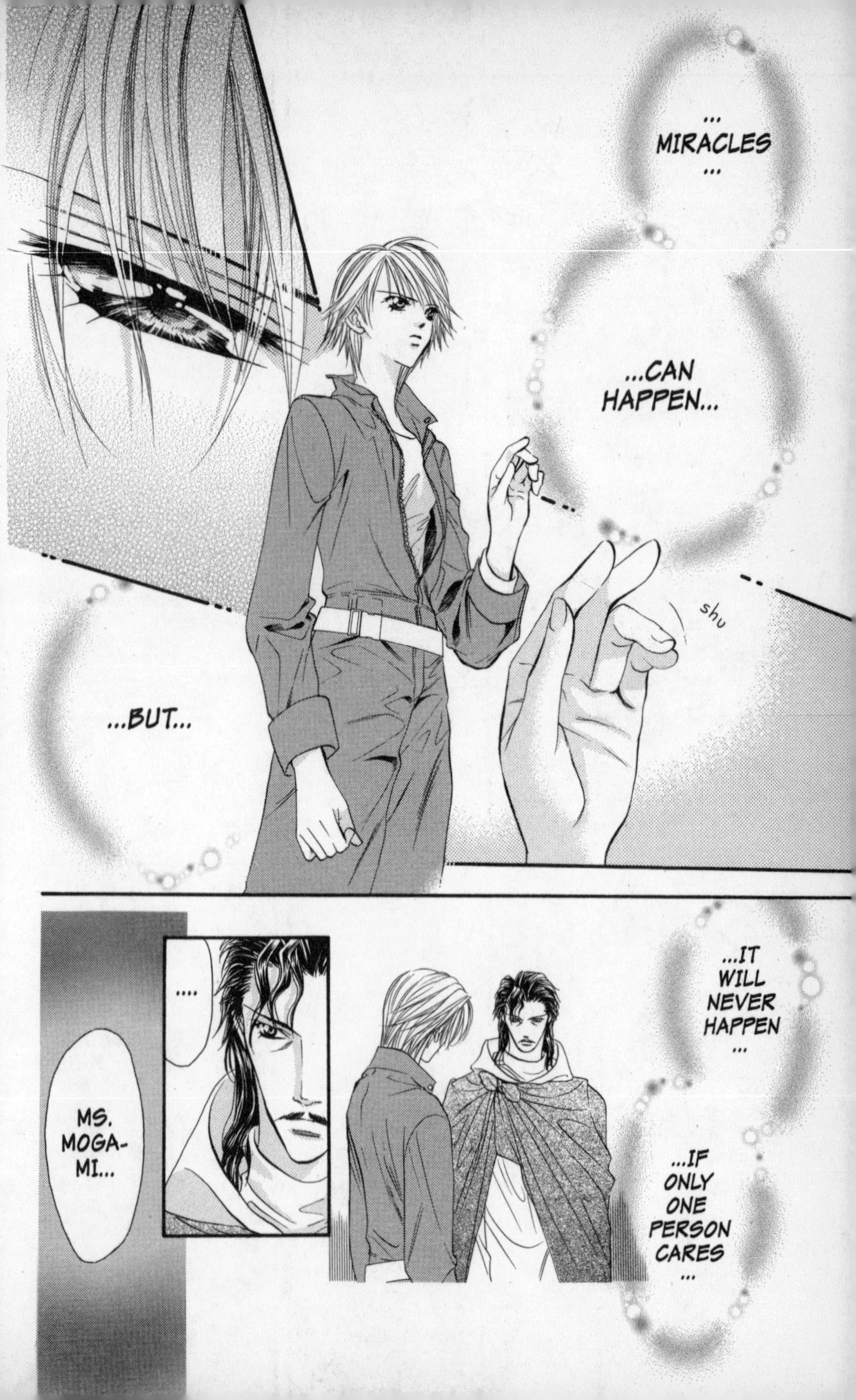

... MIRACLES ...
...CAN HAPPEN...
shu
...BUT...
...IT WILL NEVER HAPPEN ...
...IF ONLY ONE PERSON CARES ...
....
MS. MOGA-MI...

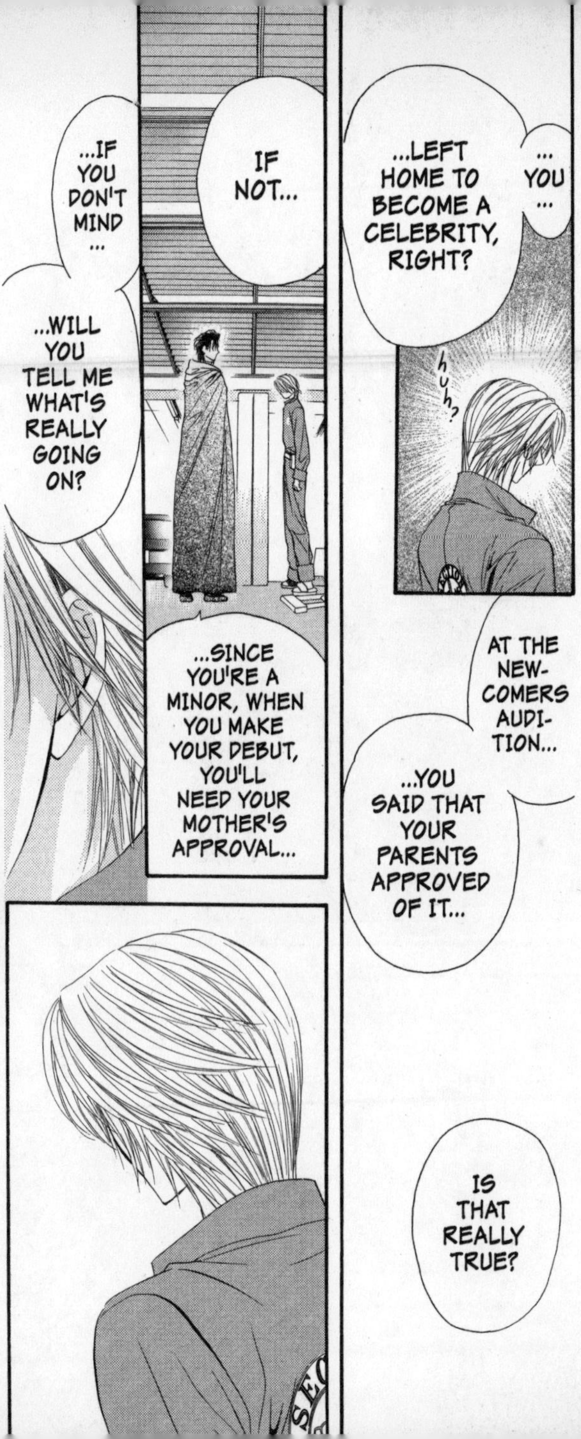
... YOU ...
...LEFT HOME TO BECOME A CELEBRITY, RIGHT?
huh?
AT THE NEWCOMERS AUDITION...
...YOU SAID THAT YOUR PARENTS APPROVED OF IT...
IS THAT REALLY TRUE?
...SINCE YOU'RE A MINOR, WHEN YOU MAKE YOUR DEBUT, YOU'LL NEED YOUR MOTHER'S APPROVAL...
IF NOT...
...IF YOU DON'T MIND...
...WILL YOU TELL ME WHAT'S REALLY GOING ON?

Shoko Aki

Shotaro's manager. I really wasn't thinking anything when I named her Shoko. When I thought about it later...

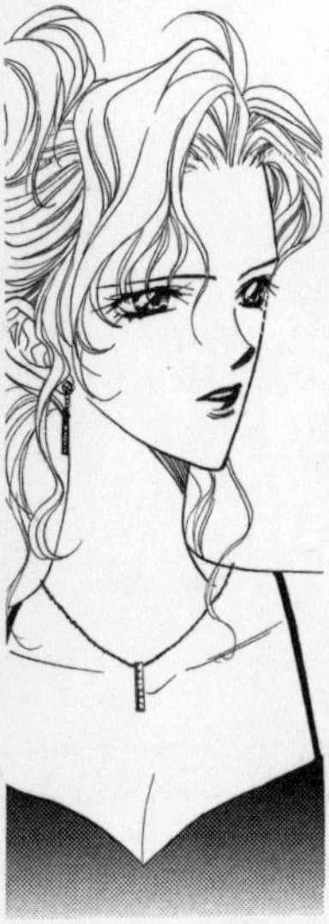

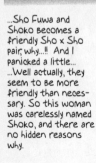

...Sho Fuwa and Shoko becomes a friendly Sho x Sho pair, why...!! And I panicked a little... ...Well actually, they seem to be more friendly than necessary. So this woman was carelessly named Shoko, and there are no hidden reasons why.

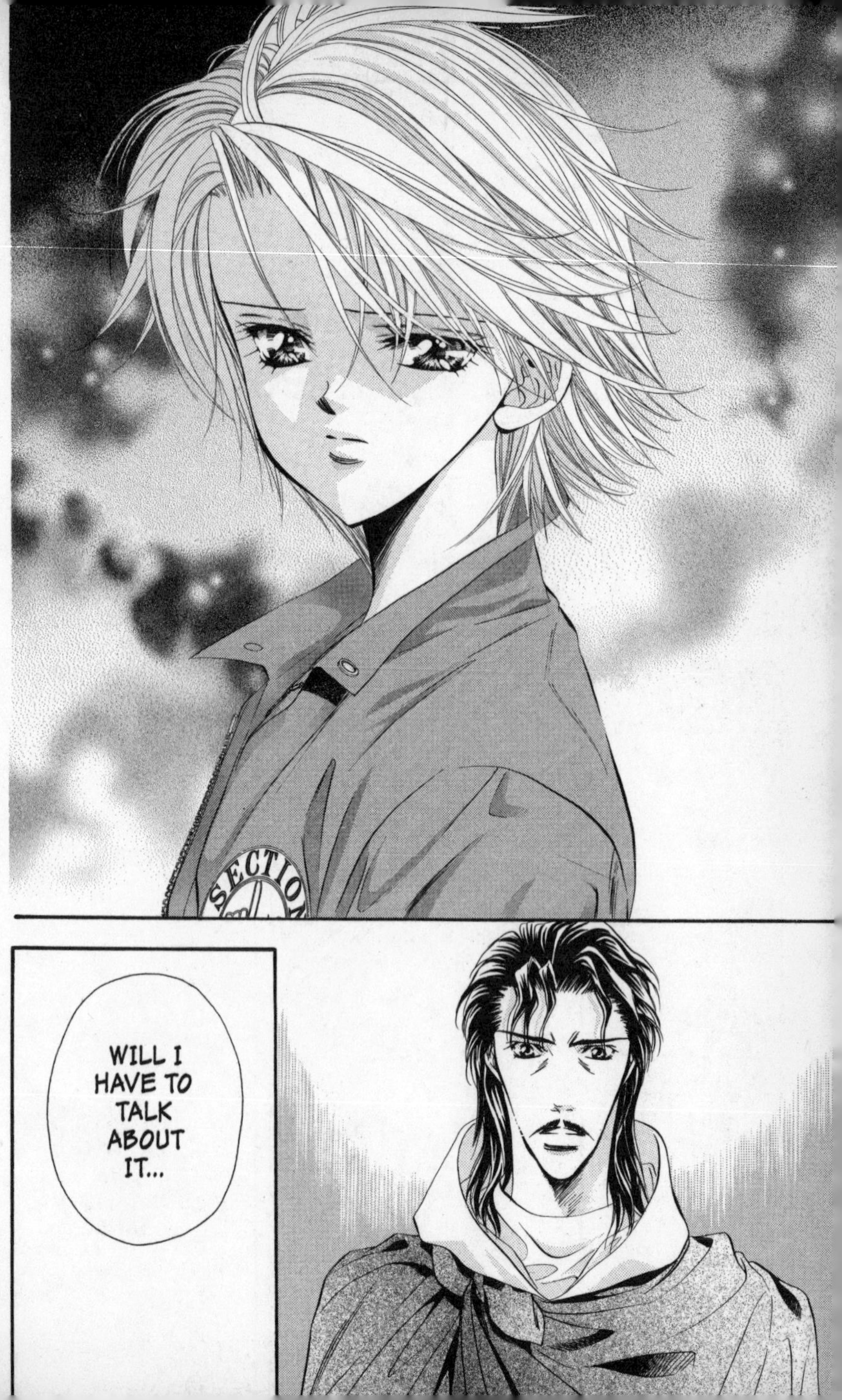
SECTION
WILL I HAVE TO TALK ABOUT IT...

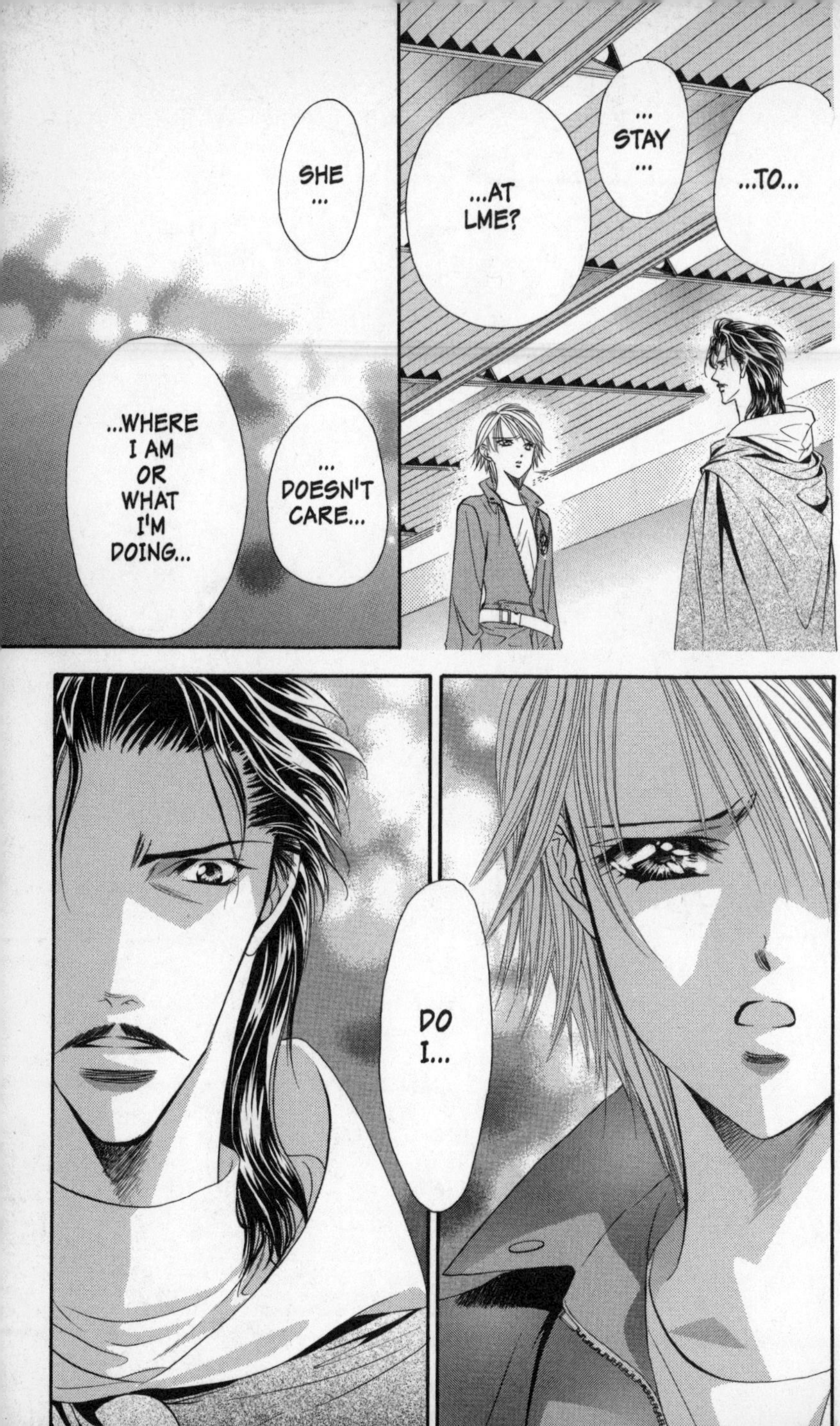
...TO...
...STAY...
...AT LME?
SHE ...
...DOESN'T CARE...
...WHERE I AM OR WHAT I'M DOING...
DO I...

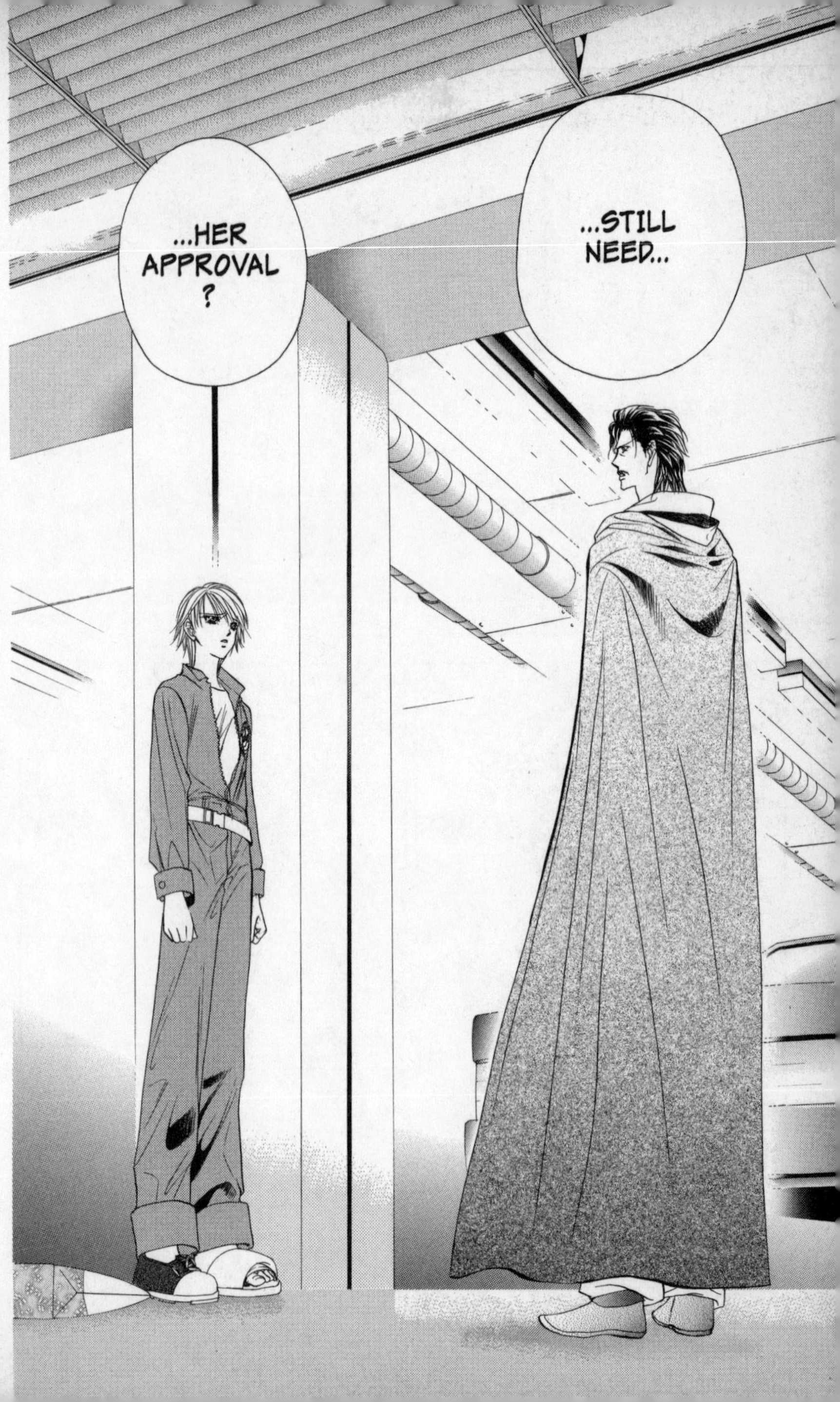
...STILL NEED...
...HER APPROVAL ?

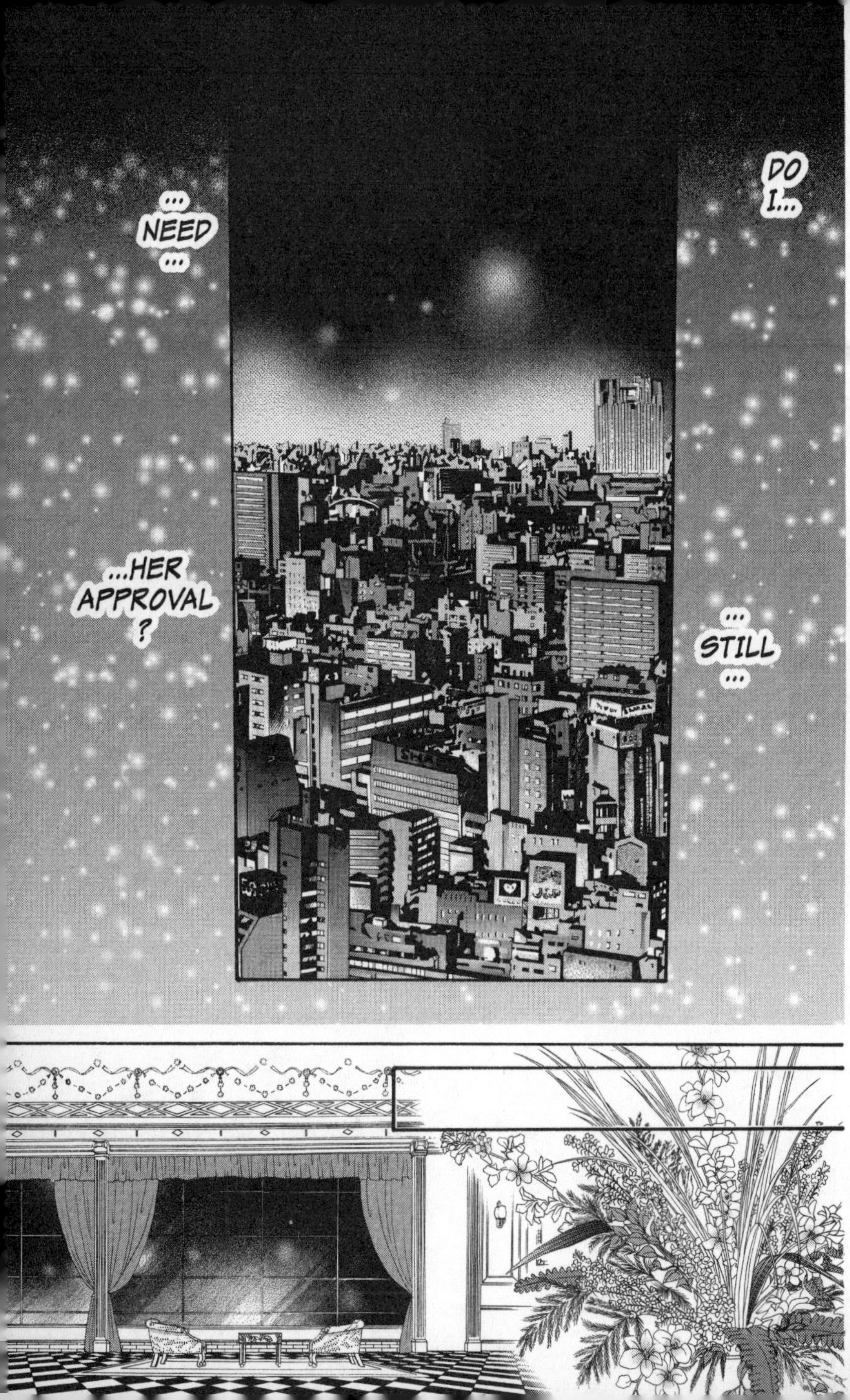
DO I...
...STILL...
...NEED...
...HER APPROVAL?

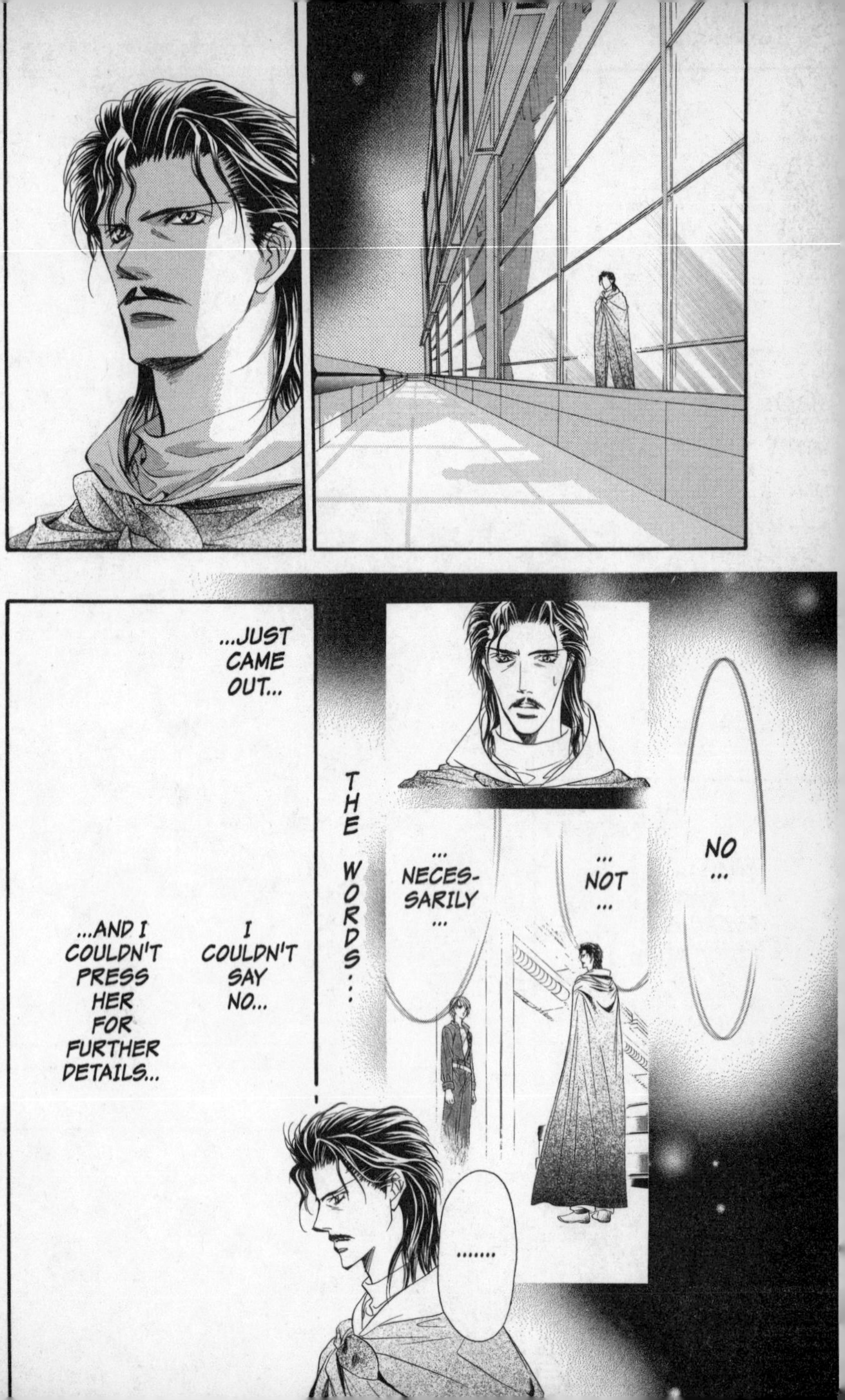
NO ...
... NOT ...
... NECES-SARILY ...
THE WORDS...
...JUST CAME OUT...
I COULDN'T SAY NO...
...AND I COULDN'T PRESS HER FOR FURTHER DETAILS...
....

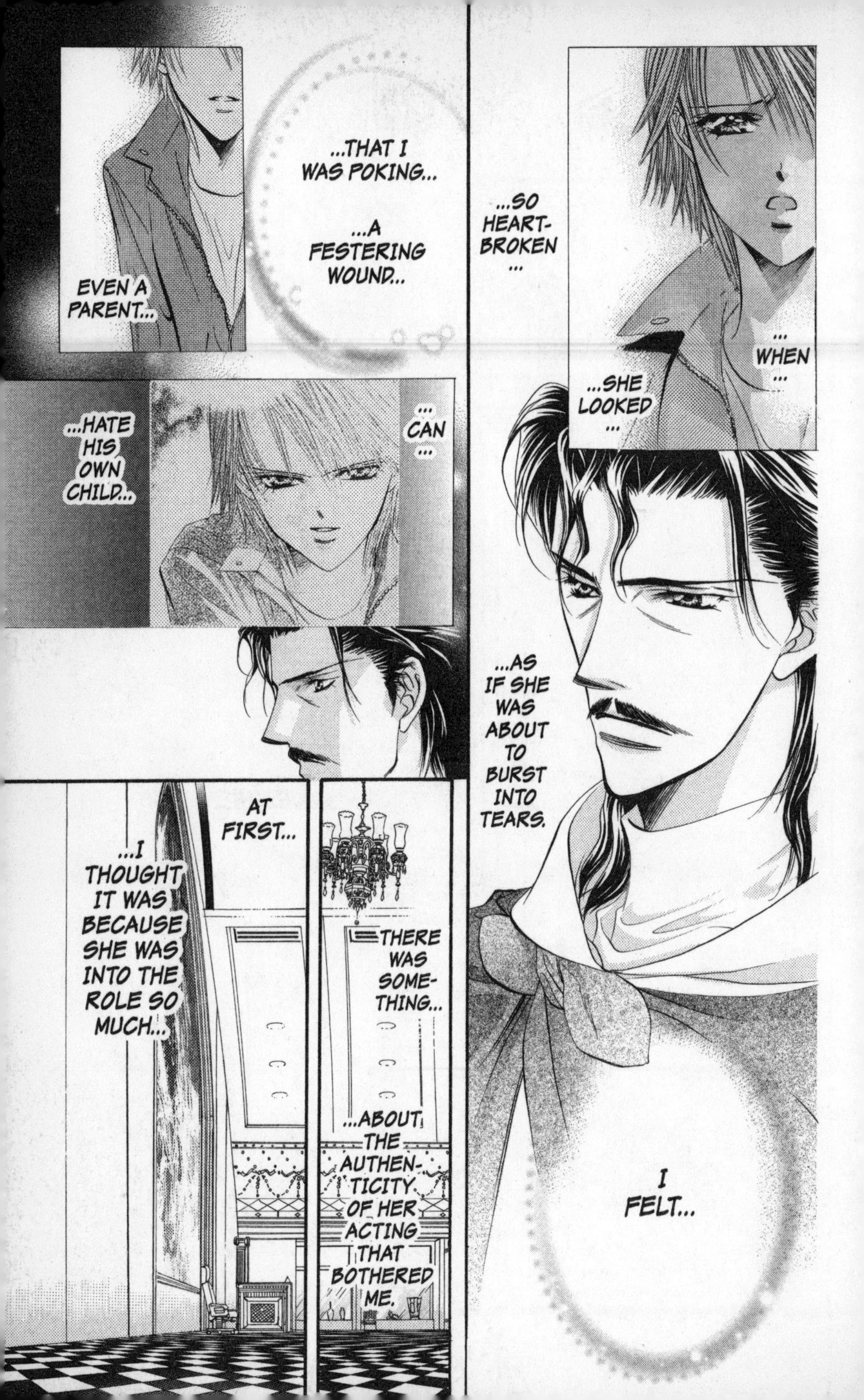

...SO HEART-BROKEN...
...WHEN...
...SHE LOOKED...
...AS IF SHE WAS ABOUT TO BURST INTO TEARS.
I FELT...
...THAT I WAS POKING...
...A FESTERING WOUND...
EVEN A PARENT...
...CAN...
...HATE HIS OWN CHILD...
AT FIRST...
...I THOUGHT IT WAS BECAUSE SHE WAS INTO THE ROLE SO MUCH...
THERE WAS SOME-THING...
...ABOUT THE AUTHEN-TICITY OF HER ACTING THAT BOTHERED ME.

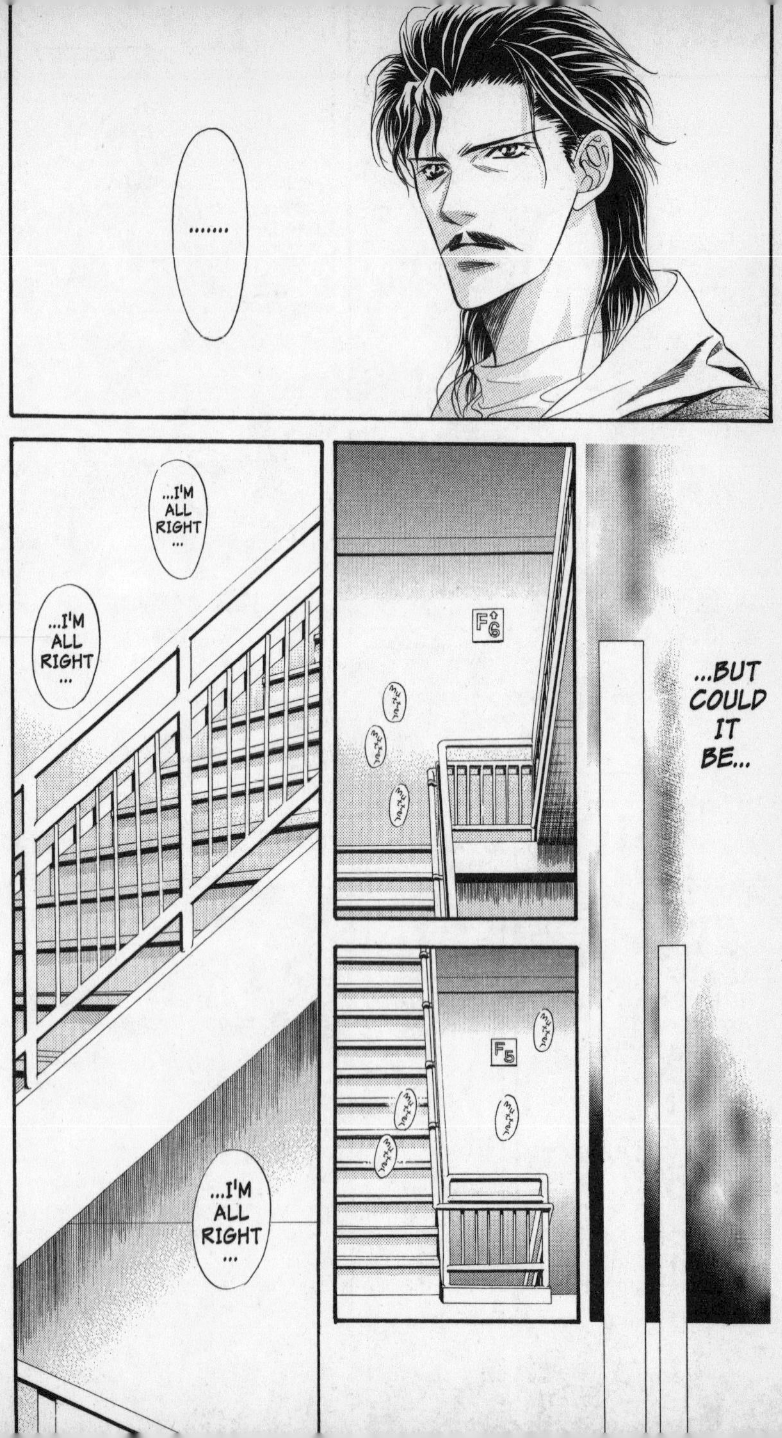
....
...BUT COULD IT BE...
F6
mutter
mutter
mutter
F5
mutter
mutter
mutter
mutter
...I'M ALL RIGHT...
...I'M ALL RIGHT...
...I'M ALL RIGHT...

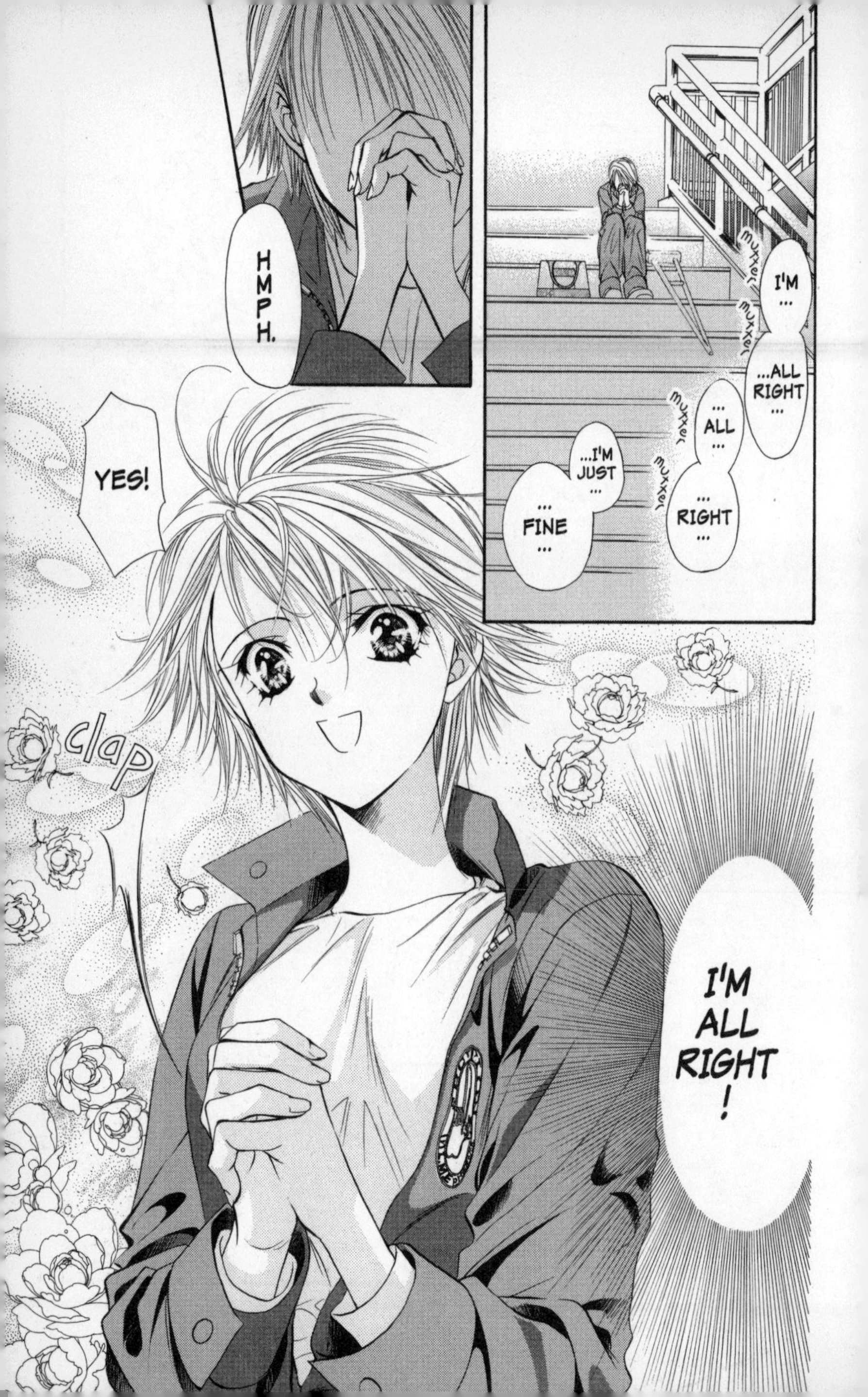
I'M ...
muxxer
...ALL RIGHT ...
muxxer
... ALL ...
muxxer
... RIGHT ...
muxxer
...I'M JUST ...
... FINE ...
HMPH.
YES!
clap
I'M ALL RIGHT!

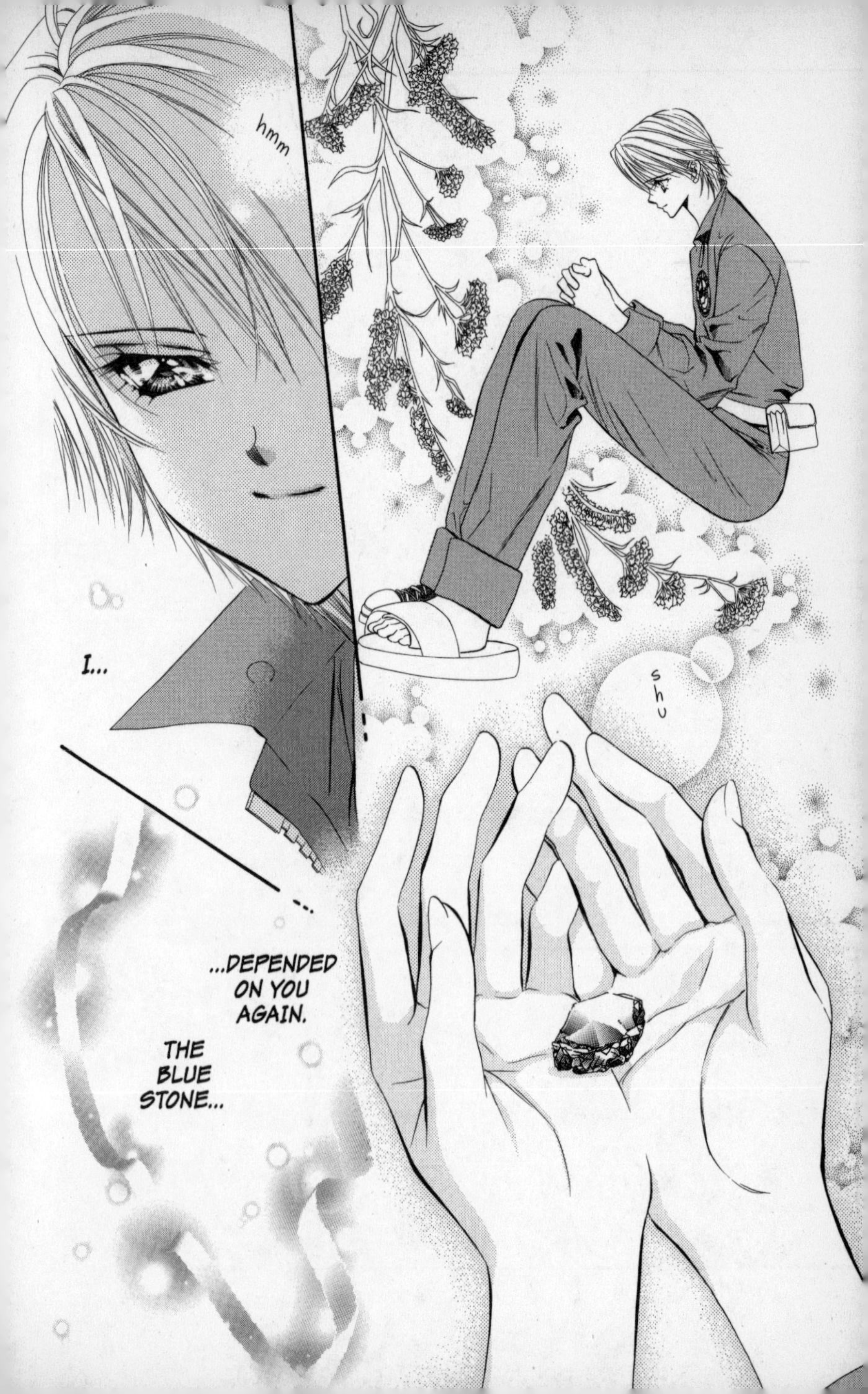
shu
hmm
I...
...DEPENDED ON YOU AGAIN.
THE BLUE STONE...

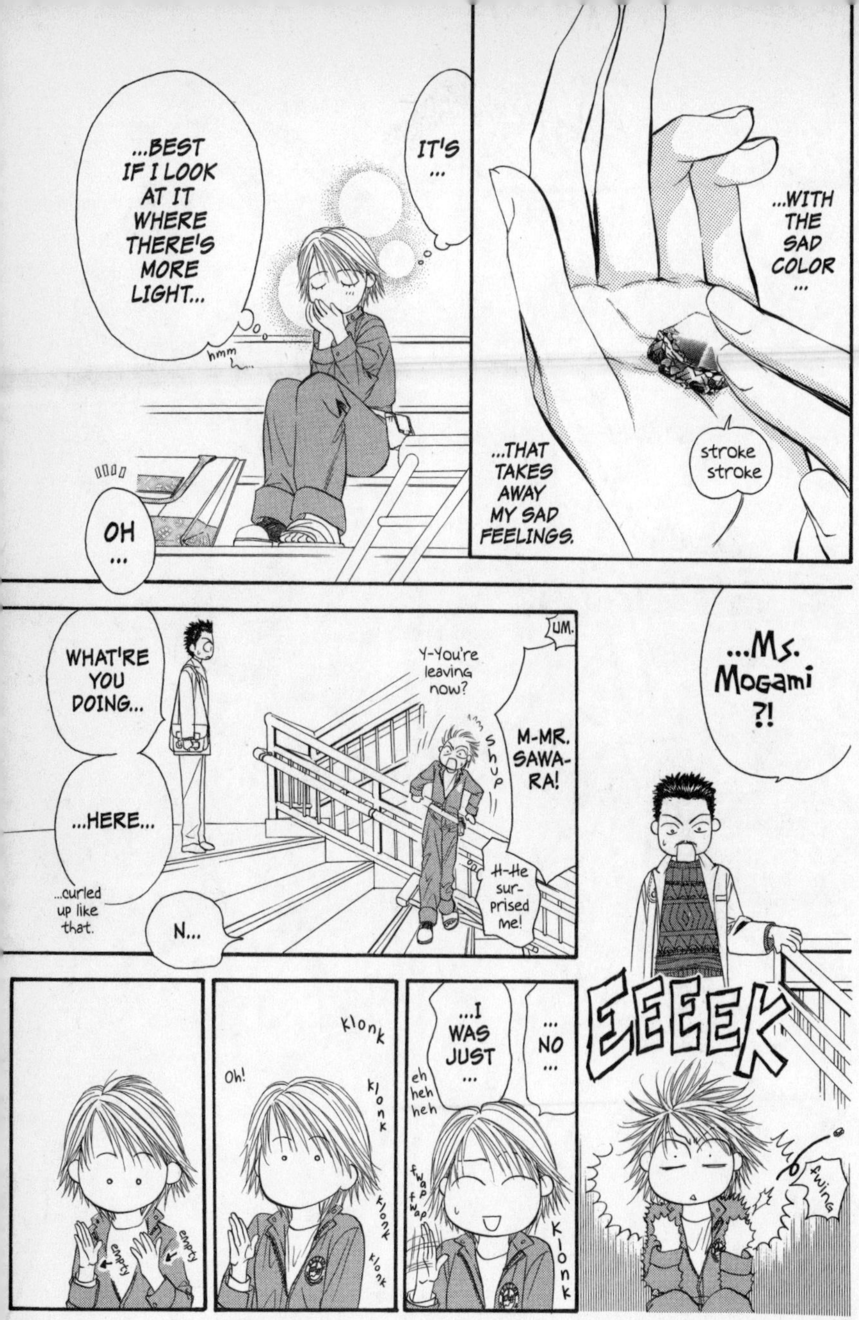
...WITH THE SAD COLOR ...
...THAT TAKES AWAY MY SAD FEELINGS.
stroke stroke
IT'S ...
...BEST IF I LOOK AT IT WHERE THERE'S MORE LIGHT...
hmm
OH ...
...Ms. Mogami ?!
UM.
M-MR. SAWARA!
Y-You're leaving now?
shup
H-He surprised me!
WHAT'RE YOU DOING...
...HERE...
...curled up like that.
N...
EEEEK
fwing
... NO ...
...I WAS JUST ...
eh heh heh
fwap fwap
klonk
Oh!
klonk
klonk
klonk
klonk
empty
empty

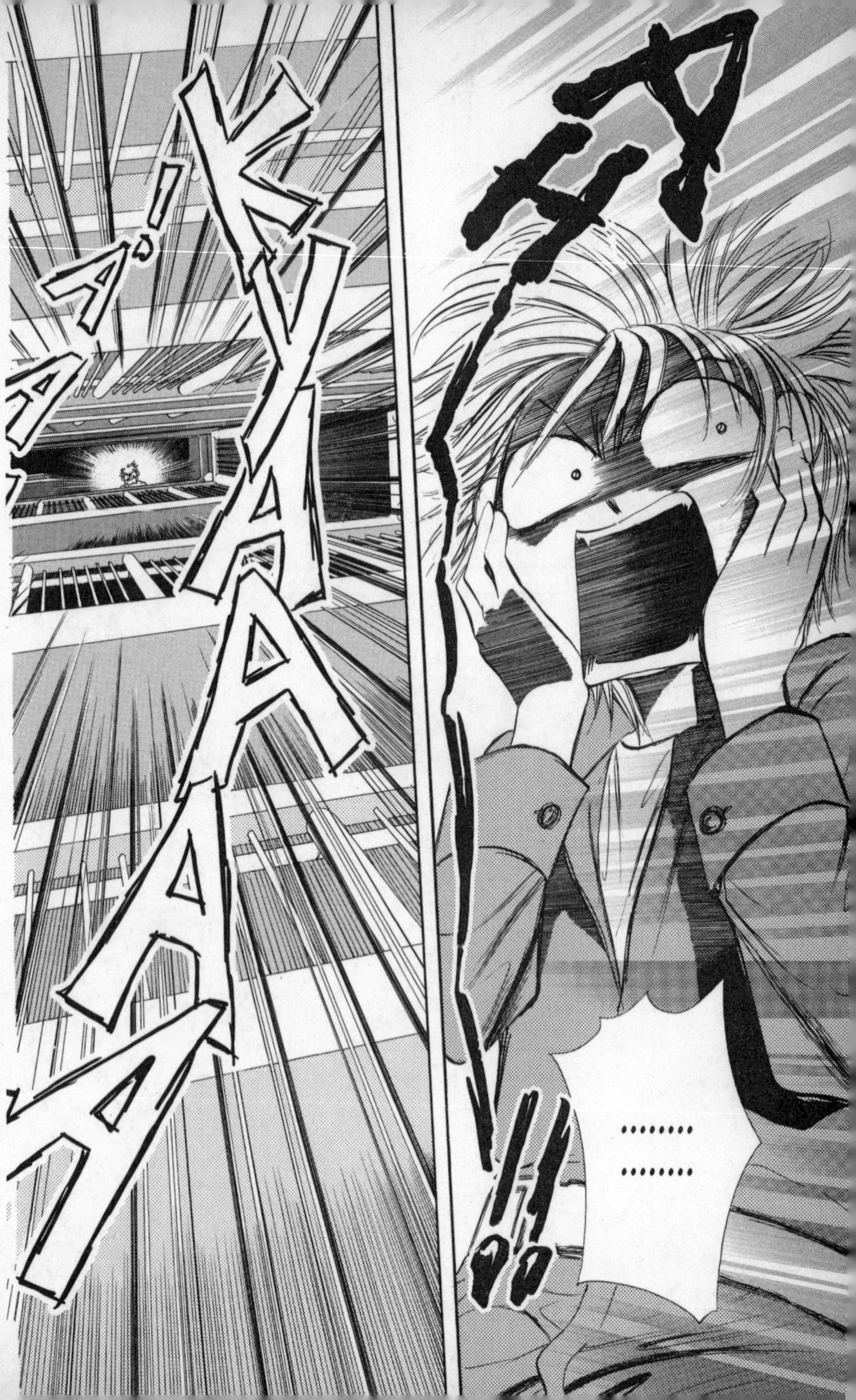
....
....

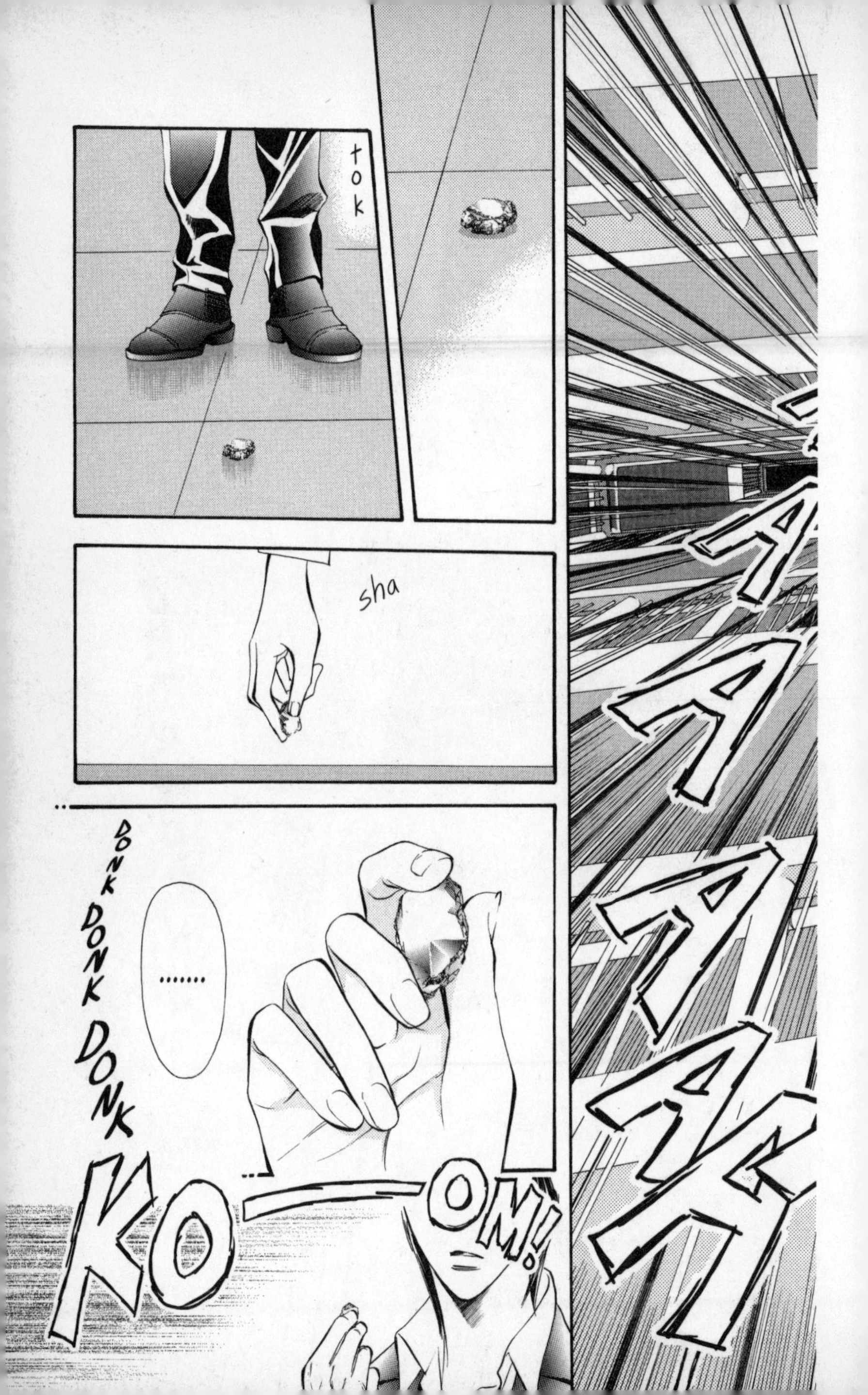
AAAAAA
tok
sha
....
DONK DONK DONK
KO—OM!

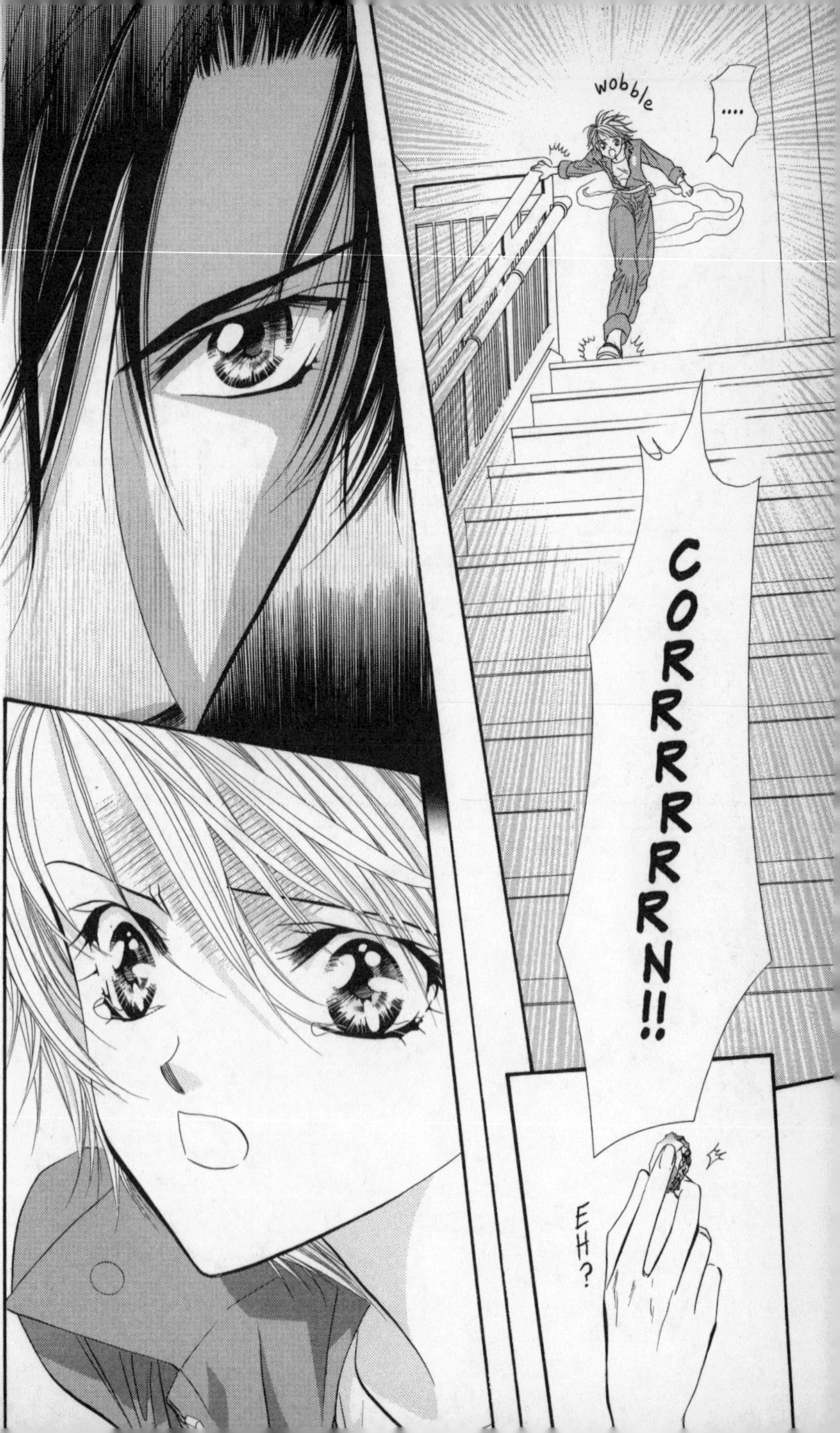
wobble
....
CORRRRRN!!
EH?

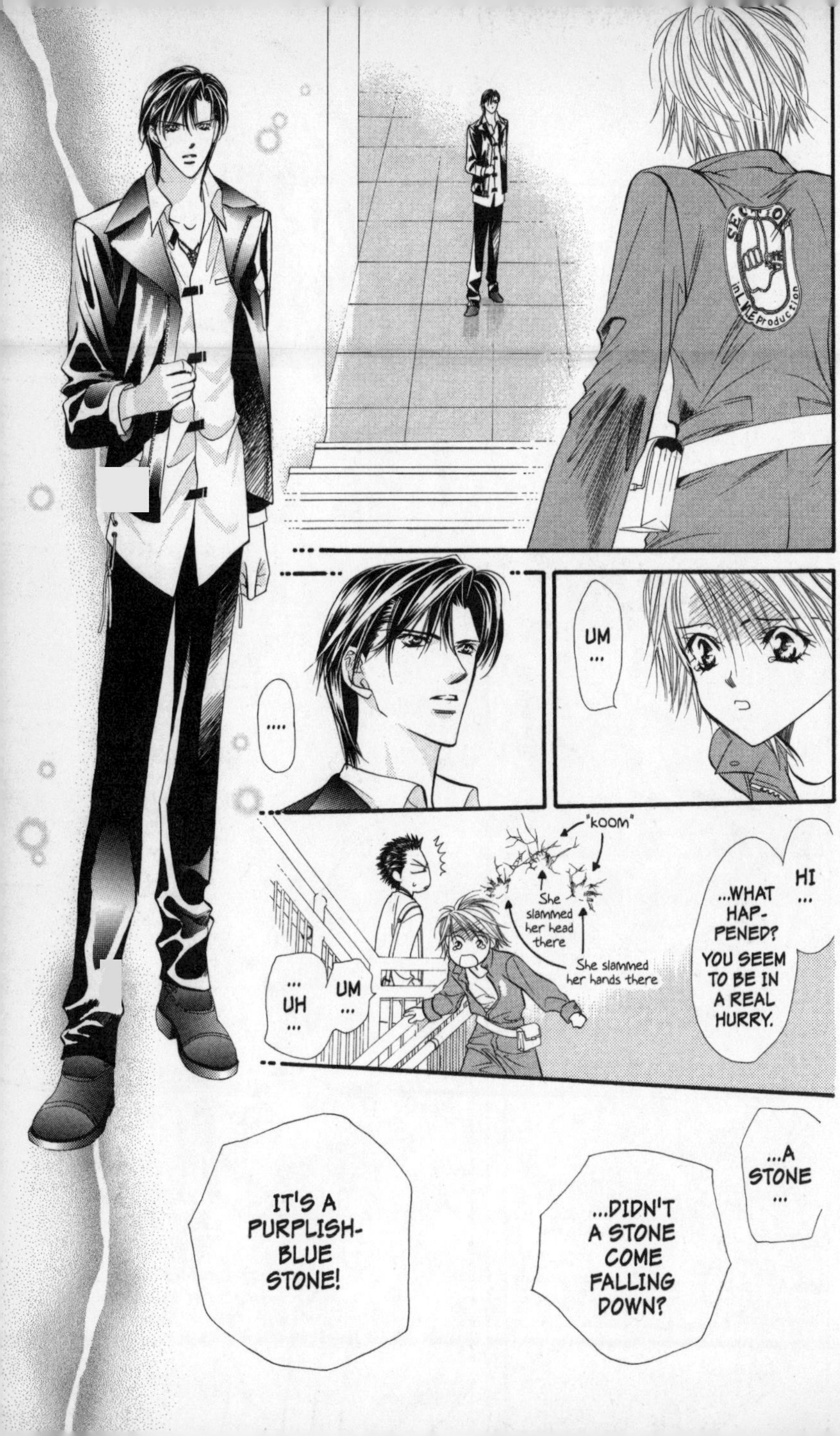
UM ...
....
HI ...
...WHAT HAP-PENED? YOU SEEM TO BE IN A REAL HURRY.
"KOOM"
She slammed her head there
She slammed her hands there
UM ...
... UH ...
...A STONE ...
...DIDN'T A STONE COME FALLING DOWN?
IT'S A PURPLISH-BLUE STONE!

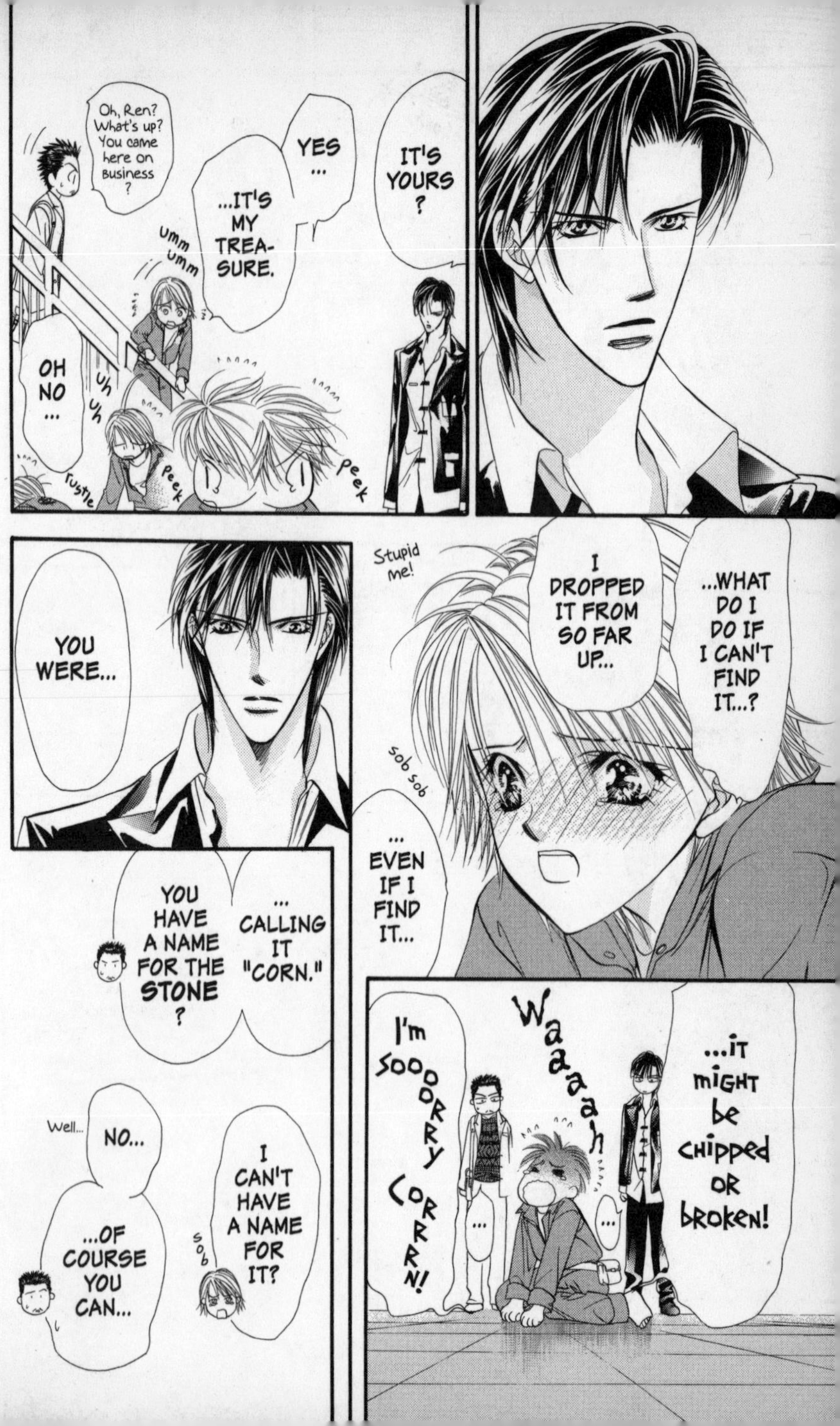
IT'S YOURS?
YES...
...IT'S MY TREASURE.
Umm umm
Oh, Ren? What's up? You came here on business?
OH NO...
uh uh
peek
Peek
rustle
Stupid me!
...WHAT DO I DO IF I CAN'T FIND IT...?
I DROPPED IT FROM SO FAR UP...
sob sob
...EVEN IF I FIND IT...
...it might be chipped or broken!
Waaaah
I'm SOOOORRY CORRRRN!
...
...
YOU WERE...
...CALLING IT "CORN."
YOU HAVE A NAME FOR THE STONE?
Well...
NO...
I CAN'T HAVE A NAME FOR IT?
sob
...OF COURSE YOU CAN...

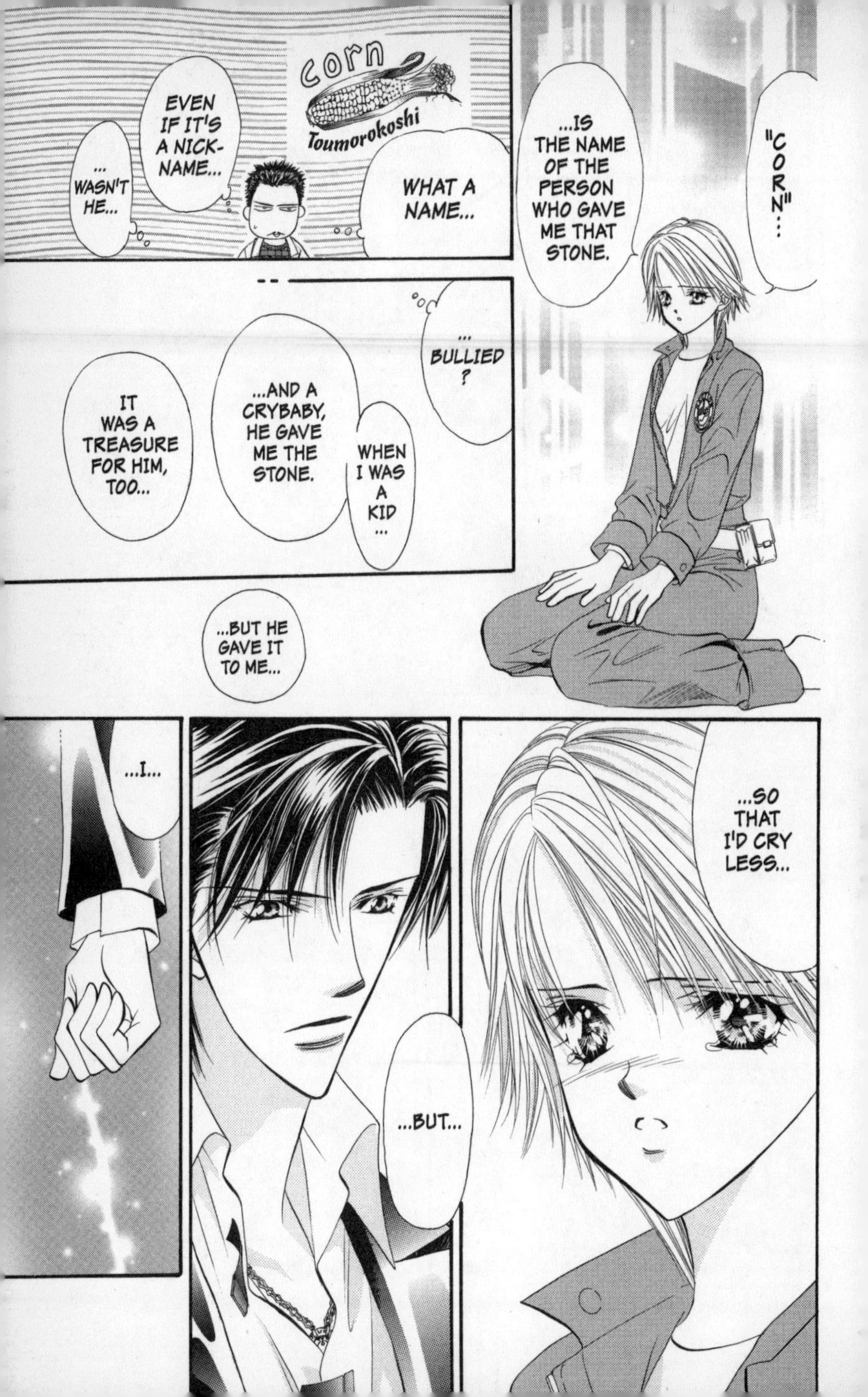
"CORN"...
...IS THE NAME OF THE PERSON WHO GAVE ME THAT STONE.
Corn
Toumorokoshi
WHAT A NAME...
EVEN IF IT'S A NICKNAME...
...WASN'T HE...
...BULLIED?
WHEN I WAS A KID...
...AND A CRYBABY, HE GAVE ME THE STONE.
IT WAS A TREASURE FOR HIM, TOO...
...BUT HE GAVE IT TO ME...
...SO THAT I'D CRY LESS...
...BUT...
...I...

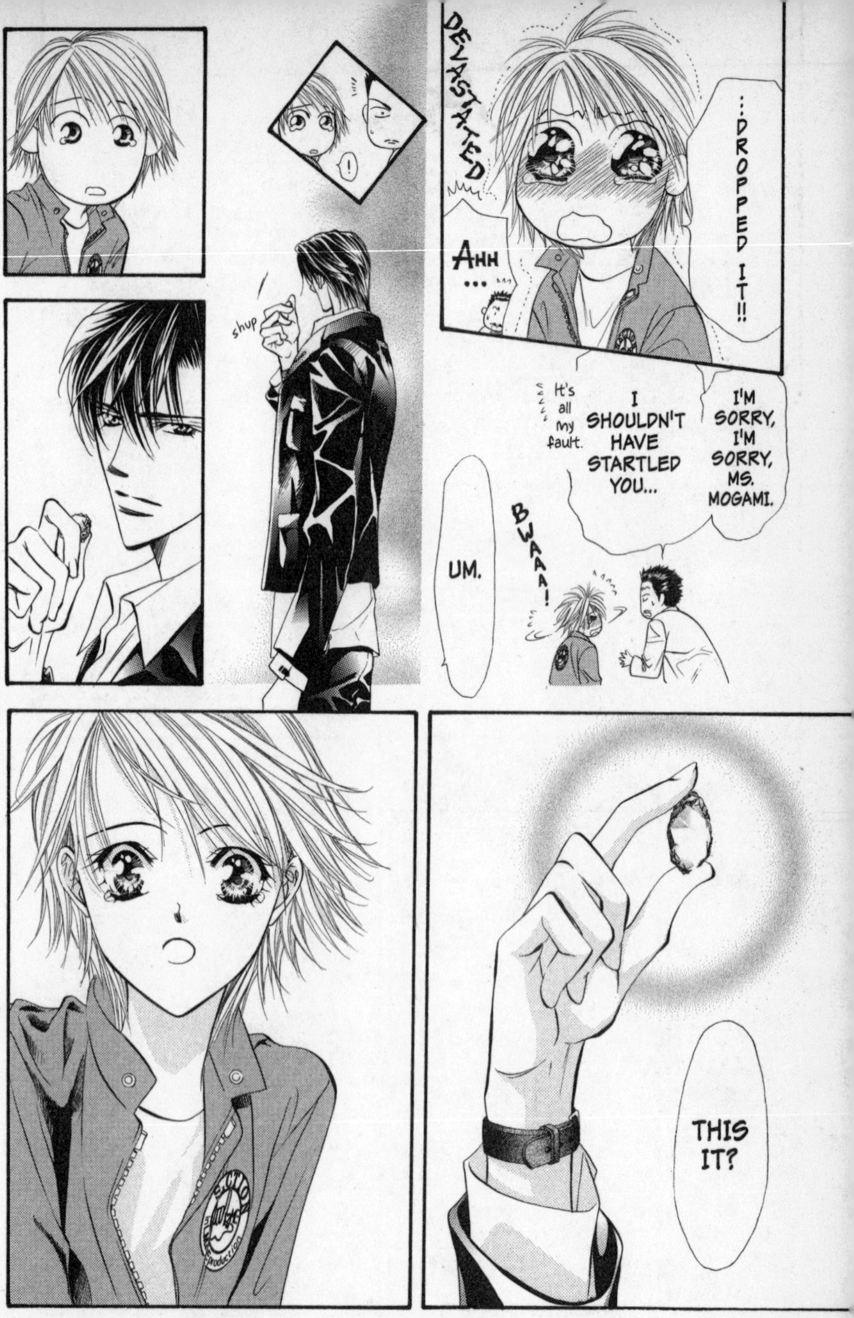
DEVASTATED
...DROPPED IT!!
AHH...
I'M SORRY, I'M SORRY, MS. MOGAMI.
I SHOULDN'T HAVE STARTLED YOU...
It's all my fault.
BWAAA!
UM.
!
shup
THIS IT?

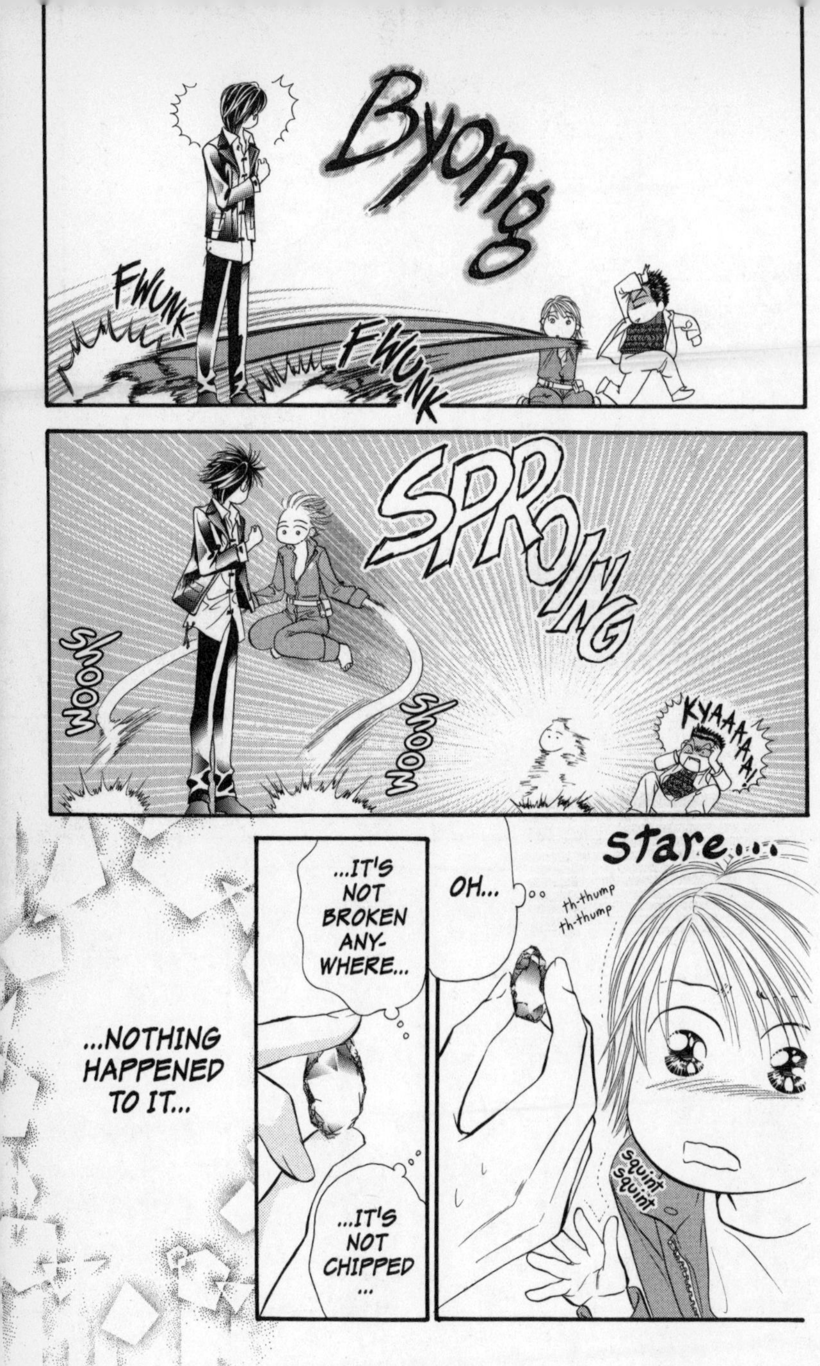
Byongo
FWUNK
FWUNK
SPROING
KYAAAAAA!
shoom
shoom
stare...
th-thump th-thump
OH...
squint squint
...IT'S NOT BROKEN ANY-WHERE...
...IT'S NOT CHIPPED...
...NOTHING HAPPENED TO IT...

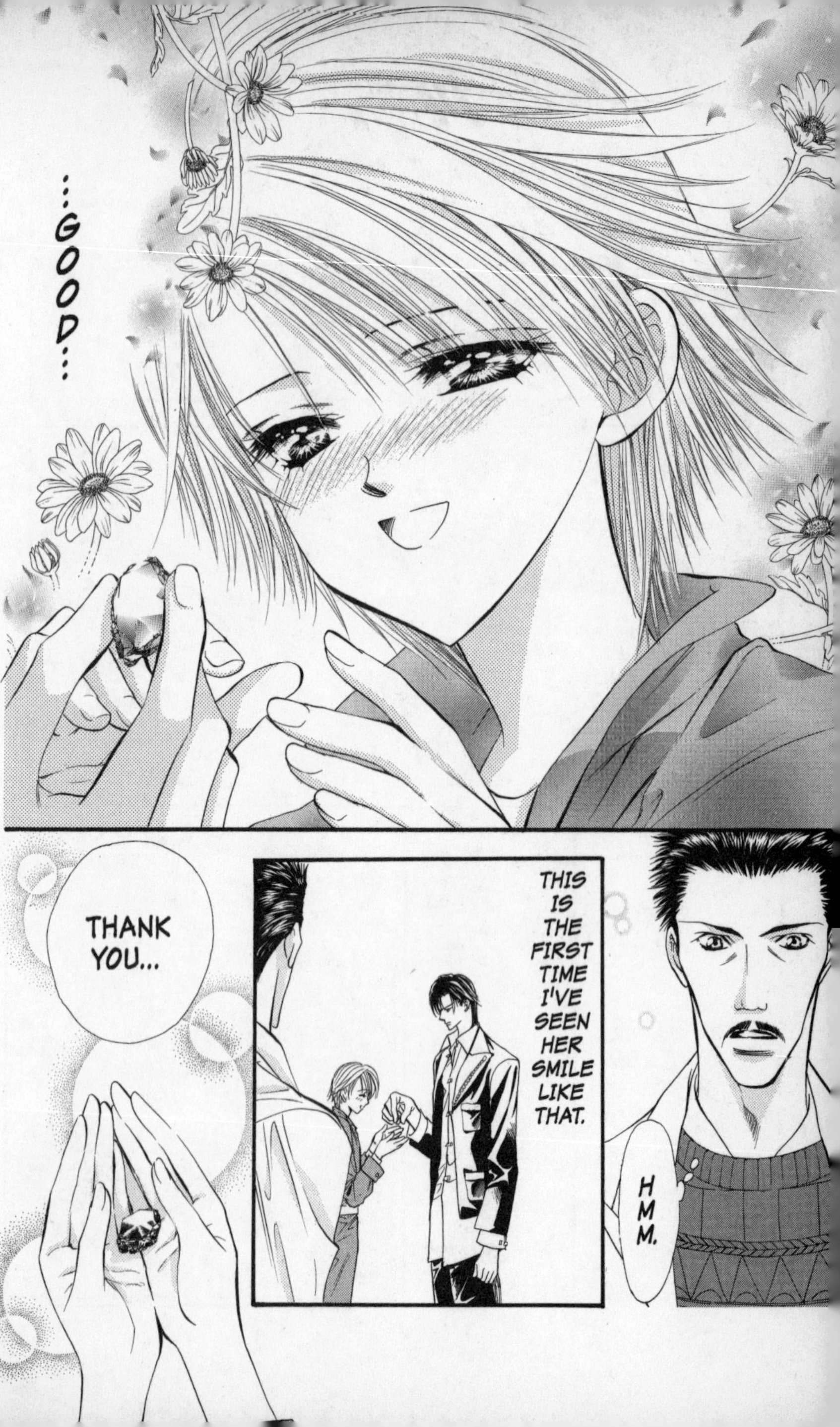
...GOOD...
HMM.
THIS IS THE FIRST TIME I'VE SEEN HER SMILE LIKE THAT.
THANK YOU...

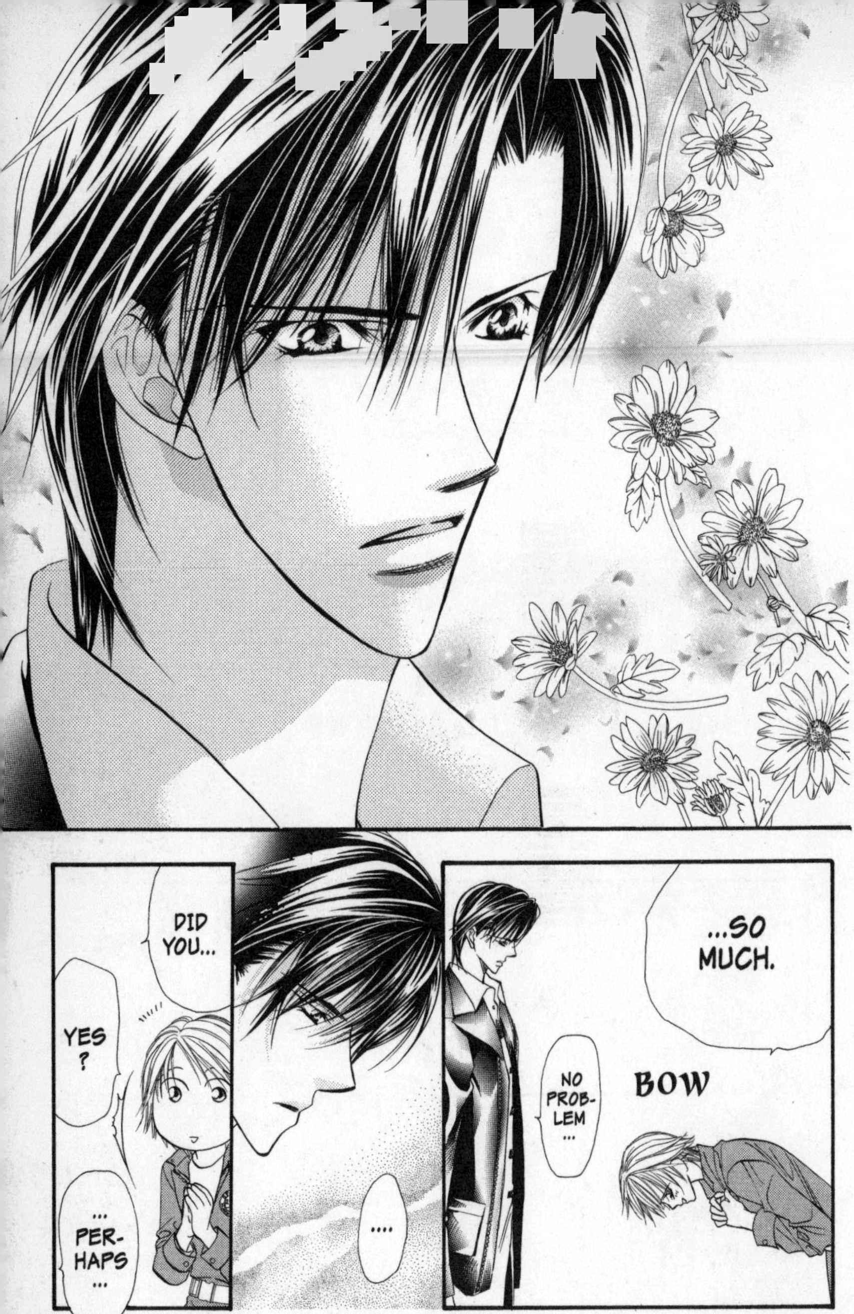
...SO MUCH.
BOW
NO PROBLEM...
....
DID YOU...
YES?
...PERHAPS...

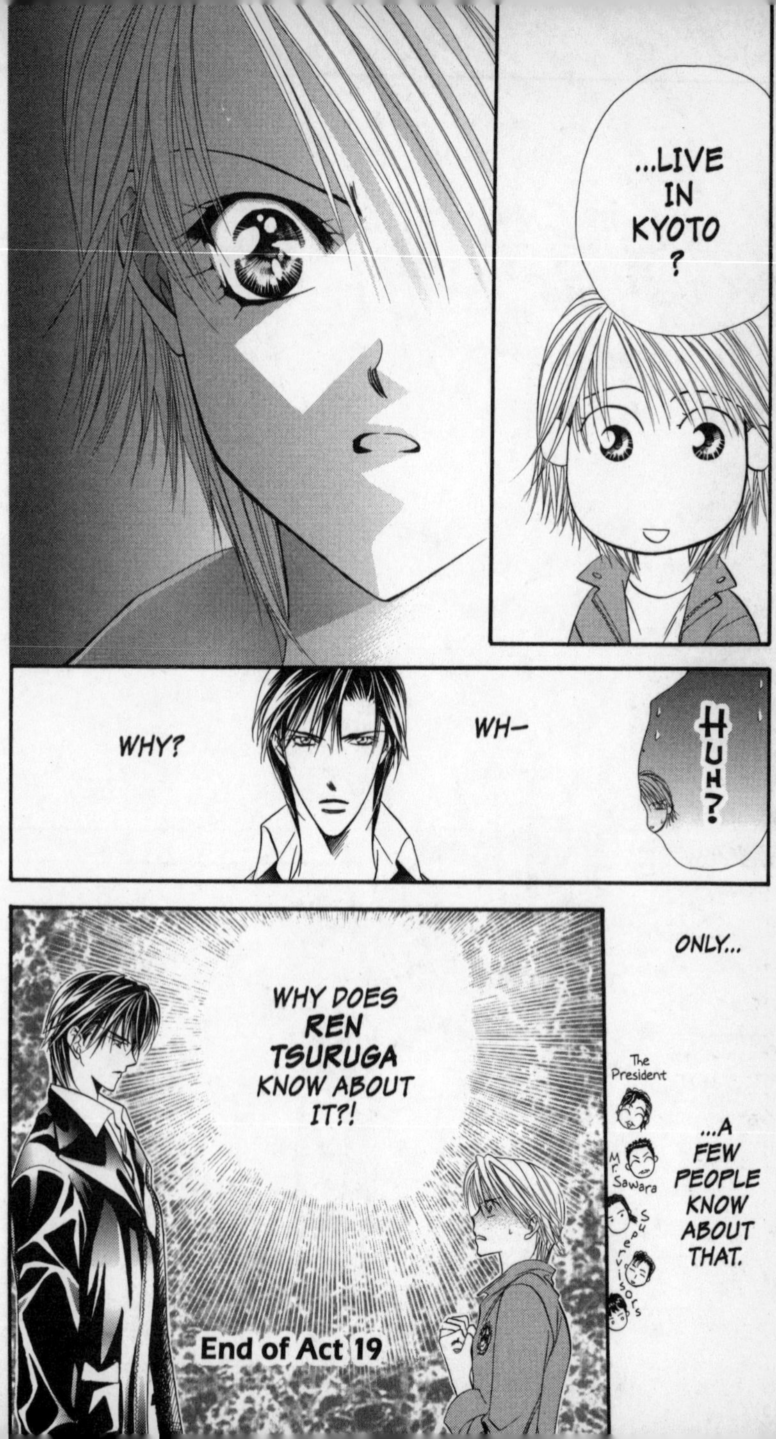
...LIVE IN KYOTO ?
HUH?
WH–
WHY?
ONLY...
The President
Mr. Sawara
Supervisors
...A FEW PEOPLE KNOW ABOUT THAT.
WHY DOES REN TSURUGA KNOW ABOUT IT?!
End of Act 19

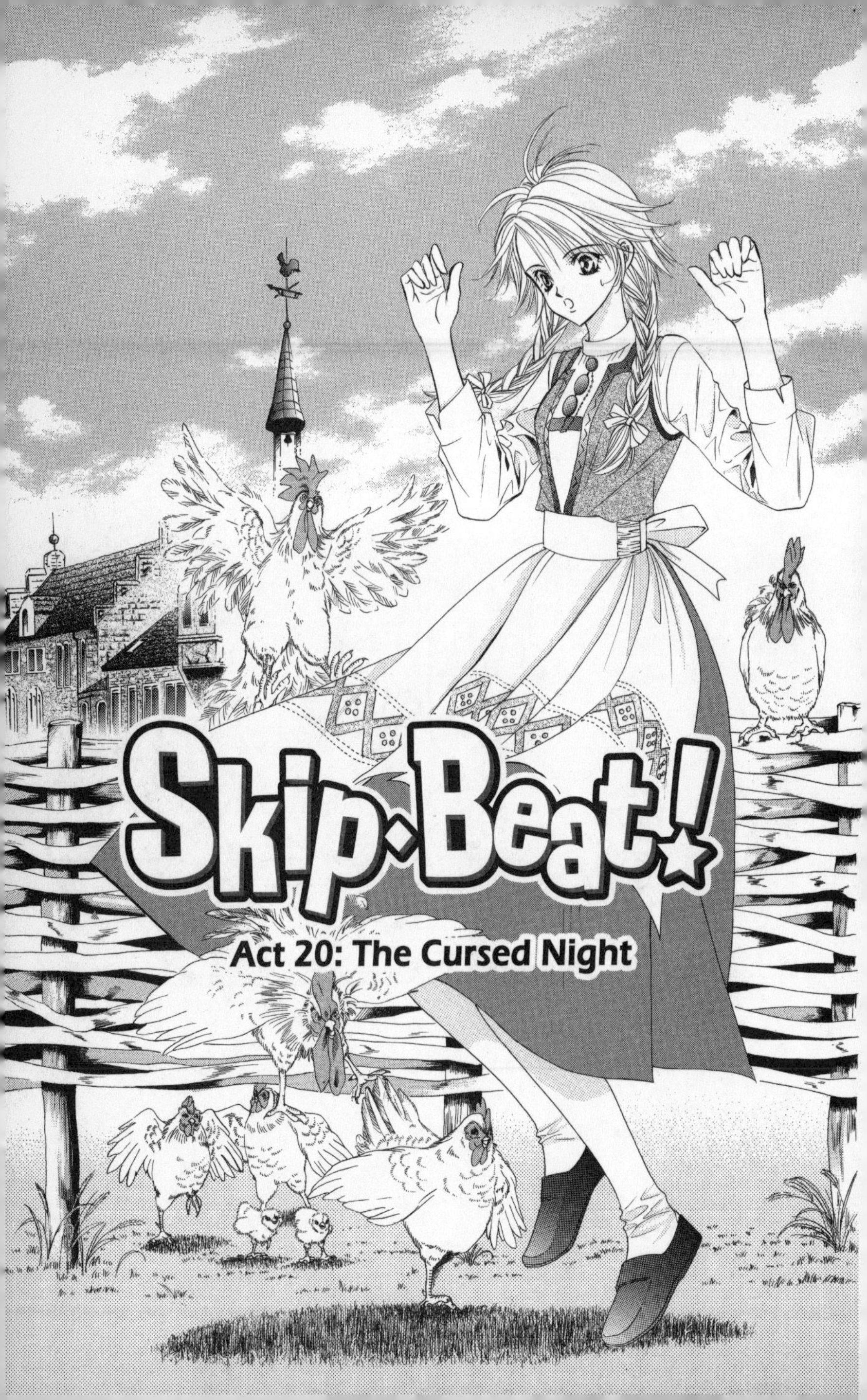
Skip·Beat!
Act 20: The Cursed Night

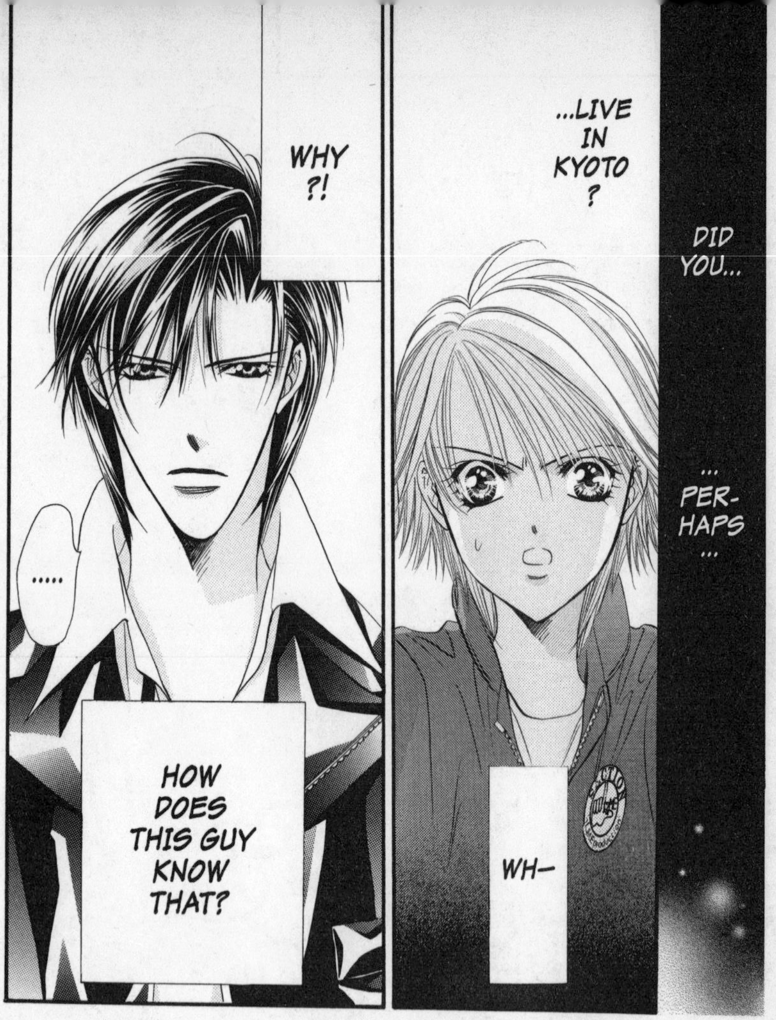
DID YOU...
...PERHAPS...
...LIVE IN KYOTO?
WH-
WHY?!
......
HOW DOES THIS GUY KNOW THAT?

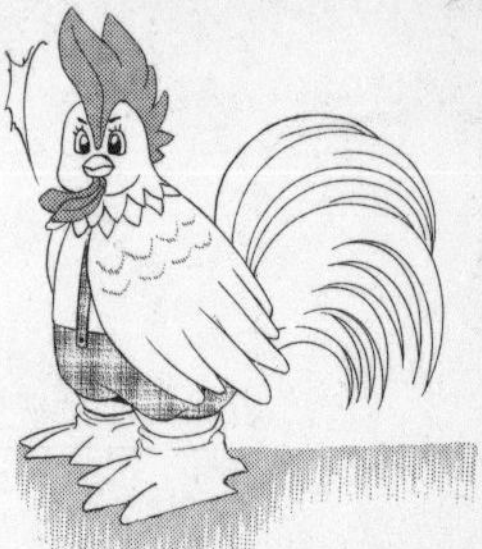

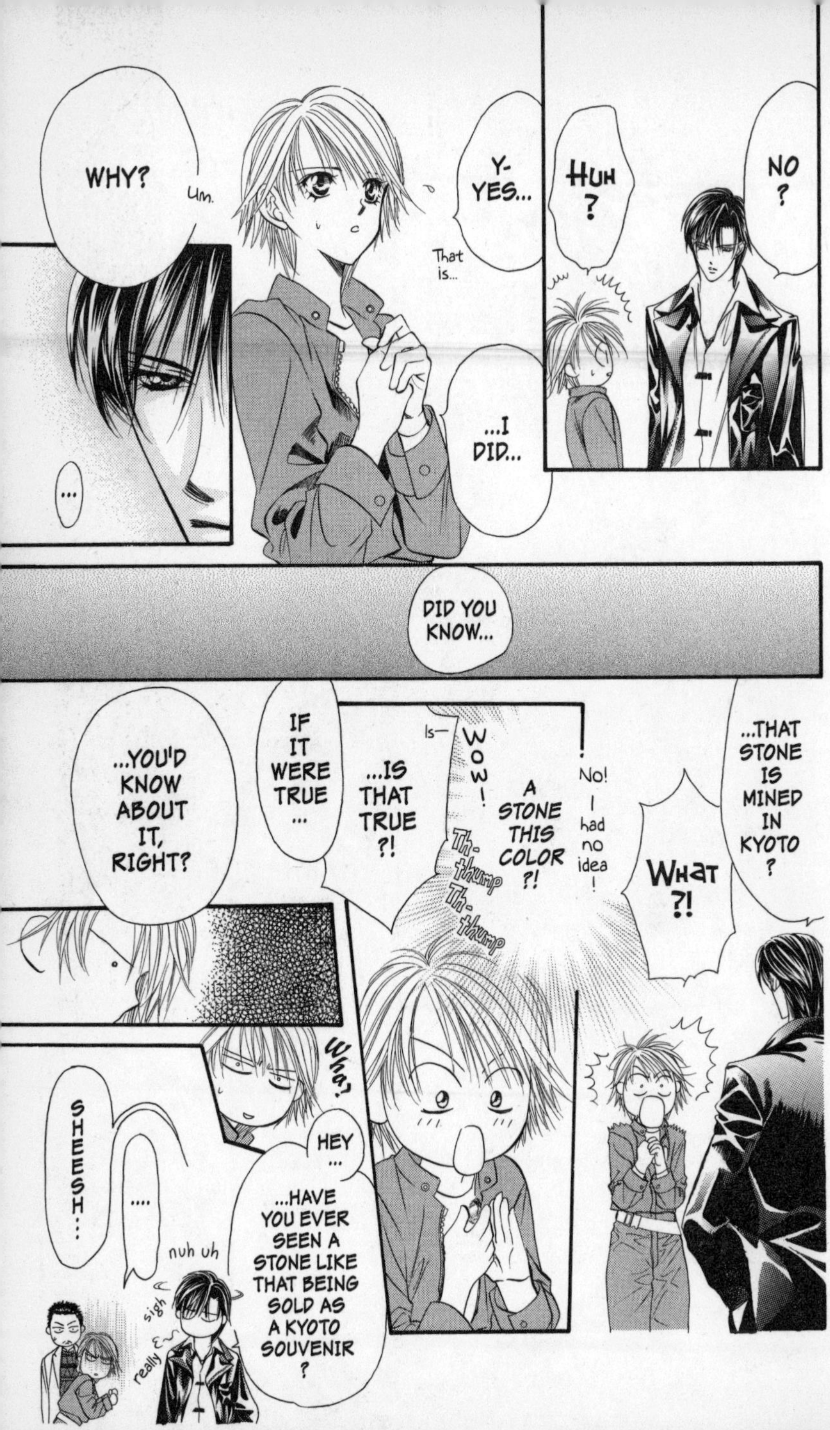
NO?
HUH?
Y-YES...
That is...
...I DID...
Um.
WHY?
...
DID YOU KNOW...
...THAT STONE IS MINED IN KYOTO?
WHAT?!
No! I had no idea!
A STONE THIS COLOR?!
WOW!
Is—
Th-thump Th-thump
...IS THAT TRUE?!
IF IT WERE TRUE...
...YOU'D KNOW ABOUT IT, RIGHT?
Wha?
HEY...
...HAVE YOU EVER SEEN A STONE LIKE THAT BEING SOLD AS A KYOTO SOUVENIR?
....
SHEESH...
nuh uh
sigh
really

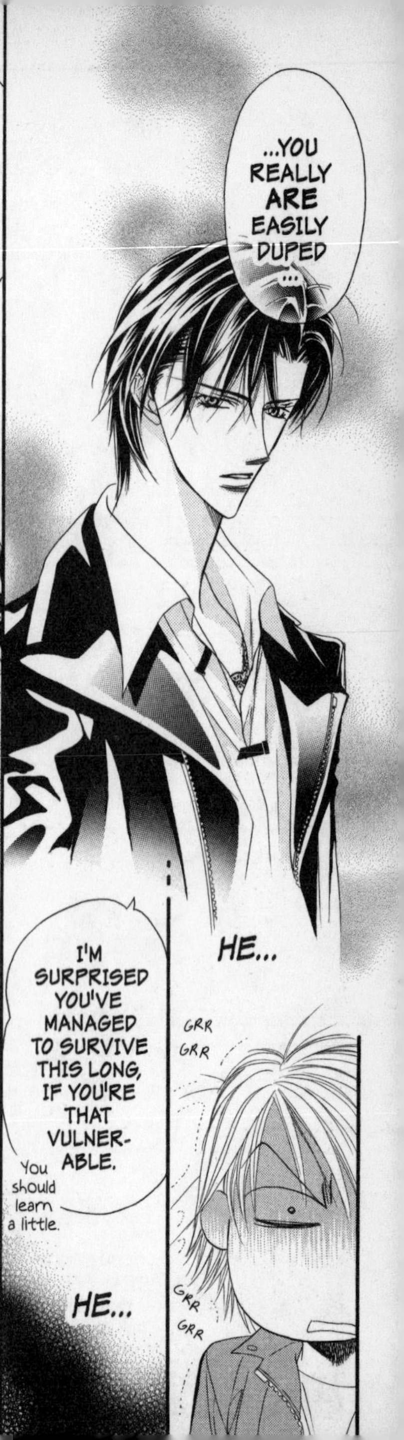
...YOU REALLY ARE EASILY DUPED...
HE...
I'M SURPRISED YOU'VE MANAGED TO SURVIVE THIS LONG, IF YOU'RE THAT VULNERABLE.
You should learn a little.
GRR GRR
HE...
GRR GRR

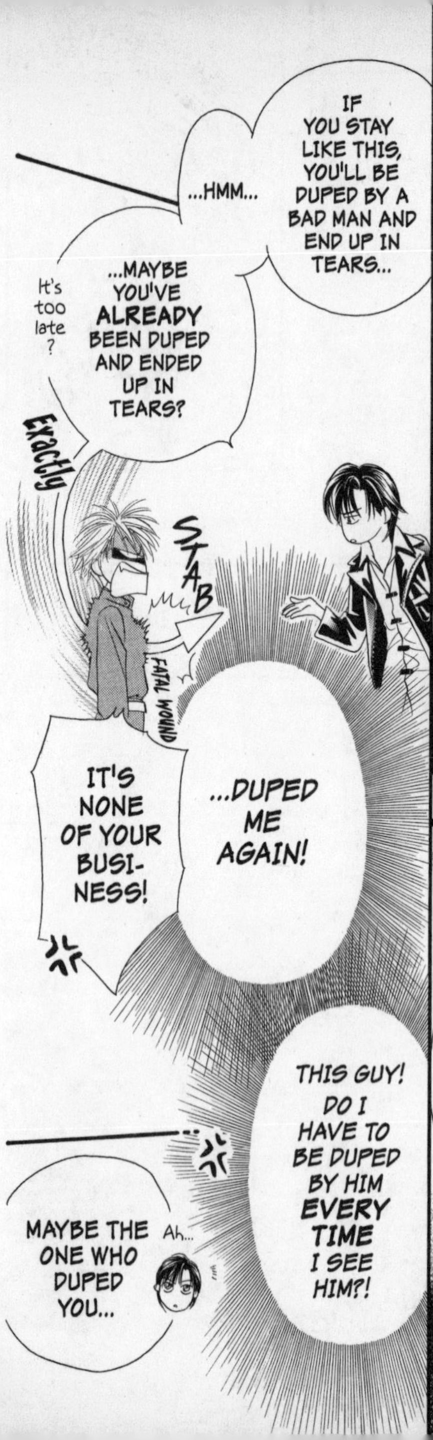
IF YOU STAY LIKE THIS, YOU'LL BE DUPED BY A BAD MAN AND END UP IN TEARS...
...HMM...
...MAYBE YOU'VE ALREADY BEEN DUPED AND ENDED UP IN TEARS?
It's too late?
Exactly
STAB
FATAL WOUND
...DUPED ME AGAIN!
IT'S NONE OF YOUR BUSINESS!
THIS GUY! DO I HAVE TO BE DUPED BY HIM EVERY TIME I SEE HIM?!
MAYBE THE ONE WHO DUPED YOU...
Ah...

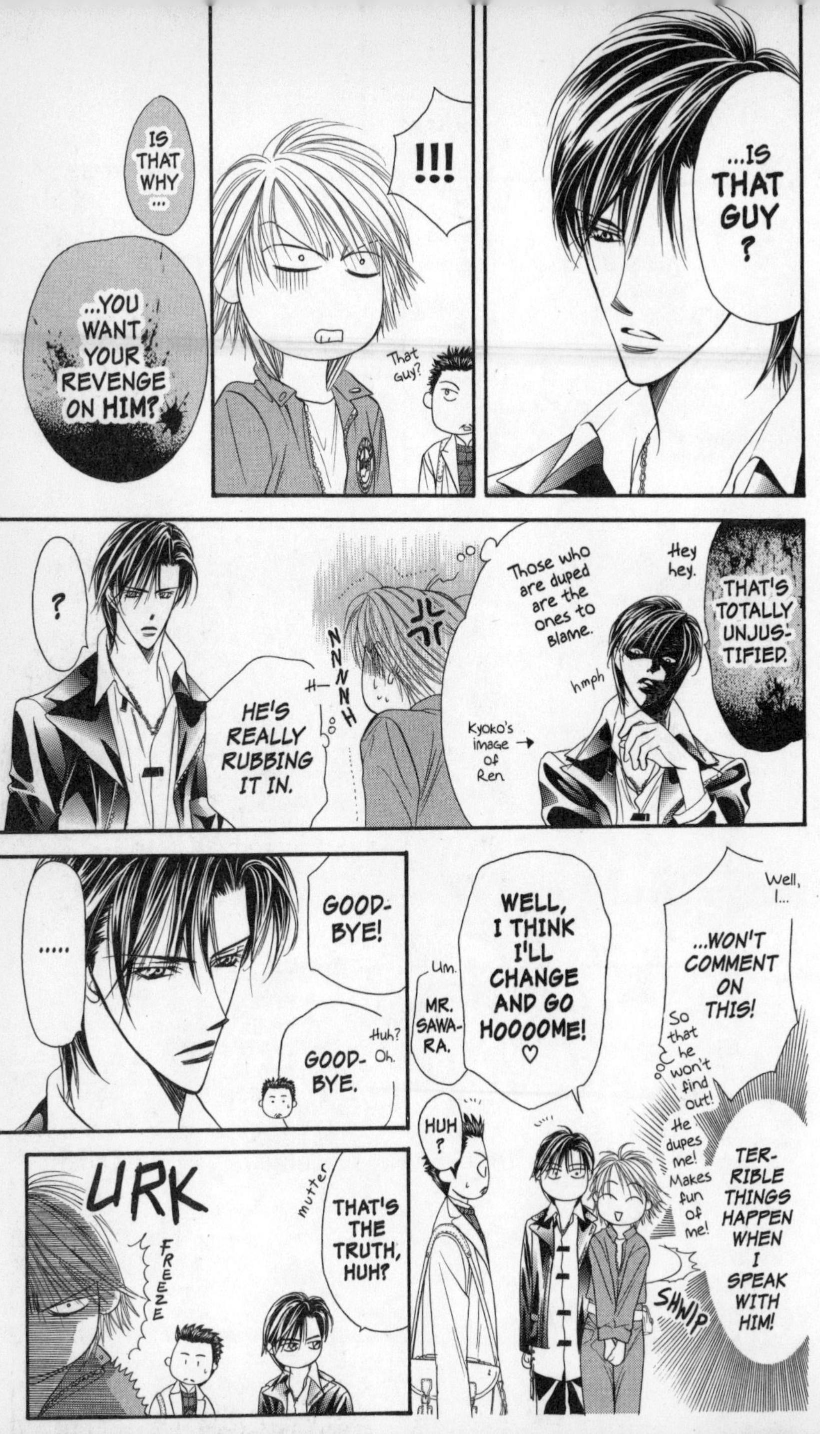
...IS THAT GUY?
!!!
That guy?
IS THAT WHY...
...YOU WANT YOUR REVENGE ON HIM?
Hey hey.
THAT'S TOTALLY UNJUS-TIFIED.
Those who are duped are the ones to blame.
hmph
Kyoko's image of Ren
NNNNH
H—
HE'S REALLY RUBBING IT IN.
?
Well, I...
...WON'T COMMENT ON THIS!
So that he won't find out!
WELL, I THINK I'LL CHANGE AND GO HOOOOME! ♡
Um.
MR. SAWA-RA.
Huh? Oh.
GOOD-BYE!
GOOD-BYE.
.....
He dupes me! Makes fun of me!
TER-RIBLE THINGS HAPPEN WHEN I SPEAK WITH HIM!
SHWIP
HUH?
mutter
THAT'S THE TRUTH, HUH?
URK
FREEZE

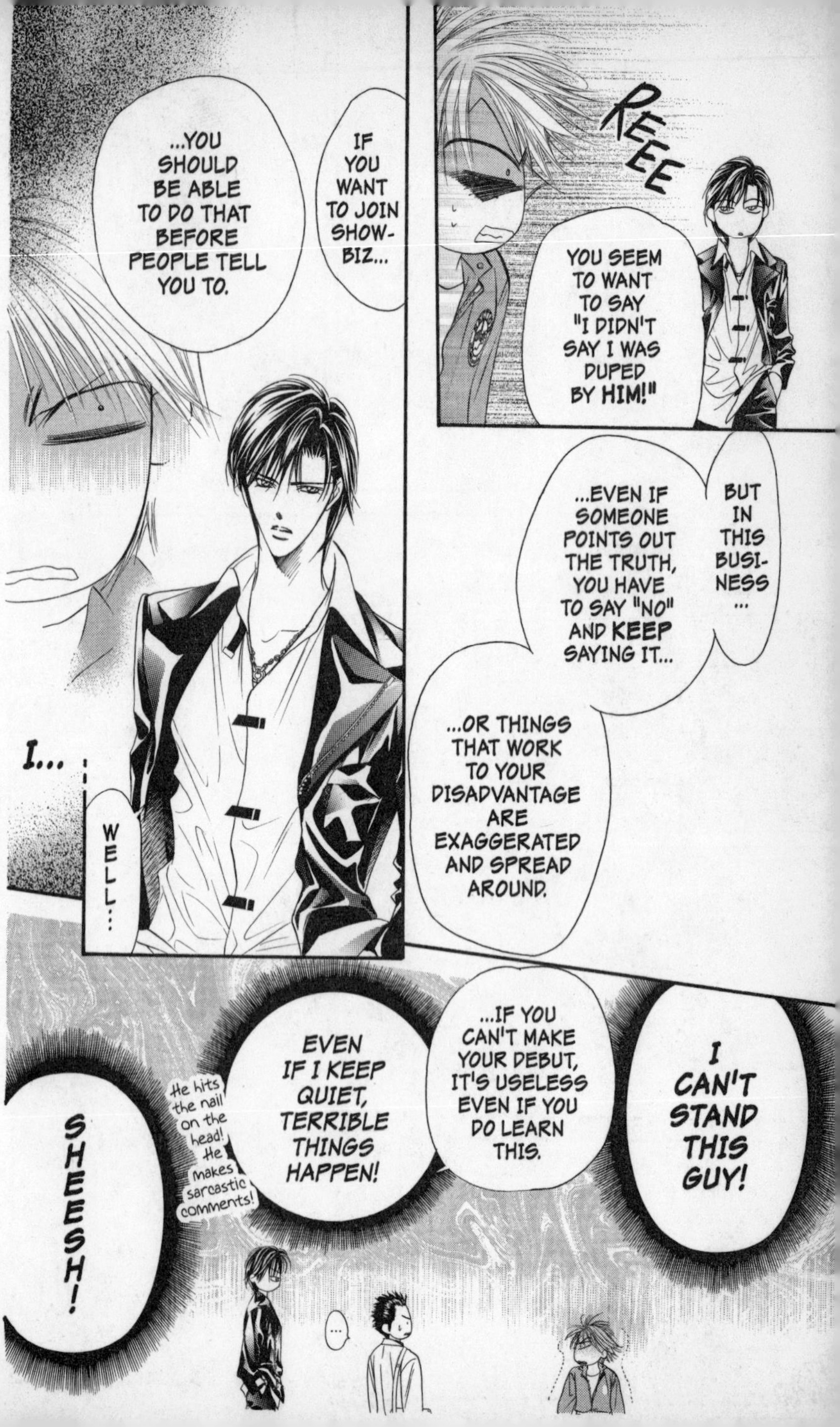
REEEE
YOU SEEM TO WANT TO SAY "I DIDN'T SAY I WAS DUPED BY HIM!"
IF YOU WANT TO JOIN SHOW-BIZ...
...YOU SHOULD BE ABLE TO DO THAT BEFORE PEOPLE TELL YOU TO.
BUT IN THIS BUSINESS...
...EVEN IF SOMEONE POINTS OUT THE TRUTH, YOU HAVE TO SAY "NO" AND KEEP SAYING IT...
...OR THINGS THAT WORK TO YOUR DISADVANTAGE ARE EXAGGERATED AND SPREAD AROUND.
I...
WELL...
I CAN'T STAND THIS GUY!
...IF YOU CAN'T MAKE YOUR DEBUT, IT'S USELESS EVEN IF YOU DO LEARN THIS.
EVEN IF I KEEP QUIET, TERRIBLE THINGS HAPPEN!
He hits the nail on the head! He makes sarcastic comments!
SHEESH!
...

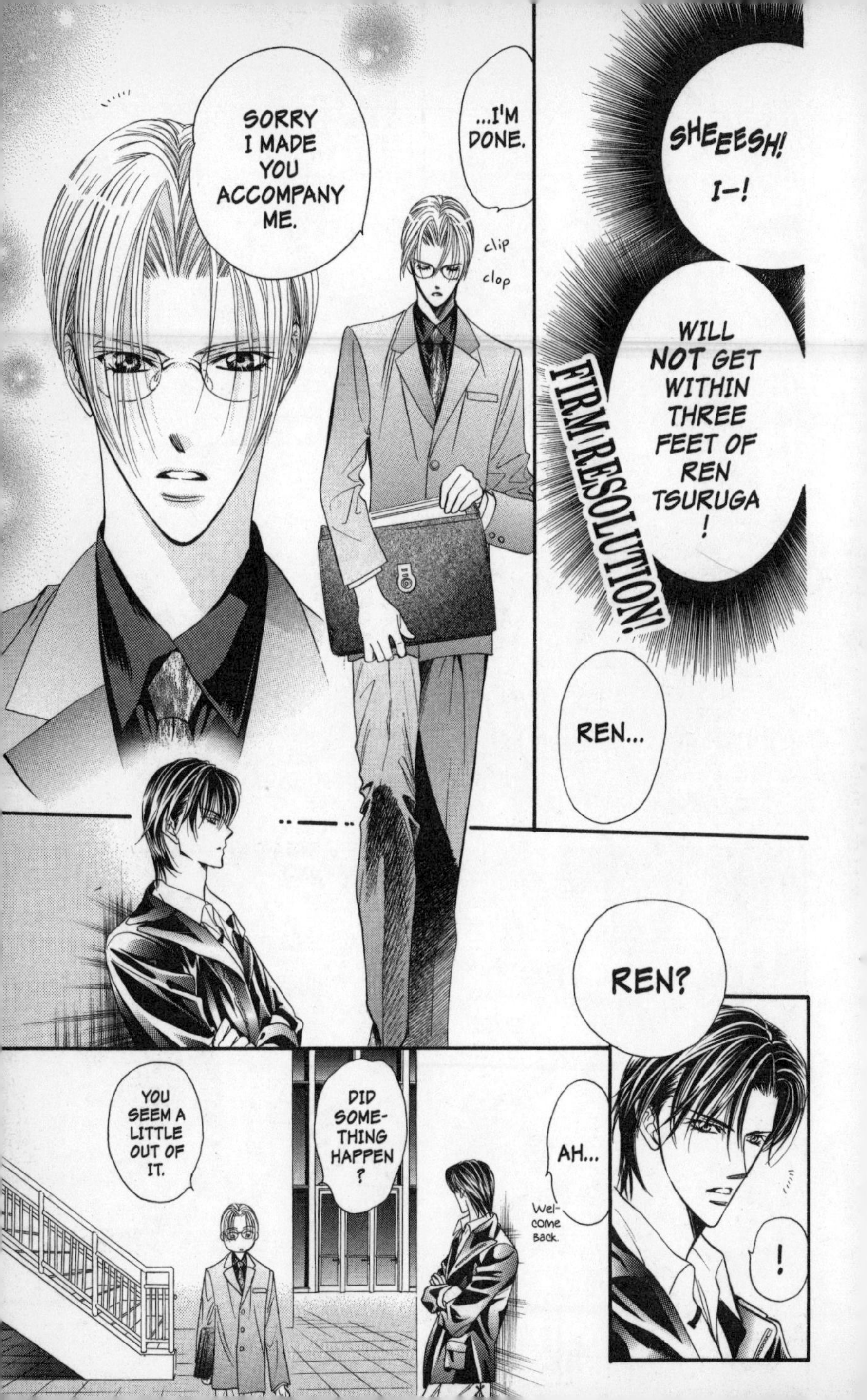
SHEEESH! I—!
WILL NOT GET WITHIN THREE FEET OF REN TSURUGA!
FIRM RESOLUTION!
REN...
...I'M DONE.
clip clop
SORRY I MADE YOU ACCOMPANY ME.
REN?
!
AH...
Wel-come back.
DID SOMETHING HAPPEN?
YOU SEEM A LITTLE OUT OF IT.

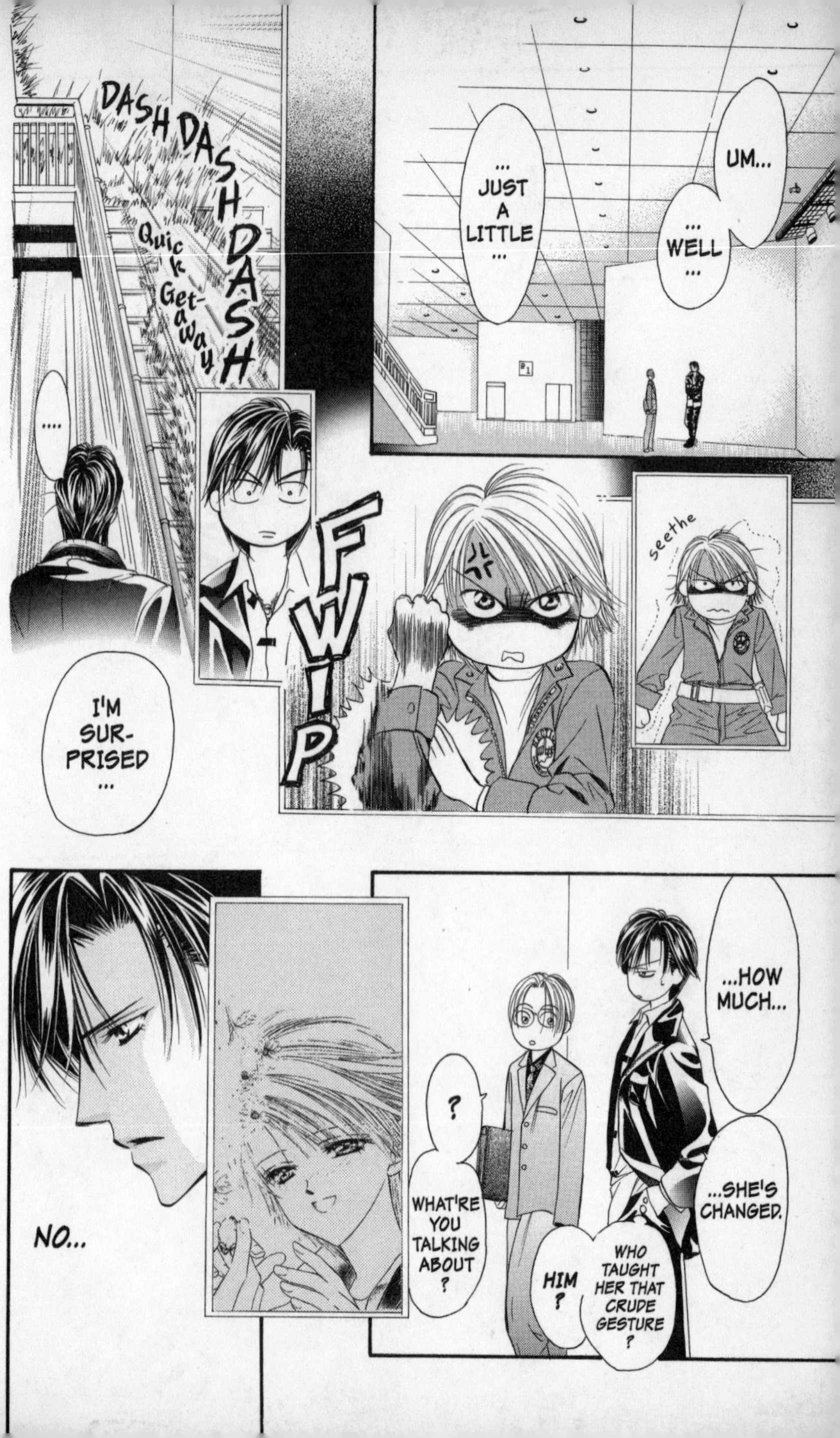
UM...
...WELL...
...JUST A LITTLE...
DASH DASH DASH DASH
Quick Get-away
seethe
FWIP
....
I'M SUR-PRISED...
...HOW MUCH...
?
...SHE'S CHANGED.
WHAT'RE YOU TALKING ABOUT?
WHO TAUGHT HER THAT CRUDE GESTURE?
HIM?
NO...

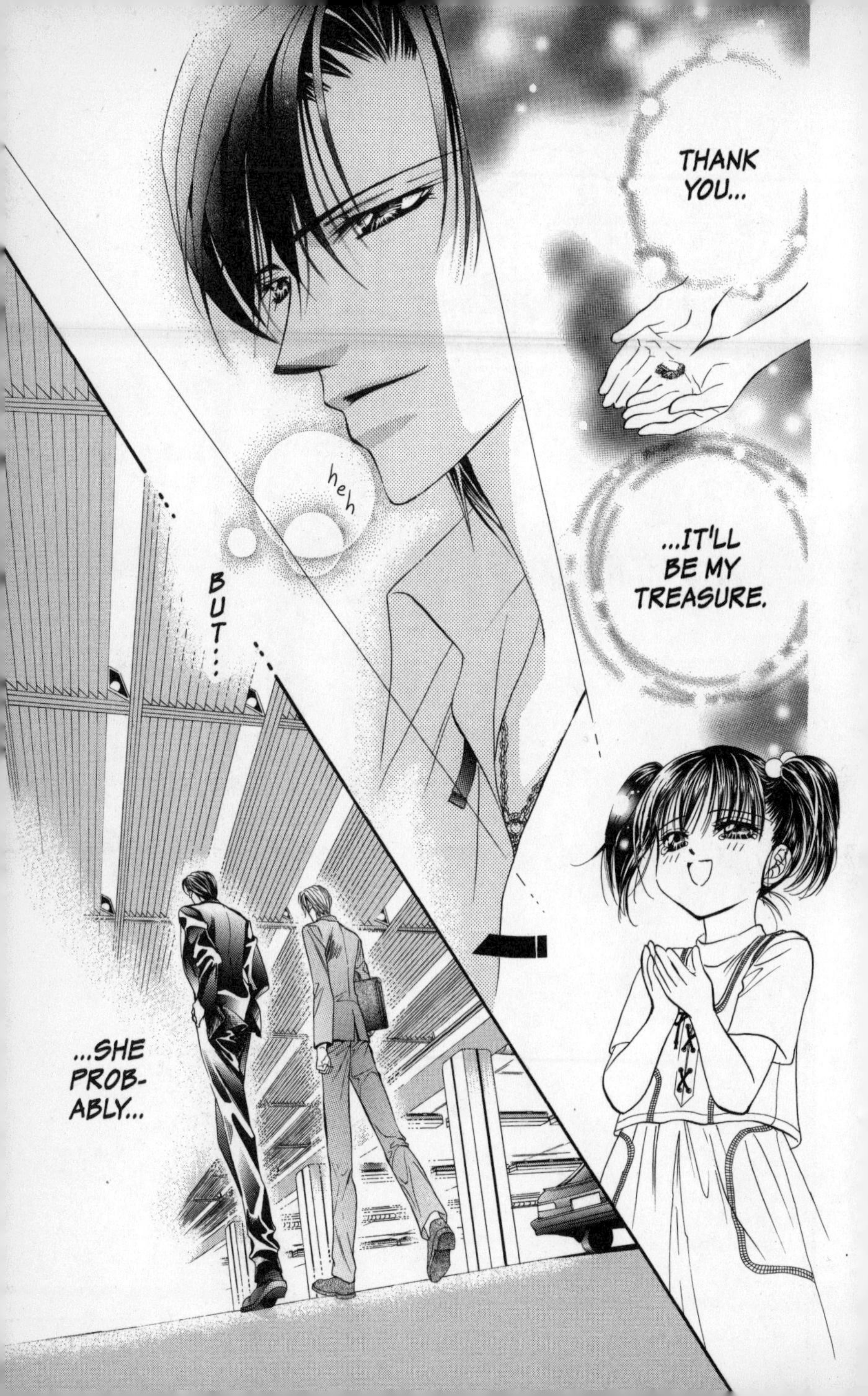
THANK YOU...
...IT'LL BE MY TREASURE.
heh
BUT...
...SHE PROBABLY...

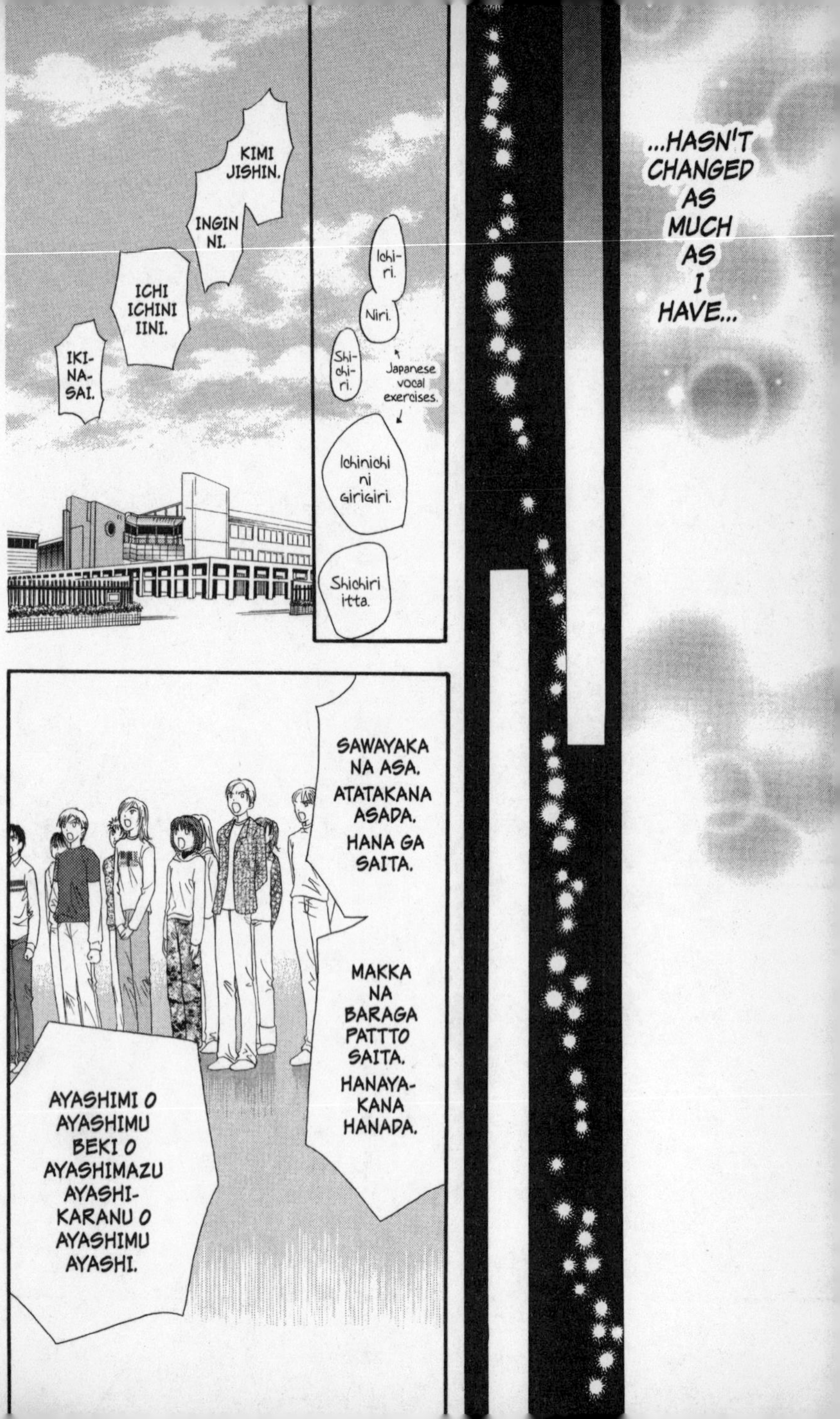
...HASN'T CHANGED AS MUCH AS I HAVE...
Ichi-ri.
Niri.
Shi-chi-ri.
Japanese vocal exercises.
Ichinichi ni girigiri.
Shichiri itta.
KIMI JISHIN.
INGIN NI.
ICHI ICHINI IINI.
IKI-NA-SAI.
SAWAYAKA NA ASA. ATATAKANA ASADA. HANA GA SAITA.
MAKKA NA BARAGA PATTTO SAITA. HANAYA-KANA HANADA.
AYASHIMI O AYASHIMU BEKI O AYASHIMAZU AYASHI-KARANU O AYASHIMU AYASHI.

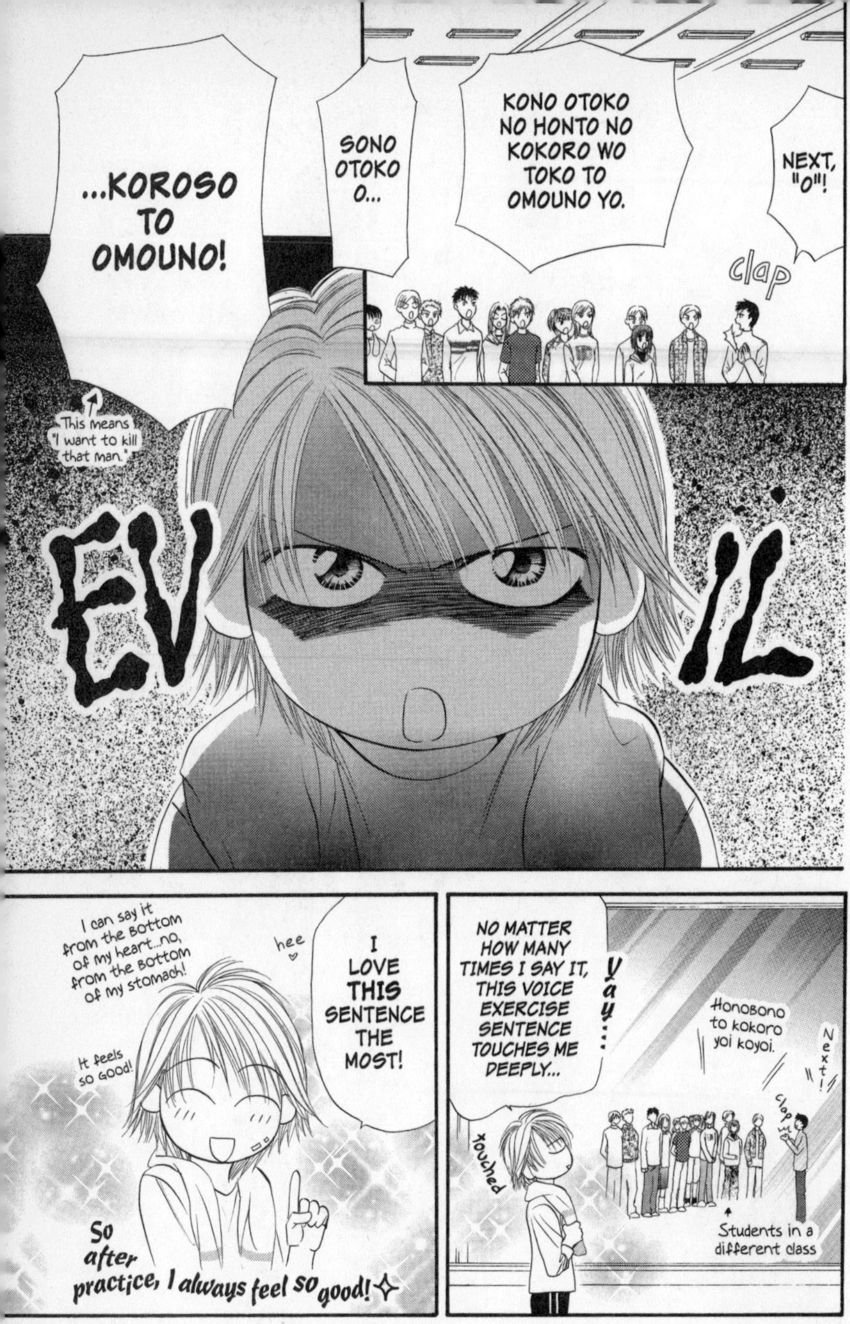
NEXT, "O"!
clap
KONO OTOKO NO HONTO NO KOKORO WO TOKO TO OMOUNO YO.
SONO OTOKO O...
...KOROSO TO OMOUNO!
This means "I want to kill that man."
EV IL
NO MATTER HOW MANY TIMES I SAY IT, THIS VOICE EXERCISE SENTENCE TOUCHES ME DEEPLY...
Yay...
Next!
Honobono to kokoro yoi koyoi.
clap
touched
Students in a different class
I LOVE THIS SENTENCE THE MOST!
hee
I can say it from the bottom of my heart...no, from the bottom of my stomach!
It feels so good!
So after practice, I always feel so good!

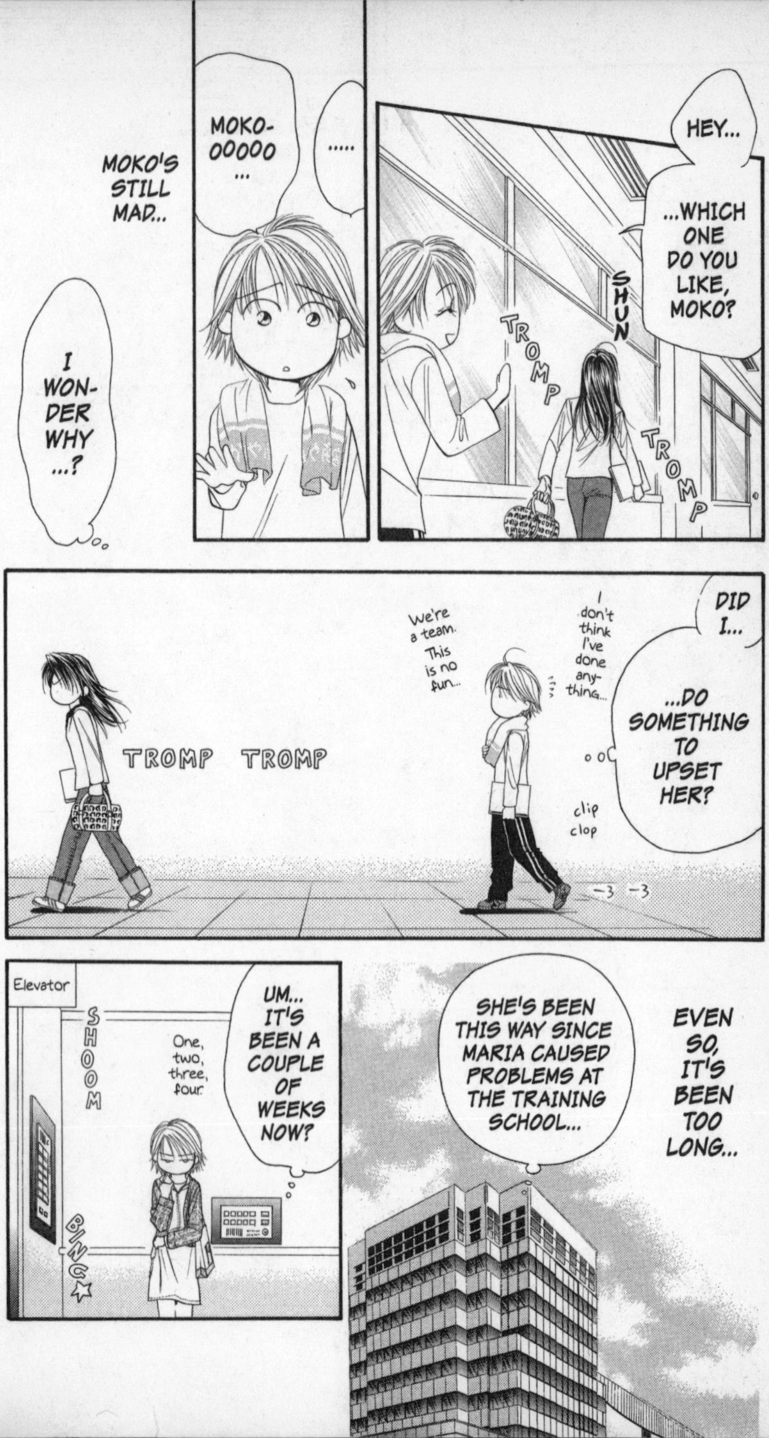
HEY...
...WHICH ONE DO YOU LIKE, MOKO?
SHUN
TROMP
TROMP
.....
MOKO-OOOOO...
MOKO'S STILL MAD...
I WONDER WHY...?
DID I...
...DO SOMETHING TO UPSET HER?
I don't think I've done anything...
We're a team. This is no fun...
clip clop
TROMP TROMP
EVEN SO, IT'S BEEN TOO LONG...
SHE'S BEEN THIS WAY SINCE MARIA CAUSED PROBLEMS AT THE TRAINING SCHOOL...
UM... IT'S BEEN A COUPLE OF WEEKS NOW?
One, two, three, four.
Elevator
SHOOM
BING☆

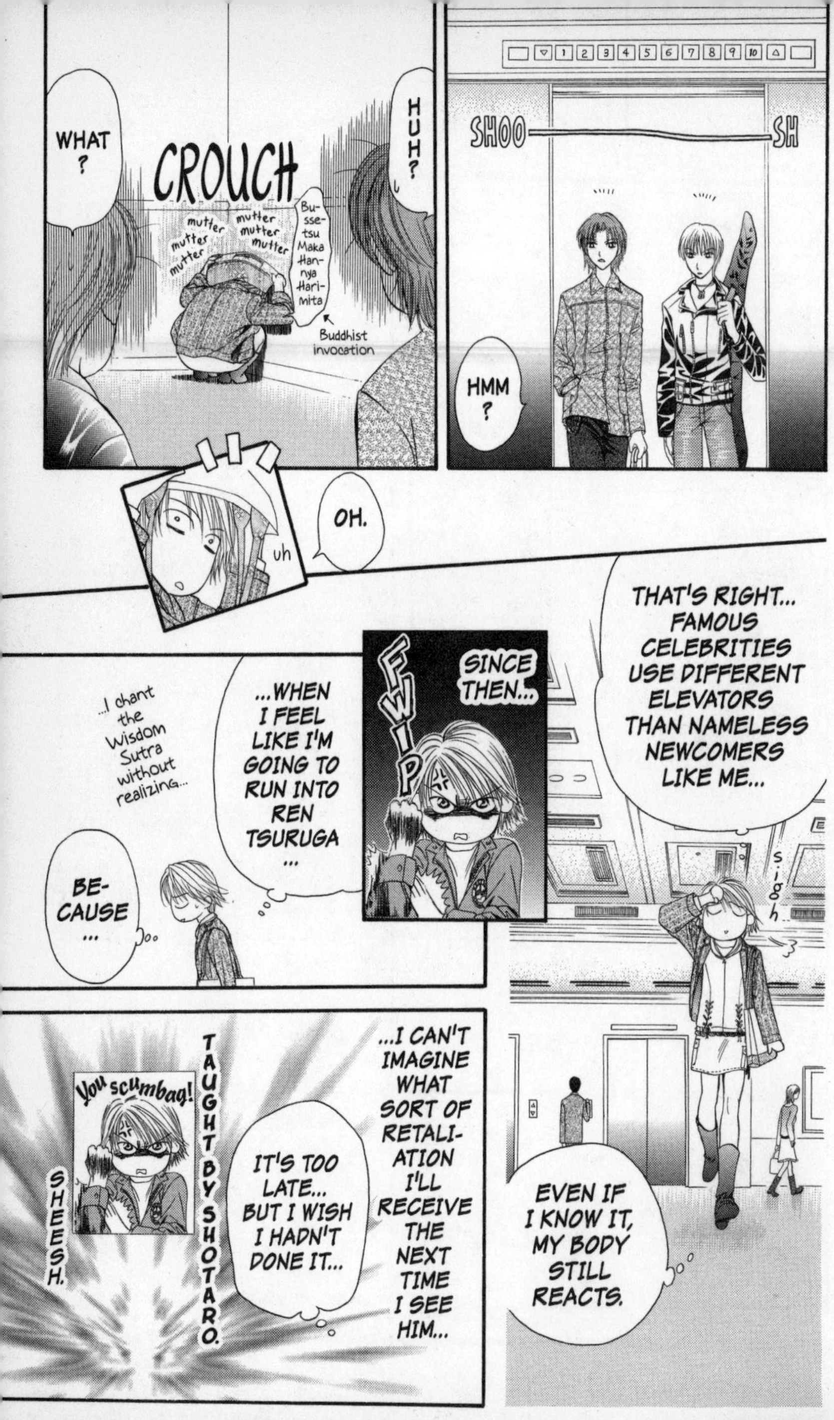
SHOO——SH
HMM?
HUH?
Bus-setsu Maka Han-nya Hari-mita
CROUCH
mutter mutter mutter mutter mutter
WHAT?
Buddhist invocation
OH.
uh
THAT'S RIGHT... FAMOUS CELEBRITIES USE DIFFERENT ELEVATORS THAN NAMELESS NEWCOMERS LIKE ME...
sigh
EVEN IF I KNOW IT, MY BODY STILL REACTS.
SINCE THEN...
FWIP
...WHEN I FEEL LIKE I'M GOING TO RUN INTO REN TSURUGA...
...I chant the Wisdom Sutra without realizing...
BE-CAUSE...
...I CAN'T IMAGINE WHAT SORT OF RETALI-ATION I'LL RECEIVE THE NEXT TIME I SEE HIM...
IT'S TOO LATE... BUT I WISH I HADN'T DONE IT...
TAUGHT BY SHOTARO.
You scumbag!
SHEESH.

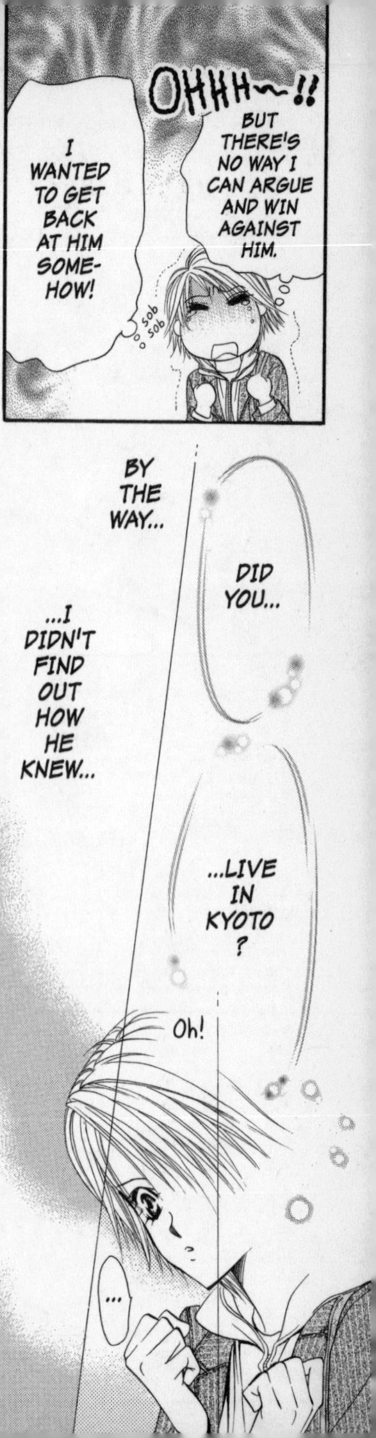
OHHH~!!
BUT THERE'S NO WAY I CAN ARGUE AND WIN AGAINST HIM.
I WANTED TO GET BACK AT HIM SOME-HOW!
sob sob
BY THE WAY...
DID YOU...
...I DIDN'T FIND OUT HOW HE KNEW...
...LIVE IN KYOTO?
Oh!
...
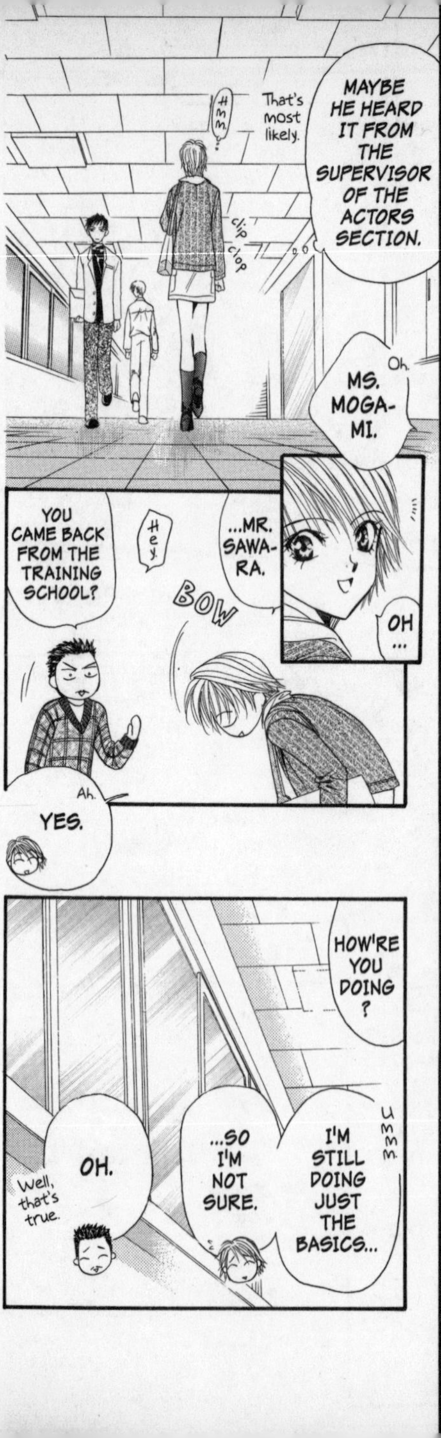
MAYBE HE HEARD IT FROM THE SUPERVISOR OF THE ACTORS SECTION.
That's most likely.
Hmm.
clip clop
Oh.
MS. MOGA-MI.
...MR. SAWA-RA.
OH ...
Hey.
YOU CAME BACK FROM THE TRAINING SCHOOL?
BOW
Ah.
YES.
HOW'RE YOU DOING?
Ummm.
I'M STILL DOING JUST THE BASICS...
...SO I'M NOT SURE.
OH.
Well, that's true.

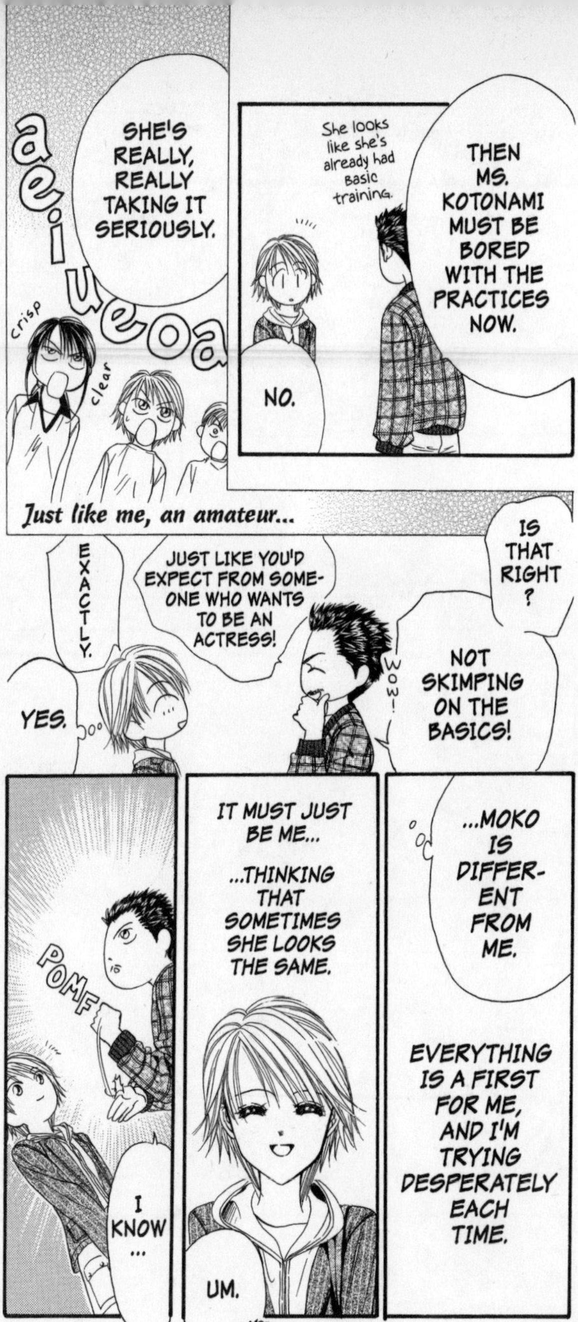
THEN MS. KOTONAMI MUST BE BORED WITH THE PRACTICES NOW.
She looks like she's already had basic training.
NO.
SHE'S REALLY, REALLY TAKING IT SERIOUSLY.
a e i u e o a
crisp
clear
Just like me, an amateur...
IS THAT RIGHT?
NOT SKIMPING ON THE BASICS!
WOW!
JUST LIKE YOU'D EXPECT FROM SOME-ONE WHO WANTS TO BE AN ACTRESS!
EXACTLY.
YES.
...MOKO IS DIFFER-ENT FROM ME.
EVERYTHING IS A FIRST FOR ME, AND I'M TRYING DESPERATELY EACH TIME.
IT MUST JUST BE ME...
...THINKING THAT SOMETIMES SHE LOOKS THE SAME.
UM.
POMF
I KNOW...

Corn

This is the stone that Kyoko secretly treasures. It's not just an ordinary stone. If you cut it and polish it, it becomes a gem. It is called Kinseiseki (cordierite). As the name implies, it is purplish blue, and another name for it is water sapphire.

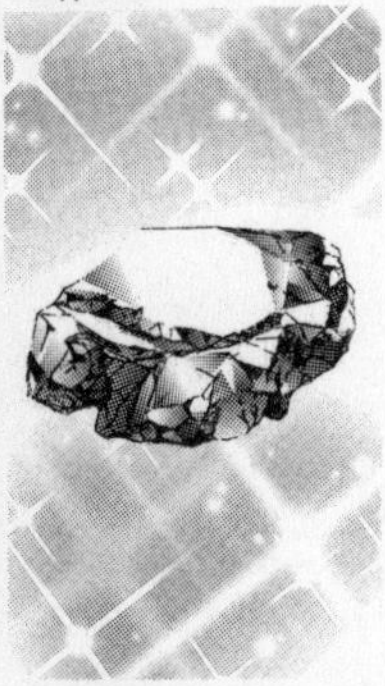

This stone is blue, but if you rotate it about 90 degrees, the blue disappears, and it becomes greenish-yellow, a mysterious(?) stone.

But when this stone is processed as a gem, it is polished so the stone looks blue from the front, and the metal mount hides the sides so that you can't see the greenish-yellow...

That sounds unfortunate, but considering the value of the gem, it is probably better to make it that way...

Reference: From Tanoshii Kobutsu Zukan (The Enjoyable Mineral Encyclopedia)

<Reference> Tanoshii Kobutsu Zukan (Soshisha)

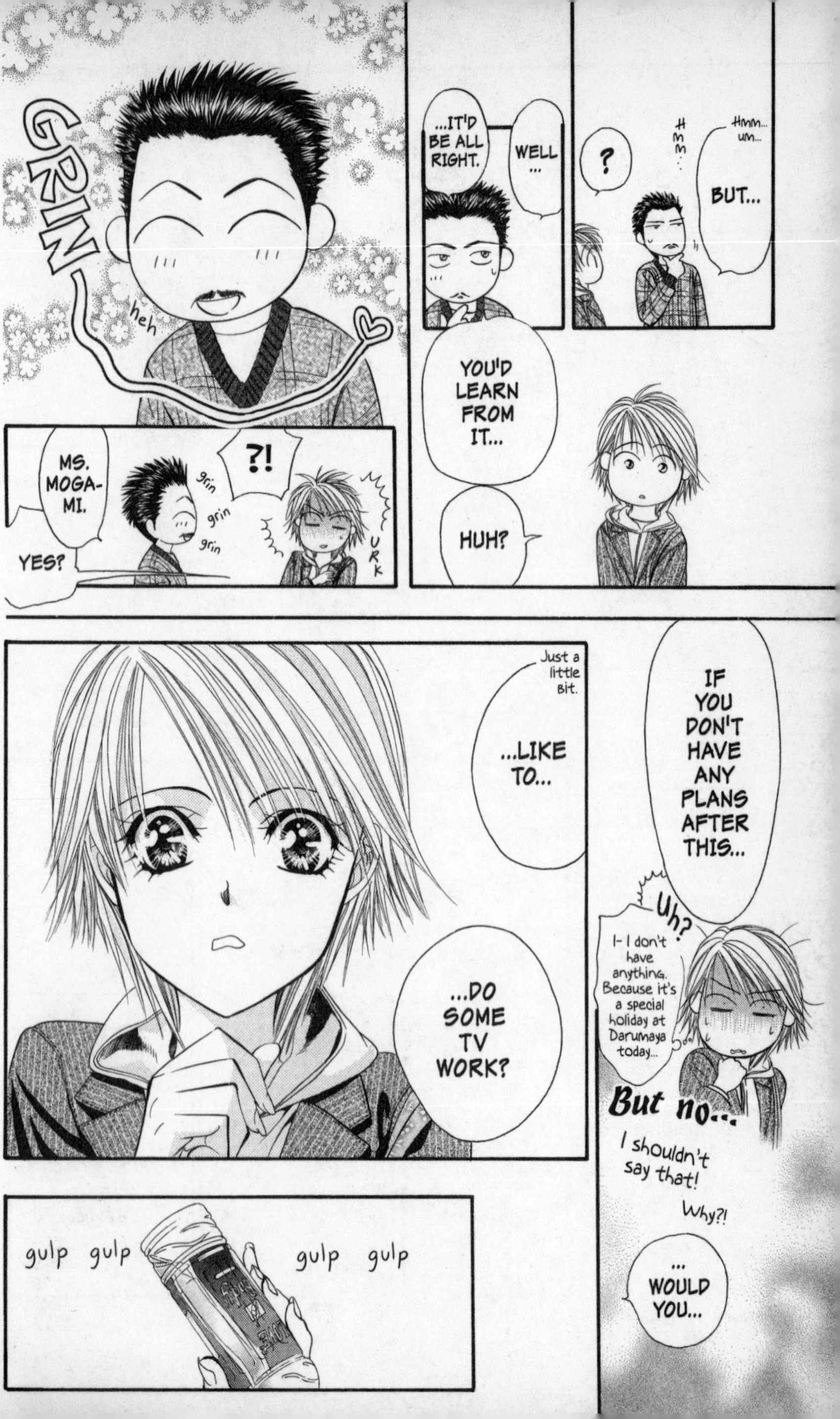
Hmm... um...
Hmm...
BUT...
?
WELL...
...IT'D BE ALL RIGHT.
YOU'D LEARN FROM IT...
HUH?
GRIN
heh
URK
?!
grin grin grin
MS. MOGA-MI.
YES?
IF YOU DON'T HAVE ANY PLANS AFTER THIS...
Uh?
I- I don't have anything. Because it's a special holiday at Darumaya today...
But no...
I shouldn't say that!
Why?!
...WOULD YOU...
Just a little bit.
...LIKE TO...
...DO SOME TV WORK?
gulp gulp
gulp gulp

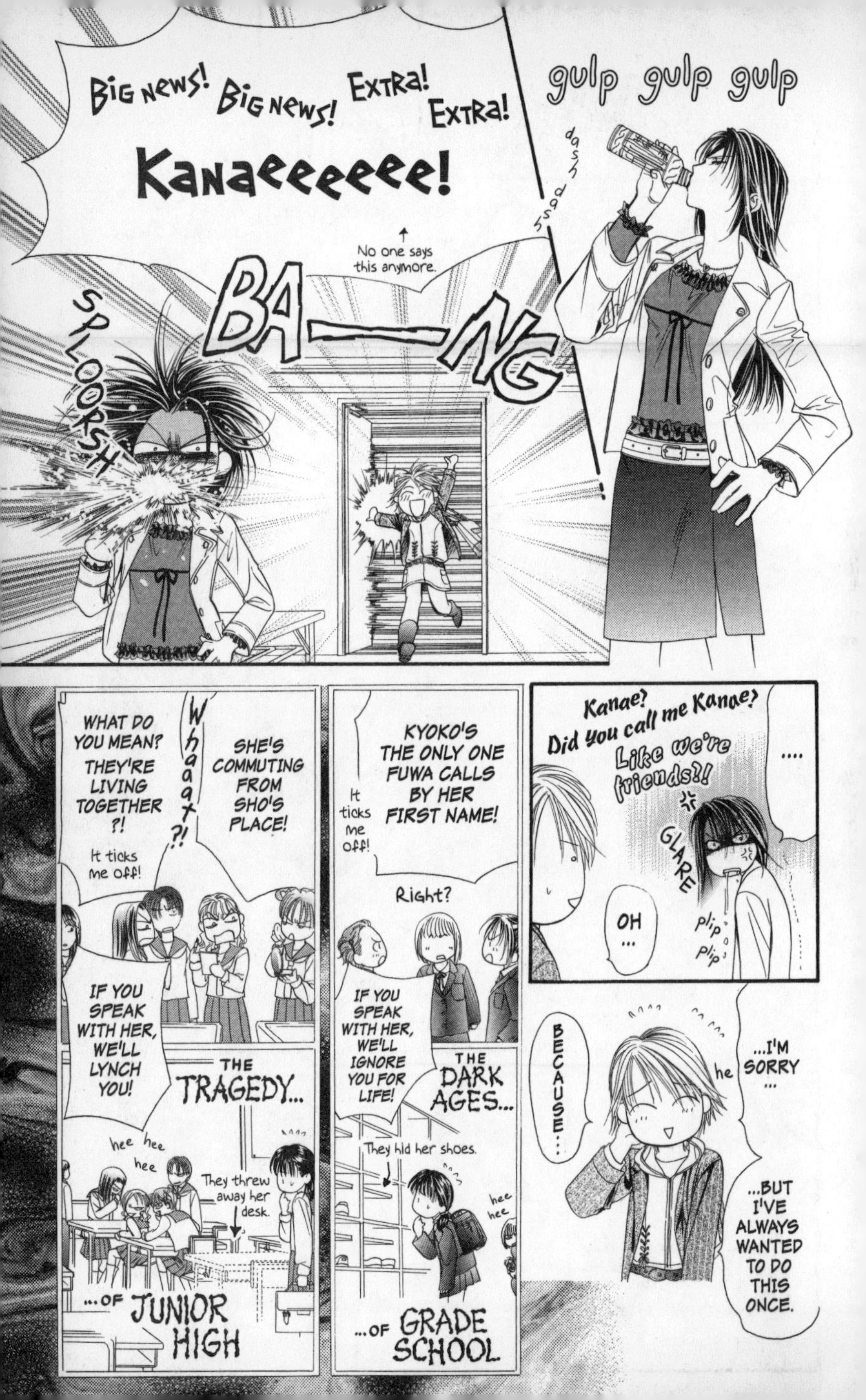
gulp gulp gulp
dash dash
Big news! Big news! Extra! Extra!
Kanaeeeeee!
No one says this anymore.
BA—NG
SPLOORSH
Kanae? Did you call me Kanae?
Like we're friends?!
....
GLARE
OH ...
plip plip
...I'M SORRY ...
he
BECAUSE...
...BUT I'VE ALWAYS WANTED TO DO THIS ONCE.
KYOKO'S THE ONLY ONE FUWA CALLS BY HER FIRST NAME!
It ticks me off!
Right?
IF YOU SPEAK WITH HER, WE'LL IGNORE YOU FOR LIFE!
THE DARK AGES...
They hid her shoes.
hee hee
...OF GRADE SCHOOL
SHE'S COMMUTING FROM SHO'S PLACE!
Whaaat?!
WHAT DO YOU MEAN? THEY'RE LIVING TOGETHER?!
It ticks me off!
IF YOU SPEAK WITH HER, WE'LL LYNCH YOU!
THE TRAGEDY...
They threw away her desk.
hee hee hee
...OF JUNIOR HIGH

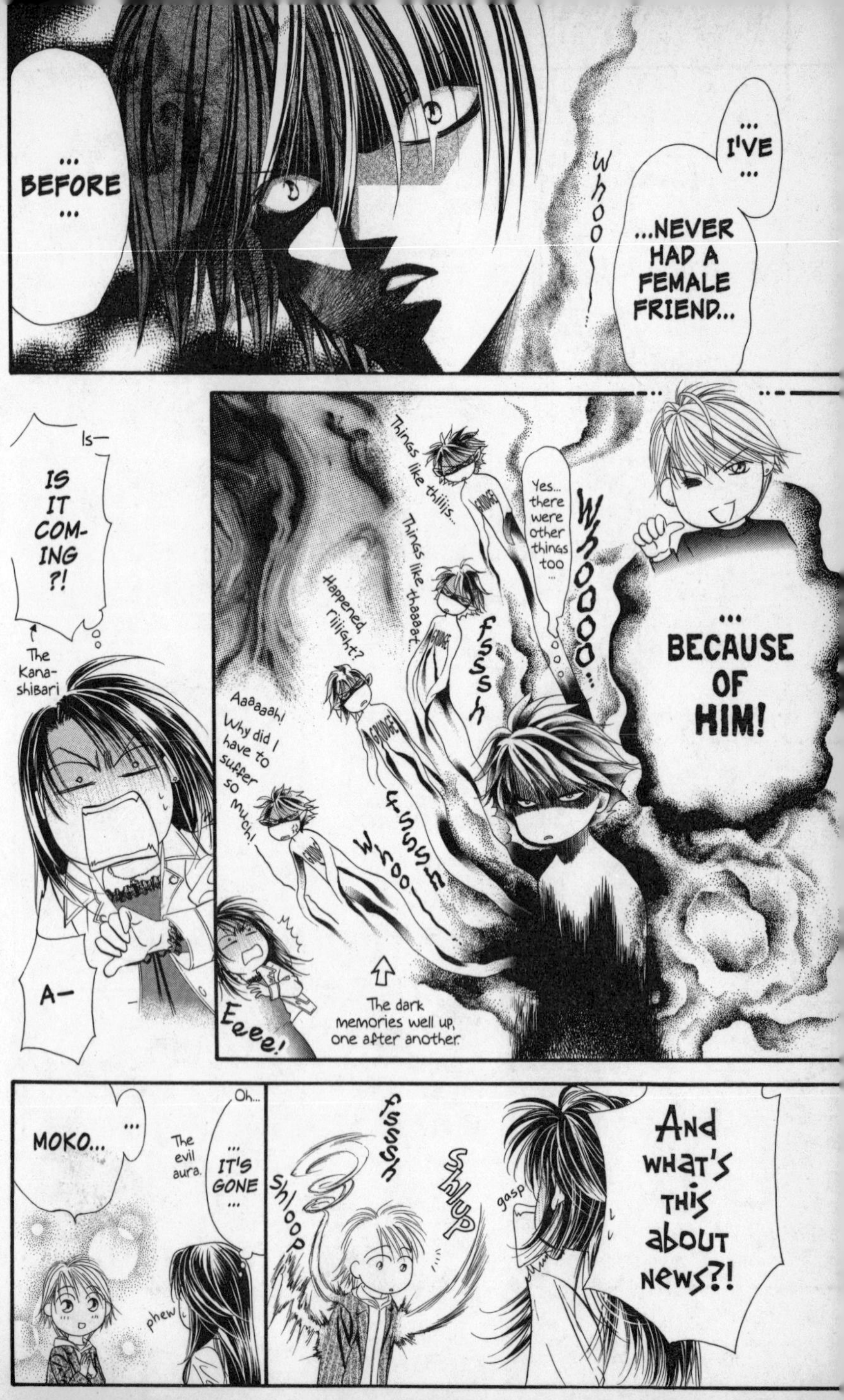

... I'VE ...
...NEVER HAD A FEMALE FRIEND...
Whoo—
... BEFORE ...
... BECAUSE OF HIM!
Yes... there were other things too ...
Whooooo...
Things like thiiiis...
GRUDGE
Things like thaaaat...
GRUDGE
fsssh
Happened, riiiight?
GRUDGE
Aaaaaah! Why did I have to suffer so much!
GRUDGE
fsssh
Whroo—
The dark memories well up, one after another.
Eeeee!
Is—
IS IT COMING?!
The Kanashibari
A—
And what's this about news?!
gasp
Shlup
fsssh
Shloop
Oh... ... IT'S GONE ...
The evil aura.
... MOKO...
phew

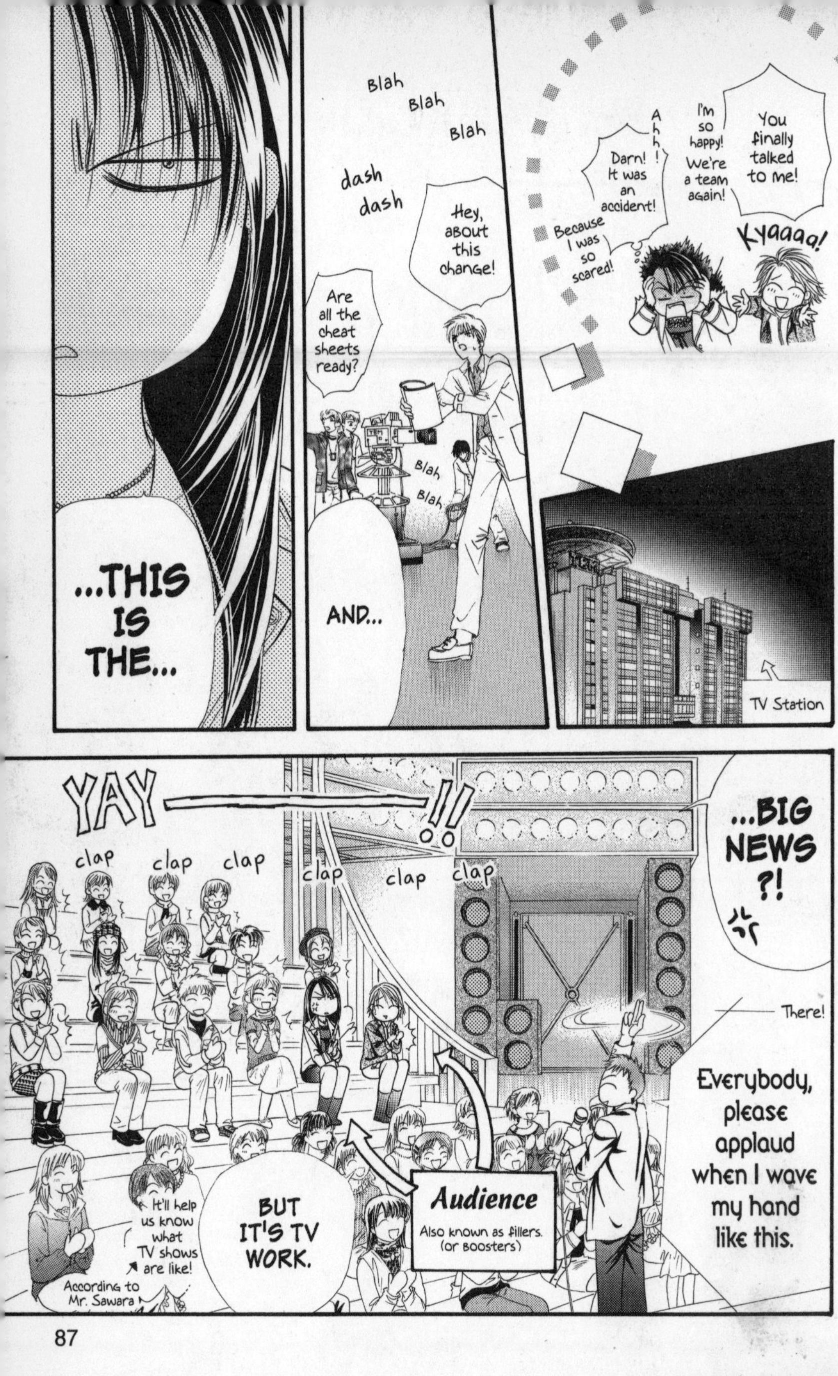
You finally talked to me!
Kyaaaa!
I'm so happy! We're a team again!
Ahh!
Darn! It was an accident!
Because I was so scared!
TV Station
Blah Blah Blah
dash dash
Hey, about this change!
Are all the cheat sheets ready?
Blah Blah
AND...
...THIS IS THE...
...BIG NEWS ?!
YAY—!!
clap clap clap clap clap clap
There!
Everybody, please applaud when I wave my hand like this.
Audience
Also known as fillers. (or boosters)
BUT IT'S TV WORK.
It'll help us know what TV shows are like!
According to Mr. Sawara

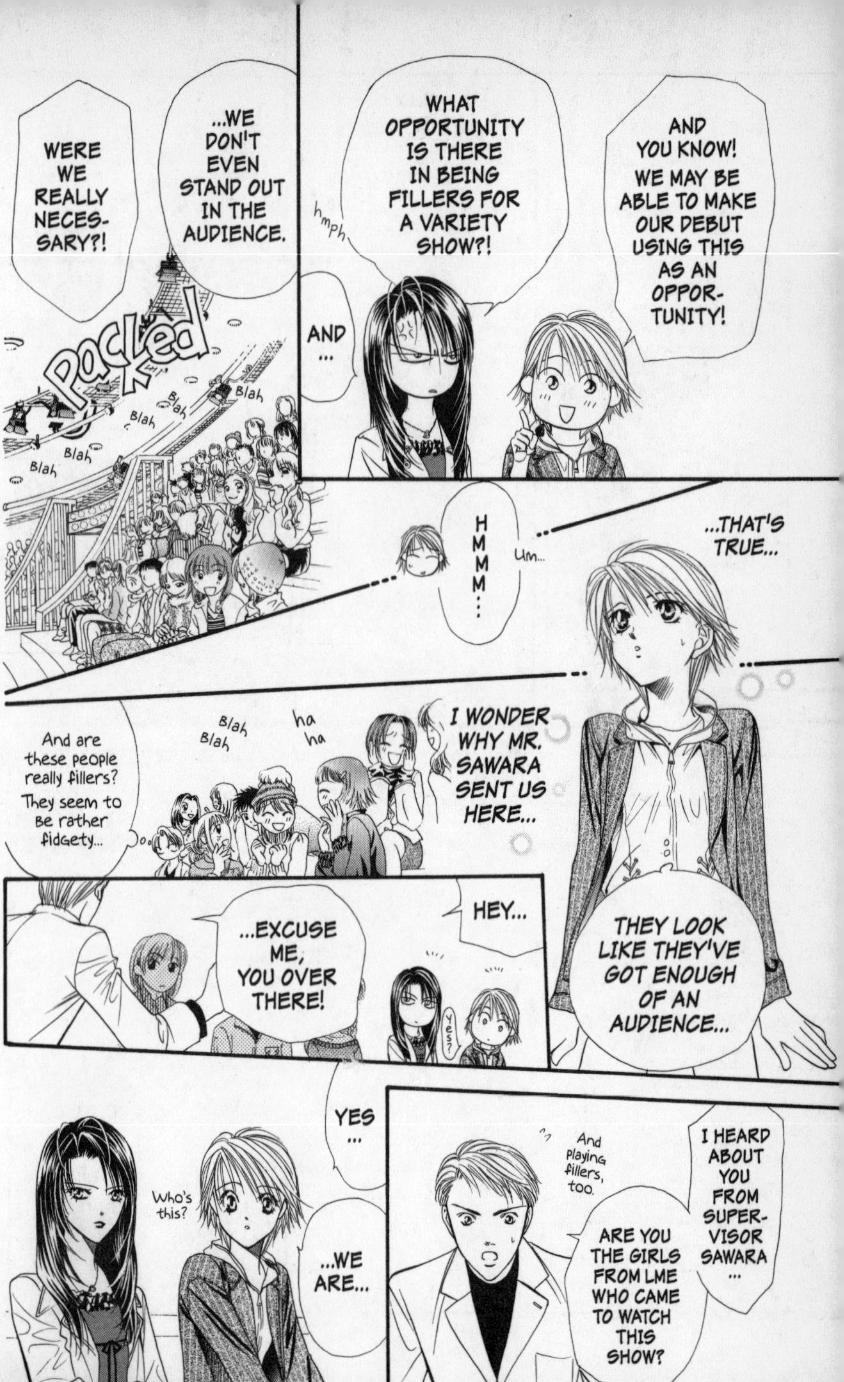
AND YOU KNOW! WE MAY BE ABLE TO MAKE OUR DEBUT USING THIS AS AN OPPOR-TUNITY!
WHAT OPPORTUNITY IS THERE IN BEING FILLERS FOR A VARIETY SHOW?!
hmph
AND ...
...WE DON'T EVEN STAND OUT IN THE AUDIENCE.
WERE WE REALLY NECES-SARY?!
Packed
Blah
Blah
Blah
Blah
...THAT'S TRUE...
HMMM...
Um...
I WONDER WHY MR. SAWARA SENT US HERE...
ha ha
Blah Blah
And are these people really fillers? They seem to be rather fidgety...
THEY LOOK LIKE THEY'VE GOT ENOUGH OF AN AUDIENCE...
HEY...
...EXCUSE ME, YOU OVER THERE!
Yes?
I HEARD ABOUT YOU FROM SUPER-VISOR SAWARA ...
And playing fillers, too.
ARE YOU THE GIRLS FROM LME WHO CAME TO WATCH THIS SHOW?
YES ...
...WE ARE...
Who's this?

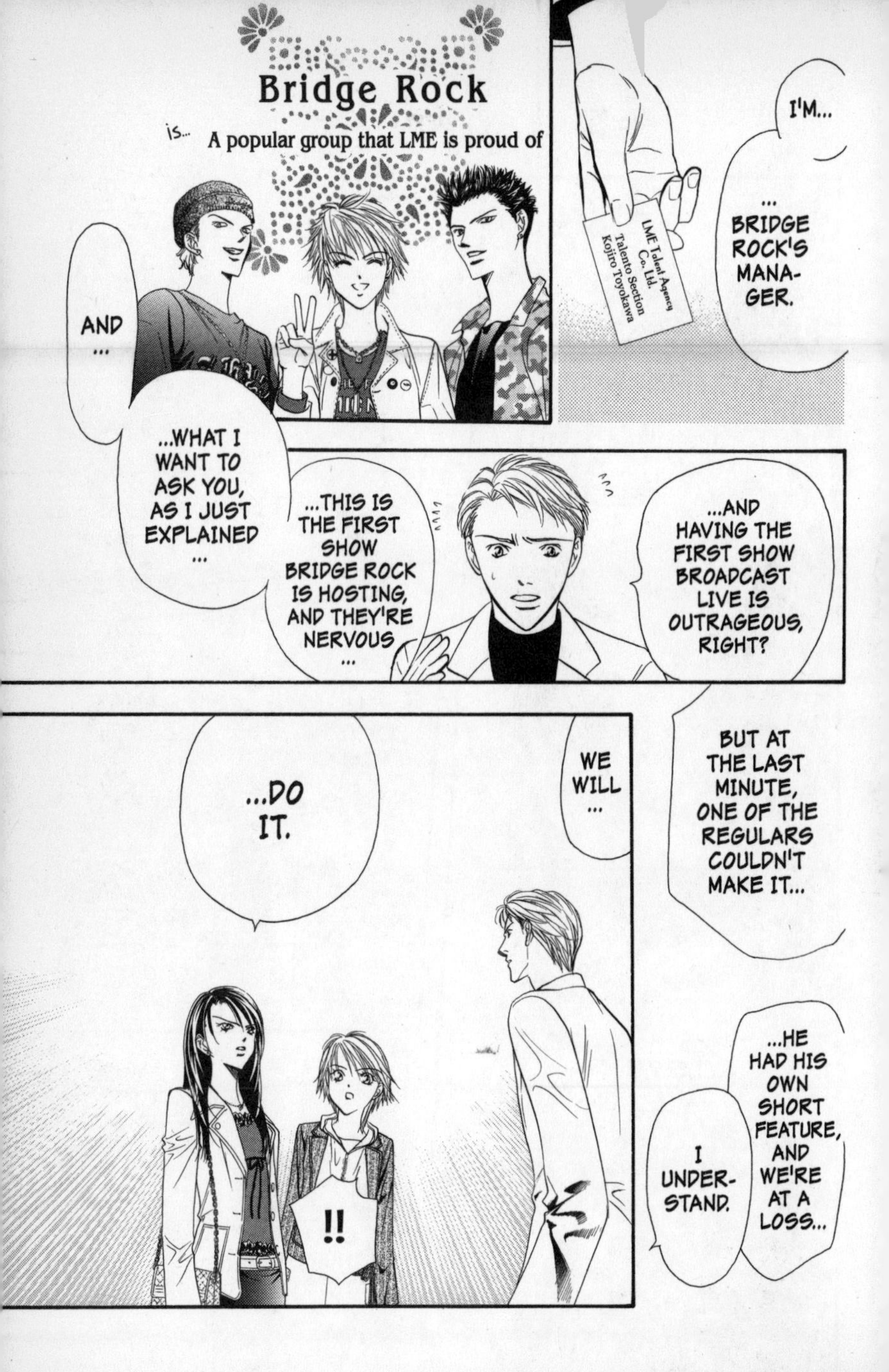
I'M...
...BRIDGE ROCK'S MANA-GER.
LME Talent Agency Co. Ltd. Talento Section Kojiro Toyokawa
Bridge Rock
is... A popular group that LME is proud of
AND...
...AND HAVING THE FIRST SHOW BROADCAST LIVE IS OUTRAGEOUS, RIGHT?
...THIS IS THE FIRST SHOW BRIDGE ROCK IS HOSTING, AND THEY'RE NERVOUS...
...WHAT I WANT TO ASK YOU, AS I JUST EXPLAINED...
BUT AT THE LAST MINUTE, ONE OF THE REGULARS COULDN'T MAKE IT...
...HE HAD HIS OWN SHORT FEATURE, AND WE'RE AT A LOSS...
I UNDER-STAND.
WE WILL...
...DO IT.
!!

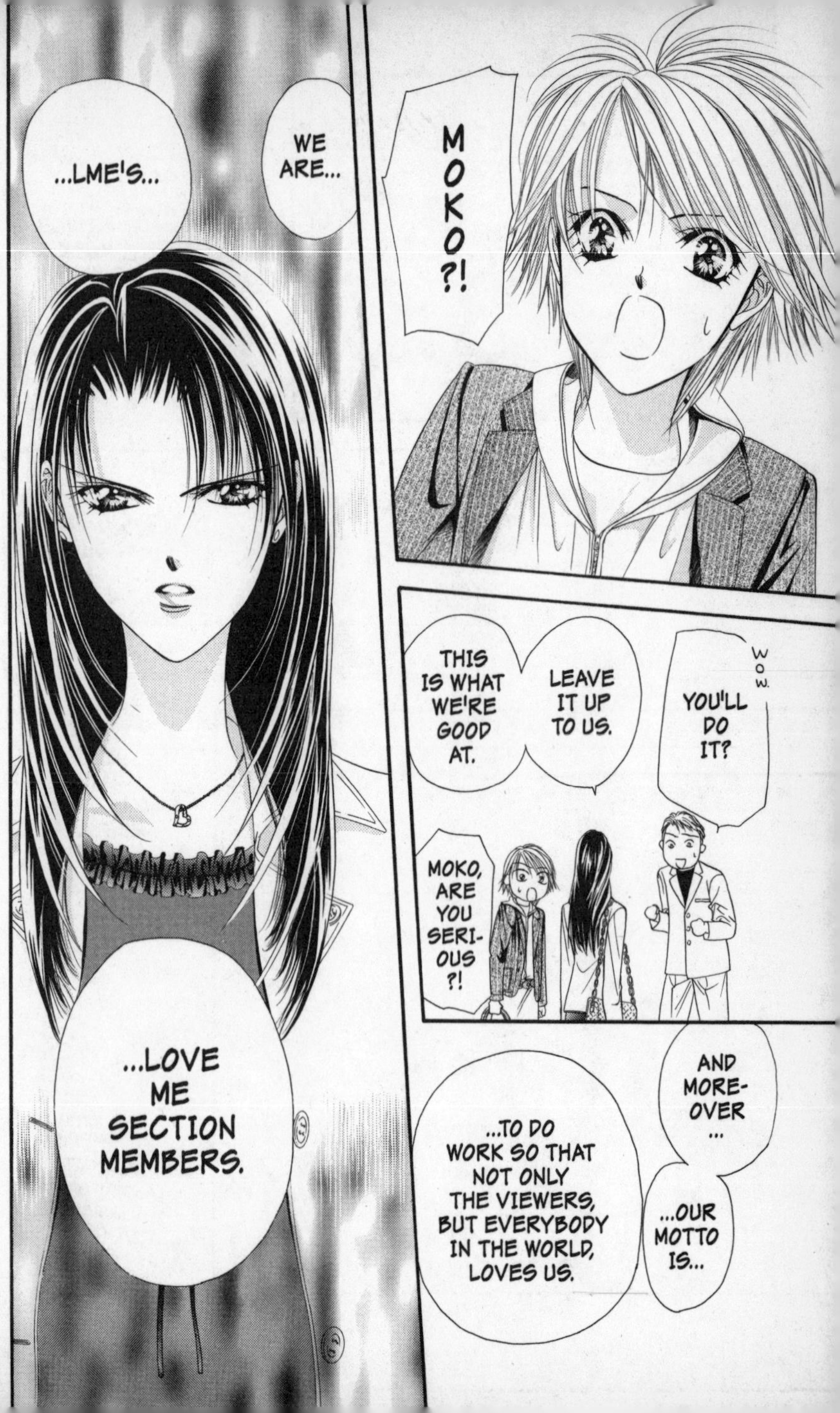
MOKO?!
WOW.
YOU'LL DO IT?
LEAVE IT UP TO US.
THIS IS WHAT WE'RE GOOD AT.
MOKO, ARE YOU SERIOUS?!
AND MOREOVER...
...OUR MOTTO IS...
...TO DO WORK SO THAT NOT ONLY THE VIEWERS, BUT EVERYBODY IN THE WORLD, LOVES US.
WE ARE...
...LME'S...
...LOVE ME SECTION MEMBERS.

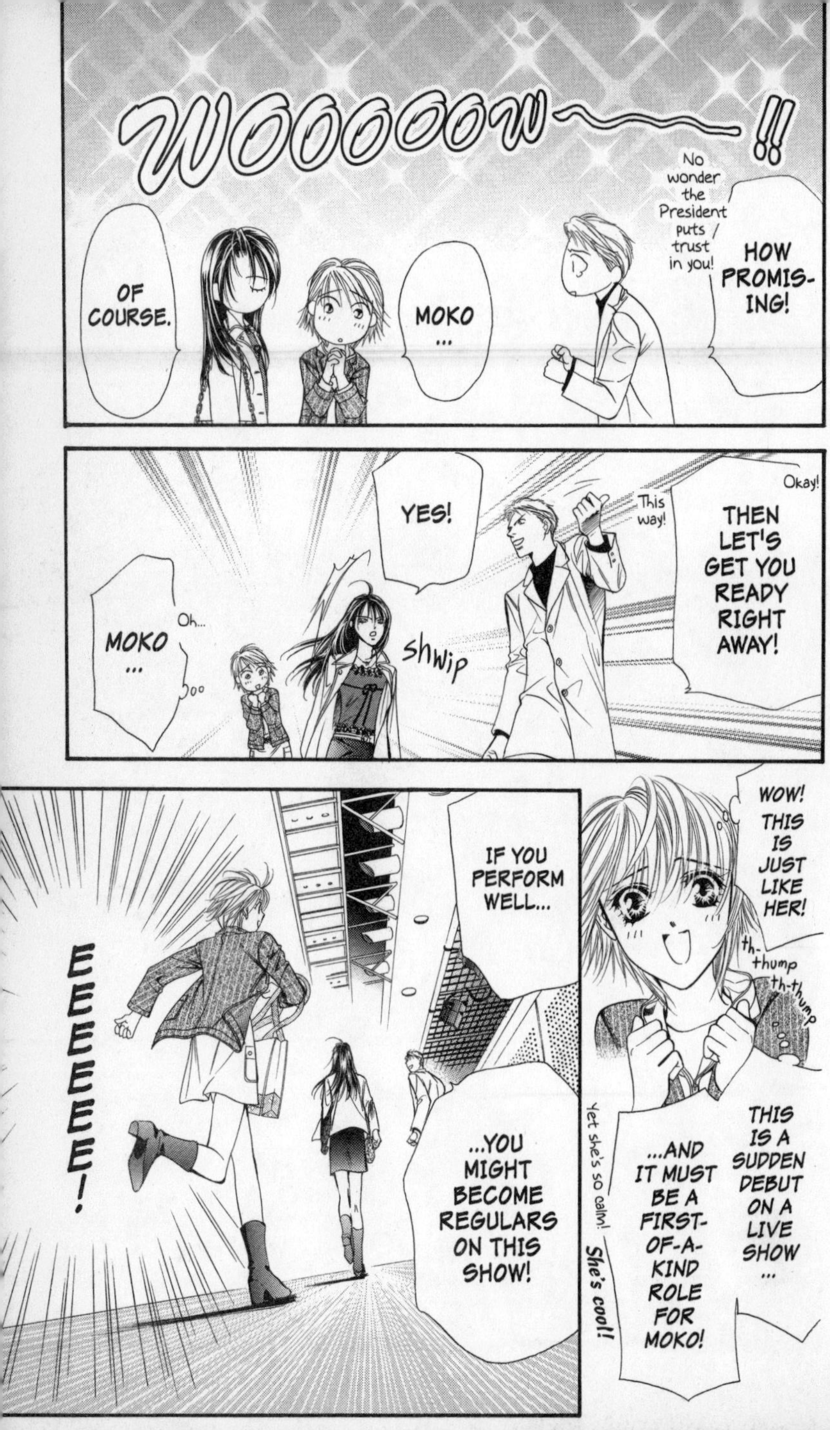

WOOOOOOW~~~!!
No wonder the President puts trust in you!
HOW PROMISING!
MOKO...
OF COURSE.
Okay!
THEN LET'S GET YOU READY RIGHT AWAY!
This way!
YES!
shwip
Oh...
MOKO...
WOW! THIS IS JUST LIKE HER!
th-thump th-thump
THIS IS A SUDDEN DEBUT ON A LIVE SHOW...
...AND IT MUST BE A FIRST-OF-A-KIND ROLE FOR MOKO!
She's cool!
Yet she's so calm!
IF YOU PERFORM WELL...
...YOU MIGHT BECOME REGULARS ON THIS SHOW!
EEEEEEE!

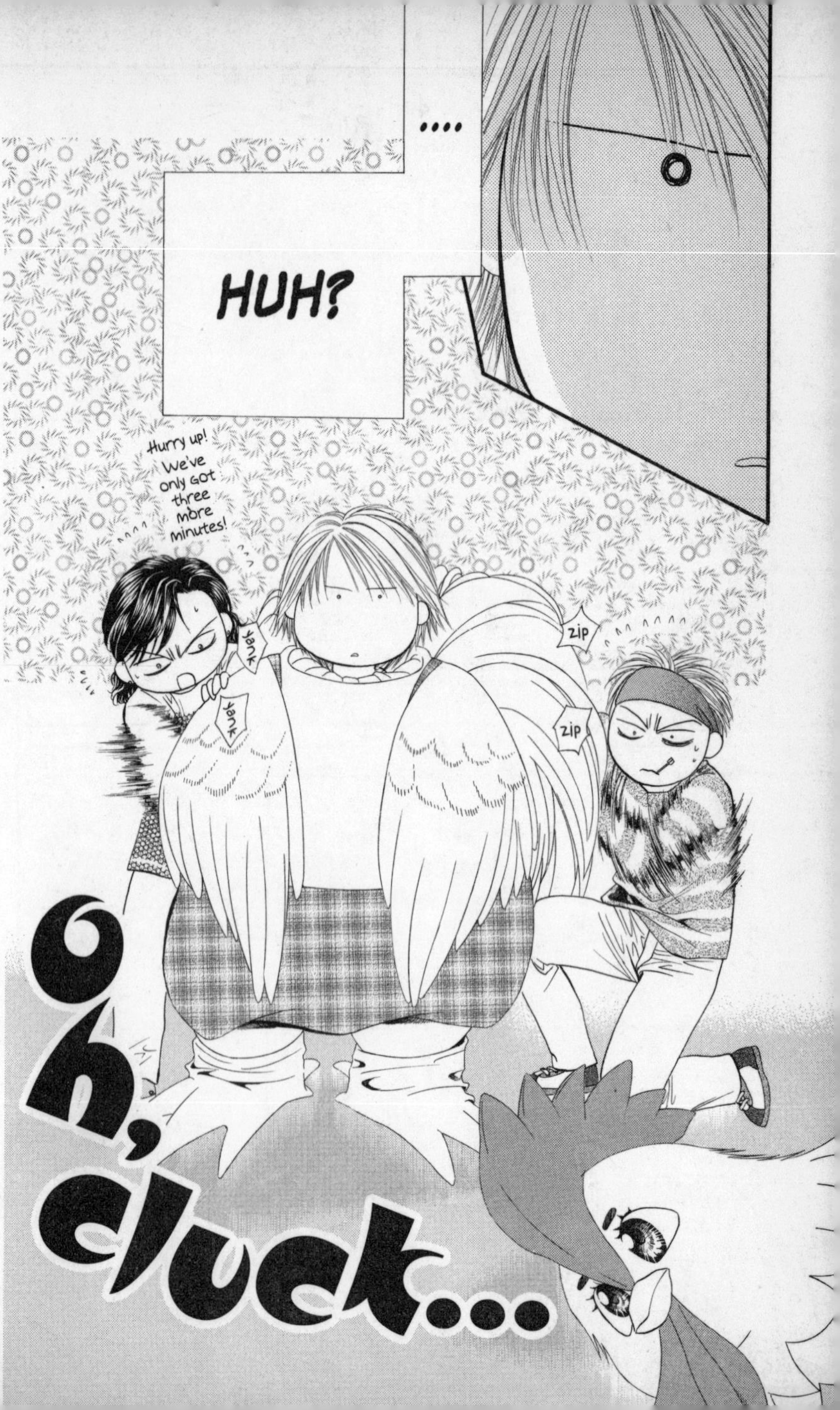
....
HUH?
Hurry up! We've only got three more minutes!
yank
yank
zip
zip
Oh, cluck...

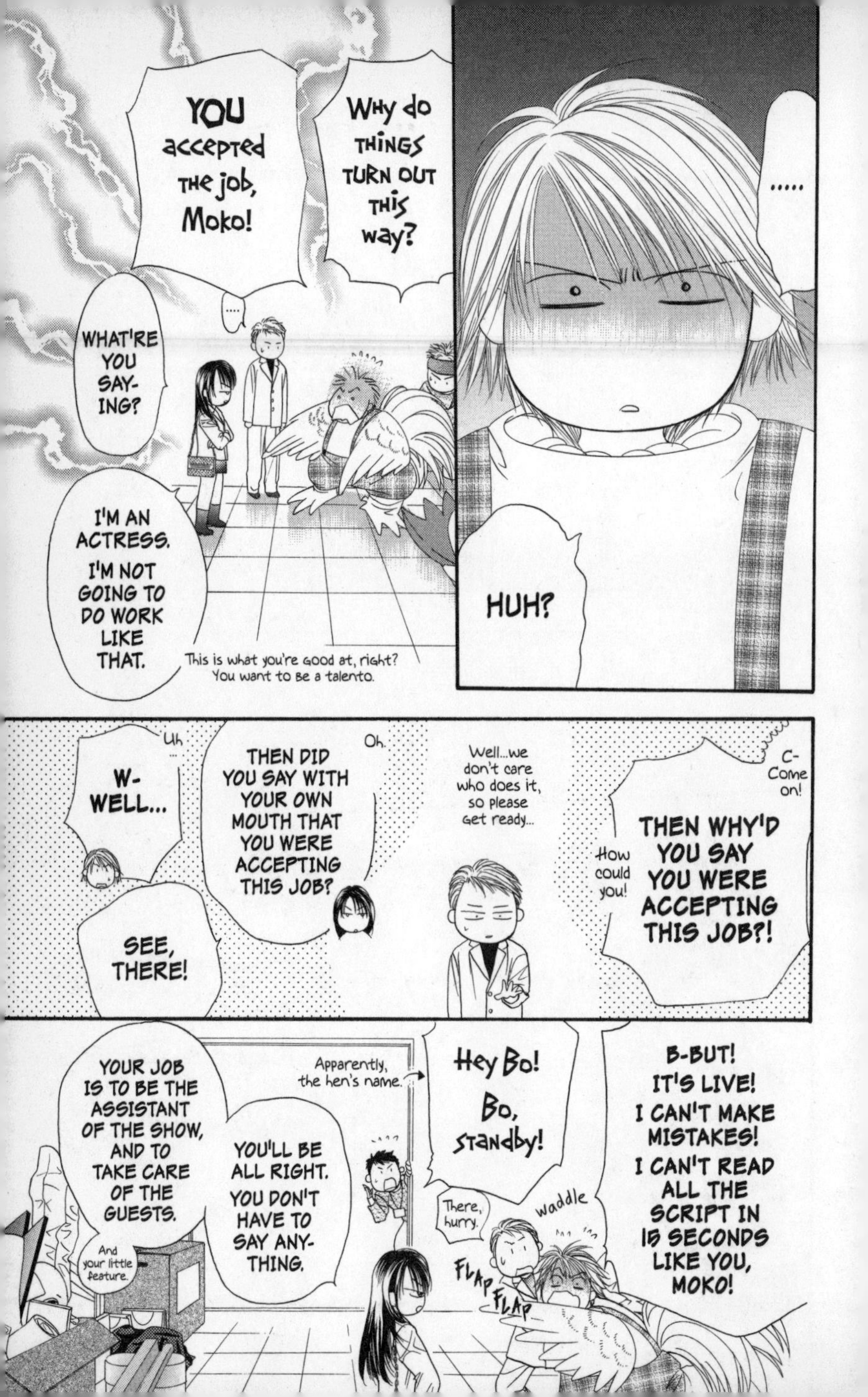
.....
HUH?
Why do things turn out this way?
YOU accepted the job, Moko!
....
WHAT'RE YOU SAYING?
I'M AN ACTRESS. I'M NOT GOING TO DO WORK LIKE THAT.
This is what you're good at, right? You want to be a talento.
C-Come on!
THEN WHY'D YOU SAY YOU WERE ACCEPTING THIS JOB?!
How could you!
Well...we don't care who does it, so please get ready...
Oh.
THEN DID YOU SAY WITH YOUR OWN MOUTH THAT YOU WERE ACCEPTING THIS JOB?
Uh...
W-WELL...
SEE, THERE!
B-BUT! IT'S LIVE! I CAN'T MAKE MISTAKES! I CAN'T READ ALL THE SCRIPT IN 15 SECONDS LIKE YOU, MOKO!
Hey Bo! Bo, standby!
Apparently, the hen's name.
waddle
There, hurry.
YOU'LL BE ALL RIGHT. YOU DON'T HAVE TO SAY ANYTHING.
YOUR JOB IS TO BE THE ASSISTANT OF THE SHOW, AND TO TAKE CARE OF THE GUESTS.
And your little feature.
FLAP FLAP

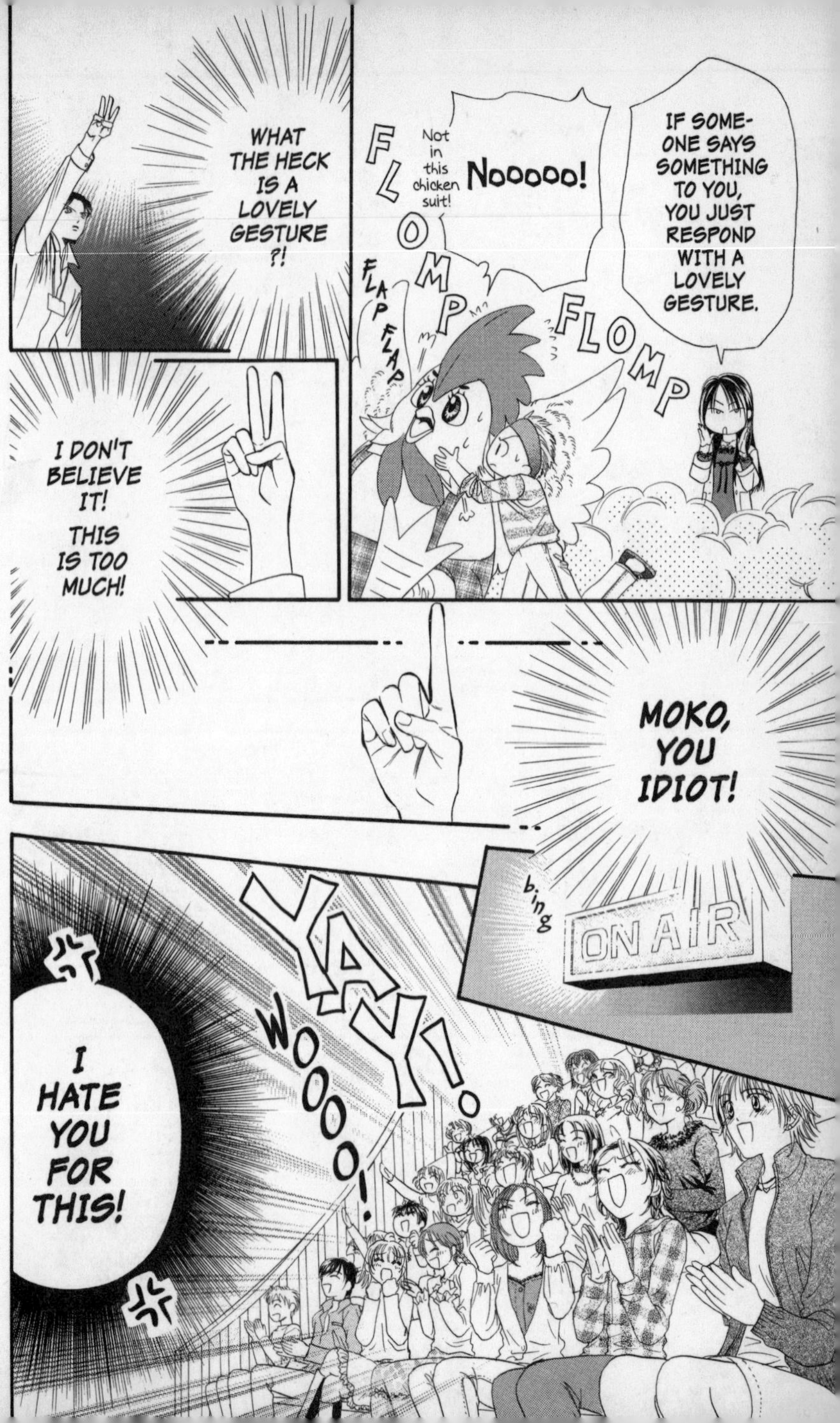
IF SOME-ONE SAYS SOMETHING TO YOU, YOU JUST RESPOND WITH A LOVELY GESTURE.
FLOMP
Nooooo!
Not in this chicken suit!
FLOMP
FLAP FLAP
WHAT THE HECK IS A LOVELY GESTURE?!
I DON'T BELIEVE IT!
THIS IS TOO MUCH!
MOKO, YOU IDIOT!
bing
ON AIR
YAY!
WOOOOO!
I HATE YOU FOR THIS!

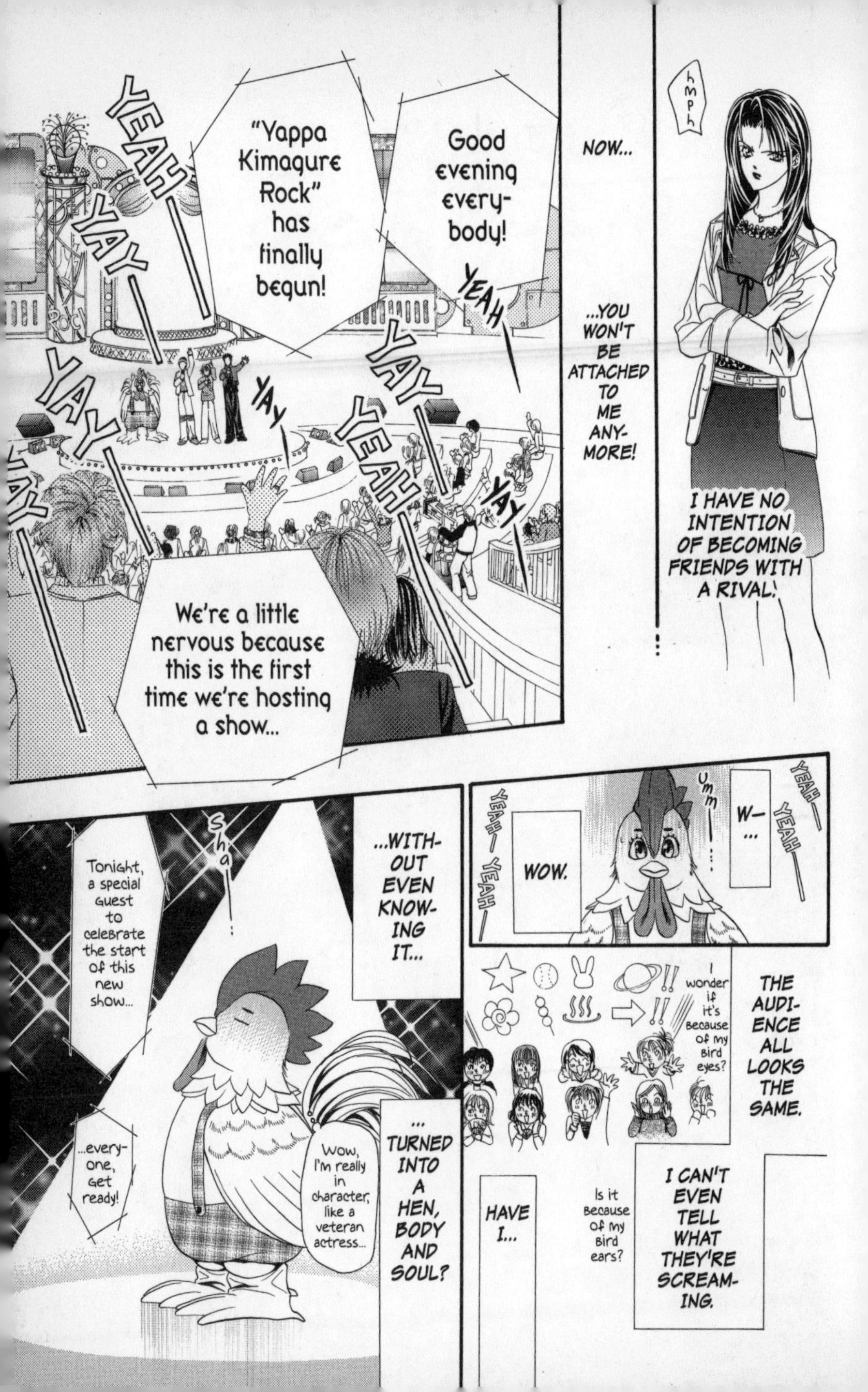
hmph
NOW...
...YOU WON'T BE ATTACHED TO ME ANYMORE!
I HAVE NO INTENTION OF BECOMING FRIENDS WITH A RIVAL!
Good evening every-body!
"Yappa Kimaqure Rock" has finally begun!
YEAH
YAY
YEAH
YAY
YEAH
YAY
YAY
YAY
YAY
We're a little nervous because this is the first time we're hosting a show...
YEAH YEAH
W—...
Umm...
WOW.
YEAH YEAH
THE AUDIENCE ALL LOOKS THE SAME.
I wonder if it's because of my Bird eyes?
I CAN'T EVEN TELL WHAT THEY'RE SCREAMING.
Is it because of my Bird ears?
HAVE I...
...WITHOUT EVEN KNOWING IT...
...TURNED INTO A HEN, BODY AND SOUL?
Sha...
Tonight, a special guest to celebrate the start of this new show...
...everyone, get ready!
Wow, I'm really in character, like a veteran actress...

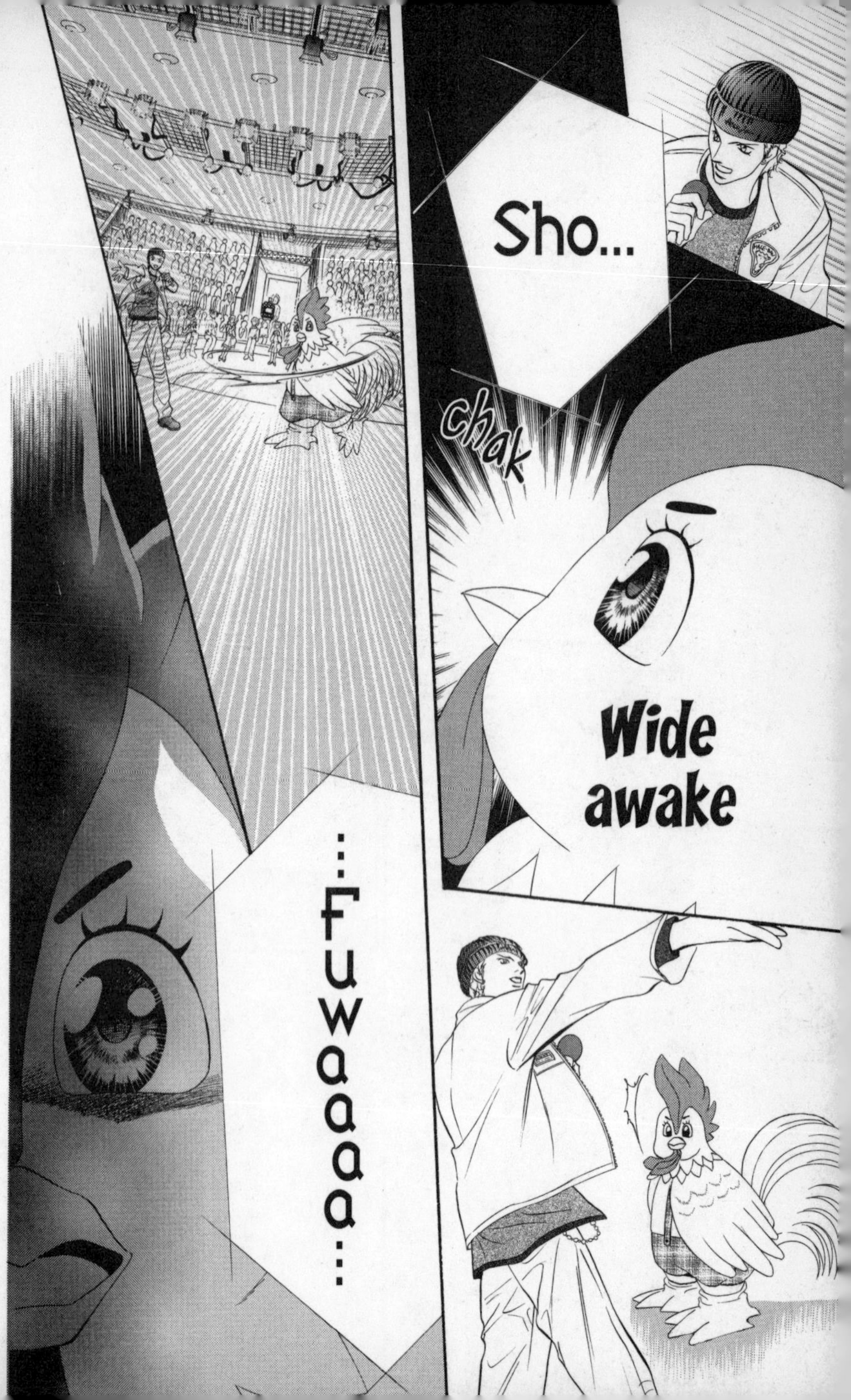
Sho...
chak
Wide awake
...Fuwaaaa...

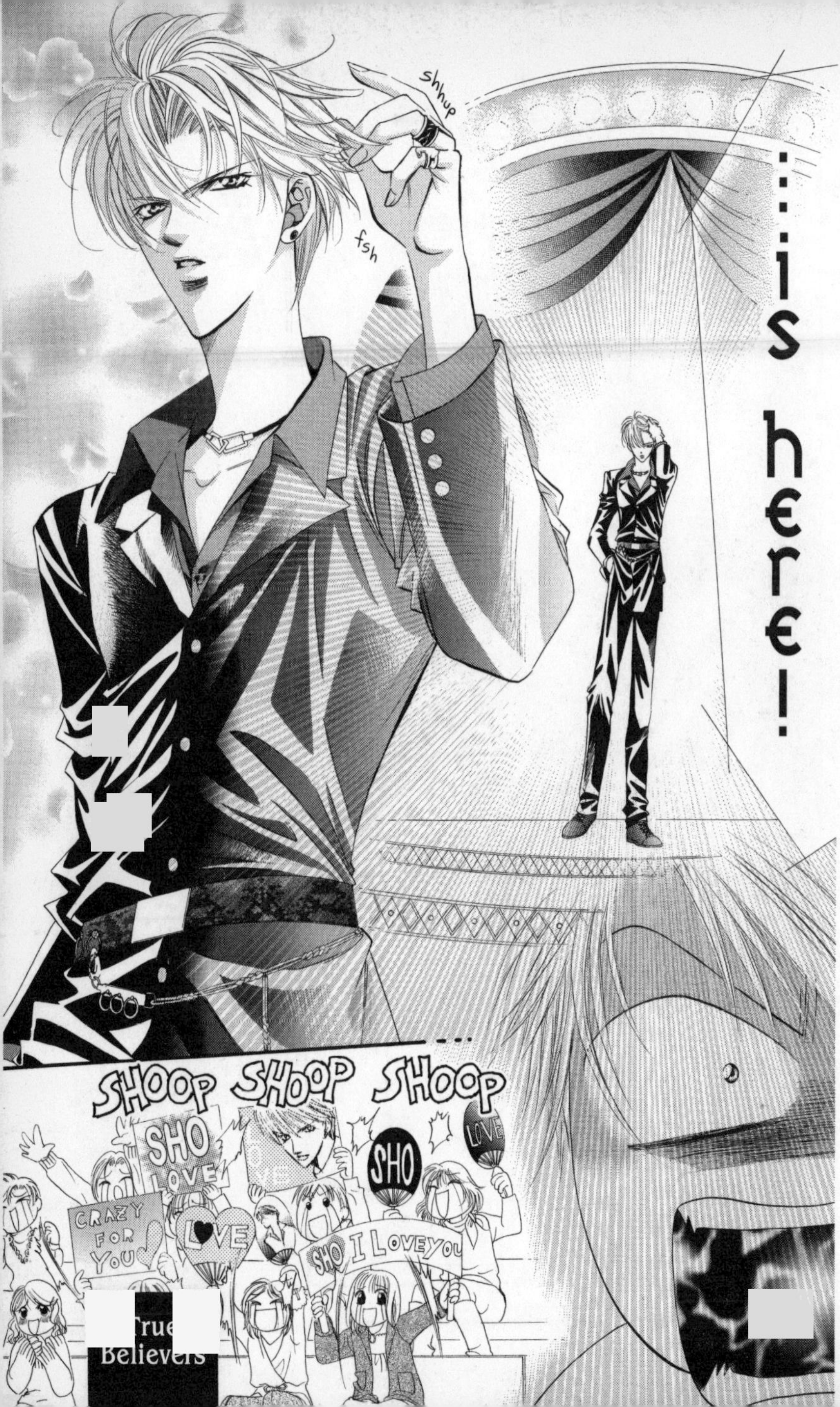
...is here!
shhup
fsh
SHOOP SHOOP SHOOP
SHO LOVE
CRAZY FOR YOU
LOVE
SHO
LOVE
SHO I LOVE YOU
True Believers

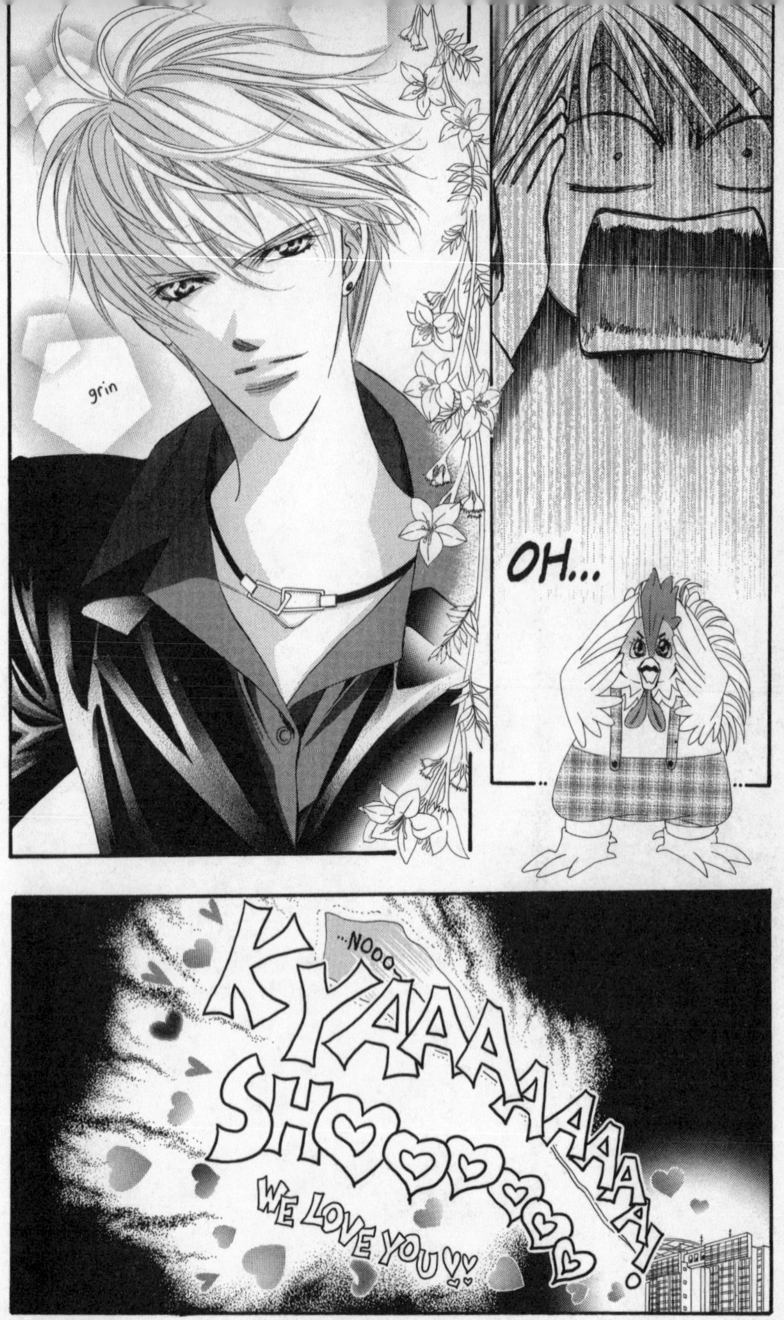
OH...
grin
...NOOO
KYAAAAAAAAAA!
SH♡♡♡♡♡♡
WE LOVE YOU♡!♡

End of Act 20

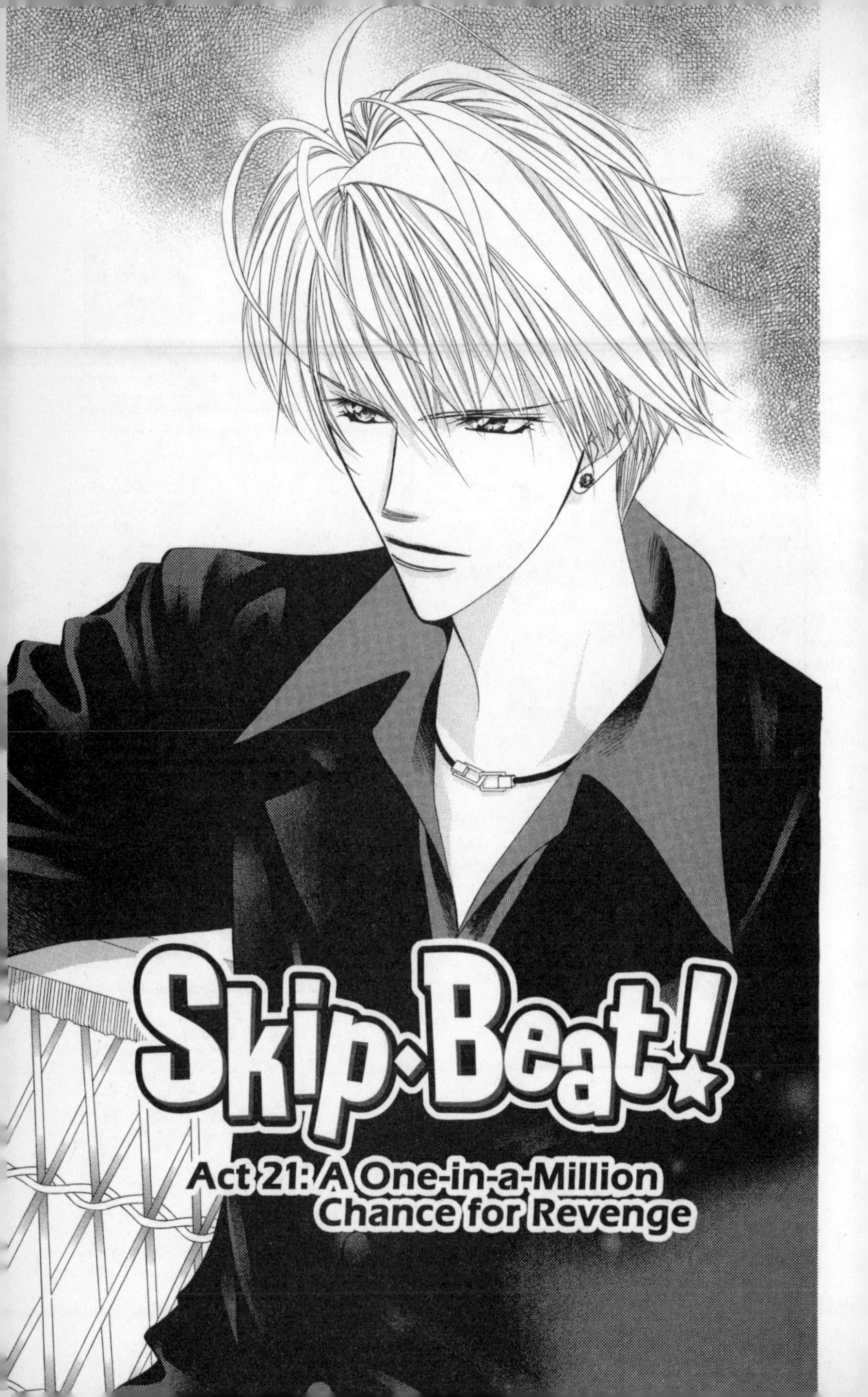
Skip·Beat!
Act 21: A One-in-a-Million Chance for Revenge

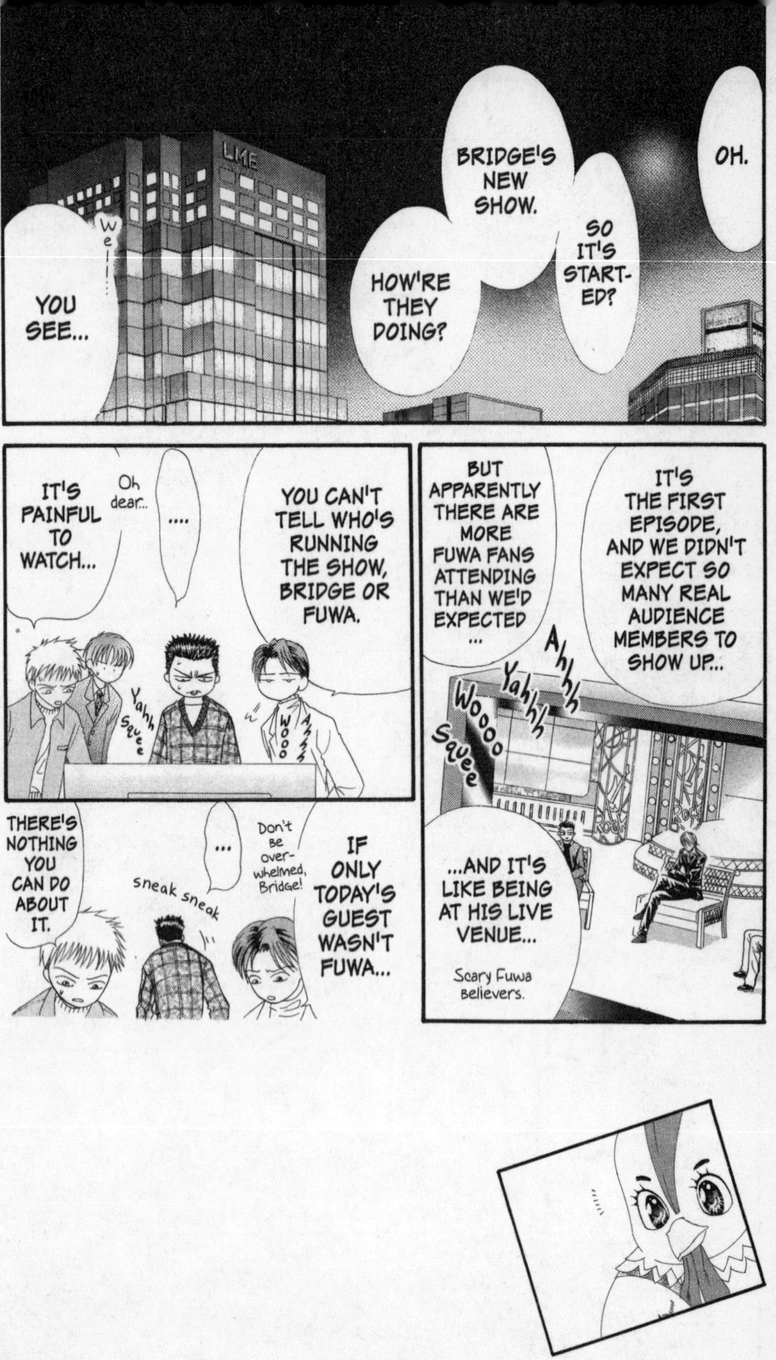
OH.
BRIDGE'S NEW SHOW.
SO IT'S START-ED?
HOW'RE THEY DOING?
Well...
YOU SEE...
IT'S THE FIRST EPISODE, AND WE DIDN'T EXPECT SO MANY REAL AUDIENCE MEMBERS TO SHOW UP...
BUT APPARENTLY THERE ARE MORE FUWA FANS ATTENDING THAN WE'D EXPECTED...
Ahhhh
Yahhh
Woooo
Squee
...AND IT'S LIKE BEING AT HIS LIVE VENUE...
Scary Fuwa believers.
YOU CAN'T TELL WHO'S RUNNING THE SHOW, BRIDGE OR FUWA.
....
Oh dear...
IT'S PAINFUL TO WATCH...
Ahhhh
Wooo
Yahh
Squee
IF ONLY TODAY'S GUEST WASN'T FUWA...
Don't be over-whelmed, Bridge!
...
sneak sneak
THERE'S NOTHING YOU CAN DO ABOUT IT.

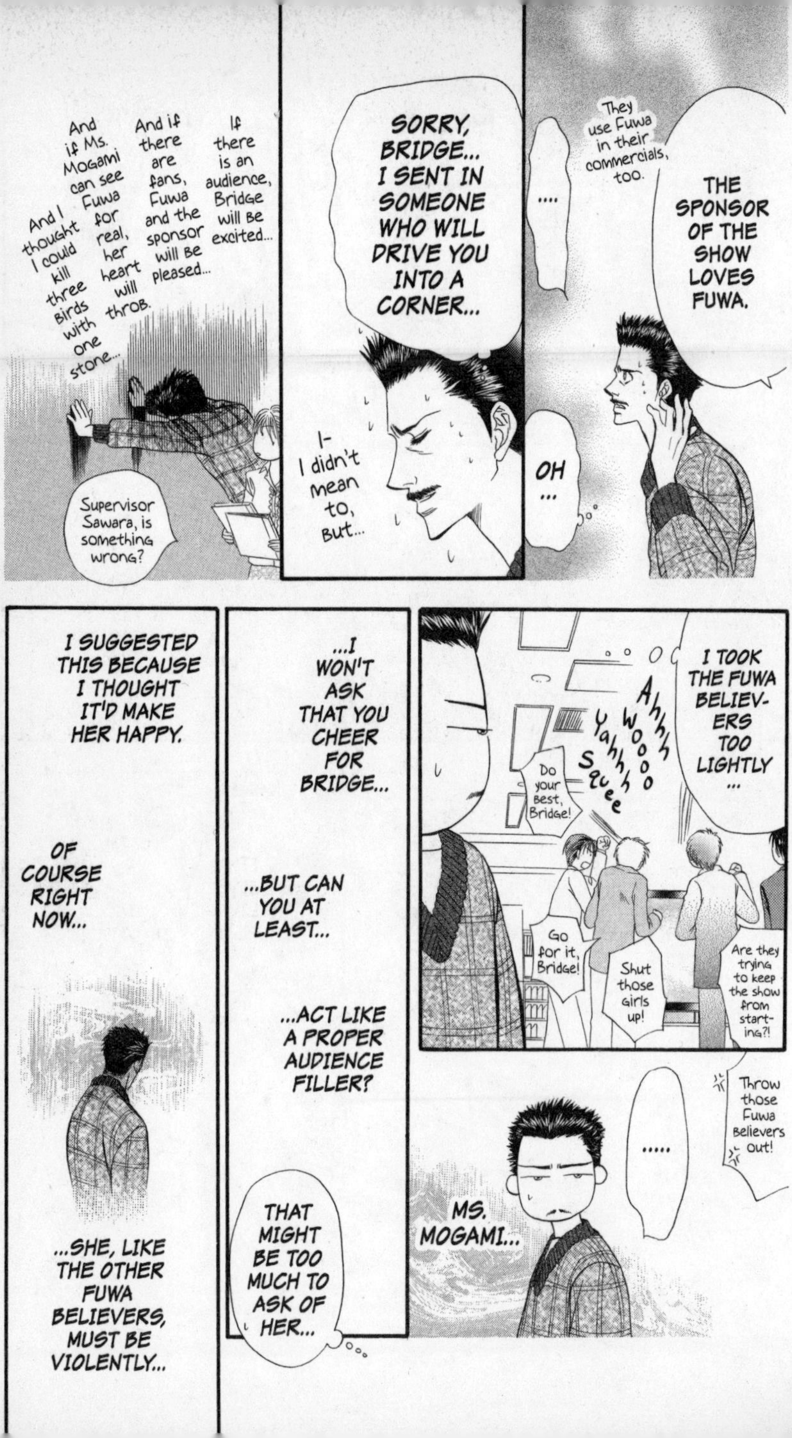
THE SPONSOR OF THE SHOW LOVES FUWA.
They use Fuwa in their commercials, too.
....
OH...
SORRY, BRIDGE... I SENT IN SOMEONE WHO WILL DRIVE YOU INTO A CORNER...
I- I didn't mean to, but...
If there is an audience, Bridge will be excited...
And if there are fans, Fuwa and the sponsor will be pleased...
And if Ms. Mogami can see Fuwa for real, her heart will throb.
And I thought I could kill three birds with one stone...
Supervisor Sawara, is something wrong?
I TOOK THE FUWA BELIEVERS TOO LIGHTLY...
Ahhh Woooo Yahhh Squee
Do your best, Bridge!
Go for it, Bridge!
Shut those girls up!
Are they trying to keep the show from starting?!
Throw those Fuwa Believers out!
.....
MS. MOGAMI...
...I WON'T ASK THAT YOU CHEER FOR BRIDGE...
...BUT CAN YOU AT LEAST...
...ACT LIKE A PROPER AUDIENCE FILLER?
THAT MIGHT BE TOO MUCH TO ASK OF HER...
I SUGGESTED THIS BECAUSE I THOUGHT IT'D MAKE HER HAPPY.
OF COURSE RIGHT NOW...
...SHE, LIKE THE OTHER FUWA BELIEVERS, MUST BE VIOLENTLY...

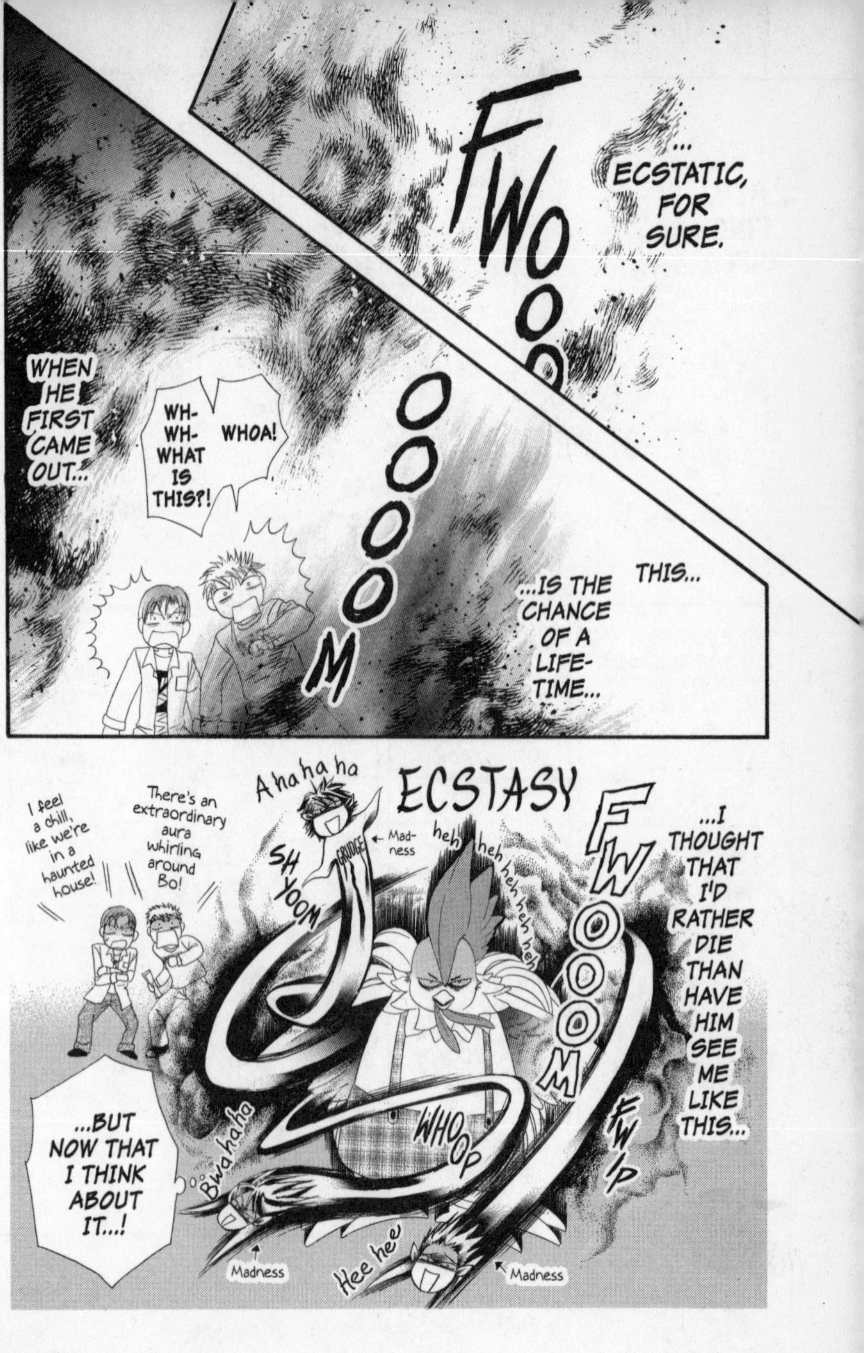

FWOOOOOOOOOM
...ECSTATIC, FOR SURE.
THIS...
...IS THE CHANCE OF A LIFE-TIME...
WHOA!
WH- WH- WHAT IS THIS?!
WHEN HE FIRST CAME OUT...
...I THOUGHT THAT I'D RATHER DIE THAN HAVE HIM SEE ME LIKE THIS...
FWOOOOOM
ECSTASY
heh heh heh heh heh
Ahahaha
Mad-ness
GRUDGE
SHYOOM
There's an extraordinary aura whirling around Bo!
I feel a chill, like we're in a haunted house!
FWIP
WHOOP
Madness
Hee hee
Madness
Bwahaha
...BUT NOW THAT I THINK ABOUT IT...!

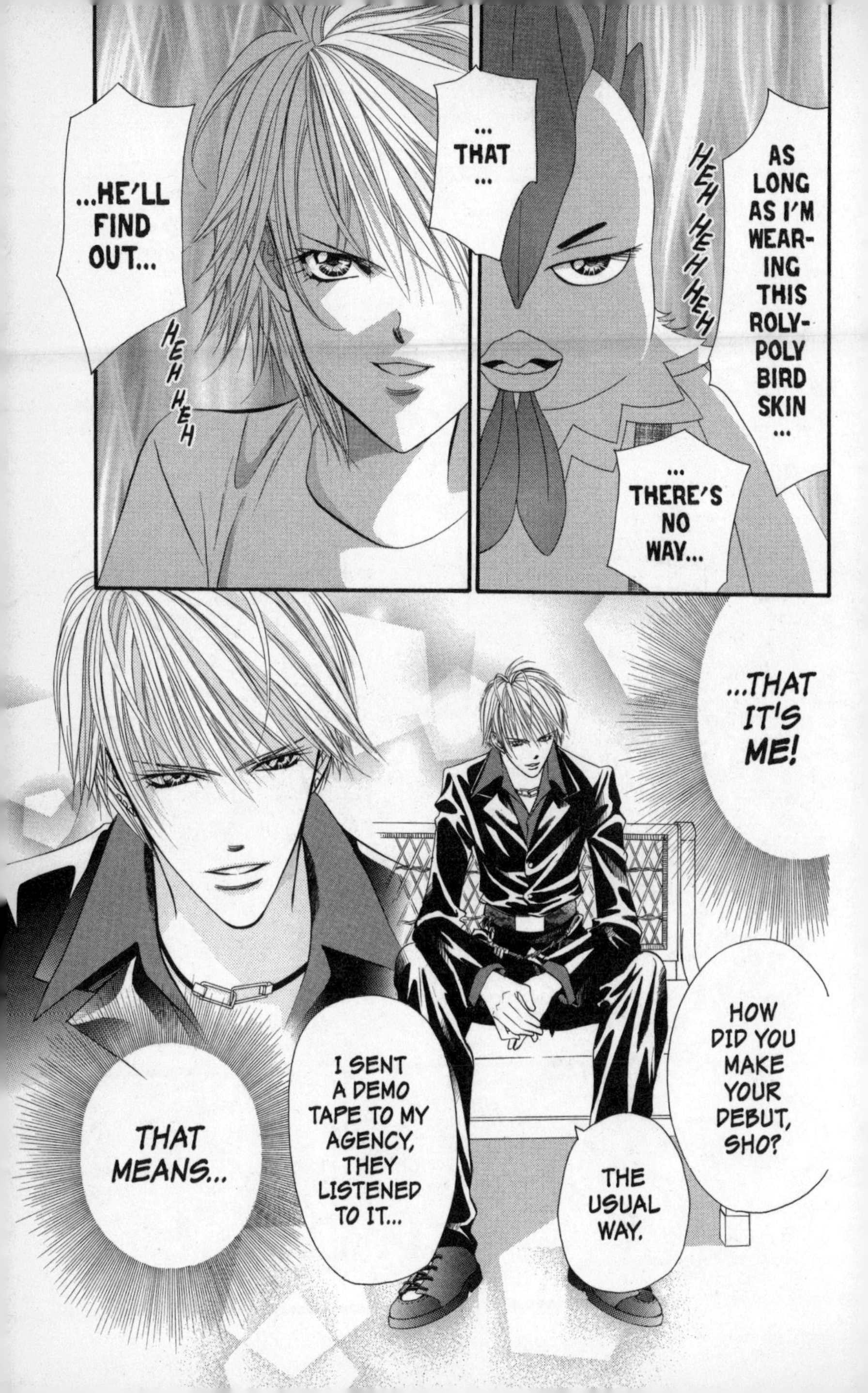
AS LONG AS I'M WEARING THIS ROLY-POLY BIRD SKIN...
HEH HEH HEH
...THERE'S NO WAY...
...THAT...
...HE'LL FIND OUT...
HEH HEH
...THAT IT'S ME!
HOW DID YOU MAKE YOUR DEBUT, SHO?
THE USUAL WAY.
I SENT A DEMO TAPE TO MY AGENCY, THEY LISTENED TO IT...
THAT MEANS...

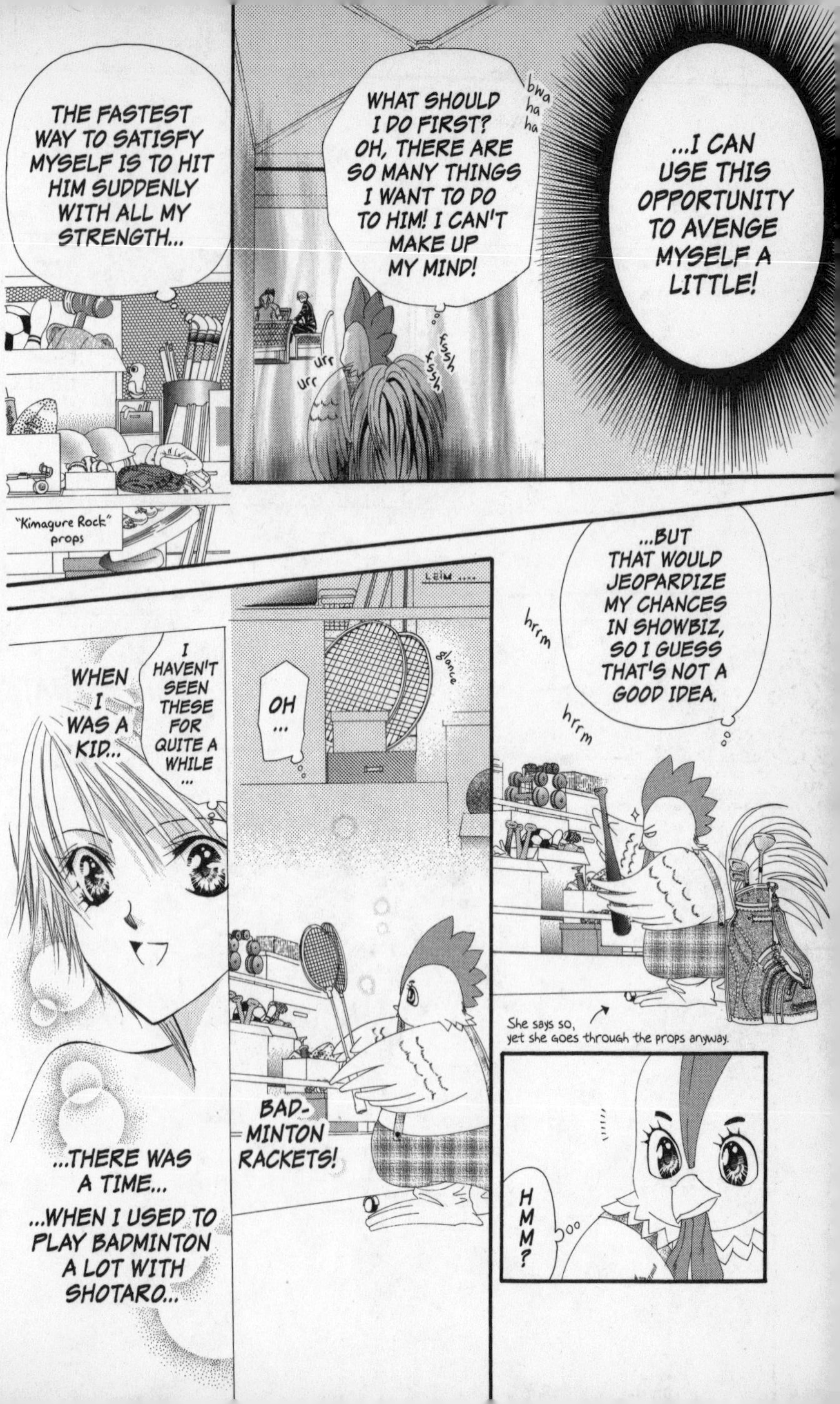
...I CAN USE THIS OPPORTUNITY TO AVENGE MYSELF A LITTLE!
bwa ha ha
WHAT SHOULD I DO FIRST? OH, THERE ARE SO MANY THINGS I WANT TO DO TO HIM! I CAN'T MAKE UP MY MIND!
fssh fssh
urr urr
THE FASTEST WAY TO SATISFY MYSELF IS TO HIT HIM SUDDENLY WITH ALL MY STRENGTH...
"Kimagure Rock" props
...BUT THAT WOULD JEOPARDIZE MY CHANCES IN SHOWBIZ, SO I GUESS THAT'S NOT A GOOD IDEA.
hrrm
hrrm
She says so, yet she goes through the props anyway.
HMM?
glance
OH ...
BAD-MINTON RACKETS!
I HAVEN'T SEEN THESE FOR QUITE A WHILE ...
WHEN I WAS A KID...
...THERE WAS A TIME...
...WHEN I USED TO PLAY BADMINTON A LOT WITH SHOTARO...

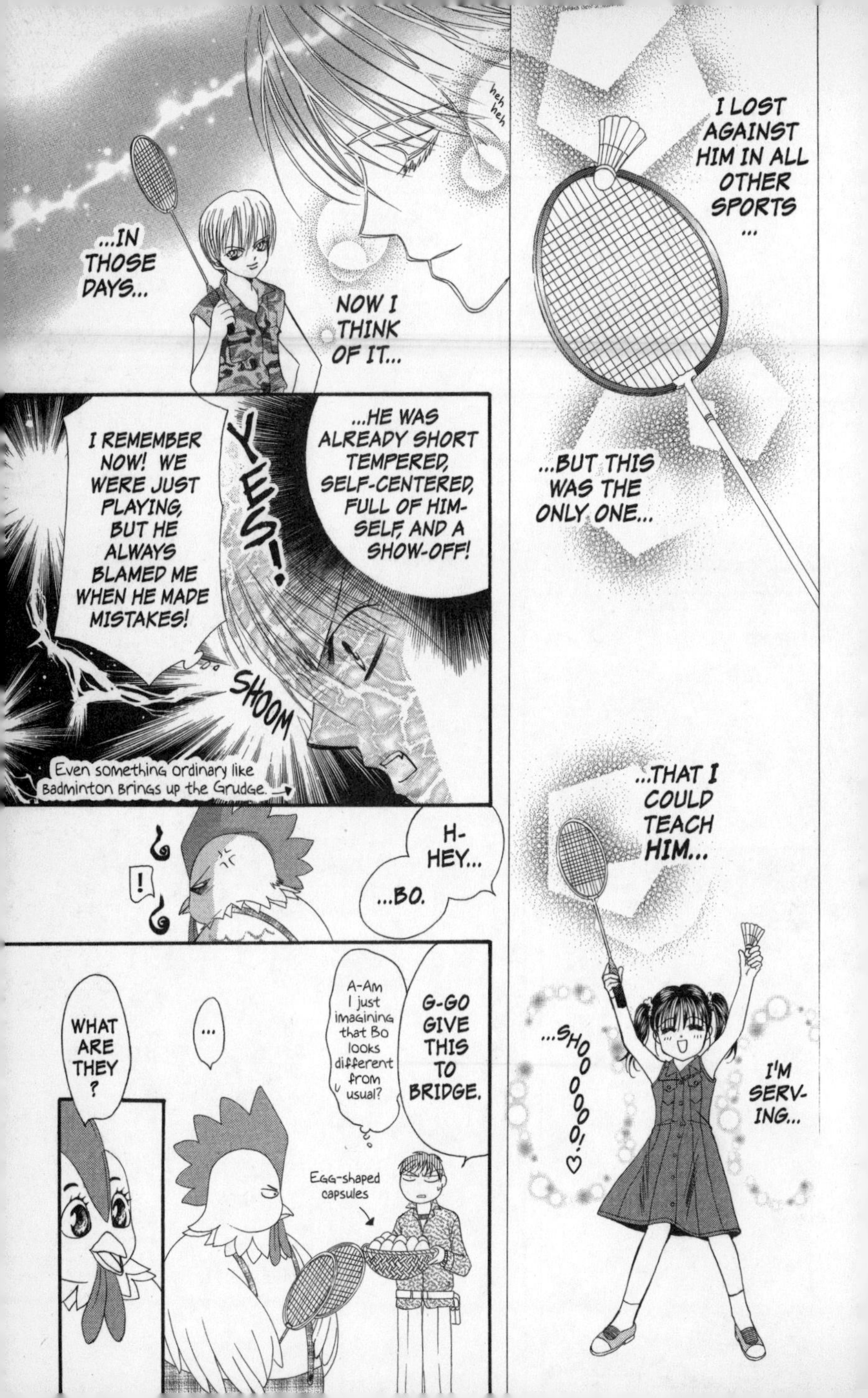
I LOST AGAINST HIM IN ALL OTHER SPORTS ...
...BUT THIS WAS THE ONLY ONE...
...THAT I COULD TEACH HIM...
I'M SERV-ING...
...SHOOOOOOO!♡
NOW I THINK OF IT...
heh heh
...IN THOSE DAYS...
...HE WAS ALREADY SHORT TEMPERED, SELF-CENTERED, FULL OF HIM-SELF, AND A SHOW-OFF!
YES!
I REMEMBER NOW! WE WERE JUST PLAYING, BUT HE ALWAYS BLAMED ME WHEN HE MADE MISTAKES!
SHOOM
Even something ordinary like Badminton Brings up the Grudge.
H-HEY... ...BO.
!
G-GO GIVE THIS TO BRIDGE.
A-Am I just imagining that Bo looks different from usual?
...
WHAT ARE THEY?
Egg-shaped capsules

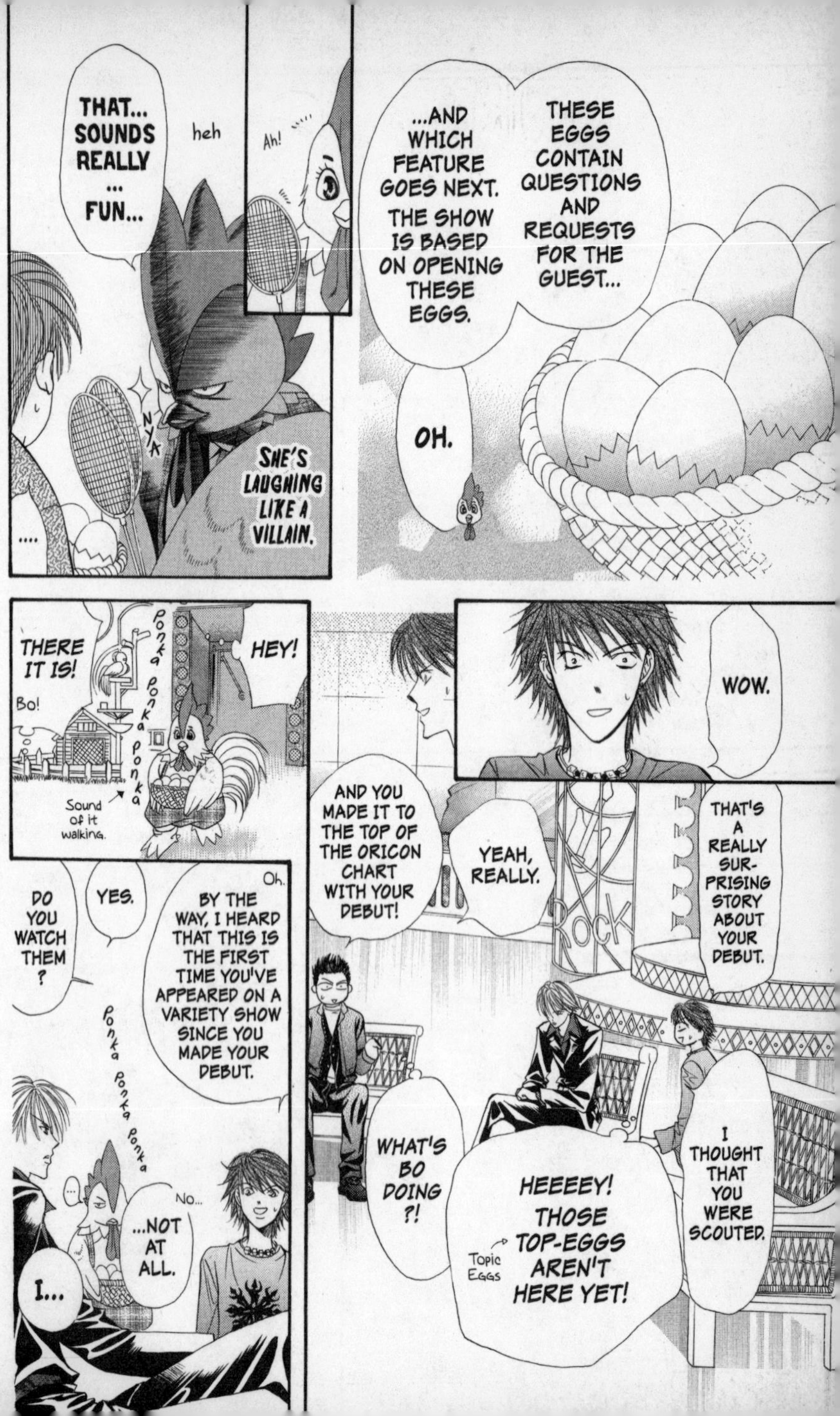
THESE EGGS CONTAIN QUESTIONS AND REQUESTS FOR THE GUEST...
...AND WHICH FEATURE GOES NEXT. THE SHOW IS BASED ON OPENING THESE EGGS.
OH.
Ah!
THAT... SOUNDS REALLY ... FUN...
heh
NYA
SHE'S LAUGHING LIKE A VILLAIN.
....
WOW.
THAT'S A REALLY SUR-PRISING STORY ABOUT YOUR DEBUT.
YEAH, REALLY.
AND YOU MADE IT TO THE TOP OF THE ORICON CHART WITH YOUR DEBUT!
I THOUGHT THAT YOU WERE SCOUTED.
HEEEEY! THOSE TOP-EGGS AREN'T HERE YET!
Topic Eggs
WHAT'S BO DOING ?!
HEY!
THERE IT IS!
Bo!
Ponka Ponka Ponka Ponka
Sound of it walking.
Oh.
BY THE WAY, I HEARD THAT THIS IS THE FIRST TIME YOU'VE APPEARED ON A VARIETY SHOW SINCE YOU MADE YOUR DEBUT.
YES.
DO YOU WATCH THEM ?
Ponka Ponka Ponka
No...
...NOT AT ALL.
...
I...

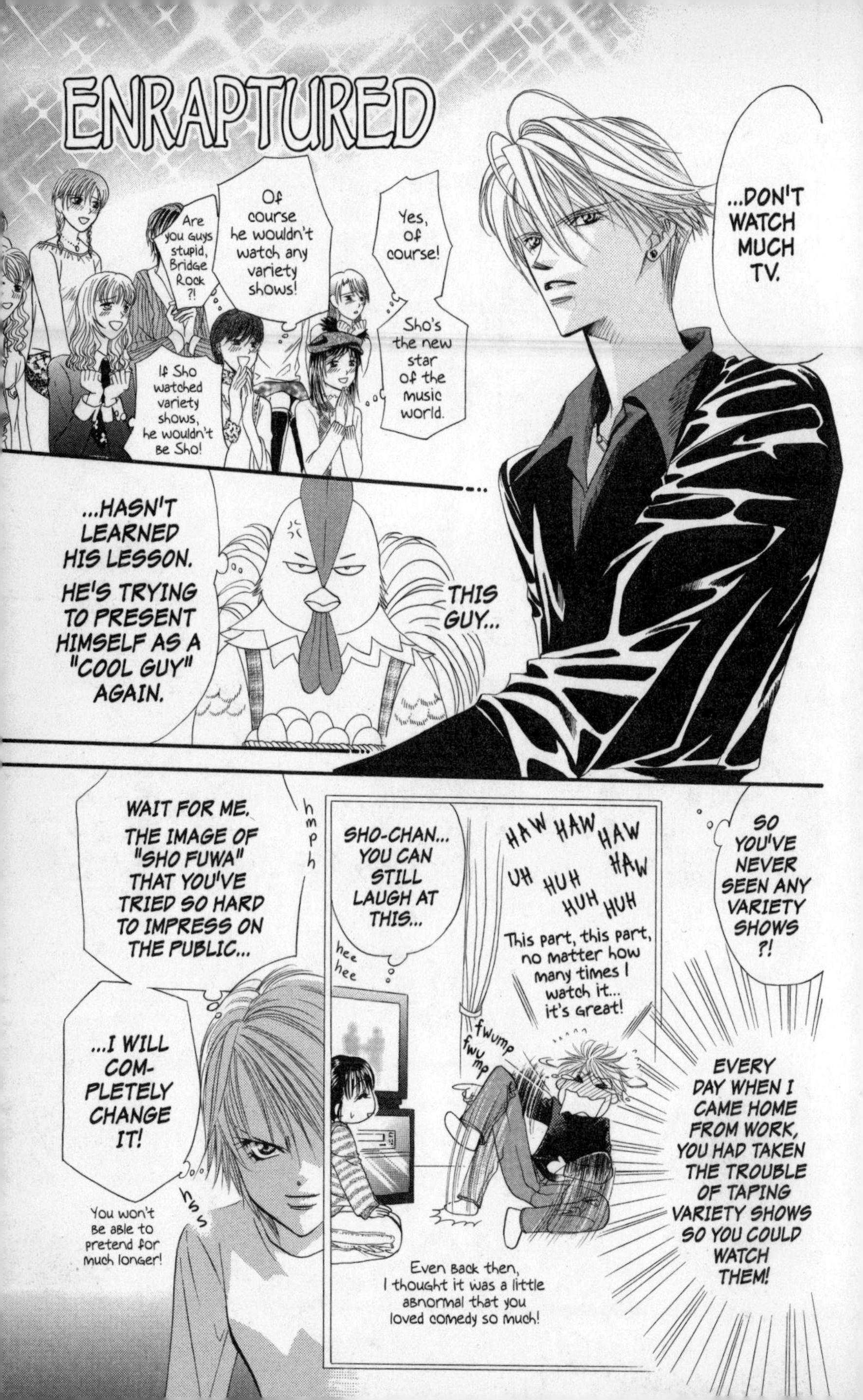
...DON'T WATCH MUCH TV.
ENRAPTURED
Yes, of course!
Sho's the new star of the music world.
Of course he wouldn't watch any variety shows!
Are you guys stupid, Bridge Rock?!
If Sho watched variety shows, he wouldn't be Sho!
THIS GUY...
...HASN'T LEARNED HIS LESSON.
HE'S TRYING TO PRESENT HIMSELF AS A "COOL GUY" AGAIN.
SO YOU'VE NEVER SEEN ANY VARIETY SHOWS?!
HAW HAW HAW HAW
UH HUH HUH HUH HUH
This part, this part, no matter how many times I watch it... it's great!
SHO-CHAN... YOU CAN STILL LAUGH AT THIS...
hee hee
fwump fwump
EVERY DAY WHEN I CAME HOME FROM WORK, YOU HAD TAKEN THE TROUBLE OF TAPING VARIETY SHOWS SO YOU COULD WATCH THEM!
Even back then, I thought it was a little abnormal that you loved comedy so much!
hmph
WAIT FOR ME.
THE IMAGE OF "SHO FUWA" THAT YOU'VE TRIED SO HARD TO IMPRESS ON THE PUBLIC...
...I WILL COM-PLETELY CHANGE IT!
hss
You won't be able to pretend for much longer!

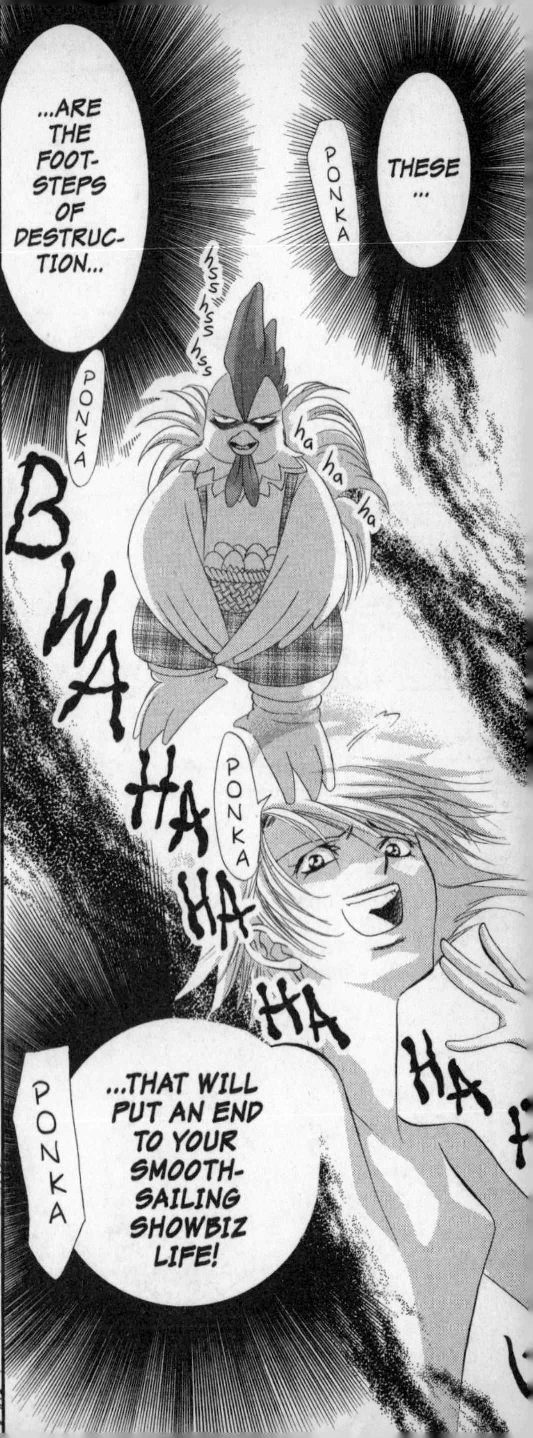
THESE...
PONKA
...ARE THE FOOT-STEPS OF DESTRUC-TION...
hss hss hss
PONKA
ha ha ha
BWAHAHAHAHA
PONKA
...THAT WILL PUT AN END TO YOUR SMOOTH-SAILING SHOWBIZ LIFE!
PONKA

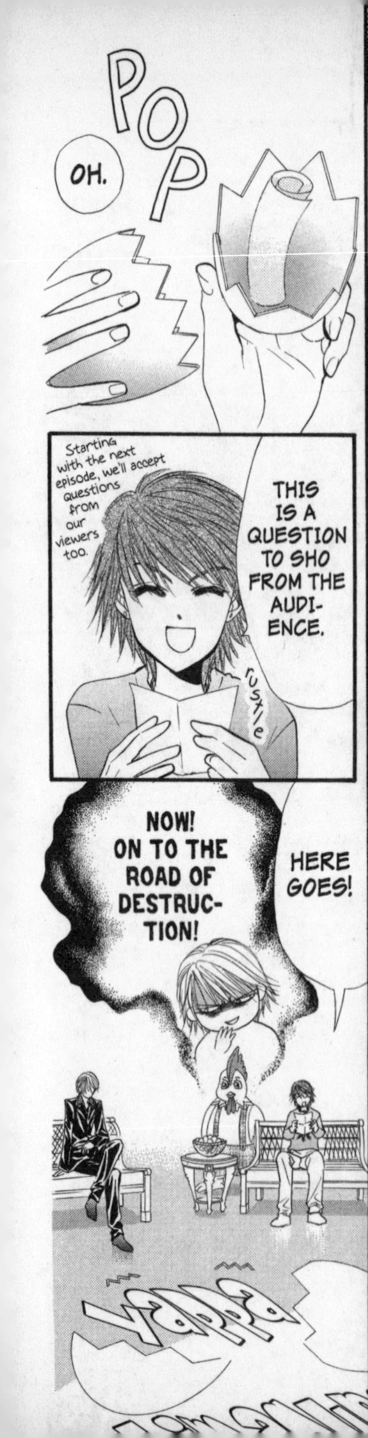
POP
OH.
THIS IS A QUESTION TO SHO FROM THE AUDI-ENCE.
Starting with the next episode, we'll accept questions from our viewers too.
rustle
HERE GOES!
NOW! ON TO THE ROAD OF DESTRUC-TION!

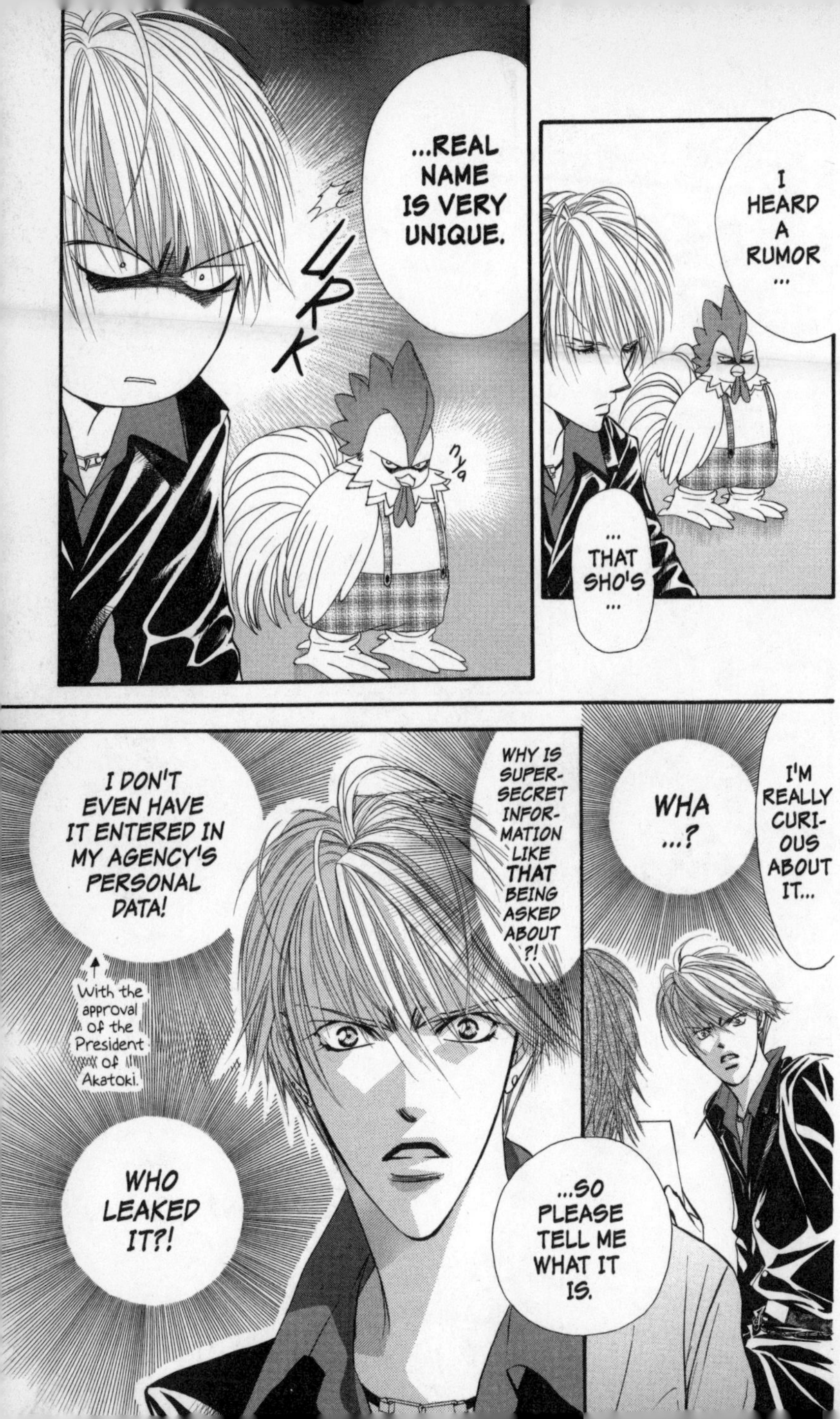
I HEARD A RUMOR...
...THAT SHO'S...
...REAL NAME IS VERY UNIQUE.
URK
nya
I'M REALLY CURIOUS ABOUT IT...
WHA...?
...SO PLEASE TELL ME WHAT IT IS.
WHY IS SUPER-SECRET INFORMATION LIKE THAT BEING ASKED ABOUT?!
I DON'T EVEN HAVE IT ENTERED IN MY AGENCY'S PERSONAL DATA!
With the approval of the President of Akatoki.
WHO LEAKED IT?!

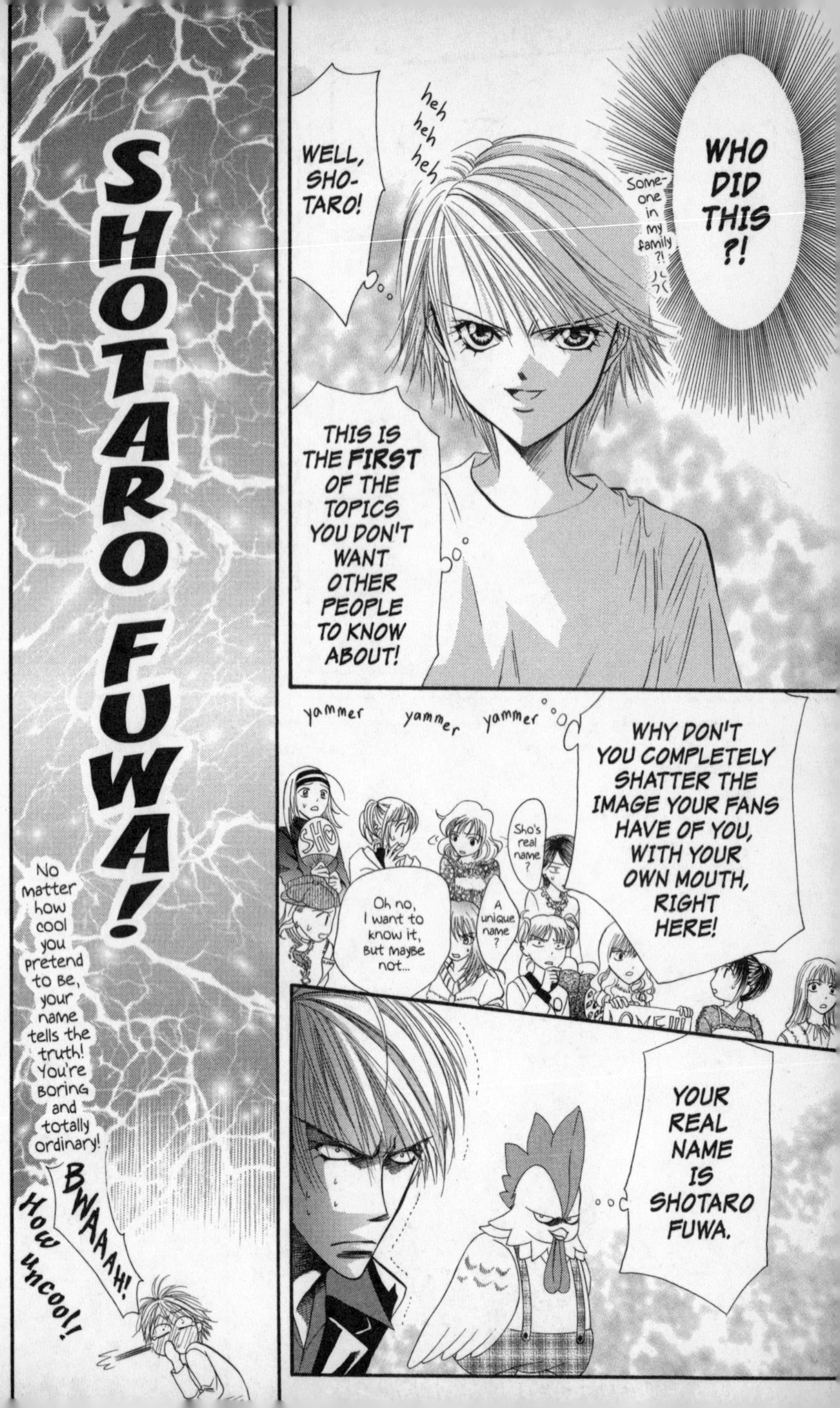
WHO DID THIS?!
Some-one in my family?!
WELL, SHO-TARO!
heh heh heh
THIS IS THE FIRST OF THE TOPICS YOU DON'T WANT OTHER PEOPLE TO KNOW ABOUT!
WHY DON'T YOU COMPLETELY SHATTER THE IMAGE YOUR FANS HAVE OF YOU, WITH YOUR OWN MOUTH, RIGHT HERE!
yammer yammer yammer
Sho's real name?
A unique name?
Oh no, I want to know it, but maybe not...
SHO
YOUR REAL NAME IS SHOTARO FUWA.
SHOTARO FUWA!
No matter how cool you pretend to be, your name tells the truth! You're boring and totally ordinary!
BWAAAAH!
How uncool!

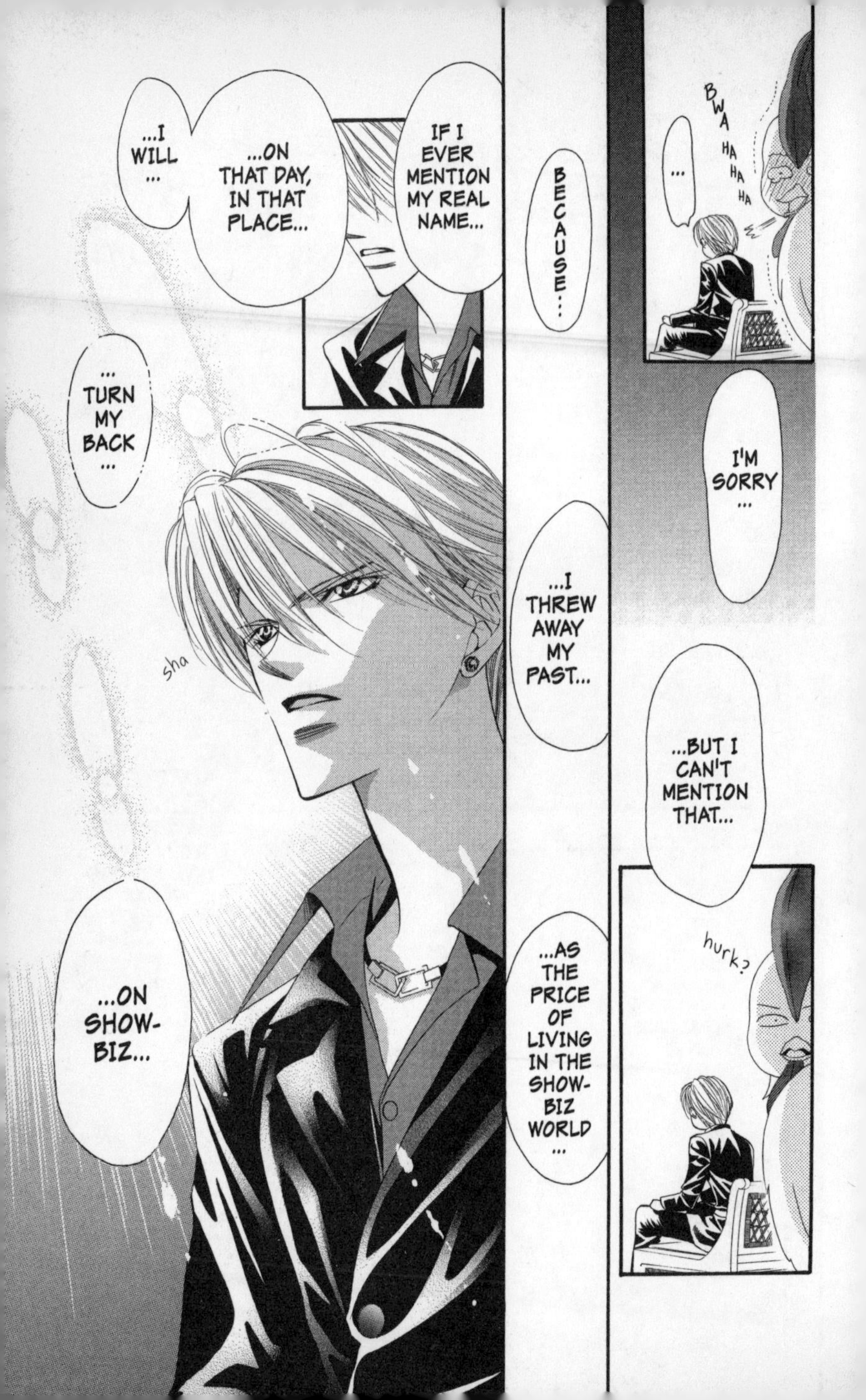
BWA HA HA HA HA
...
I'M SORRY...
...BUT I CAN'T MENTION THAT...
hurk?
BECAUSE...
...I THREW AWAY MY PAST...
...AS THE PRICE OF LIVING IN THE SHOW-BIZ WORLD...
IF I EVER MENTION MY REAL NAME...
...ON THAT DAY, IN THAT PLACE...
...I WILL...
...TURN MY BACK...
sha
...ON SHOW-BIZ...

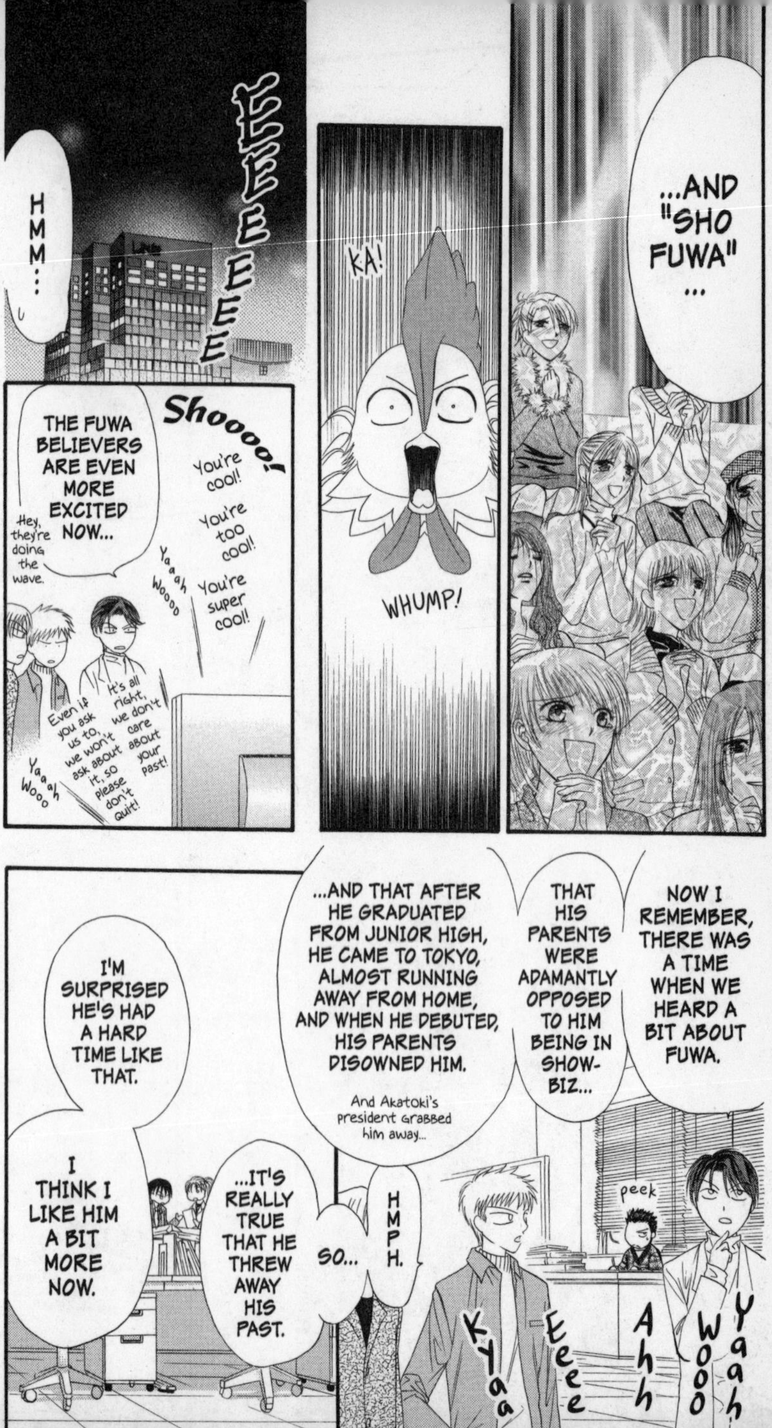
...AND "SHO FUWA" ...
KA!
WHUMP!
EEEEEEE
HMM...
Shoooooo!
THE FUWA BELIEVERS ARE EVEN MORE EXCITED NOW...
Hey, they're doing the wave.
You're cool!
You're too cool!
You're super cool!
Yaaah Woooo
It's all right, we don't care about your past!
Even if you ask us to, we won't ask about it, so please don't quit!
Yaaah Wooo
NOW I REMEMBER, THERE WAS A TIME WHEN WE HEARD A BIT ABOUT FUWA.
THAT HIS PARENTS WERE ADAMANTLY OPPOSED TO HIM BEING IN SHOW-BIZ...
...AND THAT AFTER HE GRADUATED FROM JUNIOR HIGH, HE CAME TO TOKYO, ALMOST RUNNING AWAY FROM HOME, AND WHEN HE DEBUTED, HIS PARENTS DISOWNED HIM.
And Akatoki's president grabbed him away...
I'M SURPRISED HE'S HAD A HARD TIME LIKE THAT.
peek
Yaaah Wooo Ahh Eeee Kyaa
HMPH.
SO...
...IT'S REALLY TRUE THAT HE THREW AWAY HIS PAST.
I THINK I LIKE HIM A BIT MORE NOW.

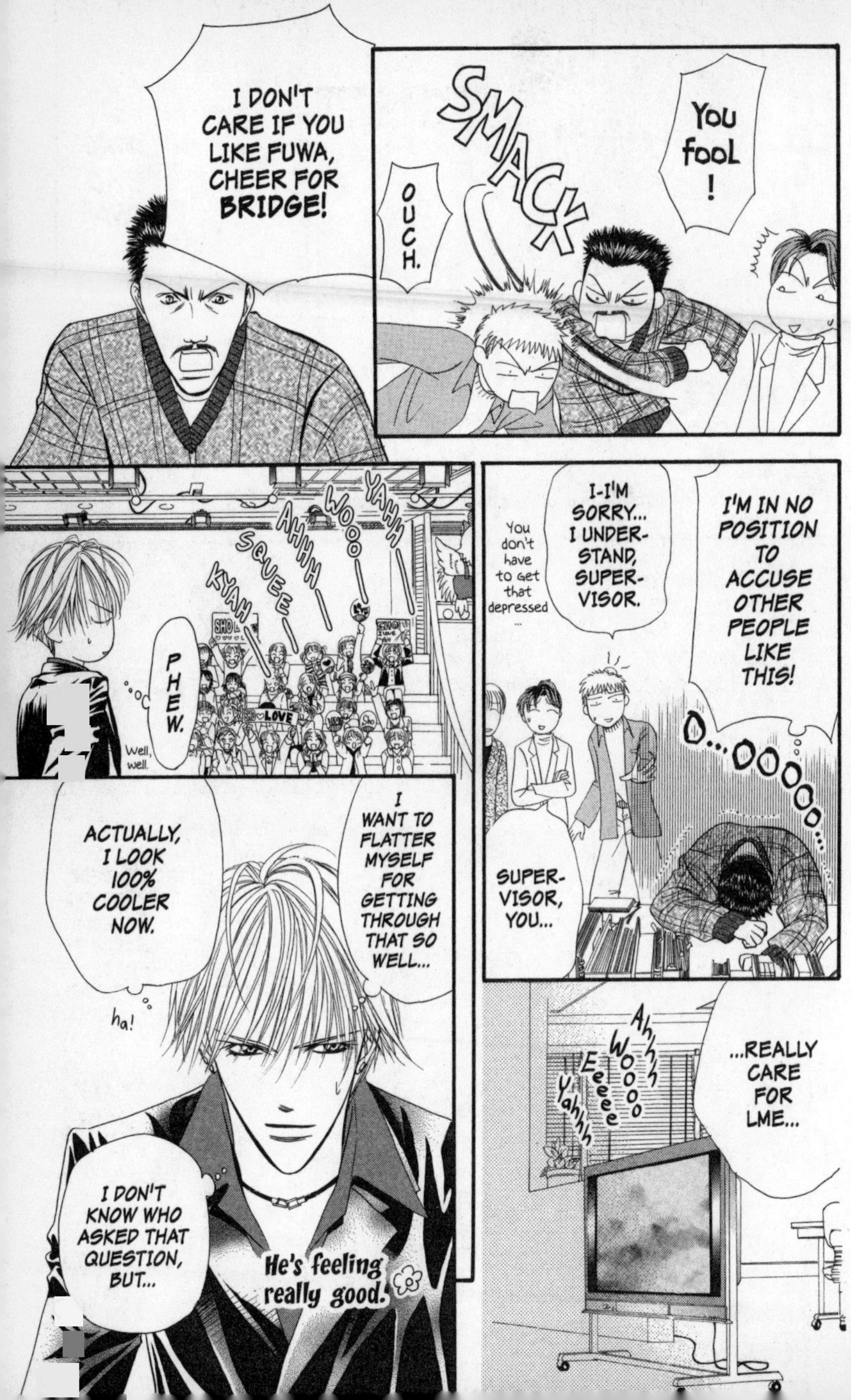
I DON'T CARE IF YOU LIKE FUWA, CHEER FOR BRIDGE!
You fool!
SMACK
OUCH.
I'M IN NO POSITION TO ACCUSE OTHER PEOPLE LIKE THIS!
I-I'M SORRY... I UNDERSTAND, SUPERVISOR.
You don't have to get that depressed...
O...OOOOO...
SUPER-VISOR, YOU...
Ahhh Wooo Eeee Yahhh
...REALLY CARE FOR LME...
YAHH WOOO AHHHH SQUEE KYAH
SHO LOVE
PHEW.
Well, well.
I WANT TO FLATTER MYSELF FOR GETTING THROUGH THAT SO WELL...
ACTUALLY, I LOOK 100% COOLER NOW.
ha!
I DON'T KNOW WHO ASKED THAT QUESTION, BUT...
He's feeling really good.

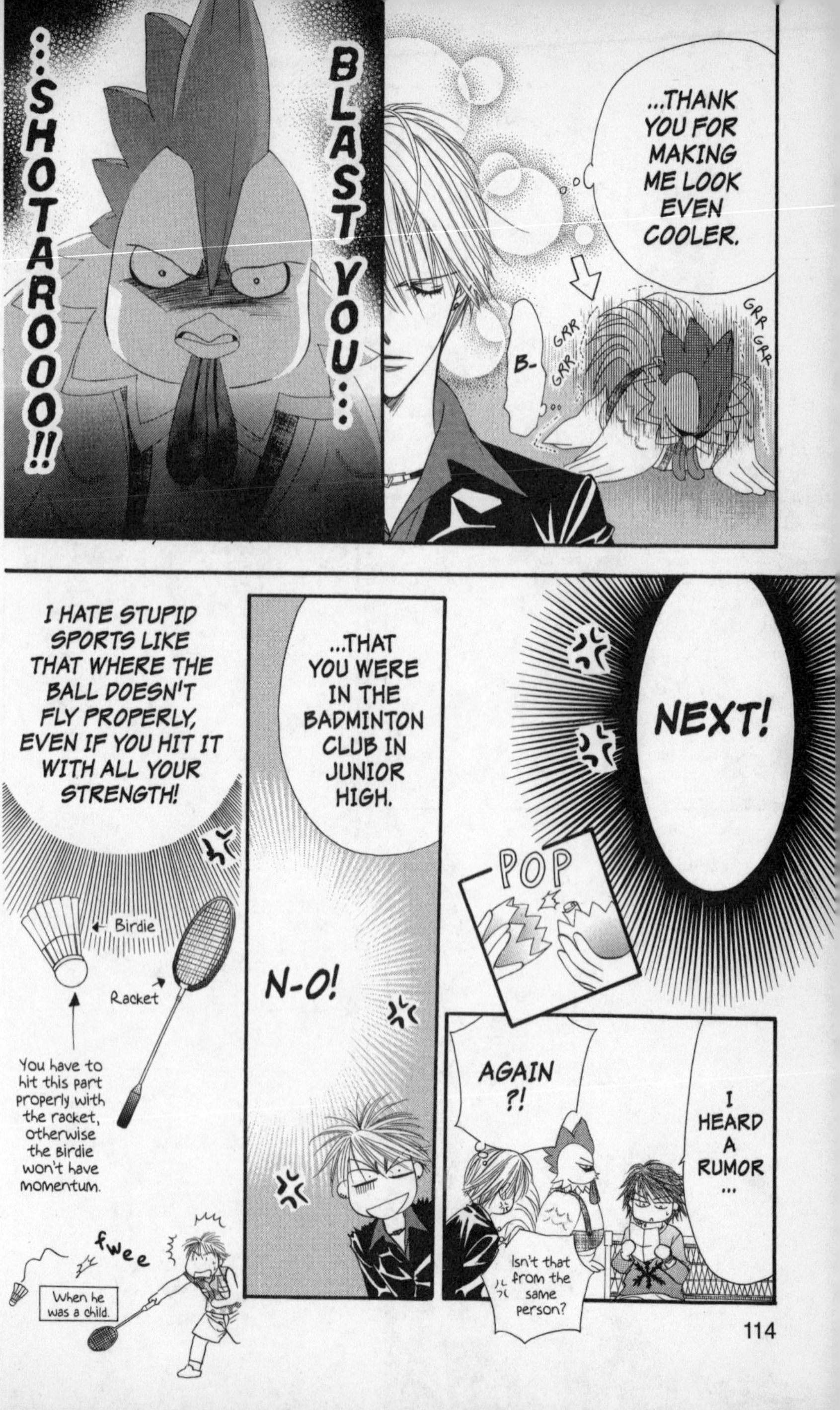
...THANK YOU FOR MAKING ME LOOK EVEN COOLER.
B-
GRR GRR
GRR GRR
BLAST YOU...
...SHOTAROOOO!!
NEXT!
POP
I HEARD A RUMOR...
AGAIN?!
Isn't that from the same person?
...THAT YOU WERE IN THE BADMINTON CLUB IN JUNIOR HIGH.
N-O!
I HATE STUPID SPORTS LIKE THAT WHERE THE BALL DOESN'T FLY PROPERLY, EVEN IF YOU HIT IT WITH ALL YOUR STRENGTH!
Birdie
Racket
You have to hit this part properly with the racket, otherwise the birdie won't have momentum.
fwee
When he was a child.

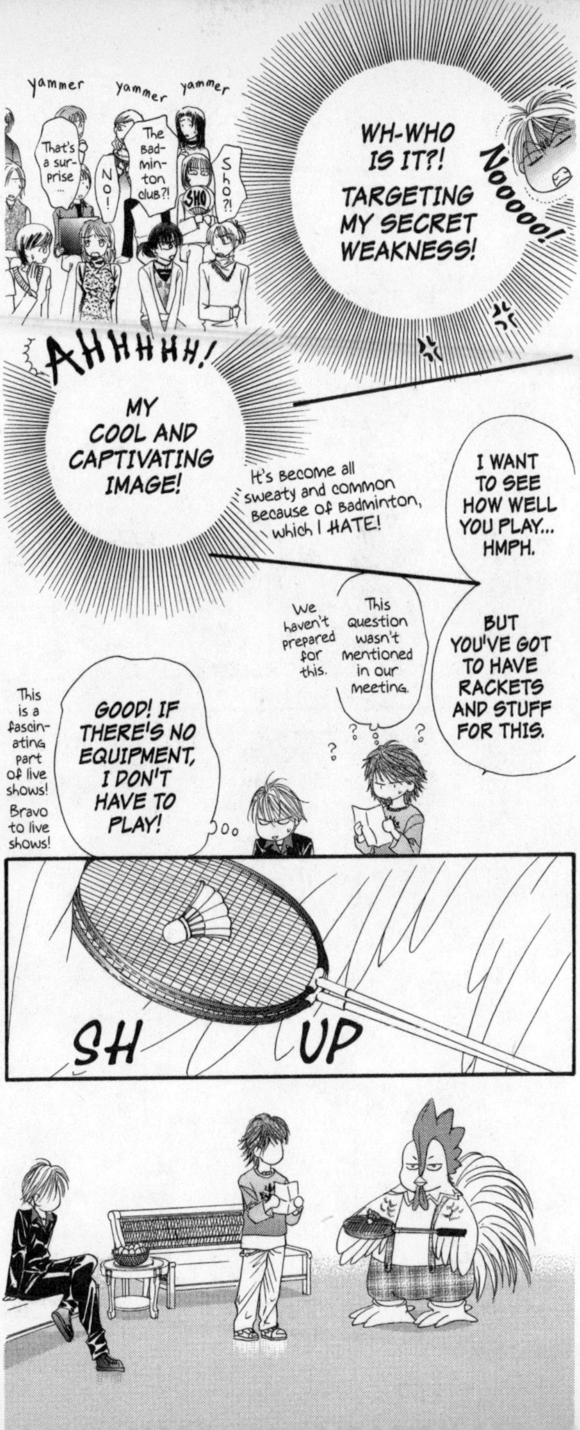
Noooooo!
WH-WHO IS IT?! TARGETING MY SECRET WEAKNESS!
yammer yammer yammer
Sho?!
SHO
The Badminton club?!
No!
That's a surprise...
I WANT TO SEE HOW WELL YOU PLAY... HMPH.
AHHHHH!
MY COOL AND CAPTIVATING IMAGE!
It's become all sweaty and common because of badminton, which I HATE!
BUT YOU'VE GOT TO HAVE RACKETS AND STUFF FOR THIS.
This question wasn't mentioned in our meeting.
We haven't prepared for this.
GOOD! IF THERE'S NO EQUIPMENT, I DON'T HAVE TO PLAY!
This is a fascinating part of live shows! Bravo to live shows!
SH UP

Bridge Rock

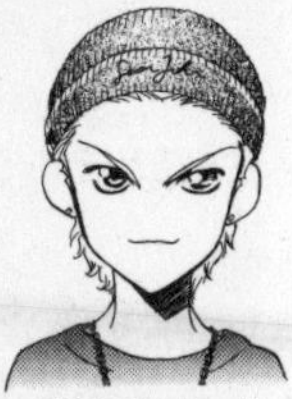

Shinichi Ishibashi
(age 18)

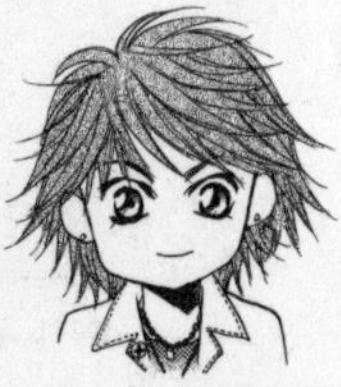

Leader: Hikaru Ishibashi
(age 20)

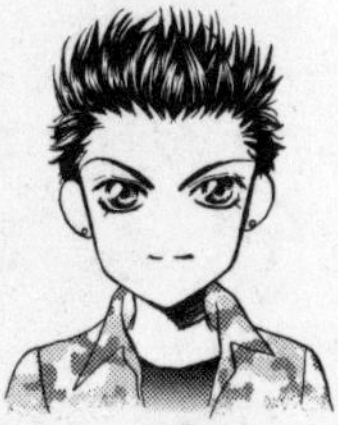

Yusei Ishibashi
(age 18)

The group name comes from their last name... ◊

Ishi (rock) Bashi (bridge)

Flip it to get Bridge Rock... (wry smile)

It's so brainless...

By the way, they all have the same last name, but they aren't related at all...

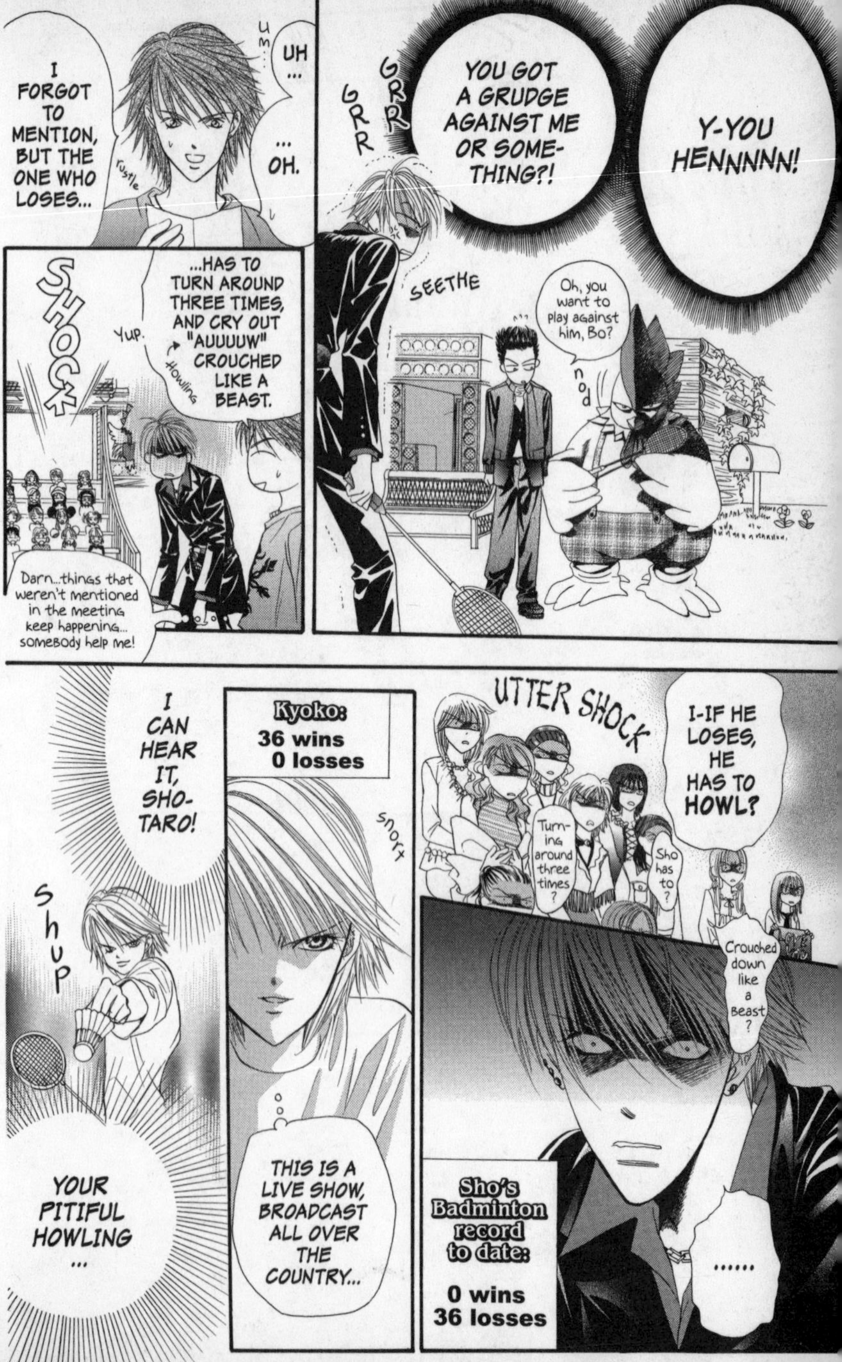
Y-YOU HENNNNN!
YOU GOT A GRUDGE AGAINST ME OR SOME-THING?!
GRR GRR
SEETHE
Oh, you want to play against him, Bo?
nod
I FORGOT TO MENTION, BUT THE ONE WHO LOSES...
um...
UH...
...OH.
rustle
...HAS TO TURN AROUND THREE TIMES, AND CRY OUT "AUUUUW" CROUCHED LIKE A BEAST.
Yup.
Howling
SHOCK
Darn...things that weren't mentioned in the meeting keep happening... somebody help me!
UTTER SHOCK
I-IF HE LOSES, HE HAS TO HOWL?
Turn-ing around three times?
Sho has to?
Crouched down like a Beast?
......
Sho's Badminton record to date:
0 wins
36 losses
Kyoko:
36 wins
0 losses
snort
THIS IS A LIVE SHOW, BROADCAST ALL OVER THE COUNTRY...
I CAN HEAR IT, SHO-TARO!
Shup
YOUR PITIFUL HOWLING...

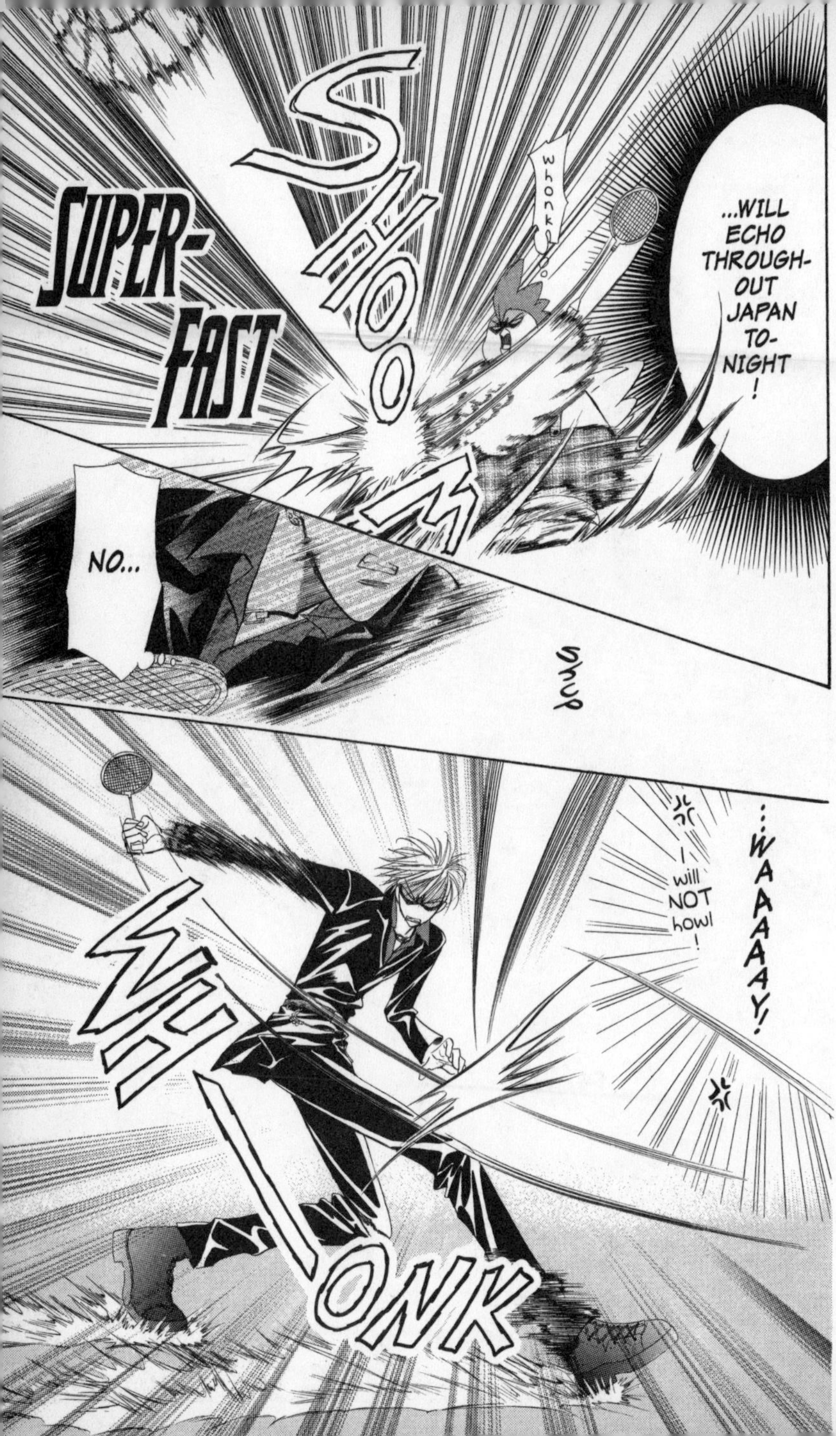
...WILL ECHO THROUGH-OUT JAPAN TO-NIGHT!
whonk
SHOOOM
SUPER-FAST
NO...
shup
...WAAAAAAY!
I will NOT howl!
WHONK

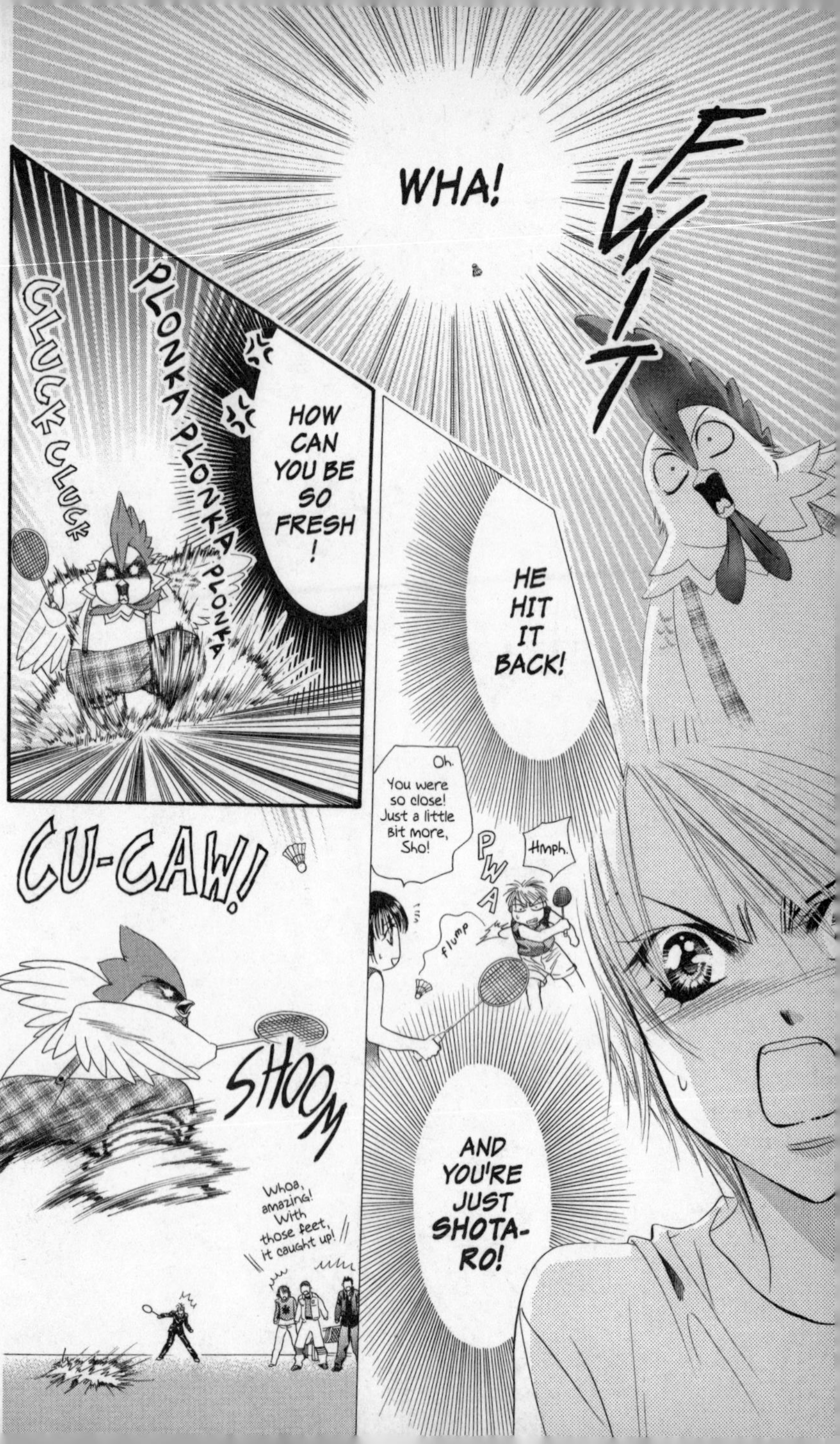
FWIT
WHA!
HE HIT IT BACK!
Oh. You were so close! Just a little bit more, Sho!
Hmph.
PWA
flump
AND YOU'RE JUST SHOTARO!
HOW CAN YOU BE SO FRESH!
PLONKA PLONKA PLONKA PLONKA
CLUCK CLUCK CLUCK
CU-CAW!
SHOOM
Whoa, amazing! With those feet, it caught up!

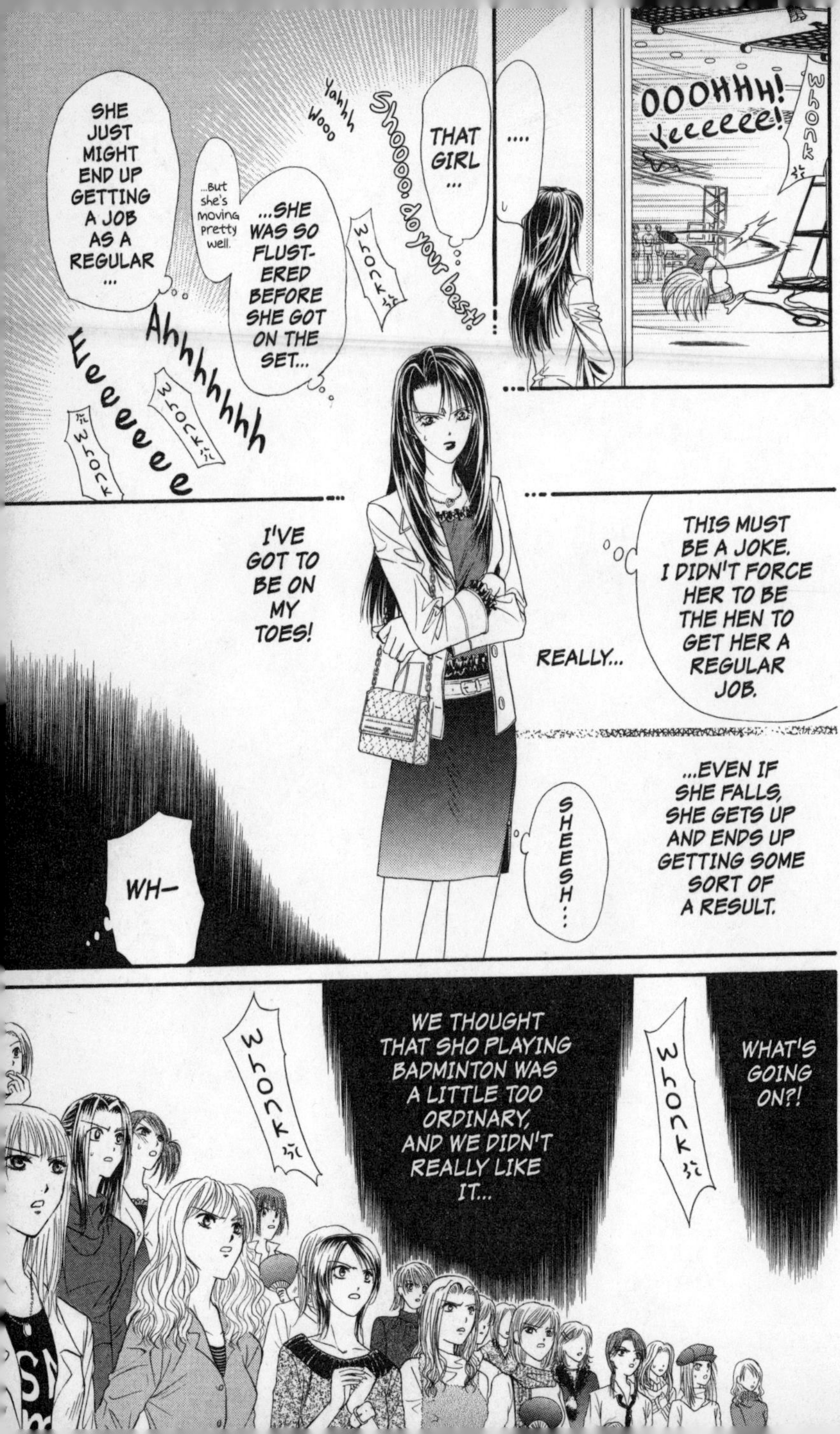
OOOHHH! Yeeeeee!
Whonk
....
THAT GIRL ...
Shoooo, do your best!
Yahhh Wooo
...SHE WAS SO FLUSTERED BEFORE SHE GOT ON THE SET...
...But she's moving pretty well.
whonk
SHE JUST MIGHT END UP GETTING A JOB AS A REGULAR ...
Ahhhhhhh
Eeeeeee
whonk
whonk
THIS MUST BE A JOKE. I DIDN'T FORCE HER TO BE THE HEN TO GET HER A REGULAR JOB.
REALLY...
I'VE GOT TO BE ON MY TOES!
...EVEN IF SHE FALLS, SHE GETS UP AND ENDS UP GETTING SOME SORT OF A RESULT.
SHEESH...
WH-
WHAT'S GOING ON?!
whonk
WE THOUGHT THAT SHO PLAYING BADMINTON WAS A LITTLE TOO ORDINARY, AND WE DIDN'T REALLY LIKE IT...
whonk

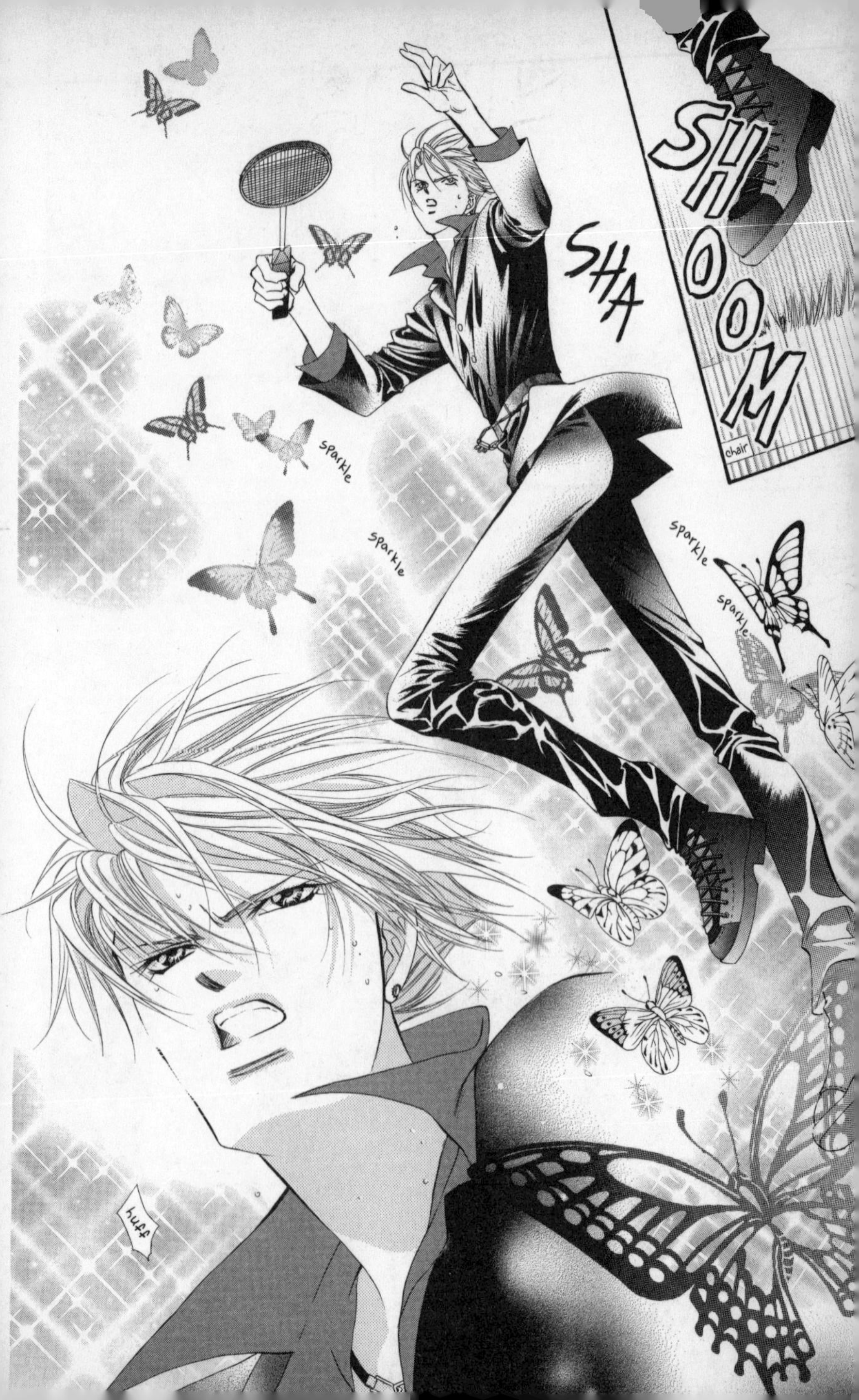
SHOOM
chair
SHA
sparkle
sparkle
sparkle
sparkle
huff

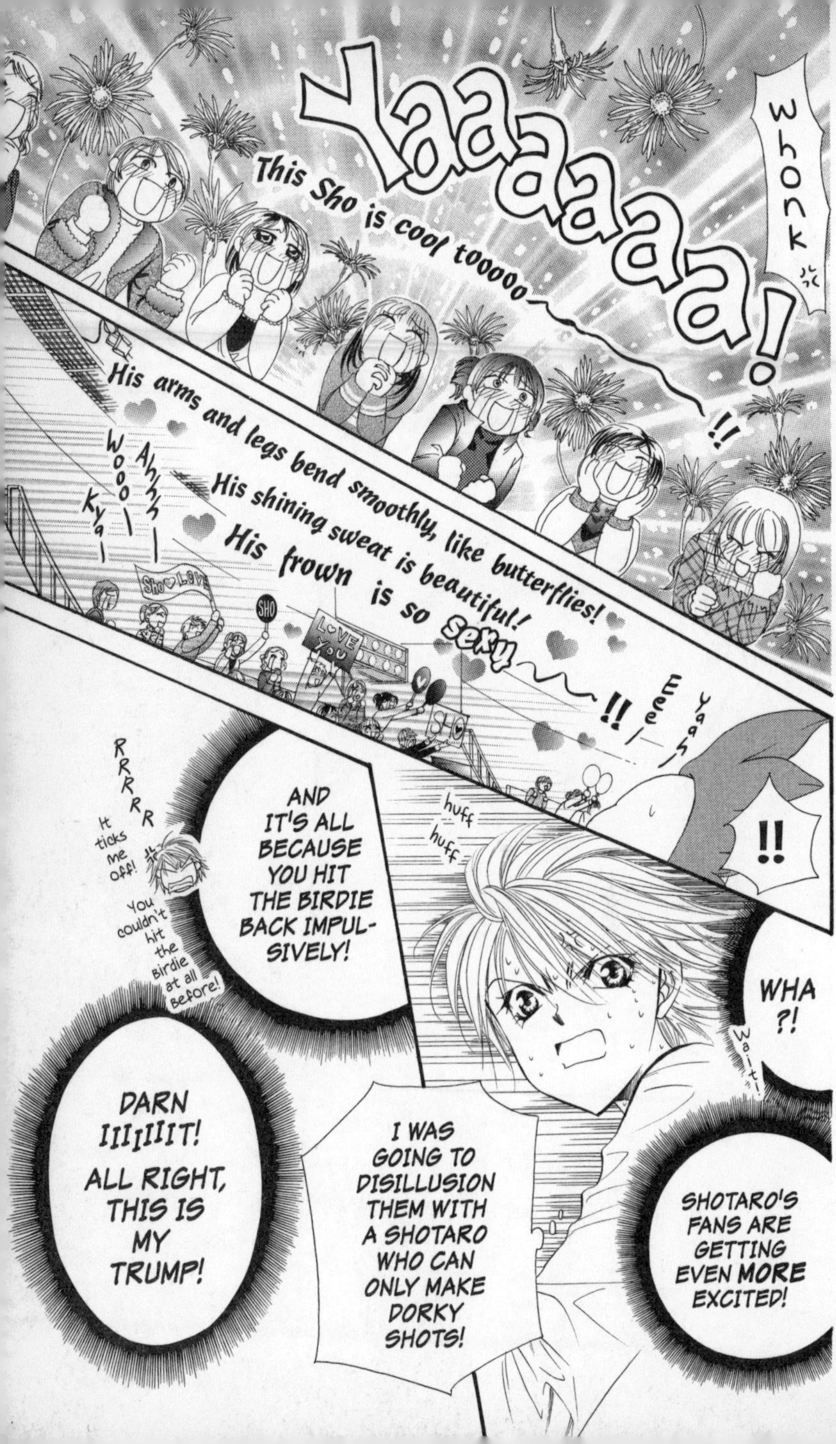
Whonk
Yaaaaaaaa!!
This Sho is cool tooooo—
His arms and legs bend smoothly, like butterflies!
His shining sweat is beautiful!
His frown is so sexy—!!
Ahhhh—
Woooo—
Kya—
Sho♥LOVE
SHO
LOVE YOU
SHO
Eeee—
Yaaah—
!!
huff huff
AND IT'S ALL BECAUSE YOU HIT THE BIRDIE BACK IMPUL-SIVELY!
RRRRR
It ticks me off!
You couldn't hit the birdie at all before!
WHA?!
Wait—
SHOTARO'S FANS ARE GETTING EVEN MORE EXCITED!
I WAS GOING TO DISILLUSION THEM WITH A SHOTARO WHO CAN ONLY MAKE DORKY SHOTS!
DARN IIIIIIIT! ALL RIGHT, THIS IS MY TRUMP!

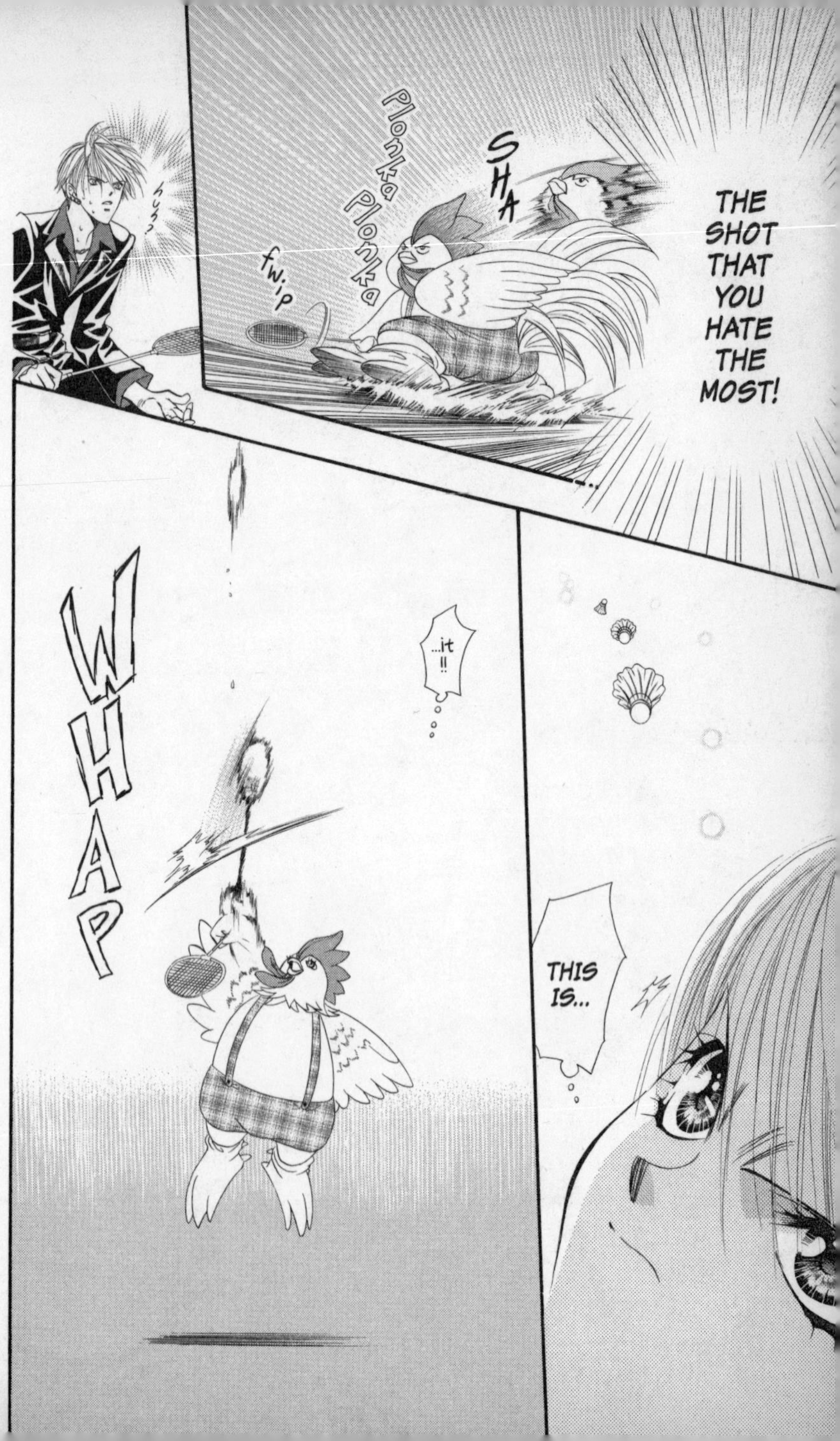
THE SHOT THAT YOU HATE THE MOST!
SHA
Plonka Plonka
fwip
THIS IS...
...it !!
WHAP

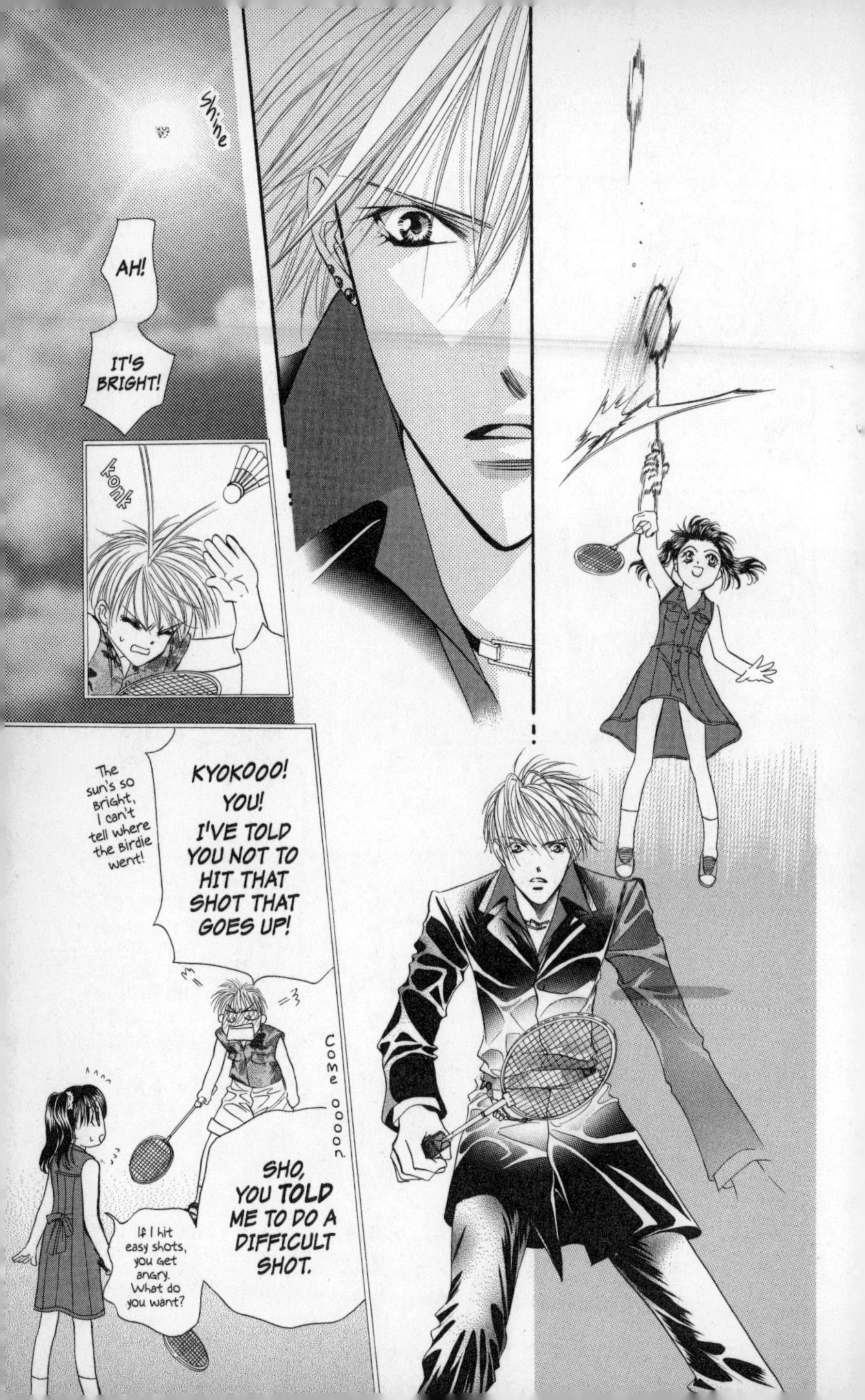
!
Shine
AH!
IT'S BRIGHT!
Konk
KYOKOOO! YOU! I'VE TOLD YOU NOT TO HIT THAT SHOT THAT GOES UP!
The sun's so bright, I can't tell where the birdie went!
Comeoooon
SHO, YOU TOLD ME TO DO A DIFFICULT SHOT.
If I hit easy shots, you get angry. What do you want?

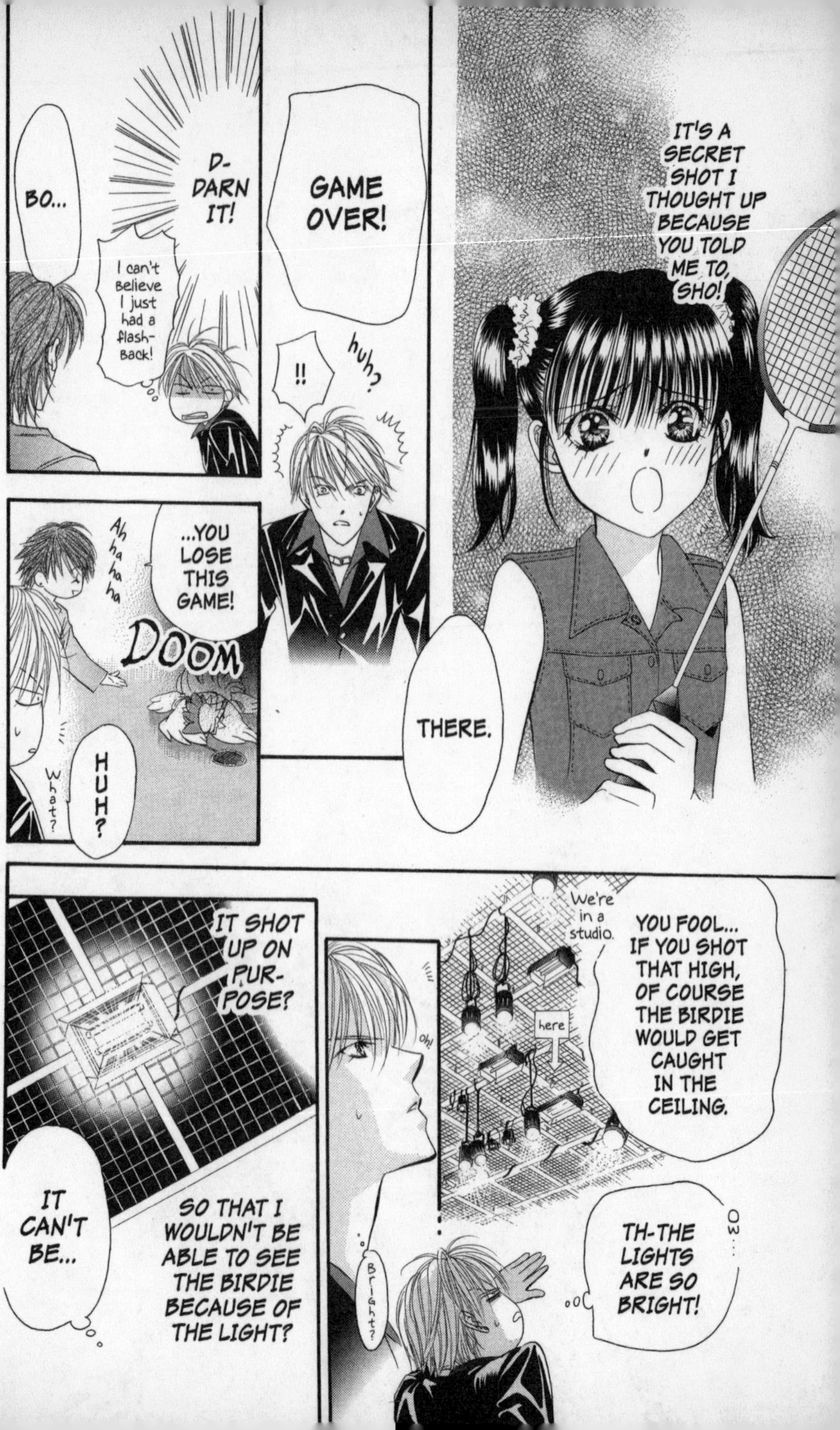
IT'S A SECRET SHOT I THOUGHT UP BECAUSE YOU TOLD ME TO, SHO!
THERE.
GAME OVER!
huh?
!!
D-DARN IT!
I can't believe I just had a flash-back!
BO...
...YOU LOSE THIS GAME!
Ah ha ha ha
DOOM
HUH?
What?
We're in a studio.
YOU FOOL... IF YOU SHOT THAT HIGH, OF COURSE THE BIRDIE WOULD GET CAUGHT IN THE CEILING.
here
TH-THE LIGHTS ARE SO BRIGHT!
Ow...
oh!
Bright?
IT SHOT UP ON PUR-POSE?
SO THAT I WOULDN'T BE ABLE TO SEE THE BIRDIE BECAUSE OF THE LIGHT?
IT CAN'T BE...

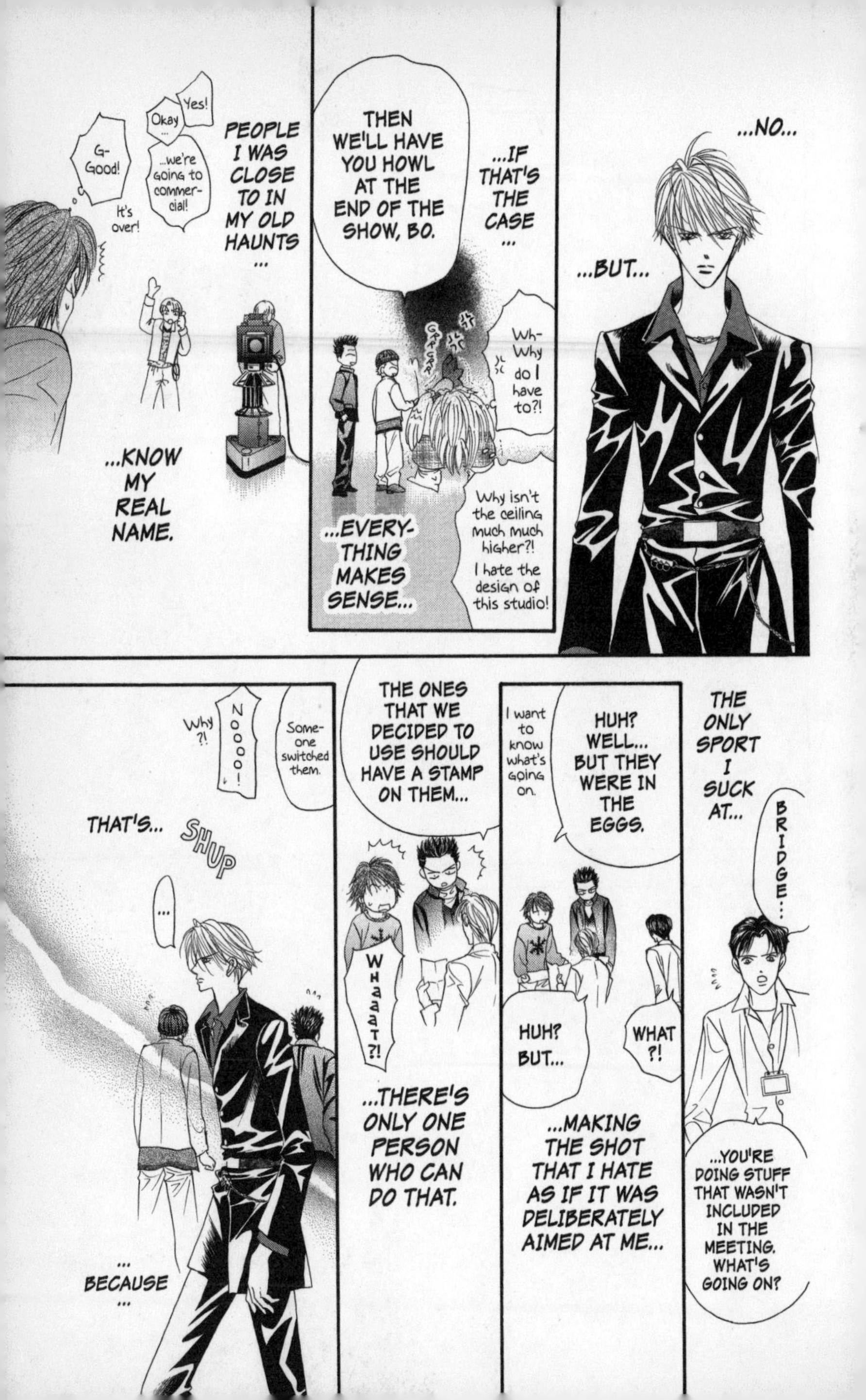

...NO...
...BUT...
...IF THAT'S THE CASE ...
THEN WE'LL HAVE YOU HOWL AT THE END OF THE SHOW, BO.
GRRR
Wh-Why do I have to?!
...EVERYTHING MAKES SENSE...
Why isn't the ceiling much much higher?! I hate the design of this studio!
PEOPLE I WAS CLOSE TO IN MY OLD HAUNTS ...
Yes!
Okay ...
...we're going to commercial!
G-Good!
It's over!
...KNOW MY REAL NAME.
THE ONLY SPORT I SUCK AT...
BRIDGE...
...YOU'RE DOING STUFF THAT WASN'T INCLUDED IN THE MEETING. WHAT'S GOING ON?
HUH? WELL... BUT THEY WERE IN THE EGGS.
I want to know what's going on.
WHAT?!
HUH? BUT...
...MAKING THE SHOT THAT I HATE AS IF IT WAS DELIBERATELY AIMED AT ME...
THE ONES THAT WE DECIDED TO USE SHOULD HAVE A STAMP ON THEM...
Whaaaat?!
...THERE'S ONLY ONE PERSON WHO CAN DO THAT.
Someone switched them.
Noooo!
Why?!
THAT'S...
SHUP
...
...BECAUSE ...

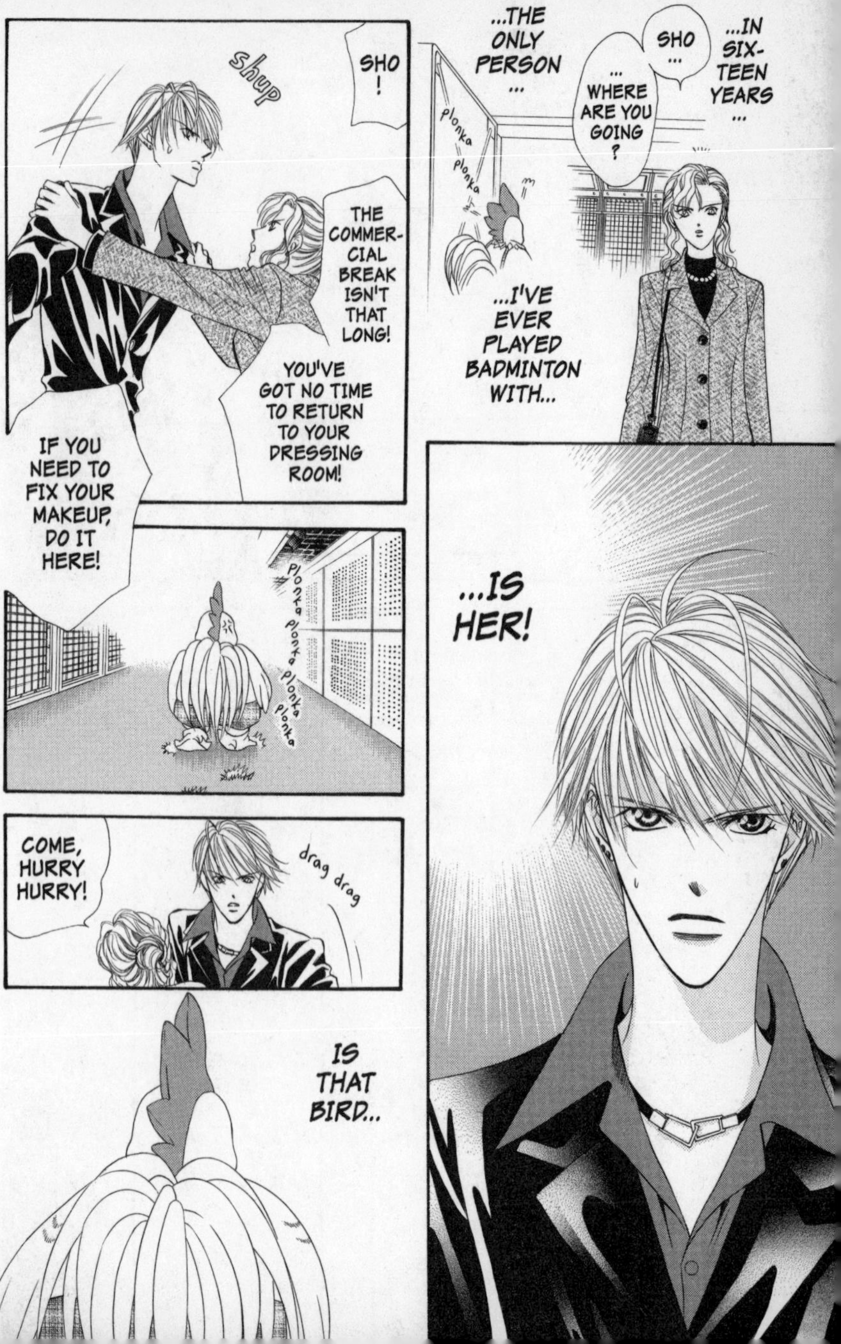
...IN SIX-TEEN YEARS...
SHO...
...WHERE ARE YOU GOING?
...THE ONLY PERSON...
plonka plonka
...I'VE EVER PLAYED BADMINTON WITH...
SHO!
shup
THE COMMERCIAL BREAK ISN'T THAT LONG!
YOU'VE GOT NO TIME TO RETURN TO YOUR DRESSING ROOM!
IF YOU NEED TO FIX YOUR MAKEUP, DO IT HERE!
...IS HER!
plonka plonka plonka plonka
COME, HURRY HURRY!
drag drag
IS THAT BIRD...

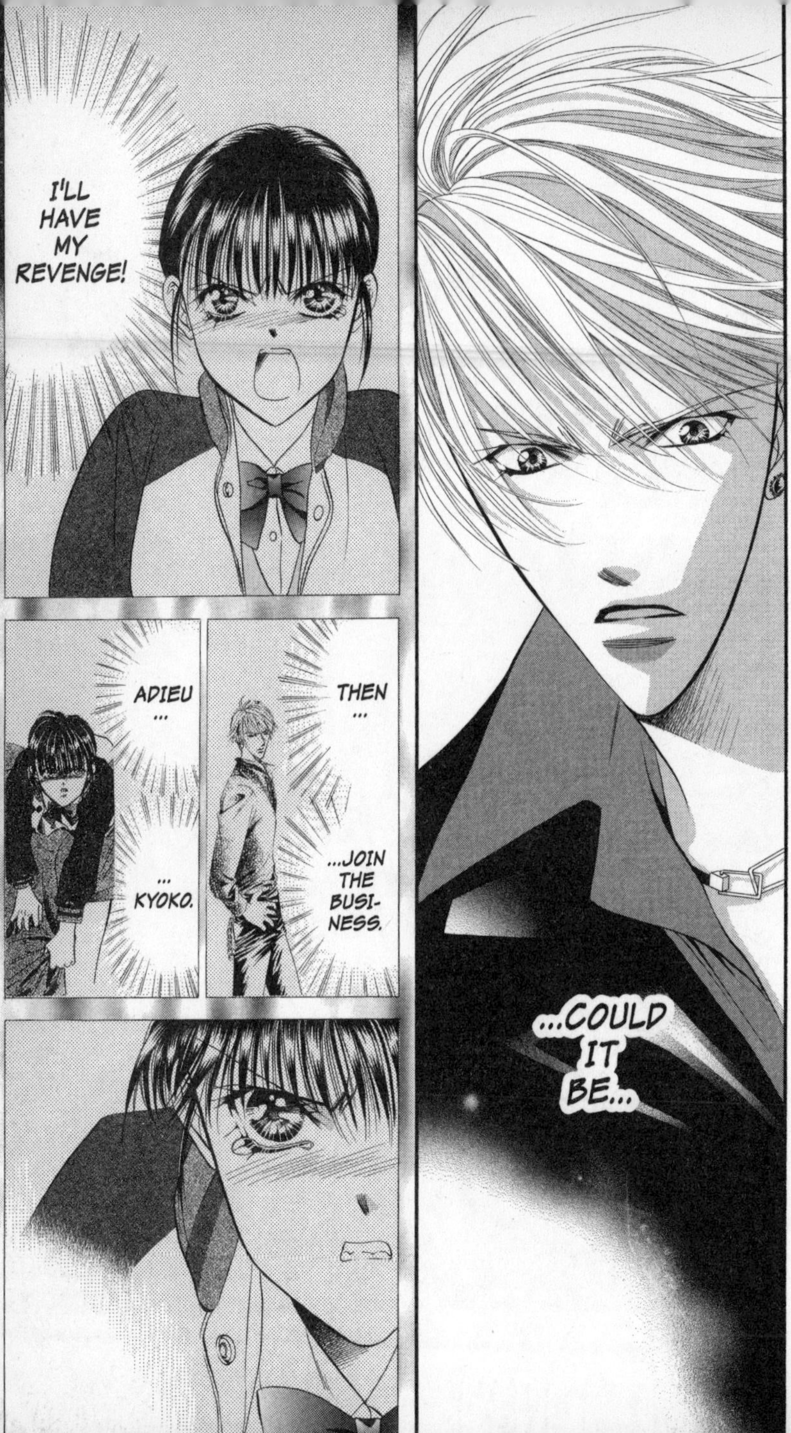
...COULD IT BE...
I'LL HAVE MY REVENGE!
THEN ...
...JOIN THE BUSI-NESS.
ADIEU ...
... KYOKO.

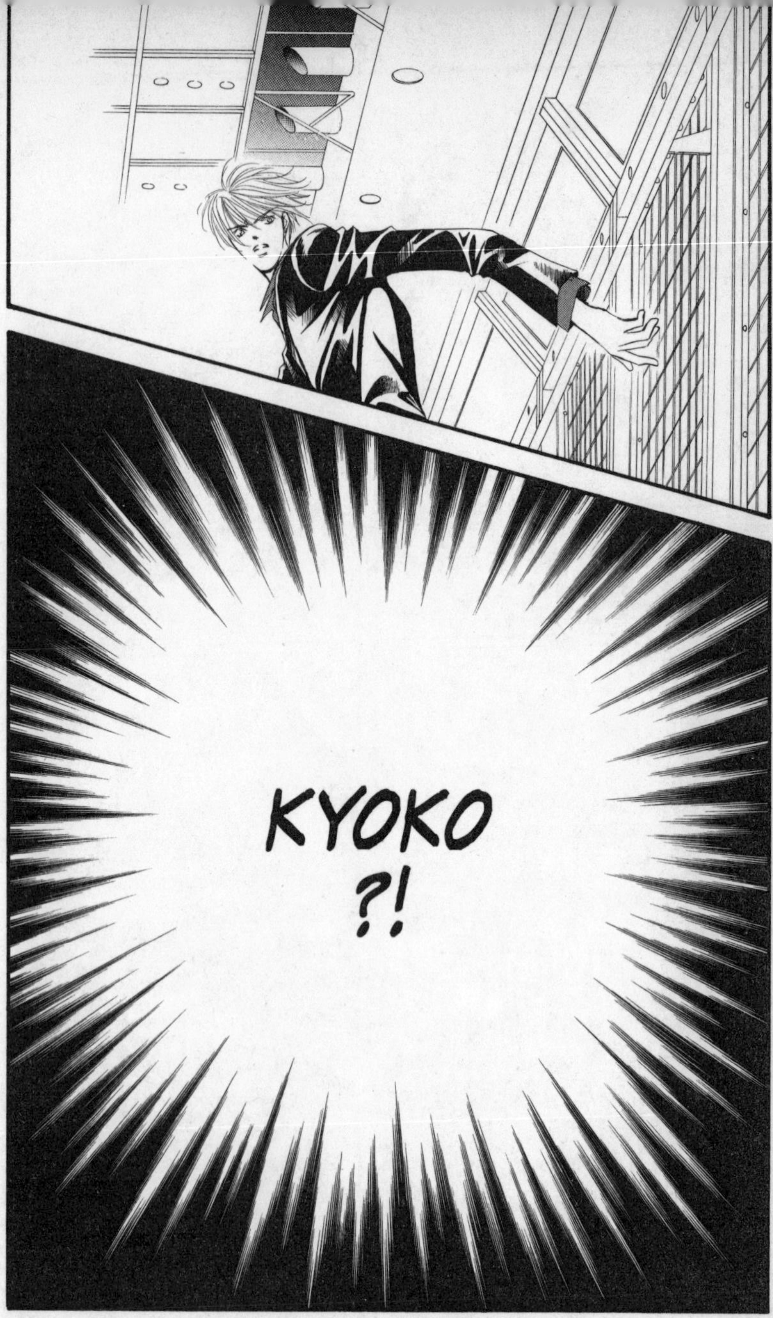
KYOKO
?!

End of Act 21

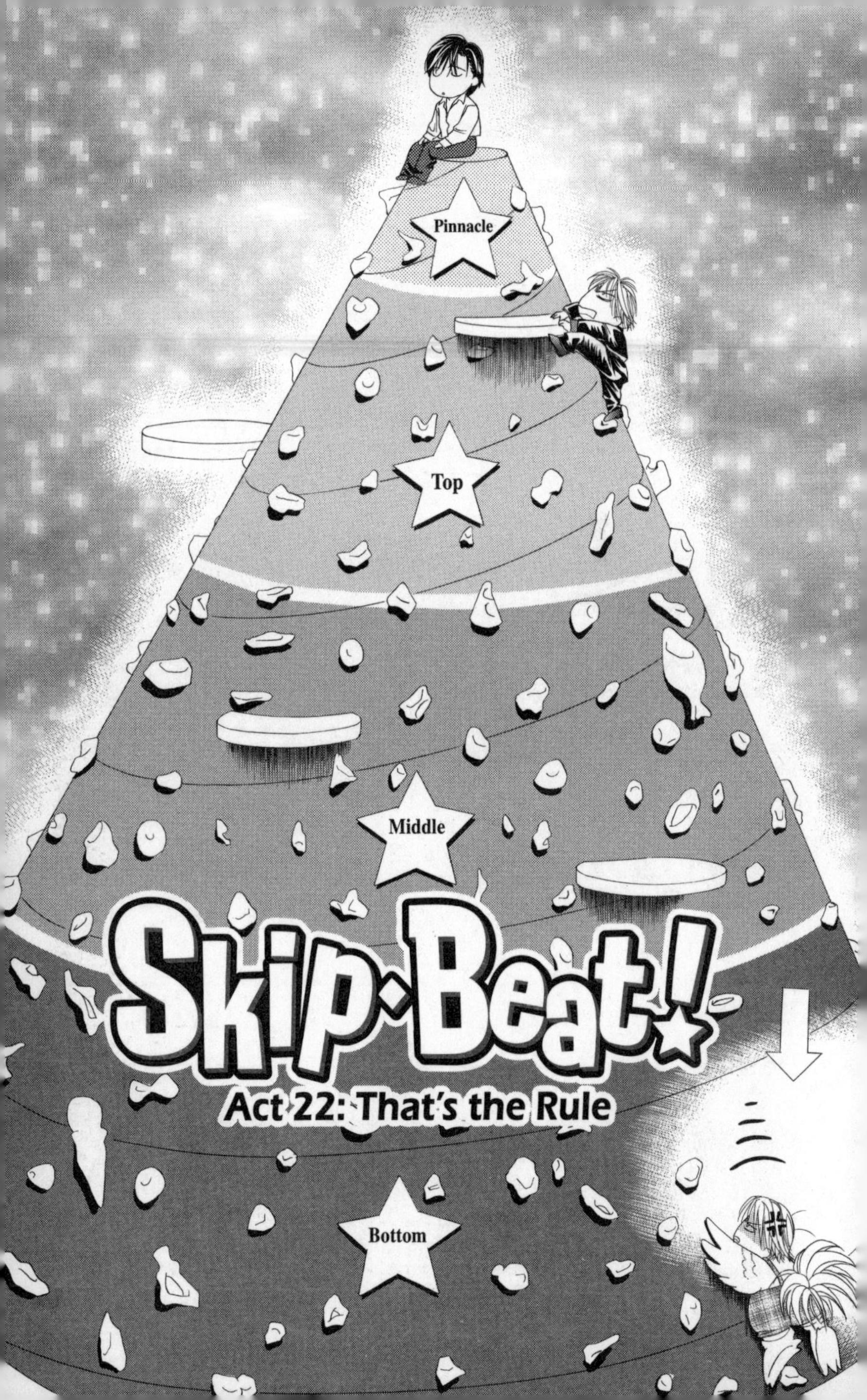
Pinnacle
Top
Middle
Skip·Beat!
Act 22: That's the Rule
Bottom

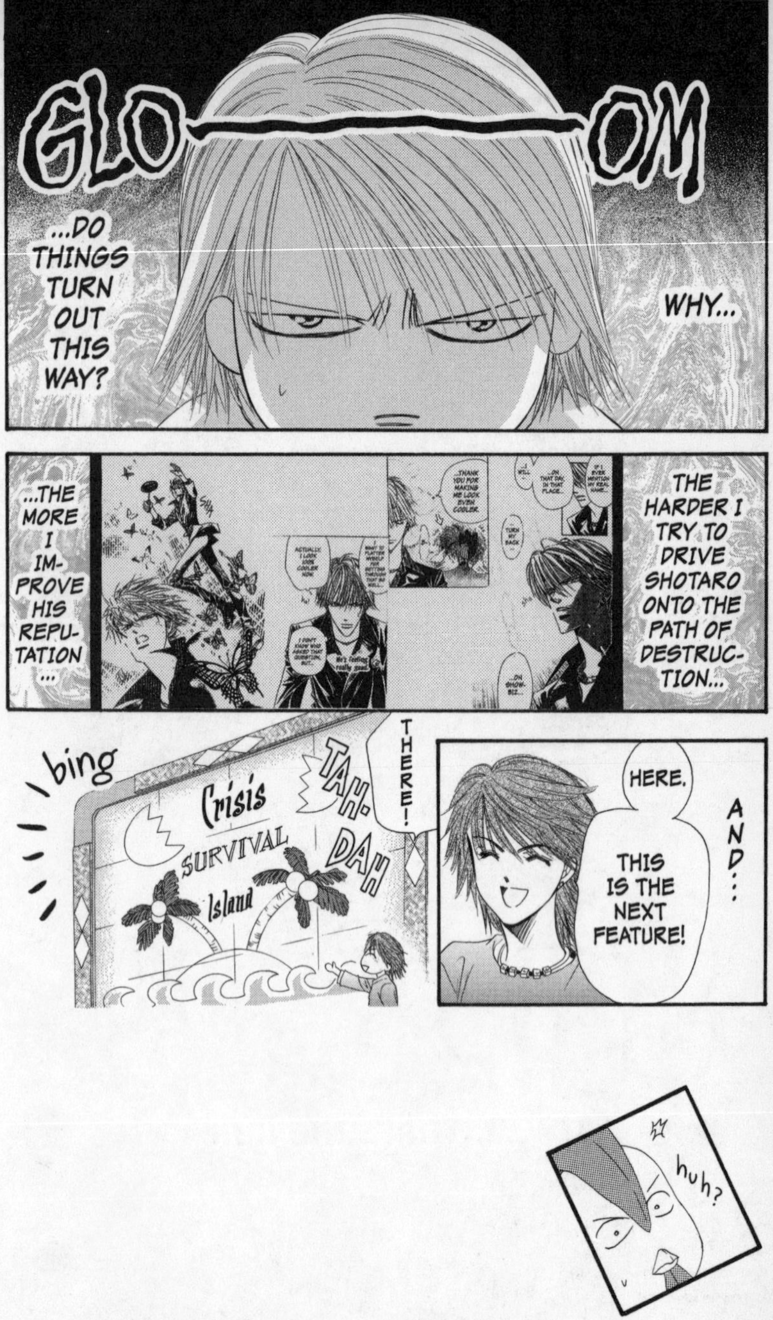
GLO———OM
WHY...
...DO THINGS TURN OUT THIS WAY?
THE HARDER I TRY TO DRIVE SHOTARO ONTO THE PATH OF DESTRUCTION...
...THE MORE I IMPROVE HIS REPUTATION...
HERE.
THIS IS THE NEXT FEATURE!
AND...
THERE!
TAH-DAH
Crisis
SURVIVAL
Island
bing
huh?

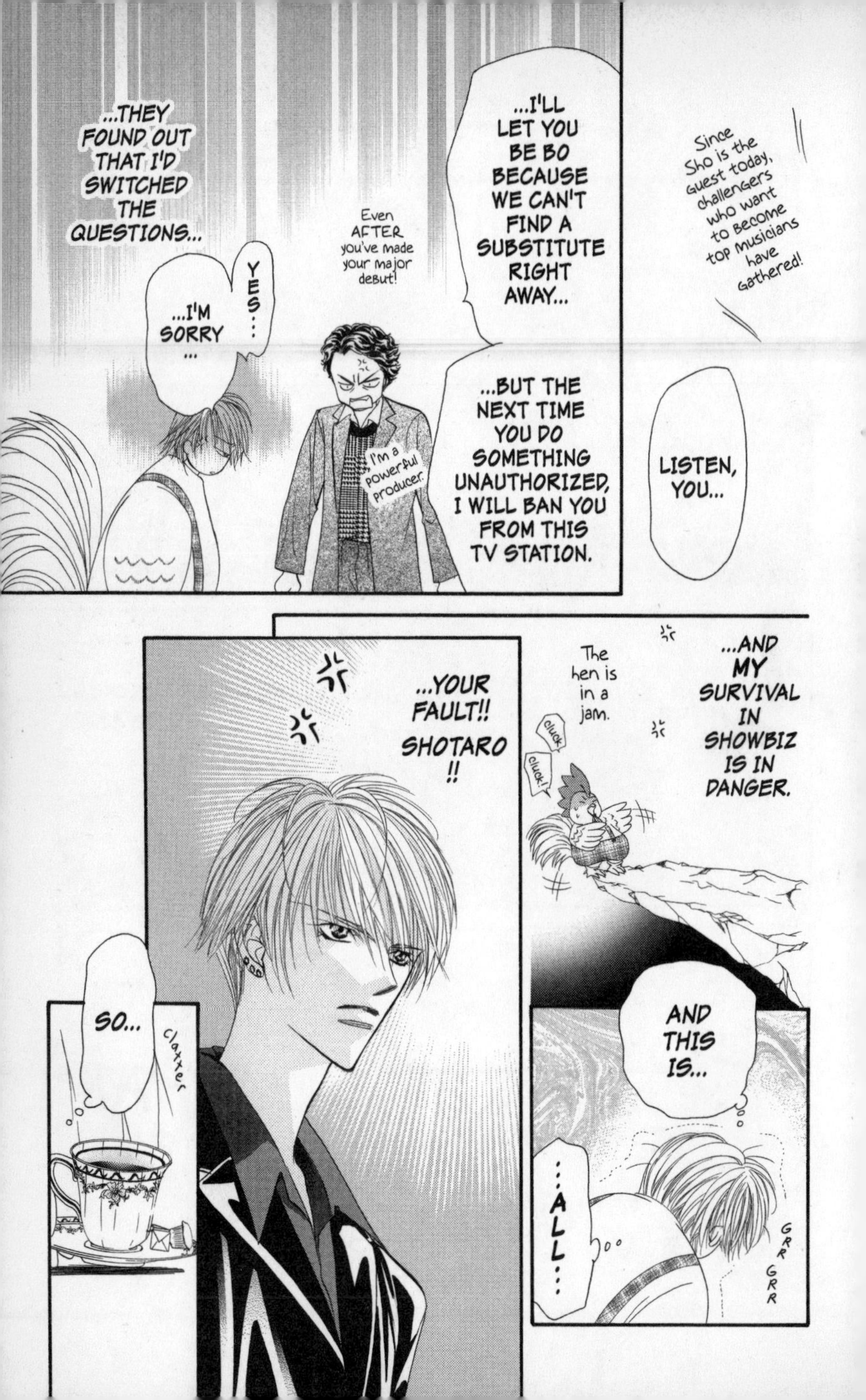
Since Sho is the guest today, challengers who want to become top musicians have gathered!
LISTEN, YOU...
...I'LL LET YOU BE BO BECAUSE WE CAN'T FIND A SUBSTITUTE RIGHT AWAY...
...BUT THE NEXT TIME YOU DO SOMETHING UNAUTHORIZED, I WILL BAN YOU FROM THIS TV STATION.
Even AFTER you've made your major debut!
I'm a powerful producer.
YES...
...I'M SORRY...
...THEY FOUND OUT THAT I'D SWITCHED THE QUESTIONS...
...AND MY SURVIVAL IN SHOWBIZ IS IN DANGER.
The hen is in a jam.
cluck
cluck!
AND THIS IS...
...ALL...
GRR GRR
...YOUR FAULT!! SHOTARO!!
SO...
Clatter

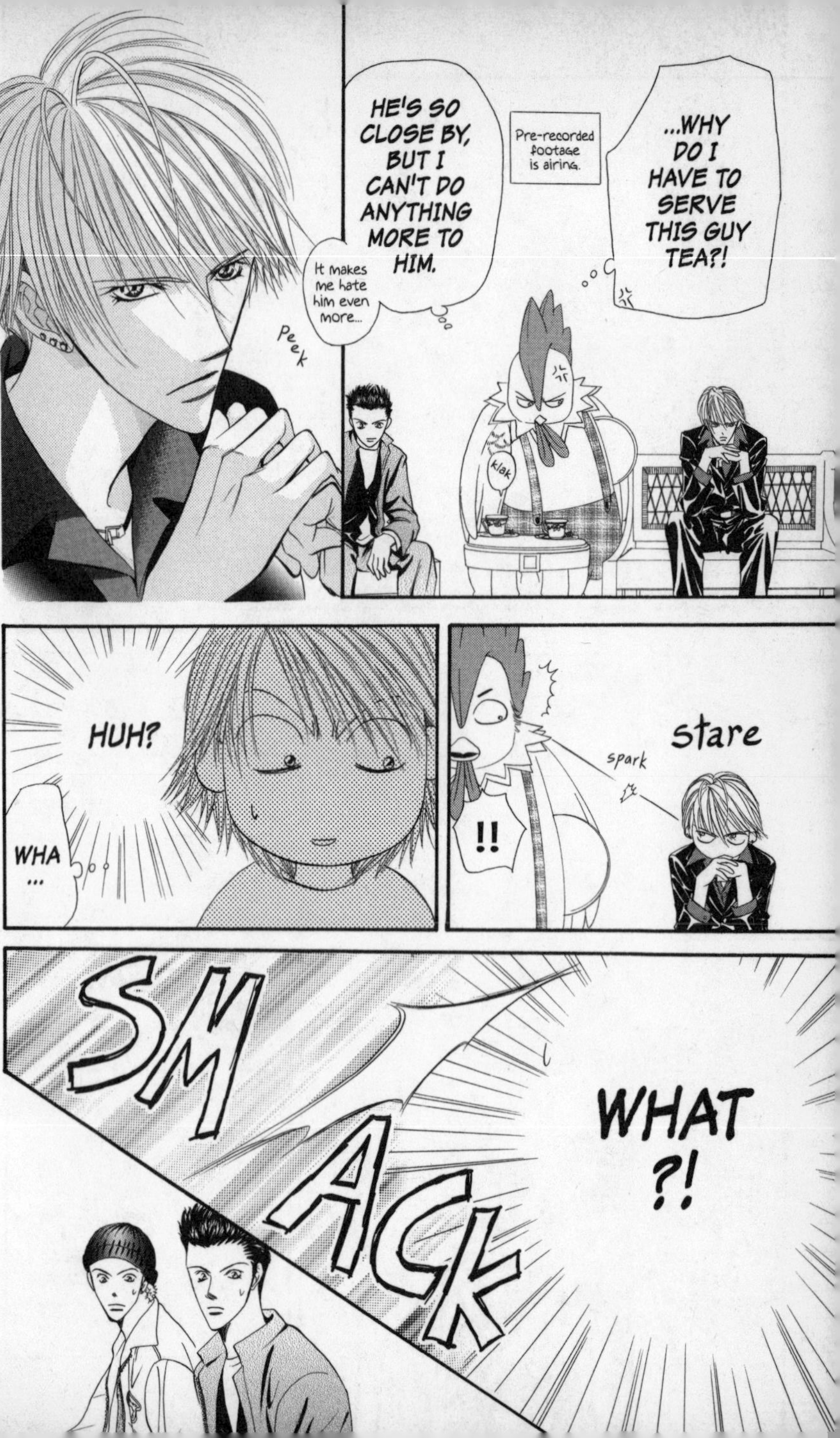
...WHY DO I HAVE TO SERVE THIS GUY TEA?!
Pre-recorded footage is airing.
HE'S SO CLOSE BY, BUT I CAN'T DO ANYTHING MORE TO HIM.
It makes me hate him even more...
klak
Peek
Stare
spark
!!
HUH?
WHA...
WHAT?!
SMACK

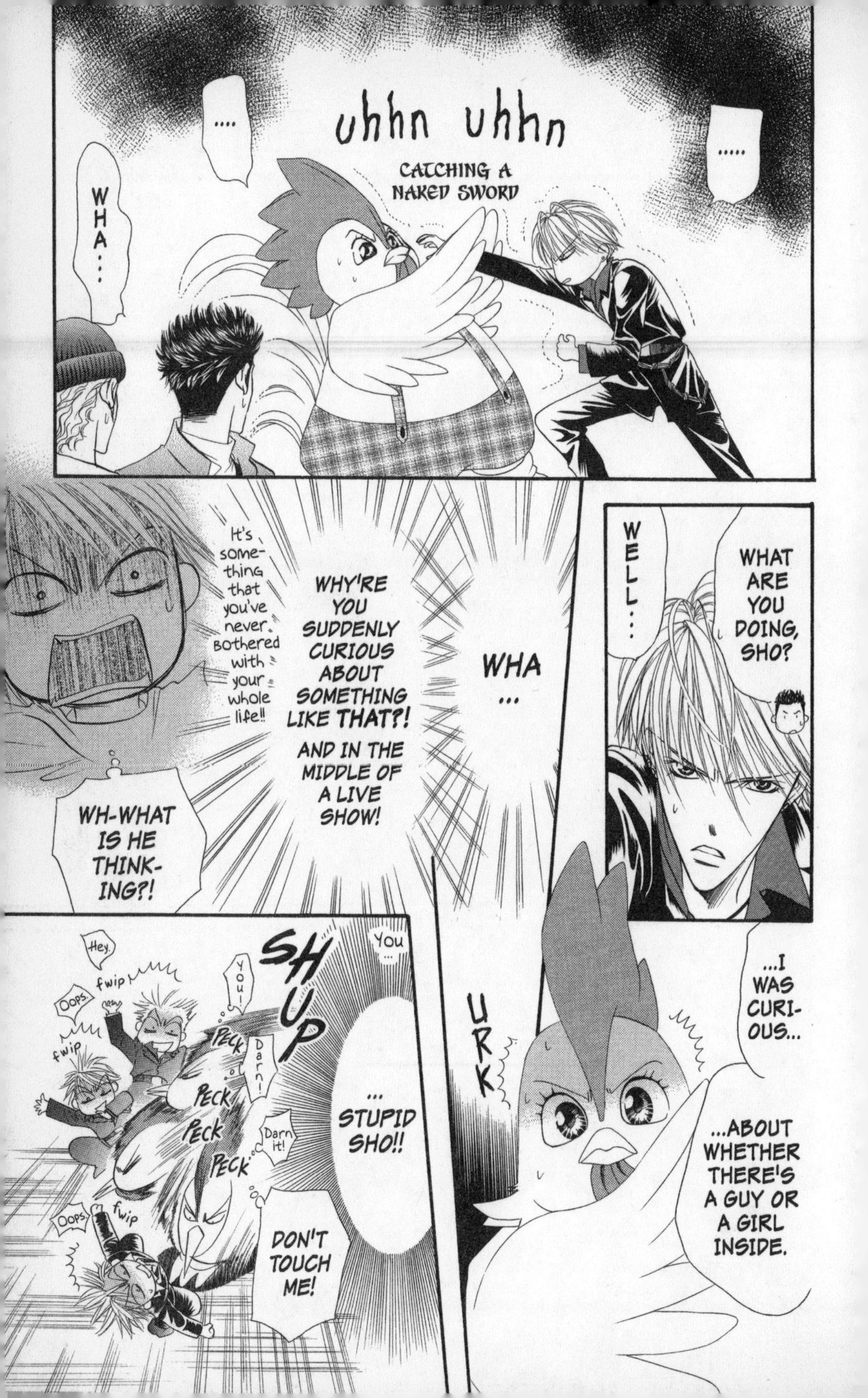
.....
uhhn uhhn
CATCHING A NAKED SWORD
....
WHA...
WHAT ARE YOU DOING, SHO?
WELL...
WHA...
WHY'RE YOU SUDDENLY CURIOUS ABOUT SOMETHING LIKE THAT?!
AND IN THE MIDDLE OF A LIVE SHOW!
It's something that you've never bothered with your whole life!!
WH-WHAT IS HE THINKING?!
URK
...I WAS CURIOUS...
...ABOUT WHETHER THERE'S A GUY OR A GIRL INSIDE.
You ...
SHUP
... STUPID SHO!!
DON'T TOUCH ME!
You!
Darn!
Darn it!
PECK
PECK
PECK
PECK
Hey.
fwip
Oops.
fwip
Oops.
fwip

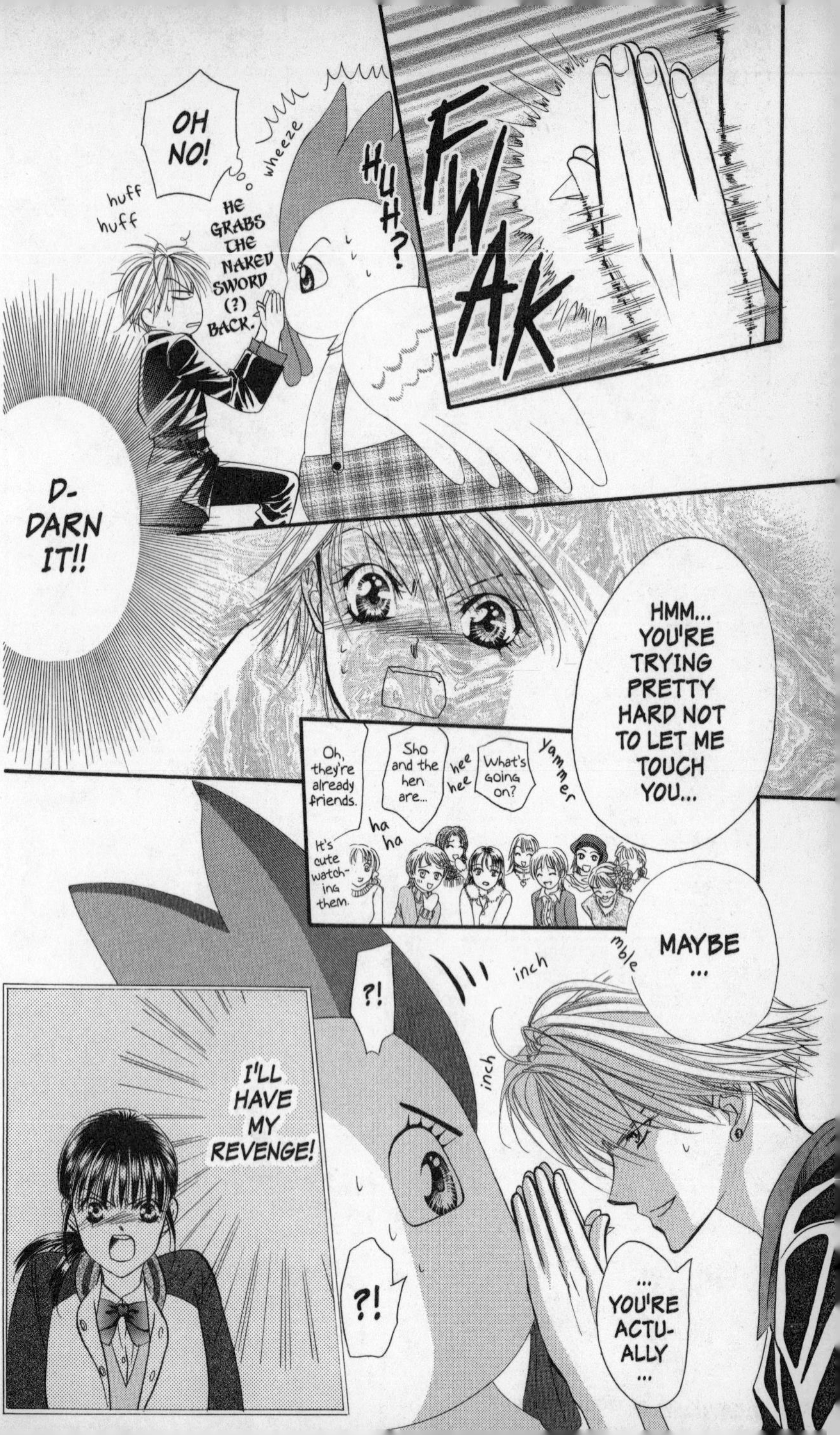
FWAK
HUH?
wheeze
OH NO!
huff huff
HE GRABS THE NAKED SWORD (?) BACK.
D-DARN IT!!
HMM... YOU'RE TRYING PRETTY HARD NOT TO LET ME TOUCH YOU...
yammer
What's going on?
hee hee
Sho and the hen are...
Oh, they're already friends.
ha ha
It's cute watching them.
MAYBE ...
mble
inch
?!
inch
... YOU'RE ACTU-ALLY ...
?!
I'LL HAVE MY REVENGE!

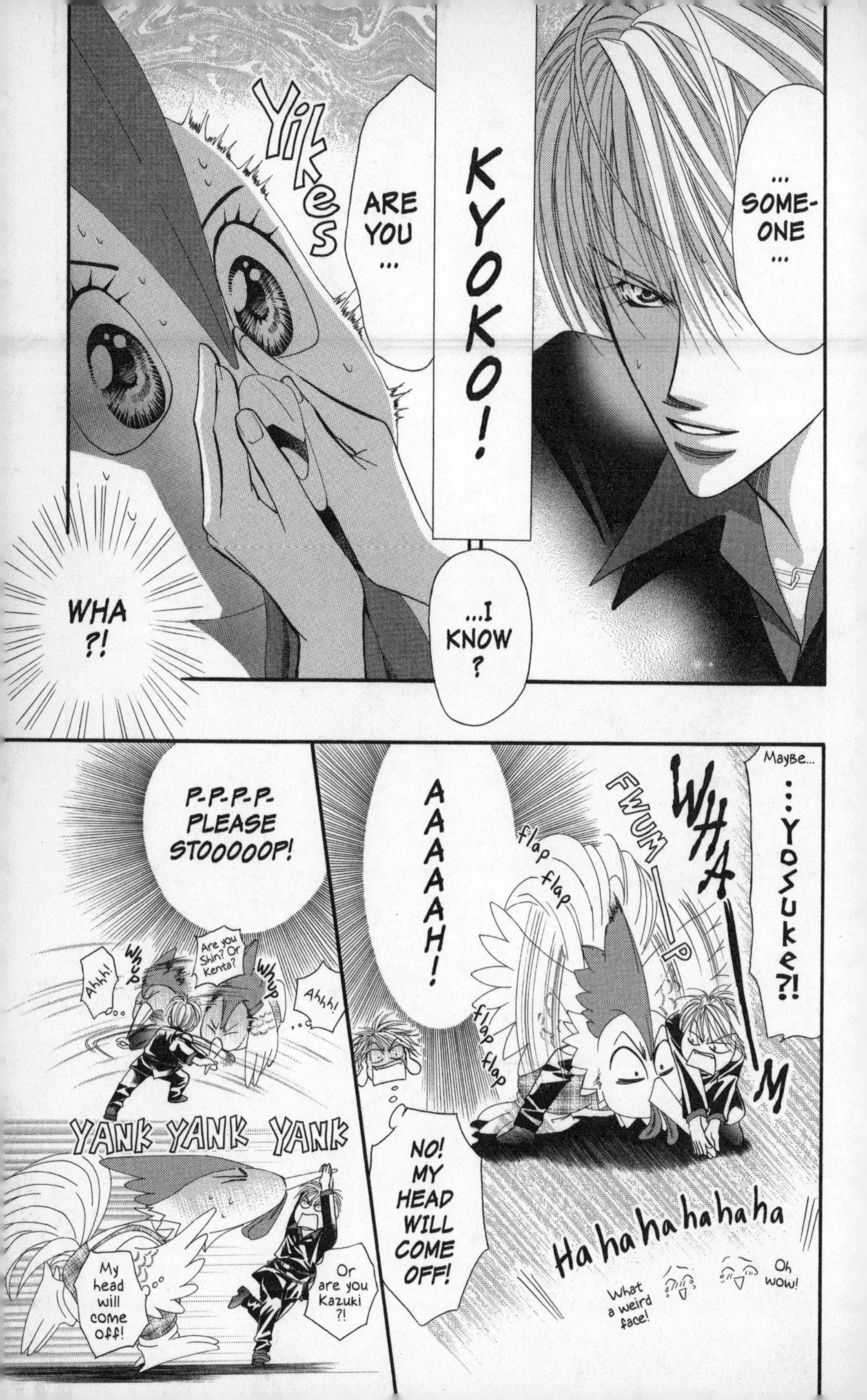

... SOME-ONE ...
KYOKO!
...I KNOW?
Yikes
ARE YOU ...
WHA ?!
Maybe...
...YOSUKE?!
WHAM—P
FWUM
flap flap
AAAAAH!
flap flap
NO! MY HEAD WILL COME OFF!
Ha ha ha ha ha ha ha
Oh wow!
What a weird face!
P-P-P-P-PLEASE STOOOOOP!
Whup
Are you Shin? Or Kenta?
Whup
Ahhh!
Ahhh!
YANK YANK YANK
Or are you Kazuki ?!
My head will come off!

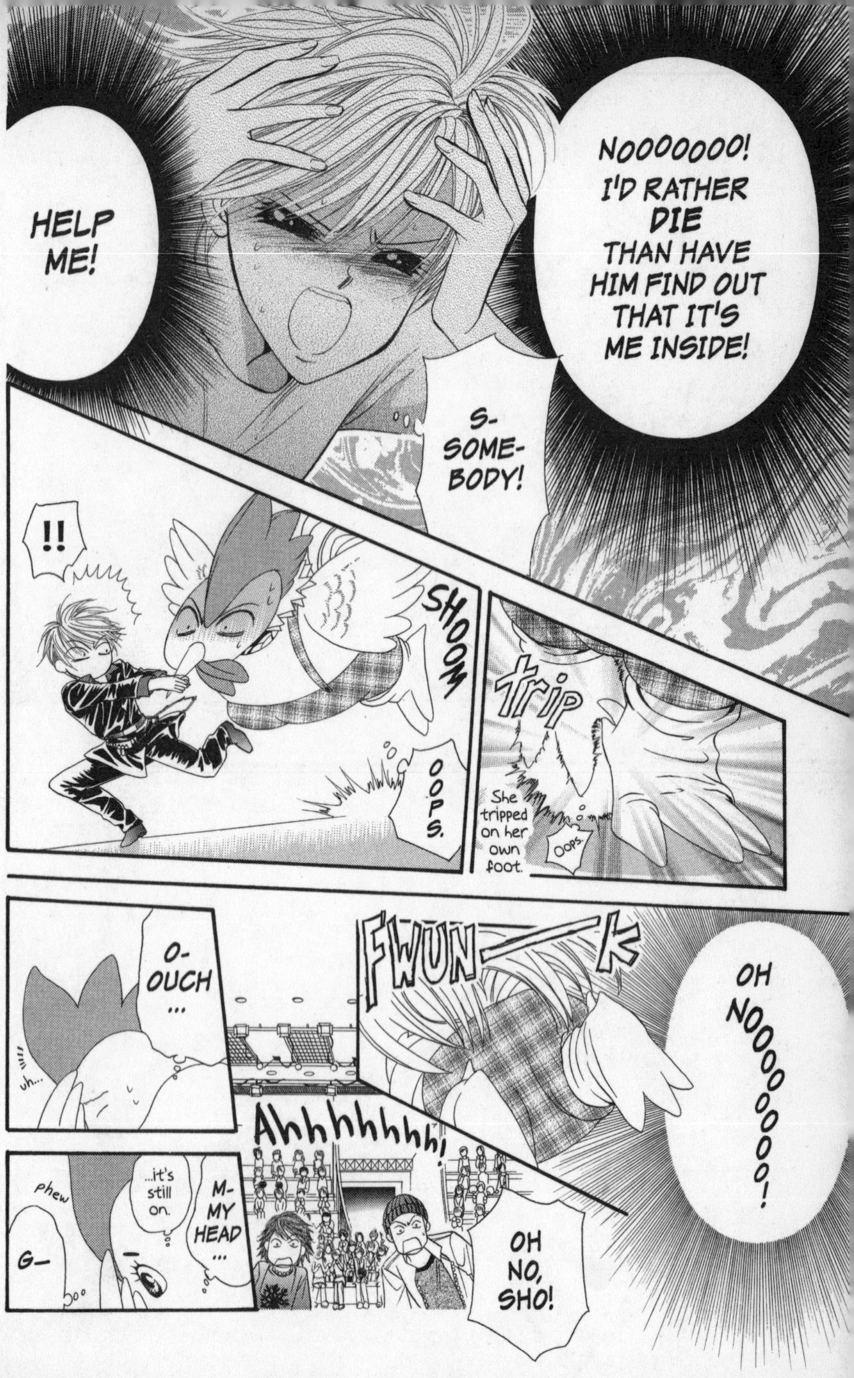
NOOOOOOO! I'D RATHER DIE THAN HAVE HIM FIND OUT THAT IT'S ME INSIDE!
HELP ME!
S-SOME-BODY!
trip
She tripped on her own foot.
Oops.
!!
SHOOM
OOPS.
FWUN—K
OH NOOOOOOOOOO!
Ahhhhhhhh!
OH NO, SHO!
O-OUCH...
uh...
M-MY HEAD...
...it's still on.
phew
G—

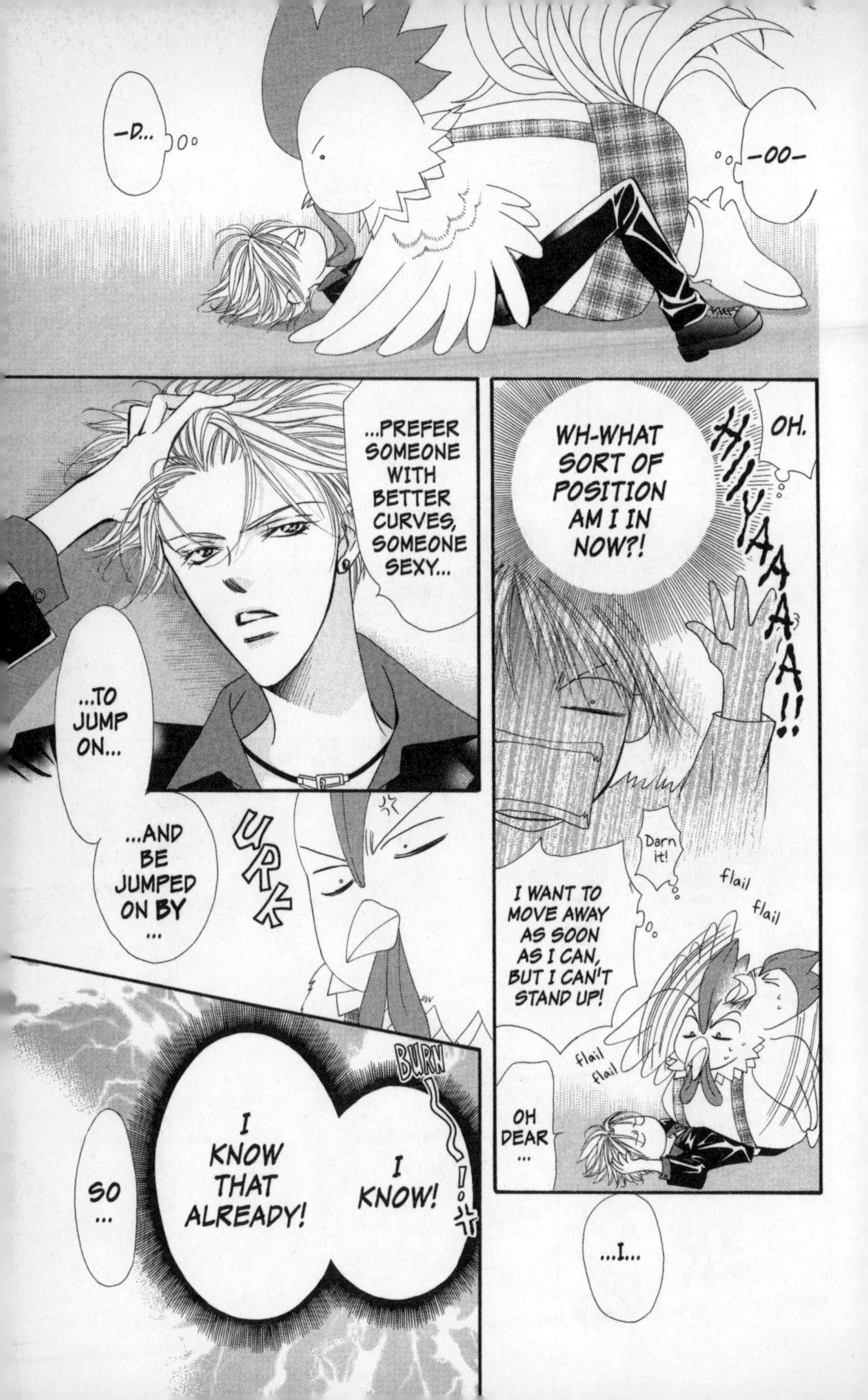

-OO-
-D...
OH.
HIIYAAAA!!
WH-WHAT SORT OF POSITION AM I IN NOW?!
...PREFER SOMEONE WITH BETTER CURVES, SOMEONE SEXY...
...TO JUMP ON...
Darn it!
I WANT TO MOVE AWAY AS SOON AS I CAN, BUT I CAN'T STAND UP!
flail
flail
flail
flail
OH DEAR...
URK
...AND BE JUMPED ON BY...
...I...
I KNOW!
BURN
I KNOW THAT ALREADY!
SO...

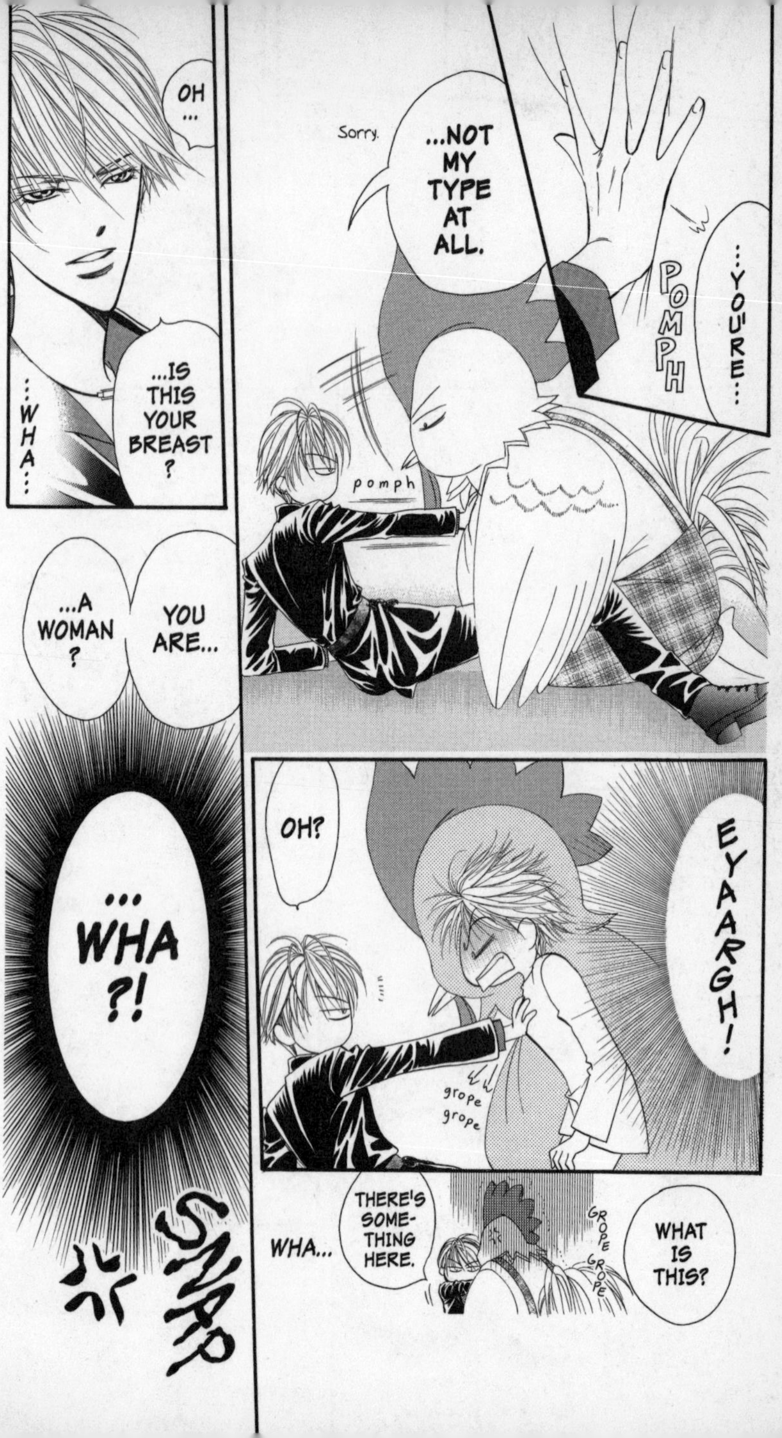

...YOU'RE...
POMPH
...NOT MY TYPE AT ALL.
Sorry.
pomph
WHAT IS THIS?
GROPE GROPE
THERE'S SOMETHING HERE.
WHA...
EYAARGH!
OH?
grope grope
OH...
...IS THIS YOUR BREAST?
...WHA...
YOU ARE...
...A WOMAN?
...WHA?!
SNAP

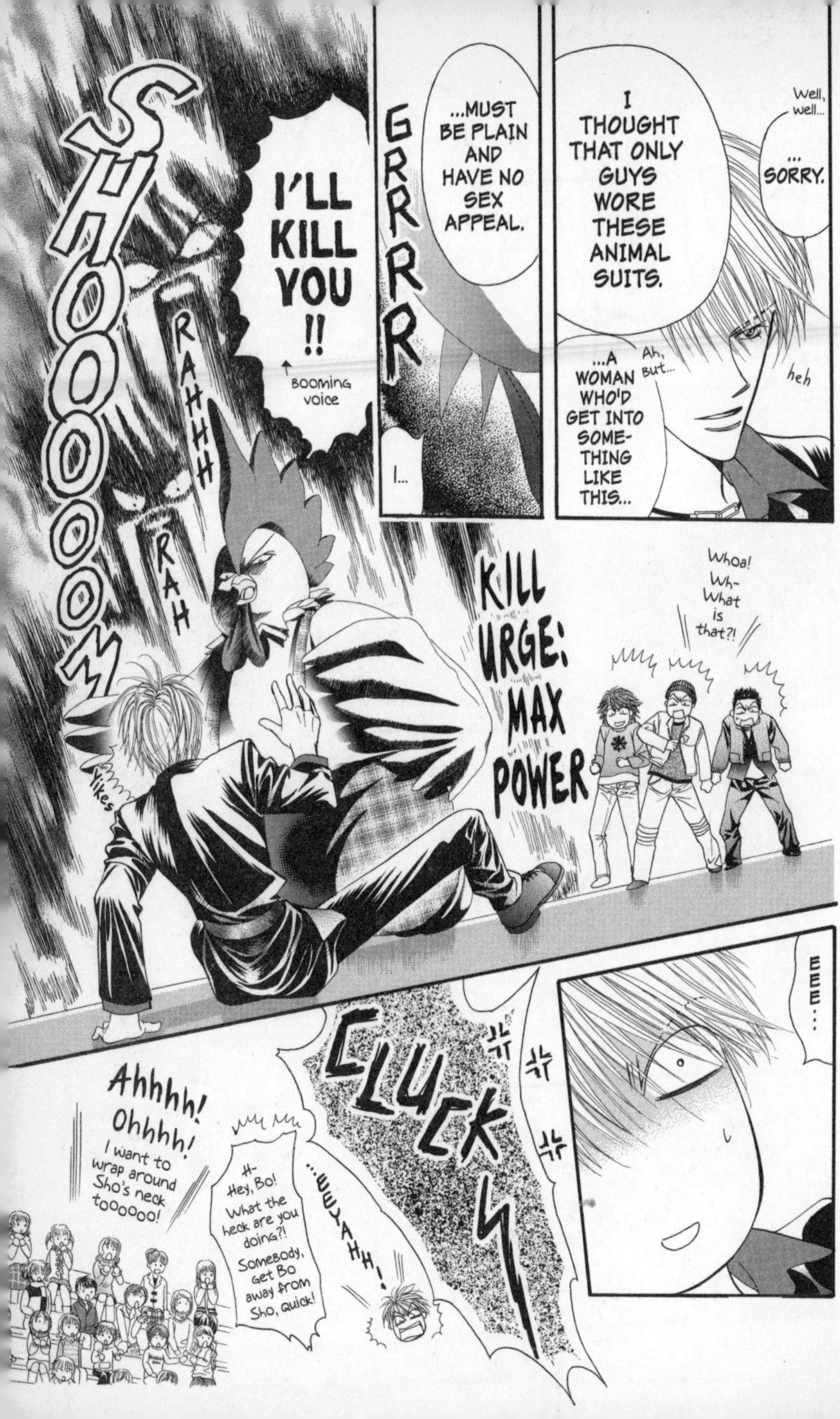
Well, well...
...SORRY.
I THOUGHT THAT ONLY GUYS WORE THESE ANIMAL SUITS.
heh
Ah, but...
...A WOMAN WHO'D GET INTO SOMETHING LIKE THIS...
...MUST BE PLAIN AND HAVE NO SEX APPEAL.
GRRRR
I...
I'LL KILL YOU!!
Booming voice
SHOOOOOOOM
RAHHHH
RAH
Whoa! Wh-What is that?!
KILL URGE: MAX POWER
Yikes
EEE...
CLUCK
...EEYAHH!
H-Hey, Bo! What the heck are you doing?! Somebody, get Bo away from Sho, quick!
Ahhhh! Ohhhh! I want to wrap around Sho's neck toooooo!

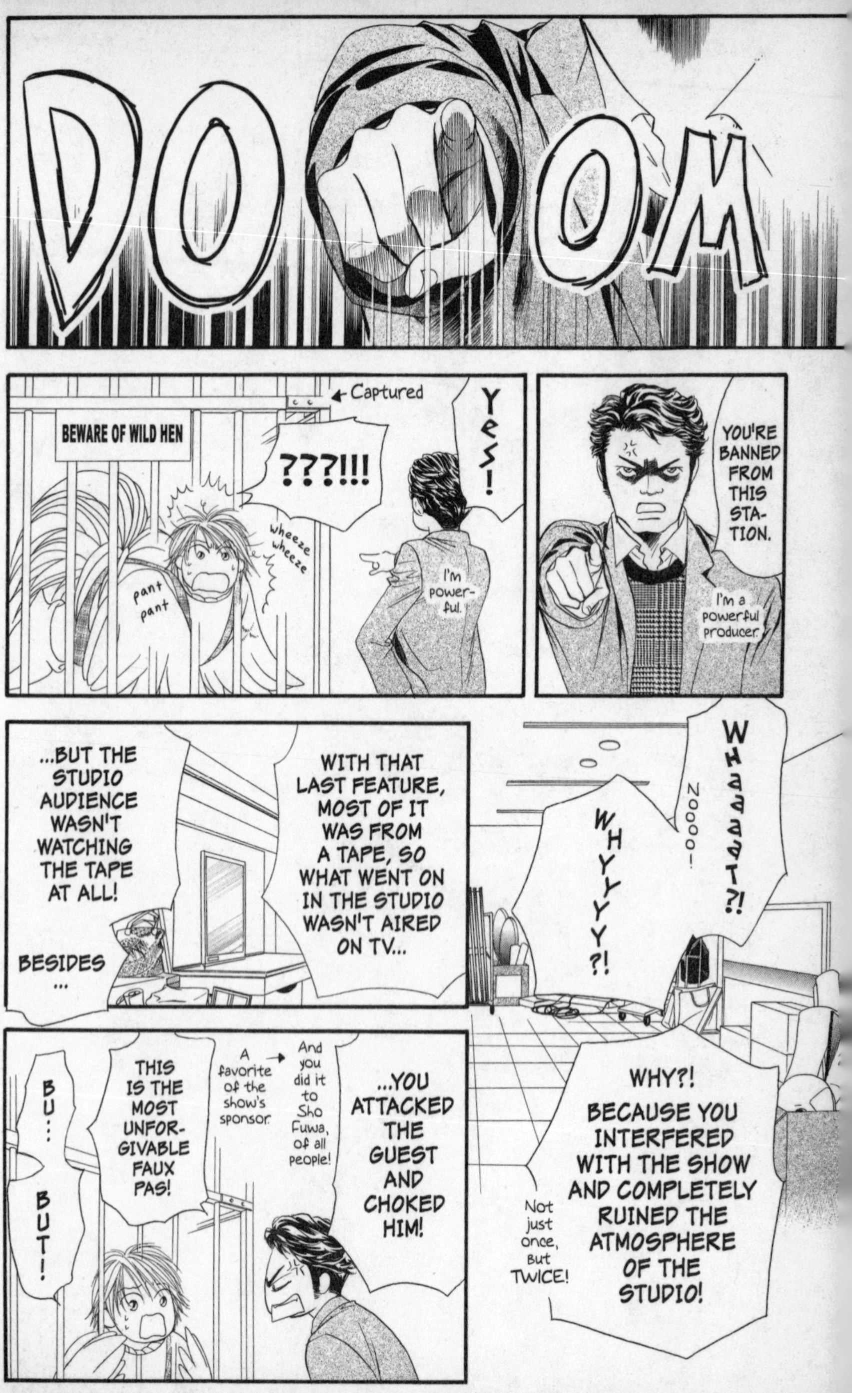
DOOOM
YOU'RE BANNED FROM THIS STATION.
I'm a powerful producer.
Yes!
I'm powerful.
Captured
???!!!
BEWARE OF WILD HEN
wheeze wheeze
pant pant
Whaaaat?!
Noooo!
WHYYYY?!
WITH THAT LAST FEATURE, MOST OF IT WAS FROM A TAPE, SO WHAT WENT ON IN THE STUDIO WASN'T AIRED ON TV...
...BUT THE STUDIO AUDIENCE WASN'T WATCHING THE TAPE AT ALL!
BESIDES...
WHY?!
BECAUSE YOU INTERFERED WITH THE SHOW AND COMPLETELY RUINED THE ATMOSPHERE OF THE STUDIO!
Not just once, but TWICE!
...YOU ATTACKED THE GUEST AND CHOKED HIM!
And you did it to Sho Fuwa, of all people!
A favorite of the show's sponsor.
THIS IS THE MOST UNFORGIVABLE FAUX PAS!
BU... BUT!

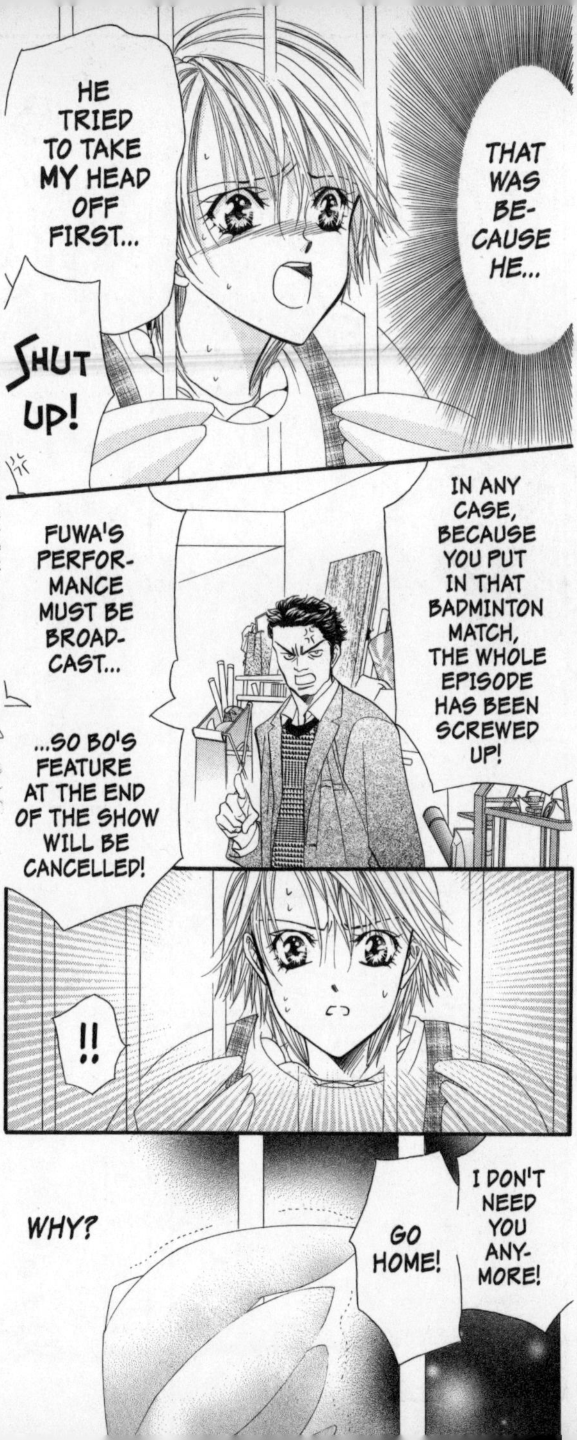
THAT WAS BE-CAUSE HE...
HE TRIED TO TAKE MY HEAD OFF FIRST...
SHUT UP!
IN ANY CASE, BECAUSE YOU PUT IN THAT BADMINTON MATCH, THE WHOLE EPISODE HAS BEEN SCREWED UP!
FUWA'S PERFOR-MANCE MUST BE BROAD-CAST...
...SO BO'S FEATURE AT THE END OF THE SHOW WILL BE CANCELLED!
!!
I DON'T NEED YOU ANY-MORE!
GO HOME!
WHY?

Bo

From the time I started *Skip Beat!* I'd told my editor that I wanted to have Kyoko do a job involving animal suits, but I didn't think that animal suit would turn out to be a hen. ♪

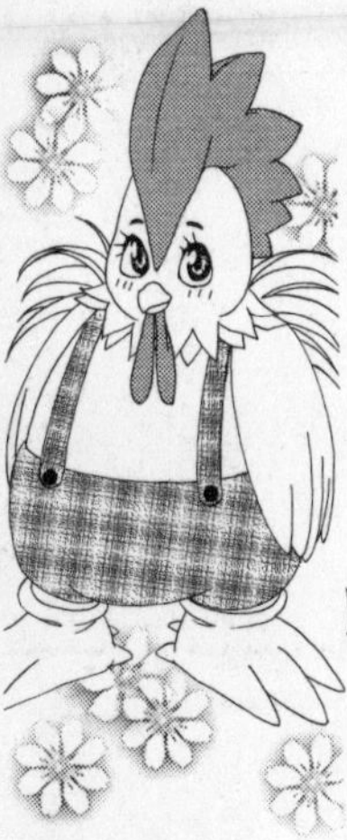

But I had this vague image of an animal suit that would be a mascot character for a talk show or a variety show (Like Manma-chan in Sanma no Manma...)...so...the animal was finally decided by trial and error after the show name "Yappa Kimagure Rock" was chosen.

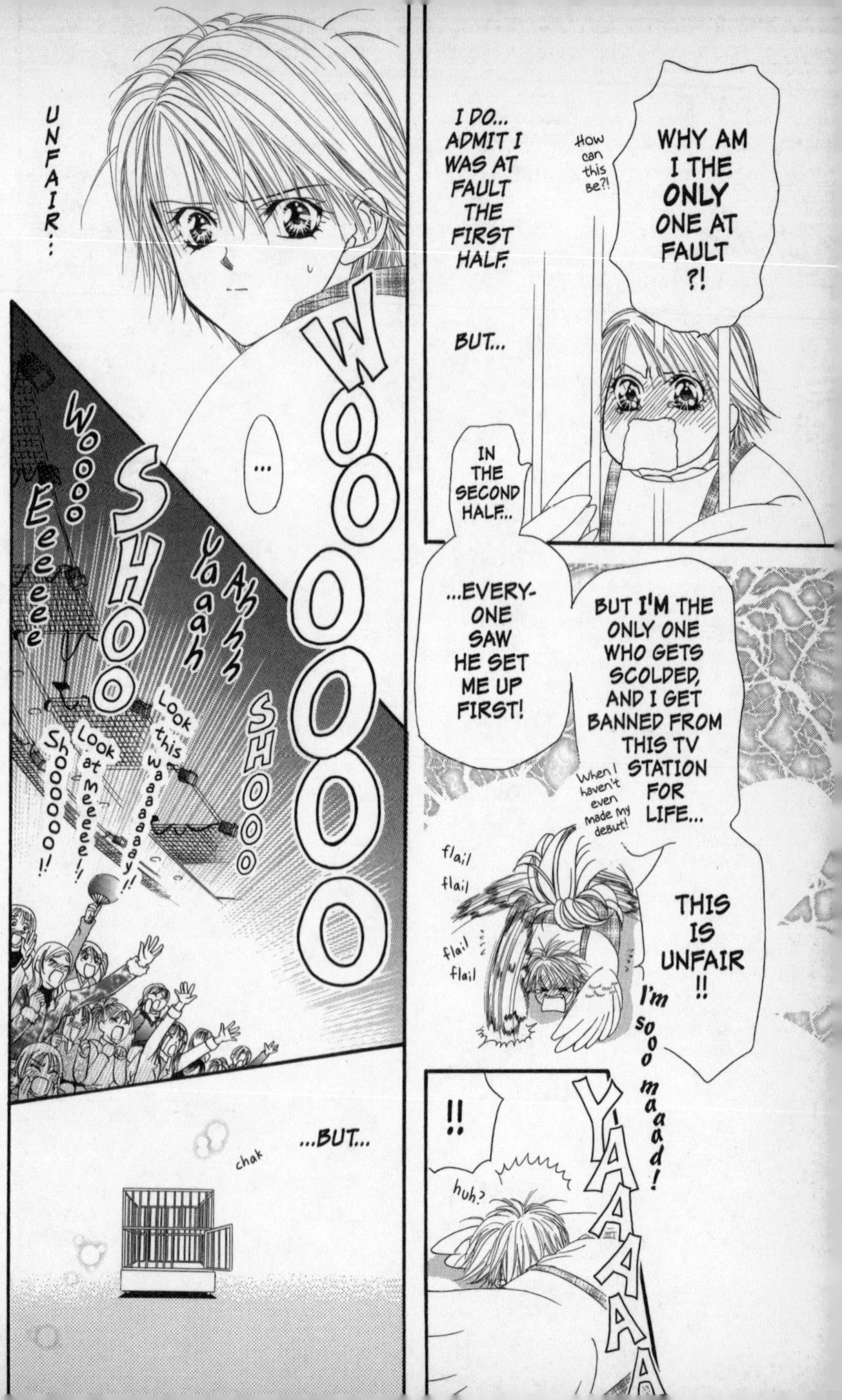
WHY AM I THE ONLY ONE AT FAULT ?!
How can this be?!
I DO... ADMIT I WAS AT FAULT THE FIRST HALF.
BUT...
IN THE SECOND HALF...
...EVERY-ONE SAW HE SET ME UP FIRST!
BUT I'M THE ONLY ONE WHO GETS SCOLDED, AND I GET BANNED FROM THIS TV STATION FOR LIFE...
When I haven't even made my debut!
flail flail
flail flail
THIS IS UNFAIR !!
I'm sooo maaad!
!!
huh?
YAAAAA
UNFAIR...
...
WOOOOOOO
SHOOOO
Ahhh Yaaaah
SHOOO
Woooo Eeeeee
Look this waaaaaaay!!
Look at meeeee!!
Shoooooo!!
...BUT...
chak

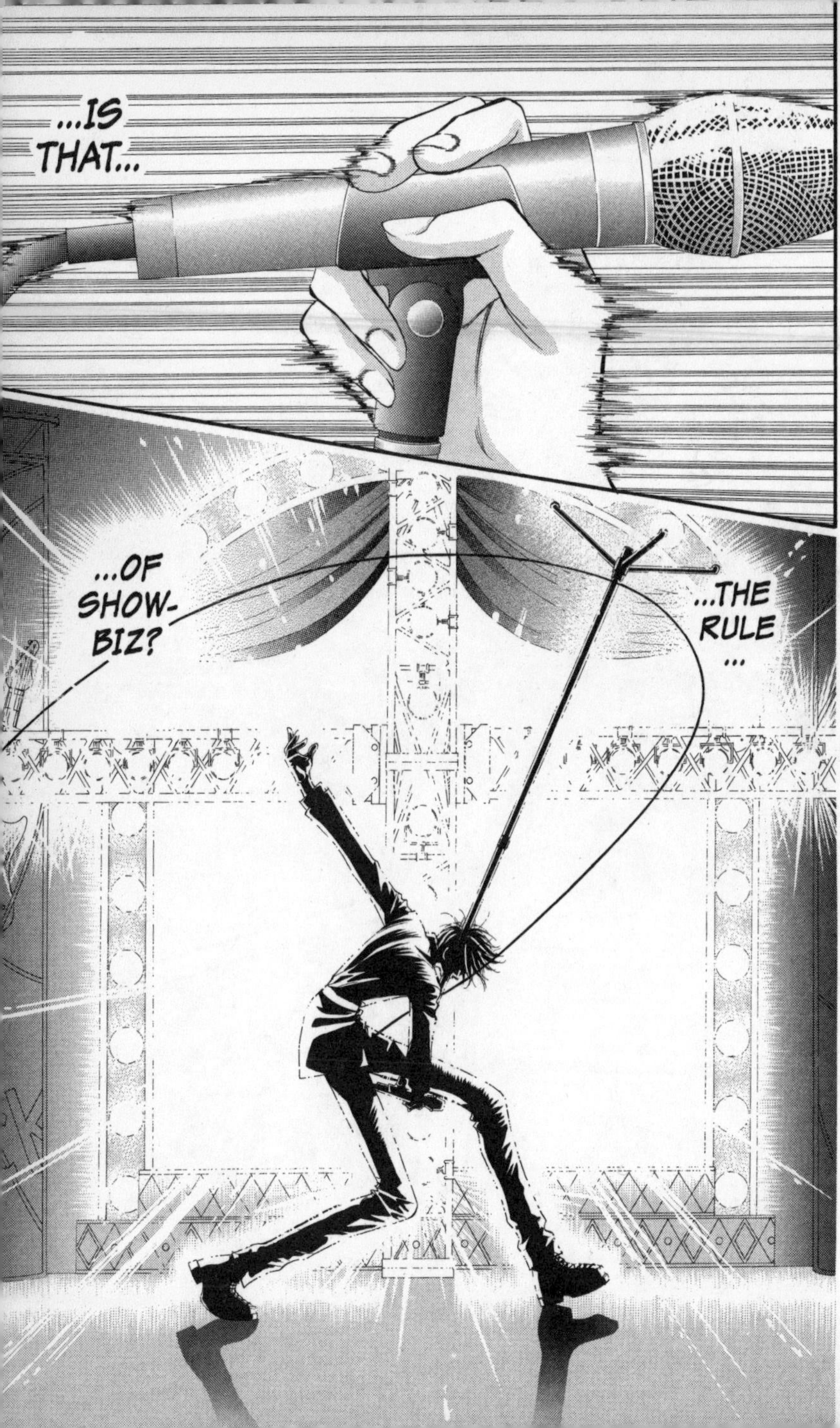
...IS THAT...
...THE RULE ...
...OF SHOW-BIZ?

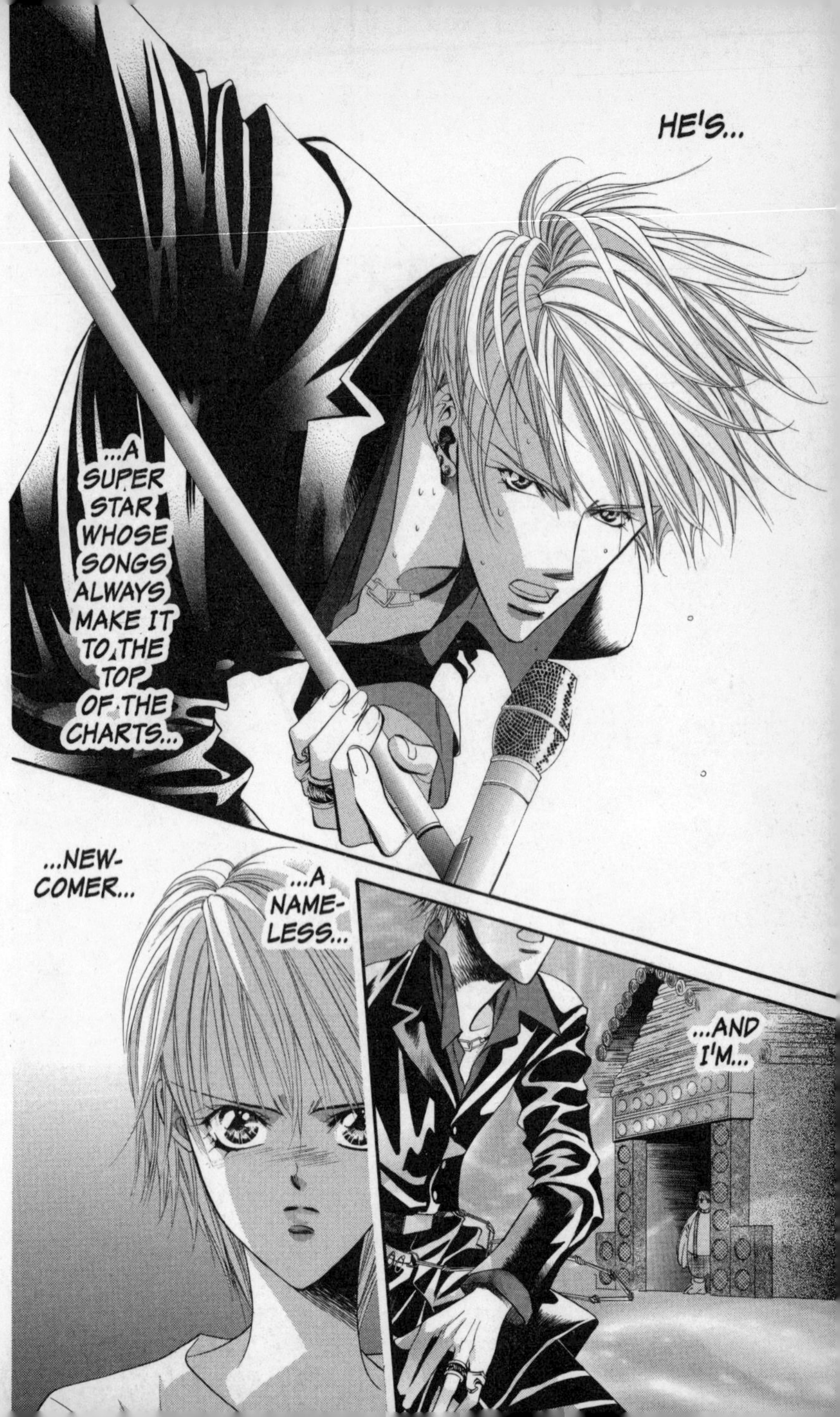
HE'S...
...A SUPER STAR WHOSE SONGS ALWAYS MAKE IT TO THE TOP OF THE CHARTS...
...AND I'M...
...A NAME-LESS...
...NEW-COMER...

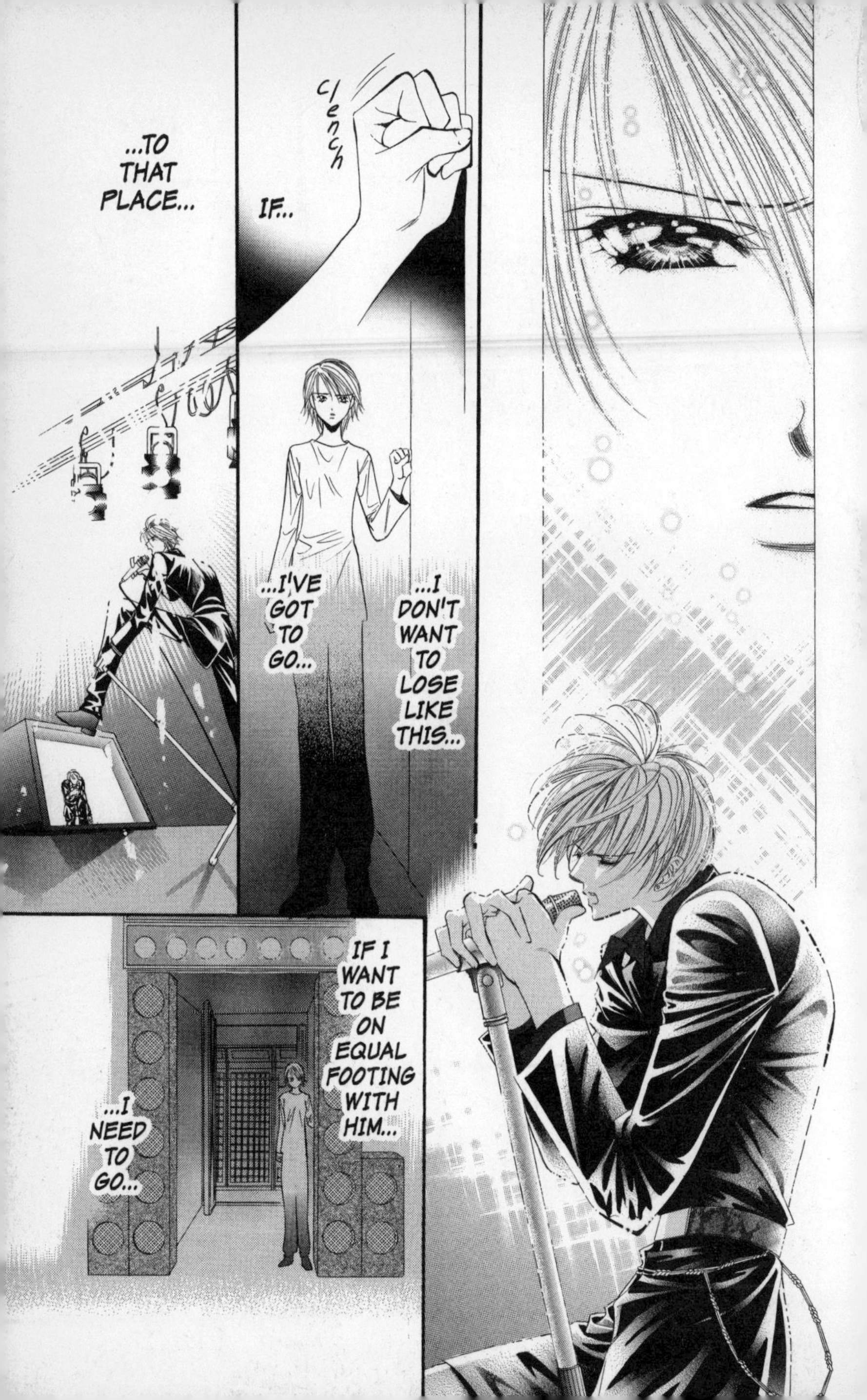
clench
IF...
...I DON'T WANT TO LOSE LIKE THIS...
...I'VE GOT TO GO...
...TO THAT PLACE...
IF I WANT TO BE ON EQUAL FOOTING WITH HIM...
...I NEED TO GO...

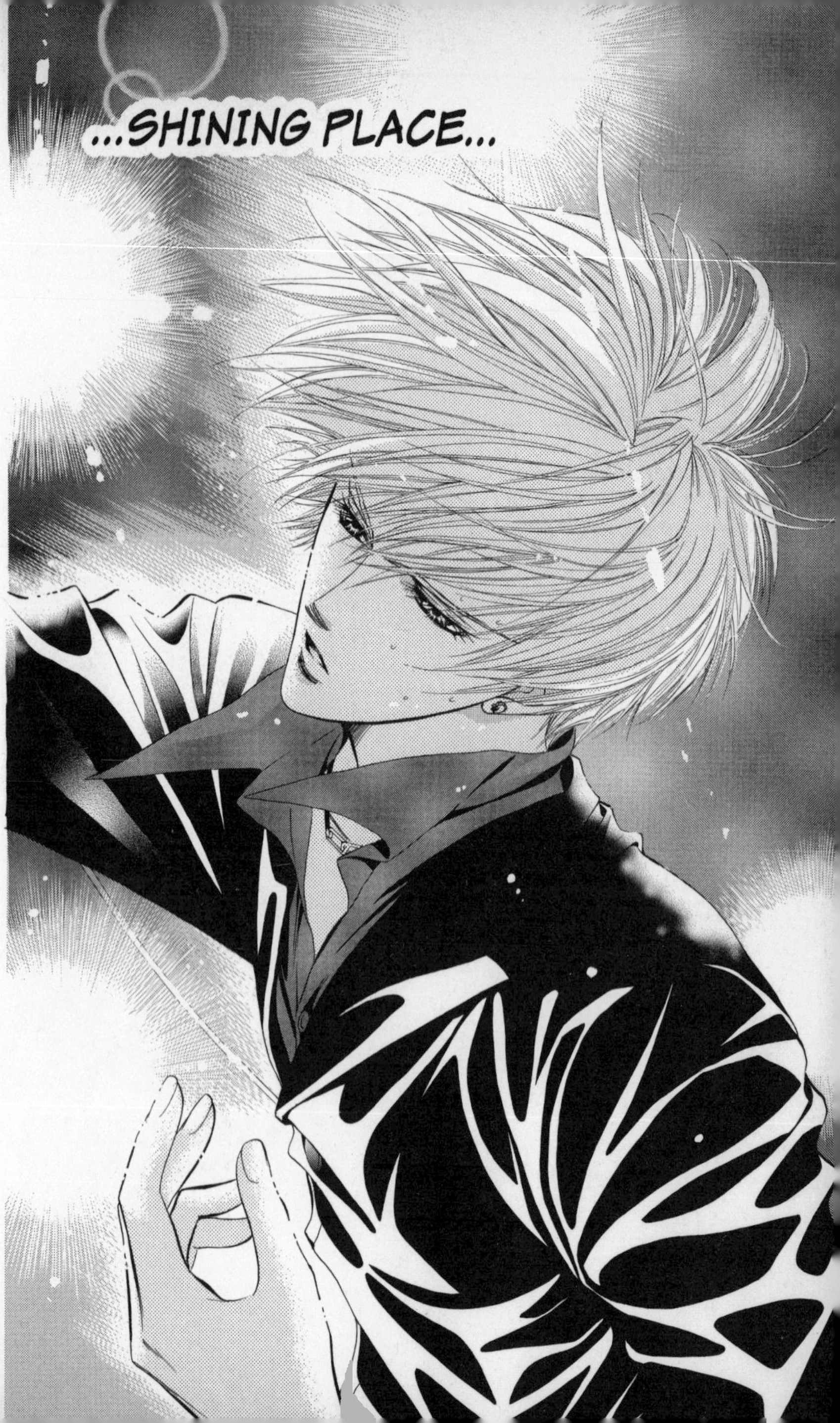
...SHINING PLACE...

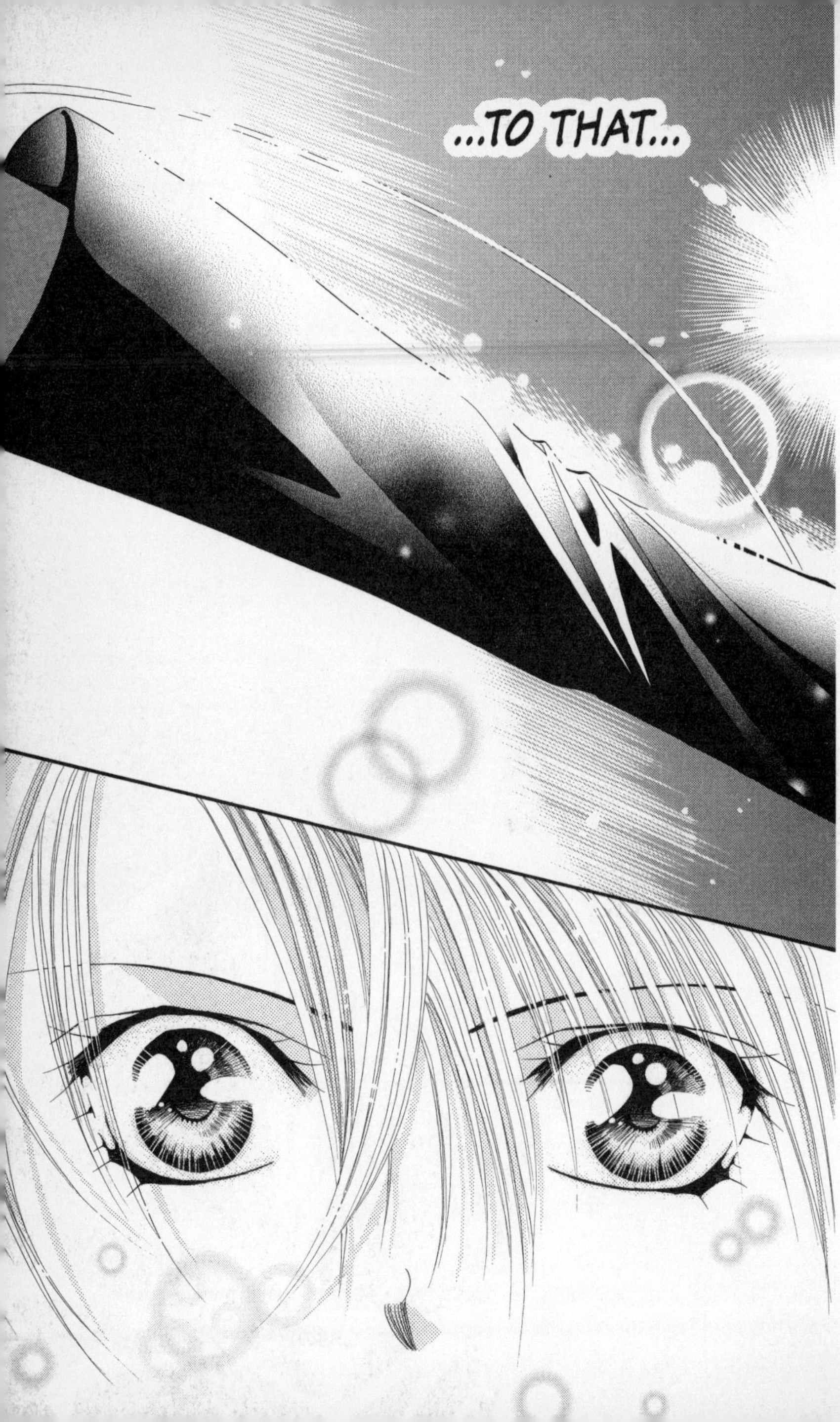
...TO THAT...

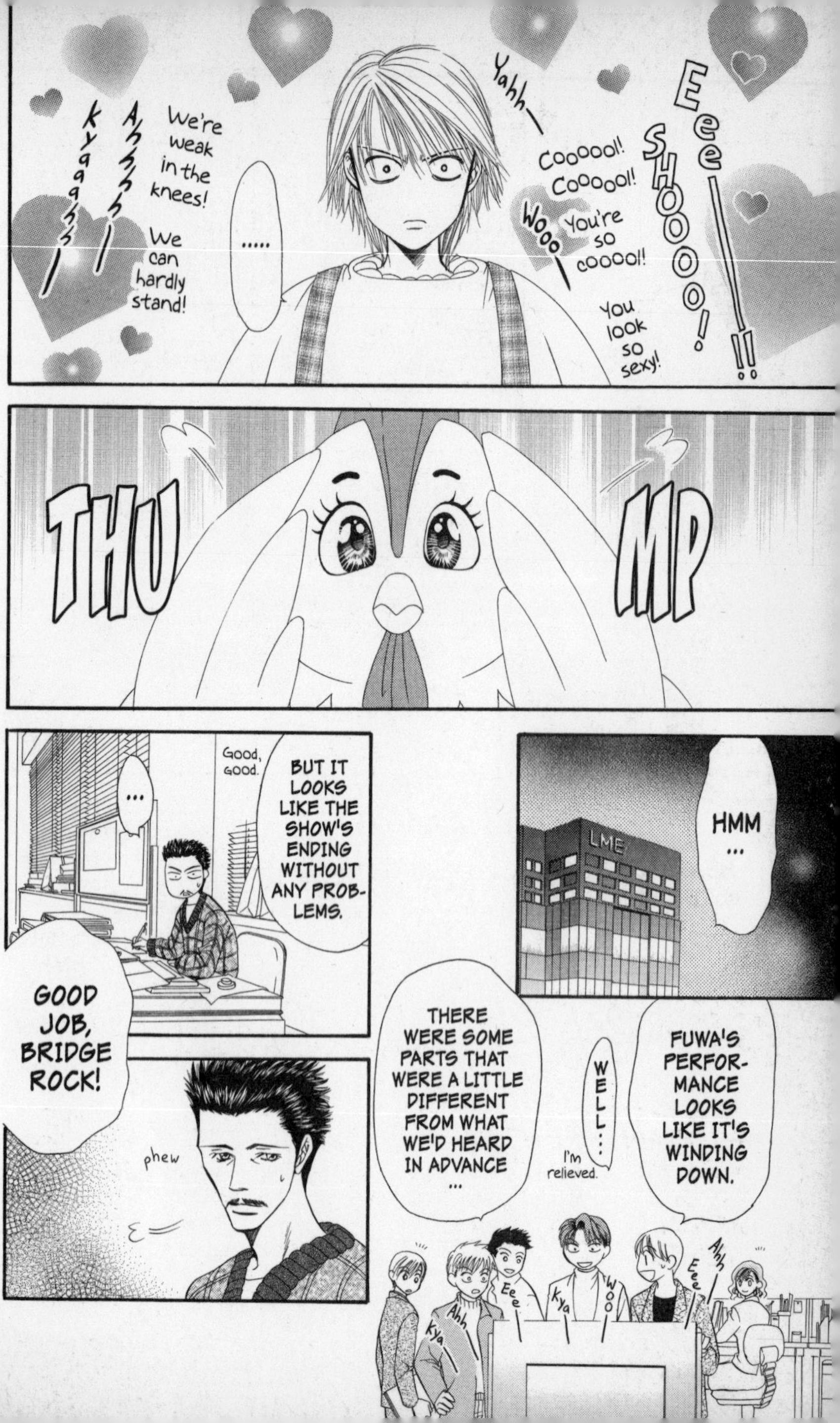
Eee—!!
SHOOOO!
Yahh—
Coooool! Coooool!
Wooo—
You're so cooool!
You look so sexy!
.....
We're weak in the knees!
We can hardly stand!
Ahhhh—
Kyaaahh—
THUMP
HMM...
BUT IT LOOKS LIKE THE SHOW'S ENDING WITHOUT ANY PROBLEMS.
Good, good.
...
FUWA'S PERFORMANCE LOOKS LIKE IT'S WINDING DOWN.
WELL...
I'm relieved.
THERE WERE SOME PARTS THAT WERE A LITTLE DIFFERENT FROM WHAT WE'D HEARD IN ADVANCE...
Ahh
Eee
Wooo
Kya
Eee
Ahh
Kya
GOOD JOB, BRIDGE ROCK!
phew

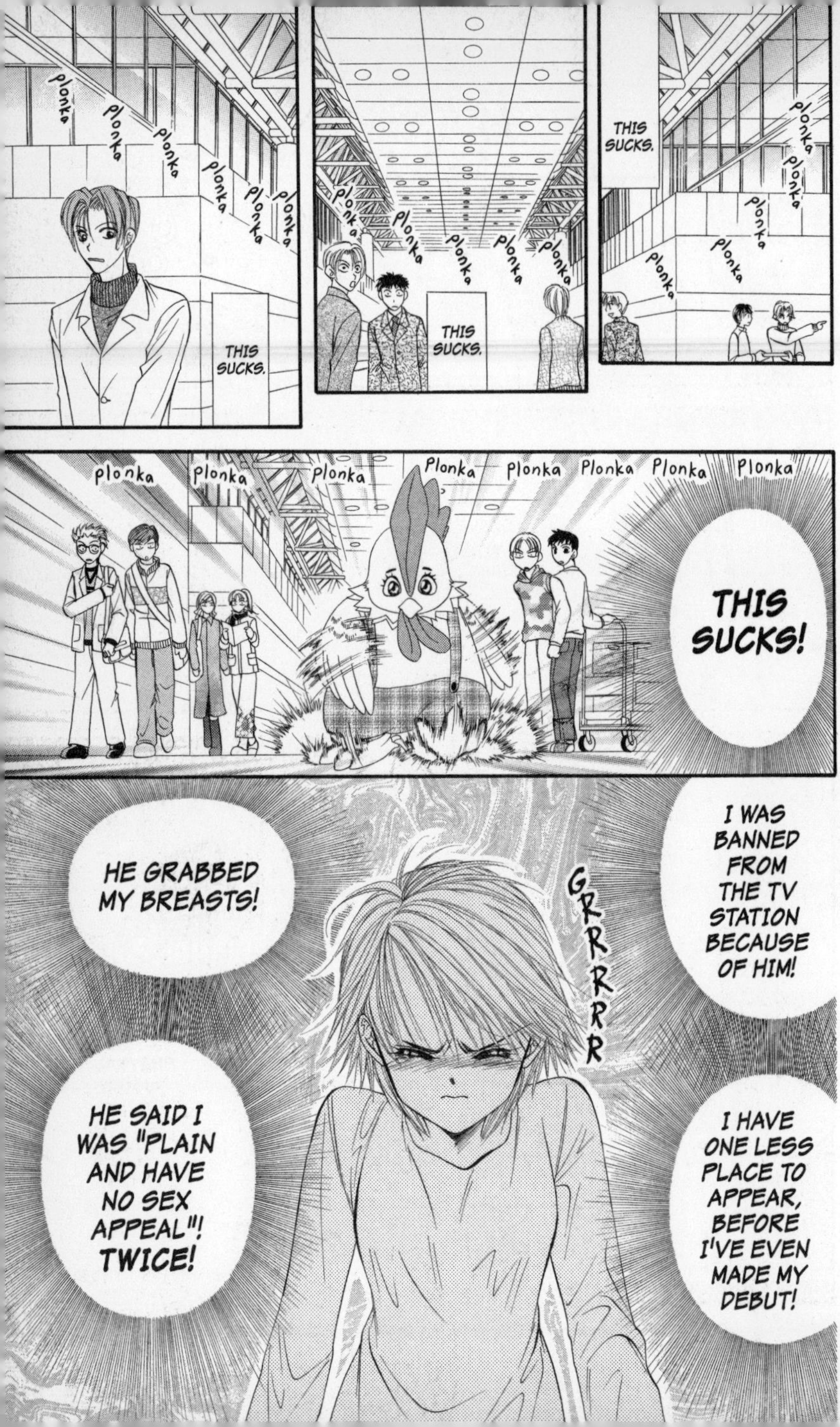
THIS SUCKS.
plonka plonka plonka plonka plonka
THIS SUCKS.
plonka plonka plonka plonka plonka plonka
THIS SUCKS.
plonka plonka plonka plonka plonka plonka
plonka plonka plonka plonka plonka plonka plonka plonka
THIS SUCKS!
I WAS BANNED FROM THE TV STATION BECAUSE OF HIM!
GRRRRRR
HE GRABBED MY BREASTS!
I HAVE ONE LESS PLACE TO APPEAR, BEFORE I'VE EVEN MADE MY DEBUT!
HE SAID I WAS "PLAIN AND HAVE NO SEX APPEAL"! TWICE!

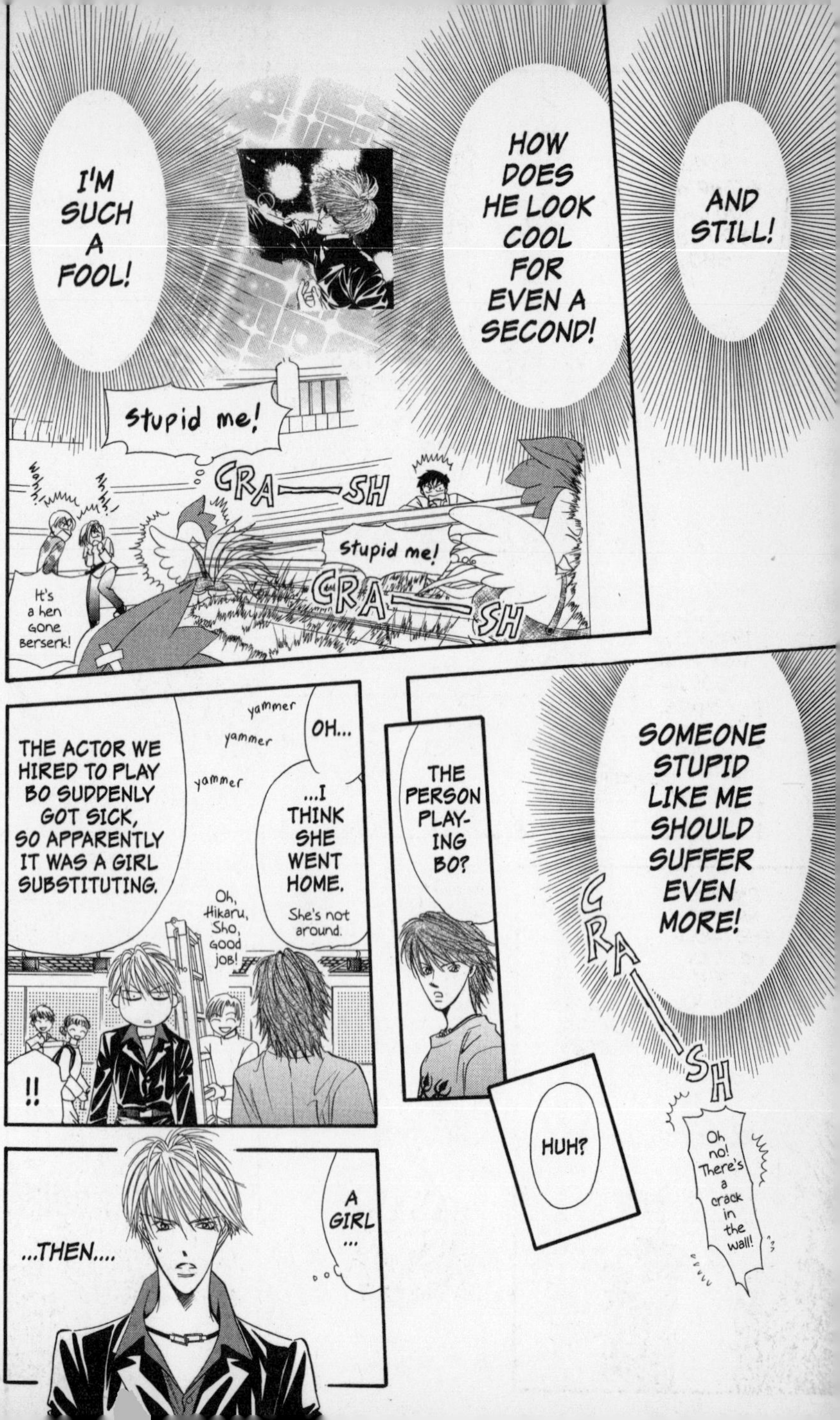
AND STILL!
HOW DOES HE LOOK COOL FOR EVEN A SECOND!
I'M SUCH A FOOL!
Stupid me!
CRA—SH
Stupid me!
CRA—SH
It's a hen gone berserk!
SOMEONE STUPID LIKE ME SHOULD SUFFER EVEN MORE!
CRA—SH
Oh no! There's a crack in the wall!
THE PERSON PLAYING BO?
HUH?
OH...
...I THINK SHE WENT HOME.
She's not around.
yammer
yammer
yammer
THE ACTOR WE HIRED TO PLAY BO SUDDENLY GOT SICK, SO APPARENTLY IT WAS A GIRL SUBSTITUTING.
Oh, Hikaru, Sho, good job!
!!
A GIRL...
...THEN....

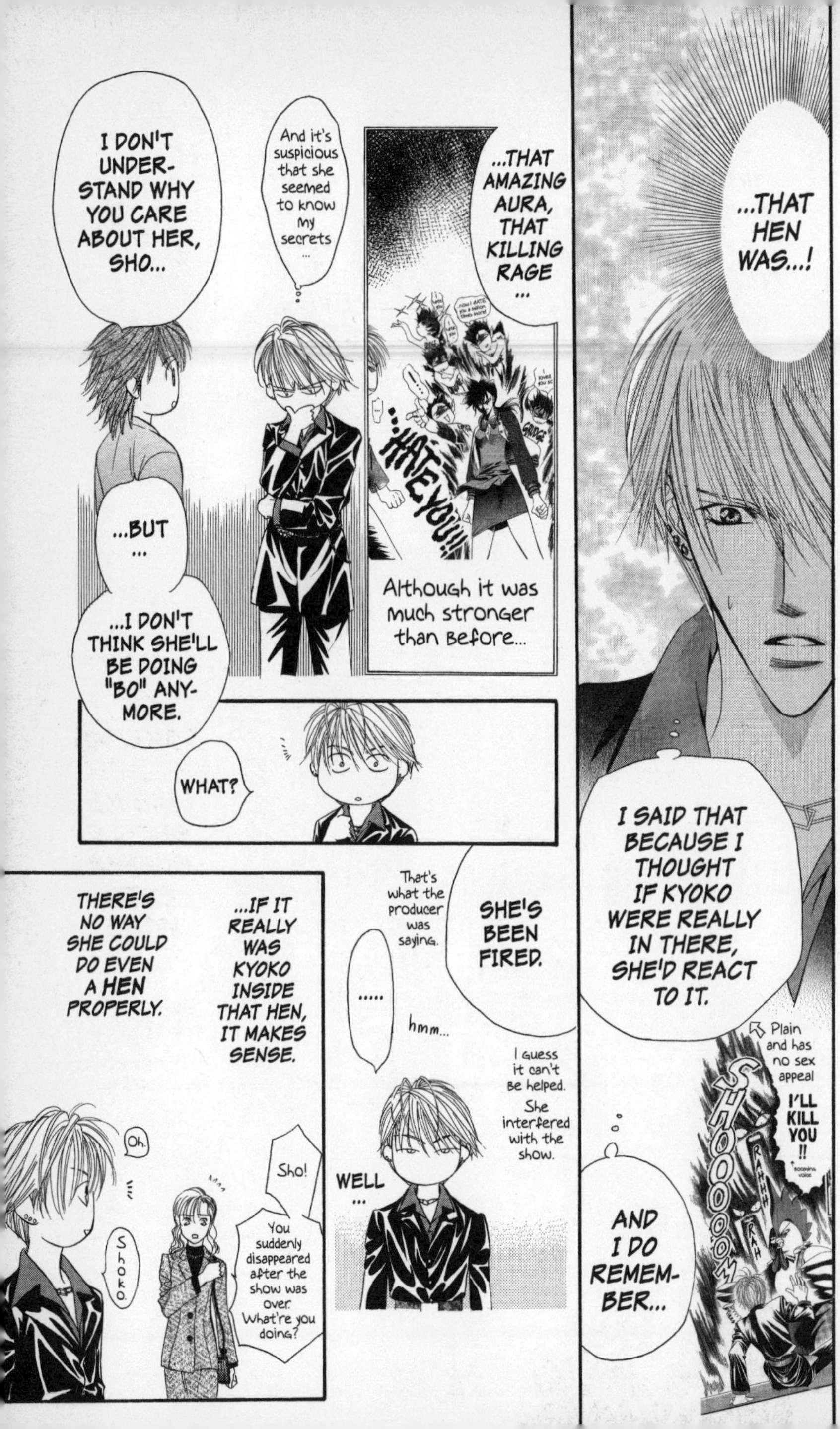

...THAT HEN WAS...!
I SAID THAT BECAUSE I THOUGHT IF KYOKO WERE REALLY IN THERE, SHE'D REACT TO IT.
Plain and has no sex appeal
I'LL KILL YOU !!
booming voice
SHOOOOOOM
RAHHH
RAH
AND I DO REMEMBER...
...THAT AMAZING AURA, THAT KILLING RAGE ...
...now I HATE you a million times more!
I loved you so
GRUDGE
...HATE YOU!!!
Although it was much stronger than before...
And it's suspicious that she seemed to know my secrets ...
I DON'T UNDERSTAND WHY YOU CARE ABOUT HER, SHO...
...BUT ...
...I DON'T THINK SHE'LL BE DOING "BO" ANYMORE.
WHAT?
SHE'S BEEN FIRED.
That's what the producer was saying.
.....
hmm...
I guess it can't be helped.
She interfered with the show.
WELL ...
...IF IT REALLY WAS KYOKO INSIDE THAT HEN, IT MAKES SENSE.
THERE'S NO WAY SHE COULD DO EVEN A HEN PROPERLY.
Sho!
You suddenly disappeared after the show was over. What're you doing?
Oh.
Shoko.

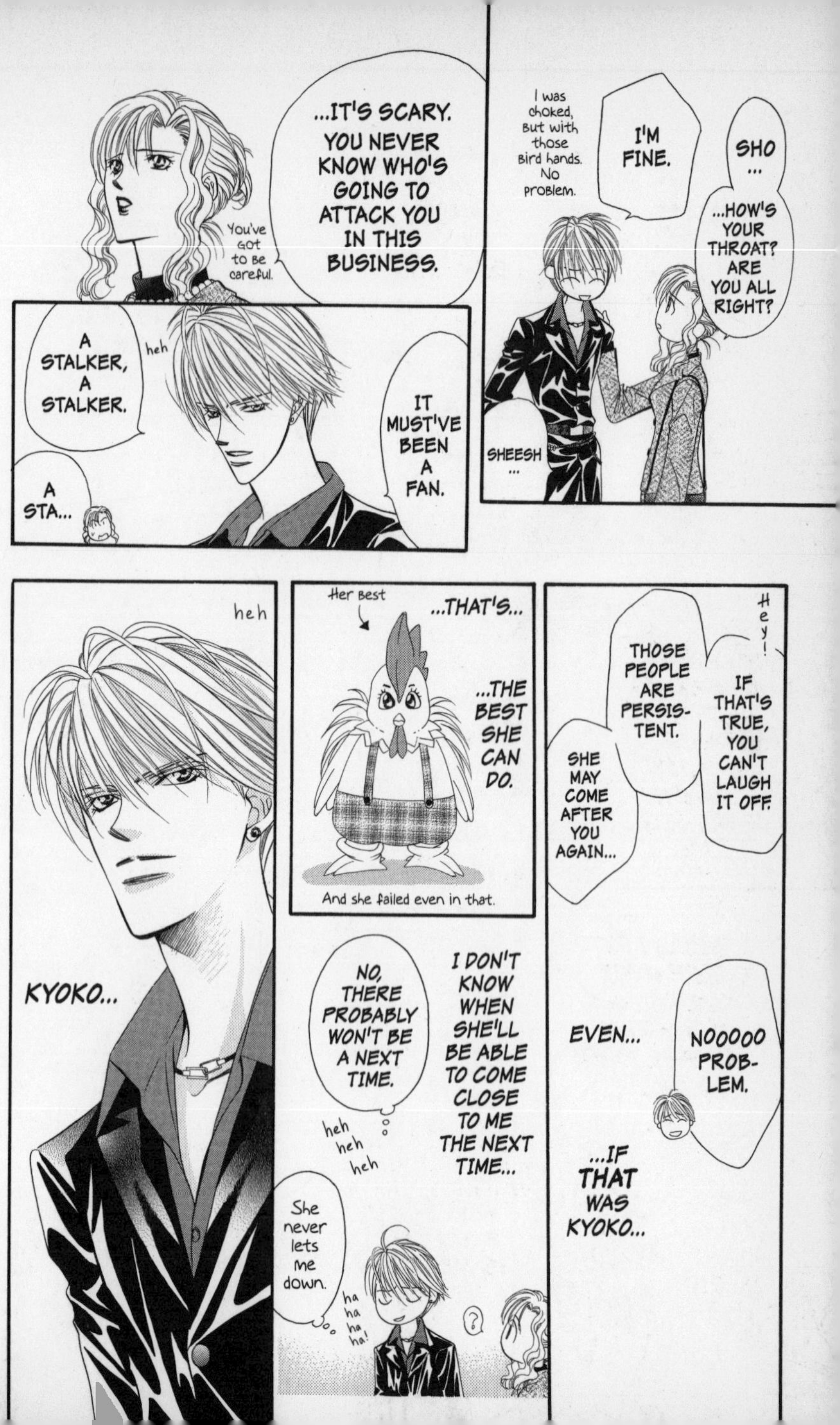
SHO ...
...HOW'S YOUR THROAT? ARE YOU ALL RIGHT?
I'M FINE.
I was choked, but with those bird hands. No problem.
SHEESH ...
...IT'S SCARY. YOU NEVER KNOW WHO'S GOING TO ATTACK YOU IN THIS BUSINESS.
You've got to be careful.
IT MUST'VE BEEN A FAN.
heh
A STALKER, A STALKER.
A STA...
Hey!
IF THAT'S TRUE, YOU CAN'T LAUGH IT OFF.
THOSE PEOPLE ARE PERSISTENT.
SHE MAY COME AFTER YOU AGAIN...
NOOOOO PROBLEM.
EVEN...
...IF THAT WAS KYOKO...
...THAT'S...
Her Best
...THE BEST SHE CAN DO.
And she failed even in that.
I DON'T KNOW WHEN SHE'LL BE ABLE TO COME CLOSE TO ME THE NEXT TIME...
NO, THERE PROBABLY WON'T BE A NEXT TIME.
heh heh heh
She never lets me down.
ha ha ha ha!
?
heh
KYOKO...

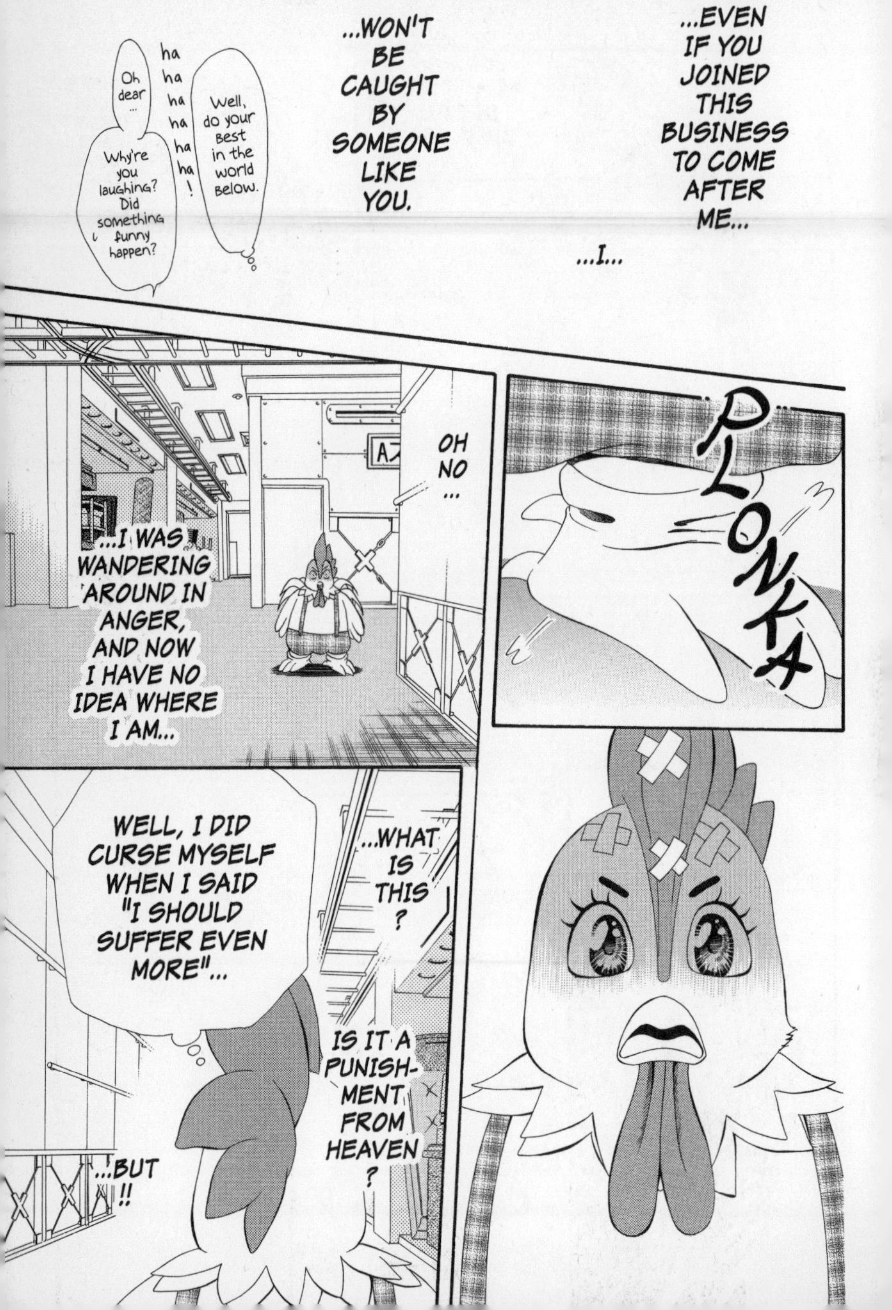
...EVEN IF YOU JOINED THIS BUSINESS TO COME AFTER ME...
...I...
...WON'T BE CAUGHT BY SOMEONE LIKE YOU.
Well, do your best in the world below.
ha ha ha ha ha ha!
Oh dear...
Why're you laughing? Did something funny happen?
PLONKA
OH NO...
...I WAS WANDERING AROUND IN ANGER, AND NOW I HAVE NO IDEA WHERE I AM...
...WHAT IS THIS?
WELL, I DID CURSE MYSELF WHEN I SAID "I SHOULD SUFFER EVEN MORE"...
IS IT A PUNISHMENT FROM HEAVEN?
...BUT!!

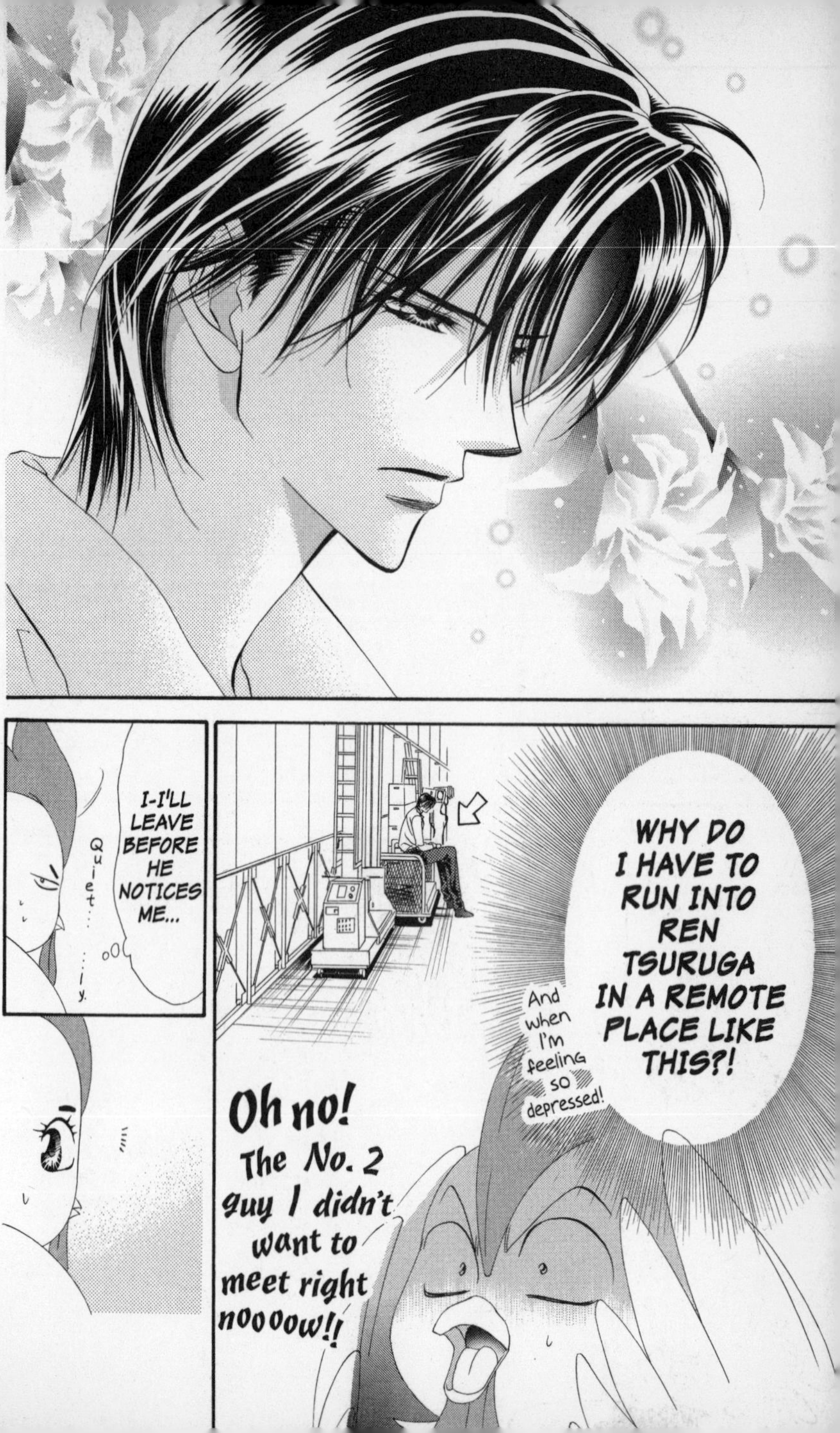
WHY DO I HAVE TO RUN INTO REN TSURUGA IN A REMOTE PLACE LIKE THIS?!
And when I'm feeling so depressed!
Oh no! The No. 2 guy I didn't want to meet right noooow!!
I-I'LL LEAVE BEFORE HE NOTICES ME...
Quiet... ...ly.

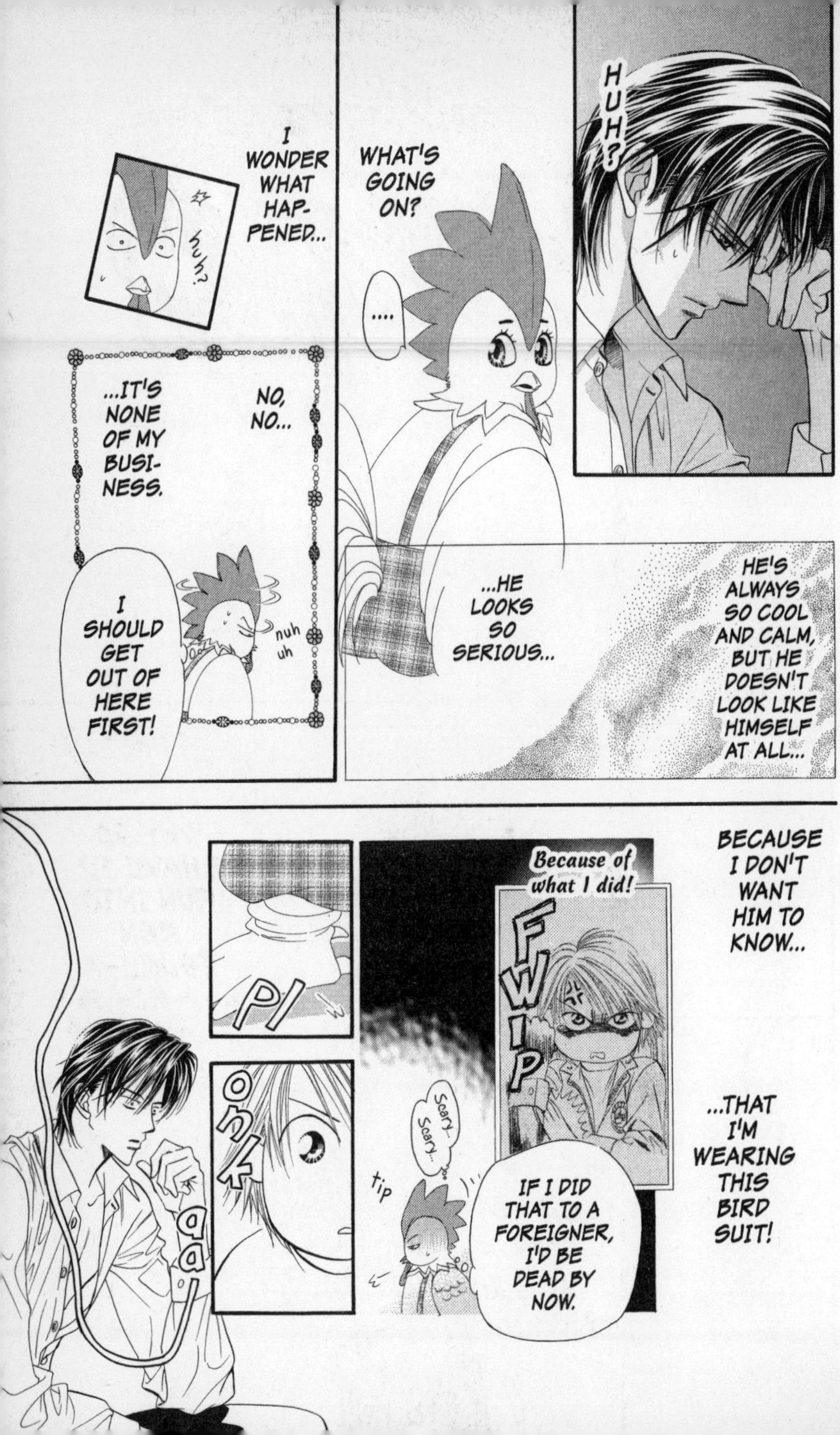

HUH?
WHAT'S GOING ON?
....
I WONDER WHAT HAP-PENED...
huh?
HE'S ALWAYS SO COOL AND CALM, BUT HE DOESN'T LOOK LIKE HIMSELF AT ALL...
...HE LOOKS SO SERIOUS...
NO, NO...
...IT'S NONE OF MY BUSI-NESS.
nuh uh
I SHOULD GET OUT OF HERE FIRST!
BECAUSE I DON'T WANT HIM TO KNOW...
...THAT I'M WEARING THIS BIRD SUIT!
Because of what I did!
FWIP
IF I DID THAT TO A FOREIGNER, I'D BE DEAD BY NOW.
Scary... Scary...
tip
PI
onk
aa

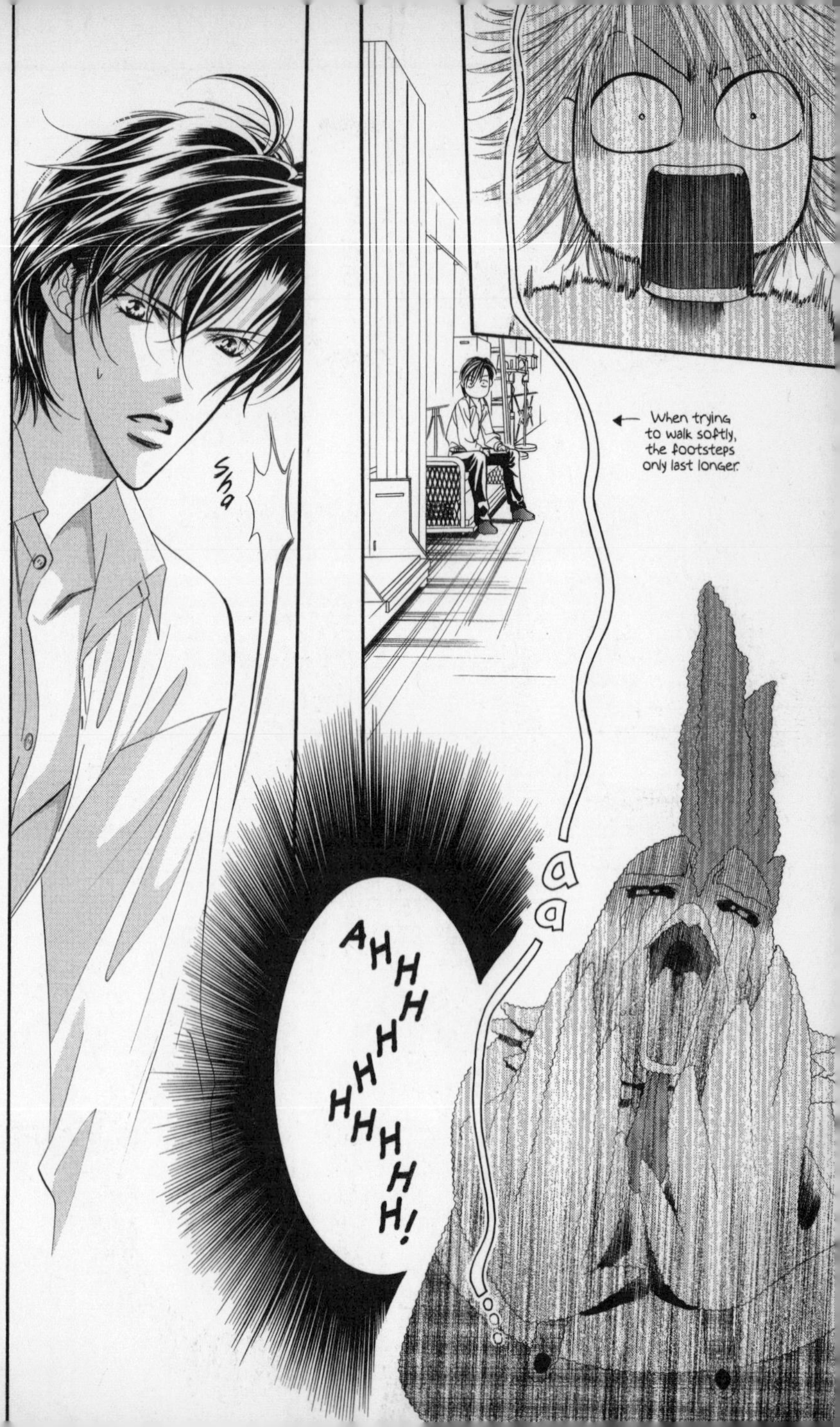
When trying to walk softly, the footsteps only last longer.
aa
AHHHHHHHHHHH!
sha

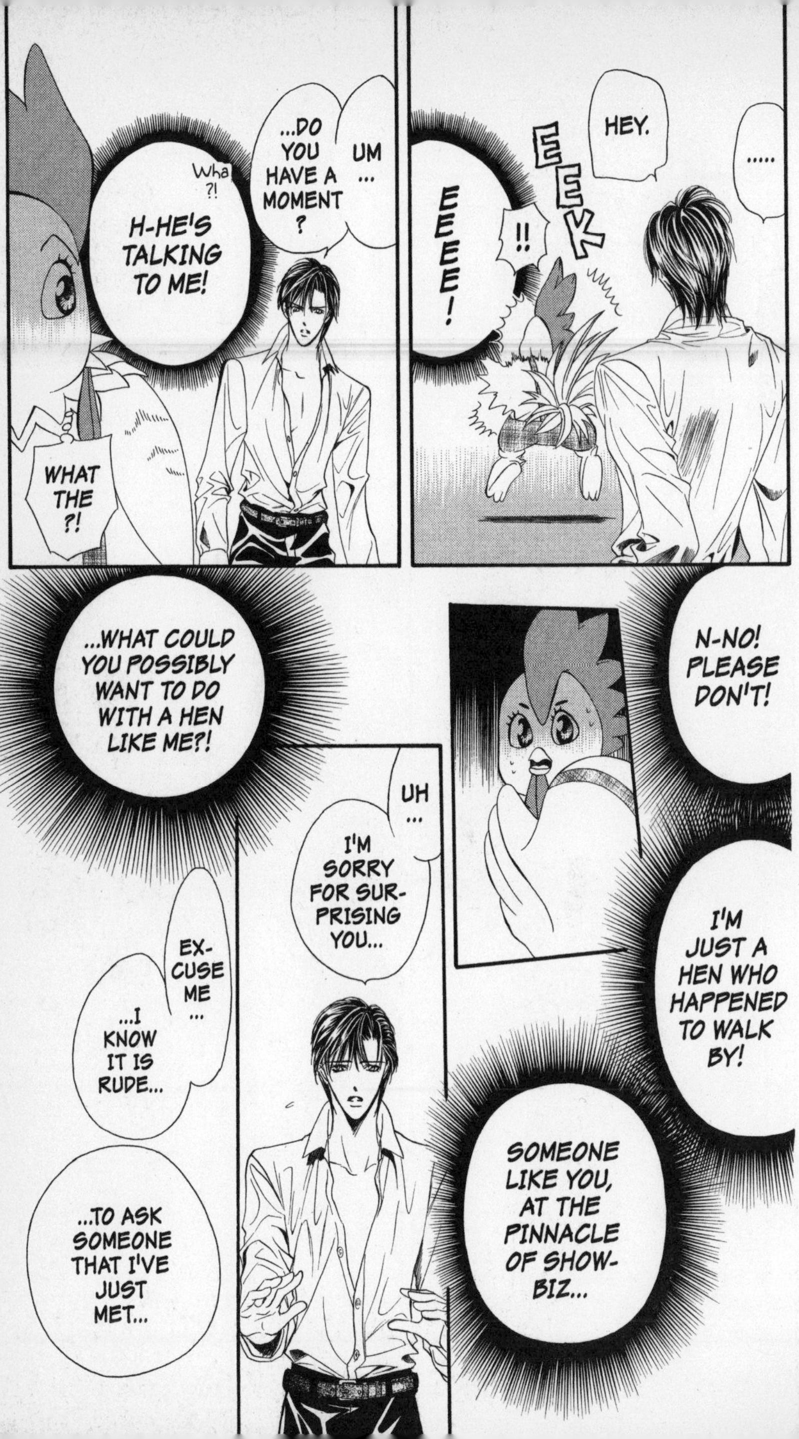
.....
HEY.
EEK
!!
EEEE!
UM ...
...DO YOU HAVE A MOMENT?
Wha ?!
H-HE'S TALKING TO ME!
WHAT THE ?!
N-NO! PLEASE DON'T!
I'M JUST A HEN WHO HAPPENED TO WALK BY!
SOMEONE LIKE YOU, AT THE PINNACLE OF SHOW-BIZ...
...WHAT COULD YOU POSSIBLY WANT TO DO WITH A HEN LIKE ME?!
UH ...
I'M SORRY FOR SUR-PRISING YOU...
EX-CUSE ME ...
...I KNOW IT IS RUDE...
...TO ASK SOMEONE THAT I'VE JUST MET...

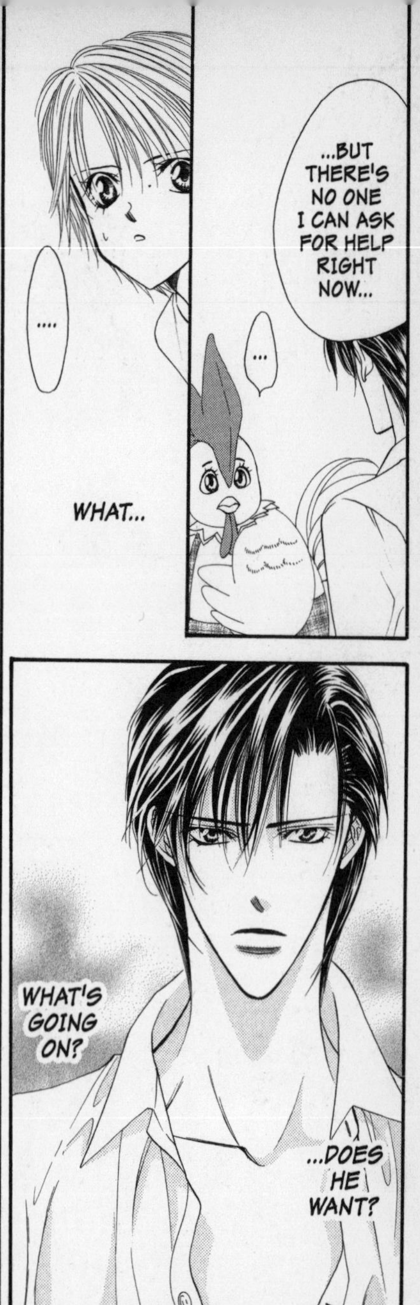
...BUT THERE'S NO ONE I CAN ASK FOR HELP RIGHT NOW...
...
....
WHAT...
WHAT'S GOING ON?
...DOES HE WANT?

End of Act 22

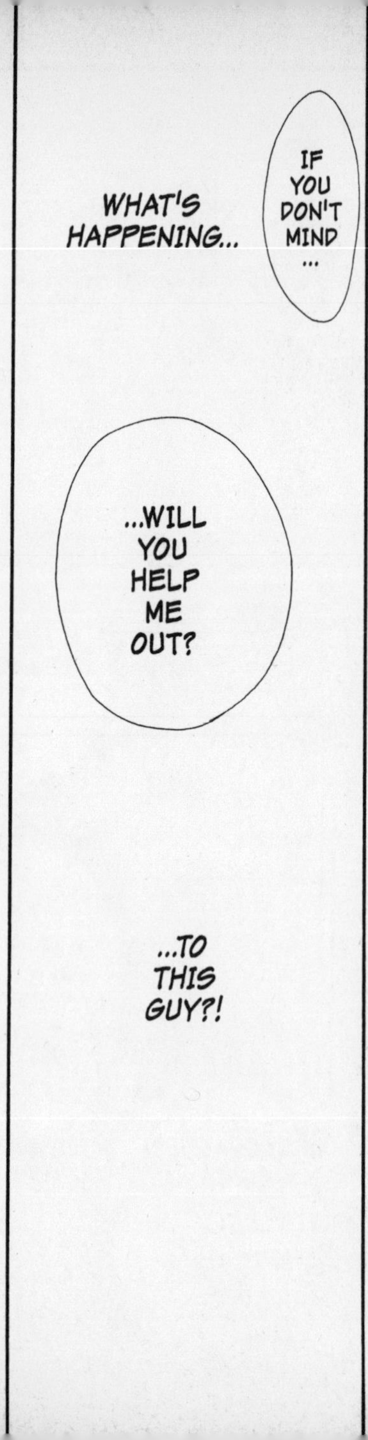
IF YOU DON'T MIND ...
WHAT'S HAPPENING...
...WILL YOU HELP ME OUT?
...TO THIS GUY?!

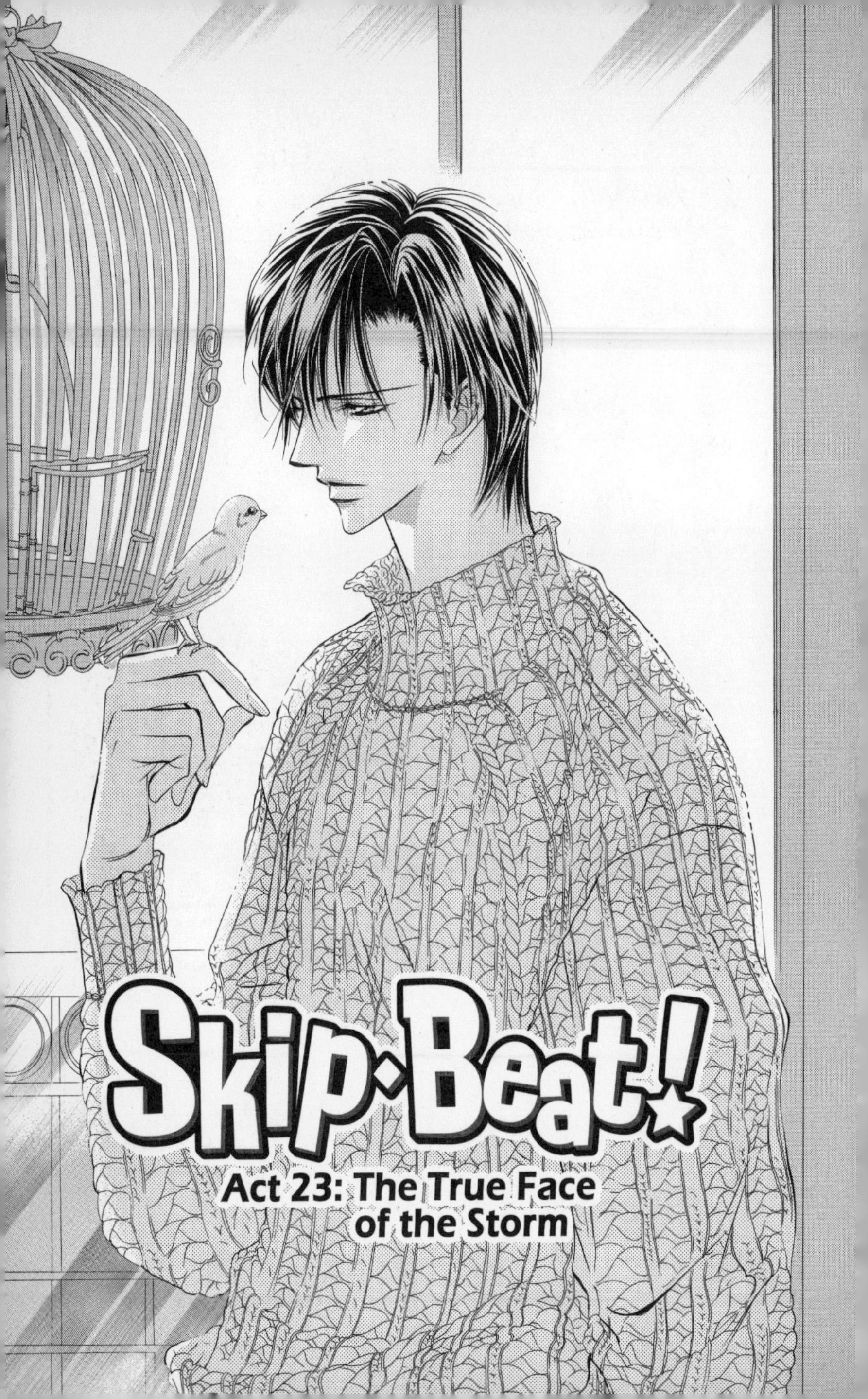
Skip·Beat!
Act 23: The True Face of the Storm

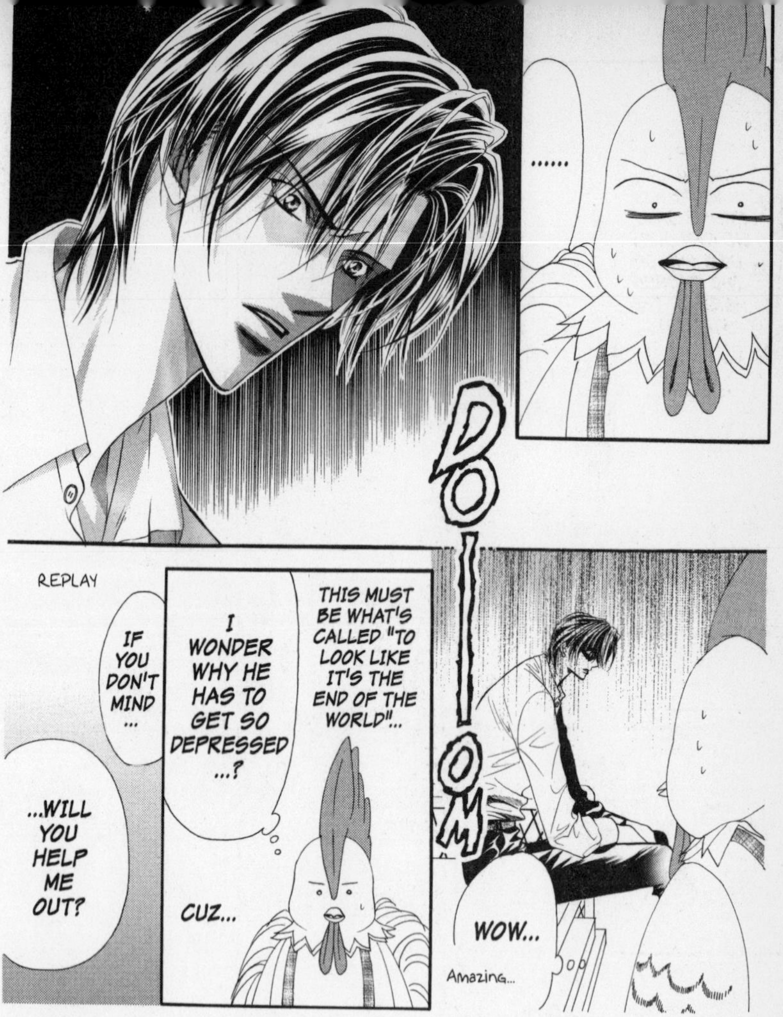
......
DOIOM
WOW...
Amazing...
THIS MUST BE WHAT'S CALLED "TO LOOK LIKE IT'S THE END OF THE WORLD"...
I WONDER WHY HE HAS TO GET SO DEPRESSED ...?
CUZ...
REPLAY
IF YOU DON'T MIND ...
...WILL YOU HELP ME OUT?

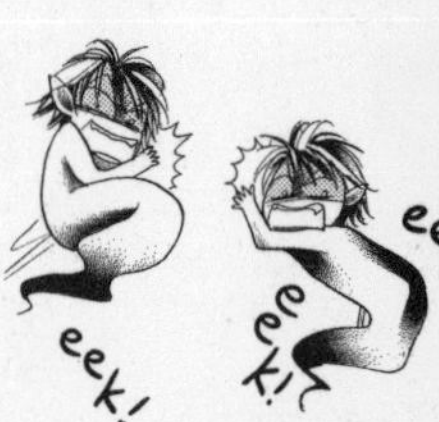
eep!
eek!
eek!

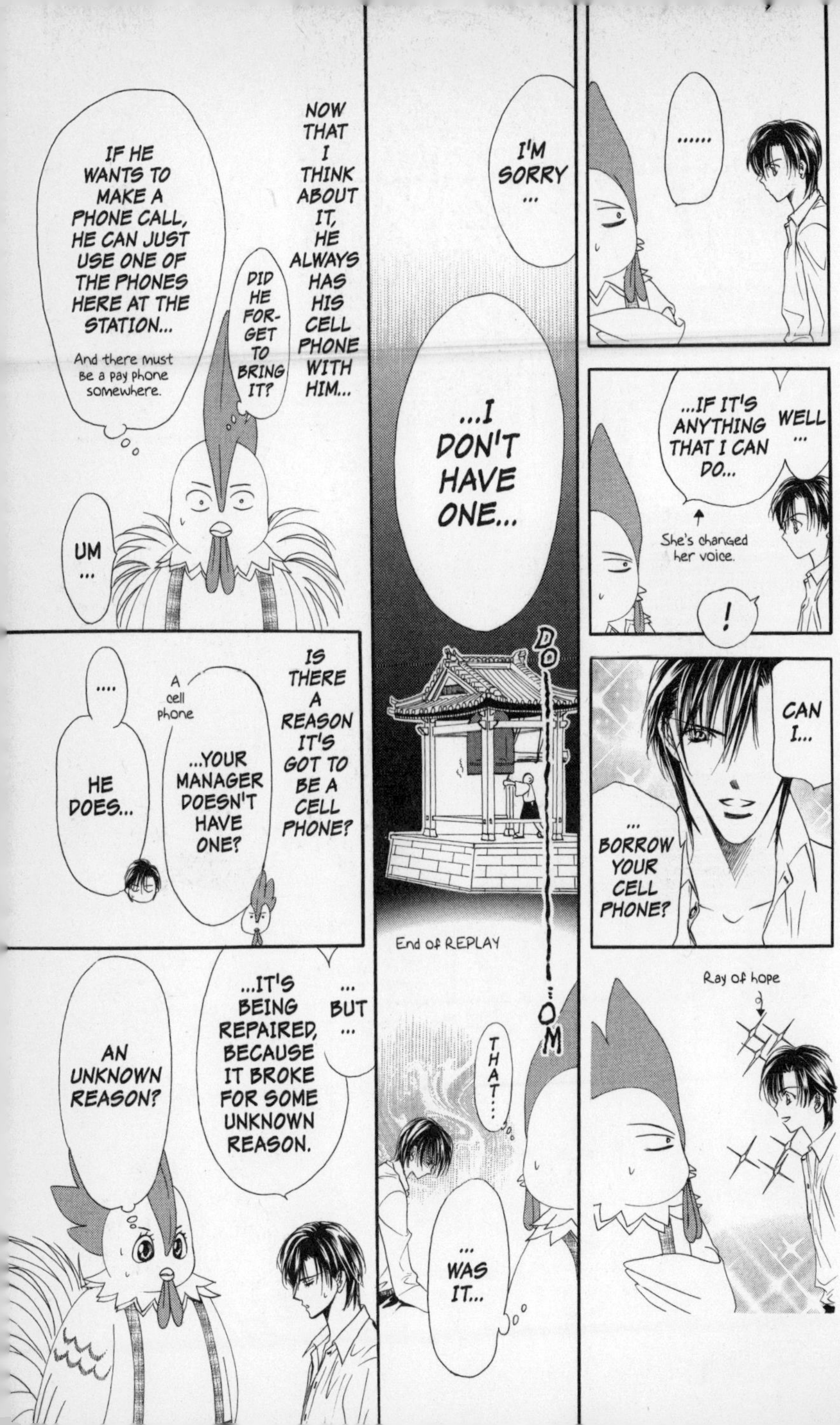
......
WELL ...
...IF IT'S ANYTHING THAT I CAN DO...
She's changed her voice.
!
CAN I...
... BORROW YOUR CELL PHONE?
Ray of hope
I'M SORRY ...
...I DON'T HAVE ONE...
DO......OM
End of REPLAY
THAT...
... WAS IT...
NOW THAT I THINK ABOUT IT, HE ALWAYS HAS HIS CELL PHONE WITH HIM...
DID HE FOR-GET TO BRING IT?
IF HE WANTS TO MAKE A PHONE CALL, HE CAN JUST USE ONE OF THE PHONES HERE AT THE STATION...
And there must be a pay phone somewhere.
UM ...
IS THERE A REASON IT'S GOT TO BE A CELL PHONE?
A cell phone
...YOUR MANAGER DOESN'T HAVE ONE?
....
HE DOES...
... BUT ...
...IT'S BEING REPAIRED, BECAUSE IT BROKE FOR SOME UNKNOWN REASON.
AN UNKNOWN REASON?

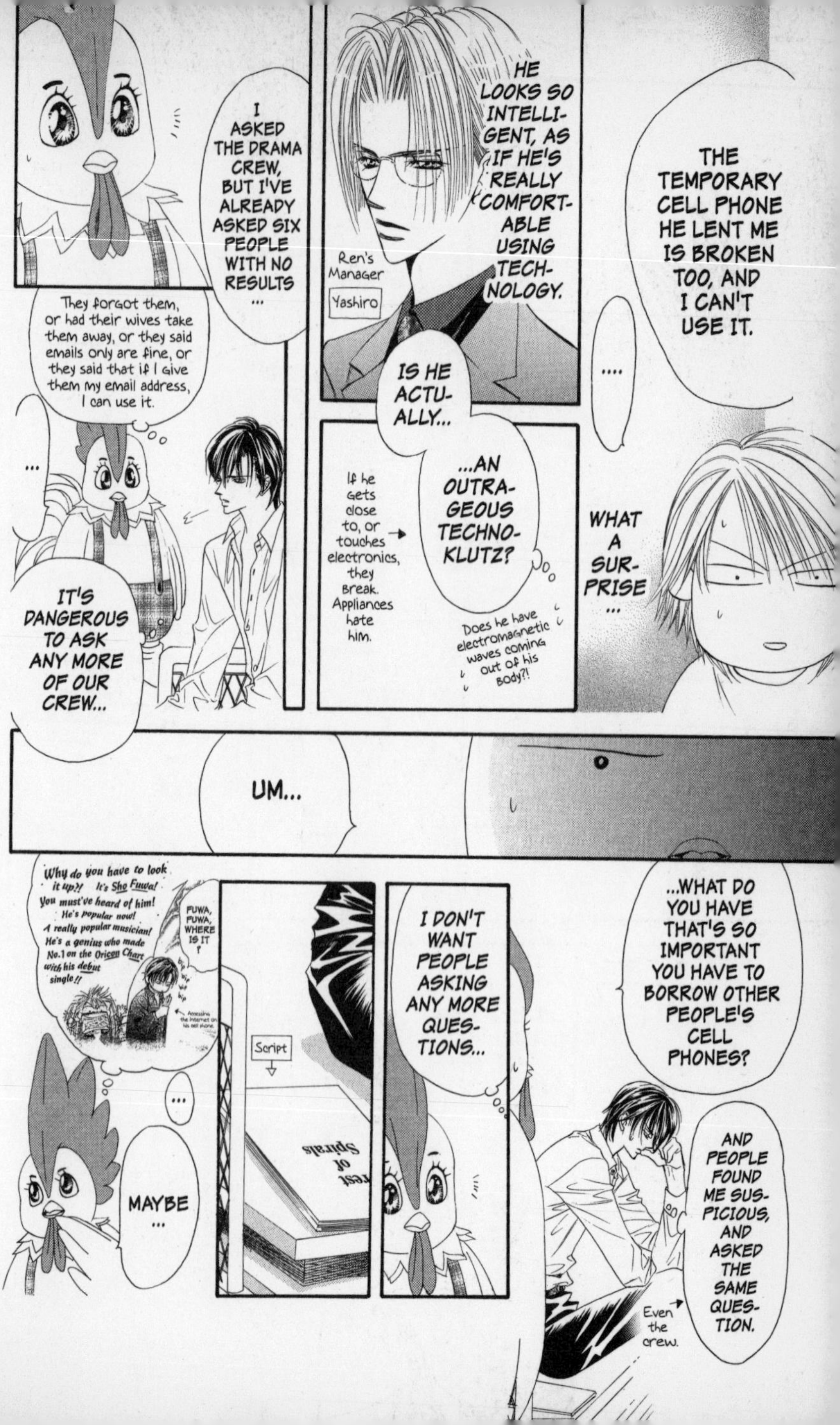
THE TEMPORARY CELL PHONE HE LENT ME IS BROKEN TOO, AND I CAN'T USE IT.
....
WHAT A SURPRISE...
HE LOOKS SO INTELLIGENT, AS IF HE'S REALLY COMFORTABLE USING TECHNOLOGY.
Ren's Manager
Yashiro
IS HE ACTUALLY...
...AN OUTRAGEOUS TECHNO-KLUTZ?
If he gets close to, or touches electronics, they break. Appliances hate him.
Does he have electromagnetic waves coming out of his body?!
I ASKED THE DRAMA CREW, BUT I'VE ALREADY ASKED SIX PEOPLE WITH NO RESULTS...
They forgot them, or had their wives take them away, or they said emails only are fine, or they said that if I give them my email address, I can use it.
...
IT'S DANGEROUS TO ASK ANY MORE OF OUR CREW...
UM...
...WHAT DO YOU HAVE THAT'S SO IMPORTANT YOU HAVE TO BORROW OTHER PEOPLE'S CELL PHONES?
AND PEOPLE FOUND ME SUSPICIOUS, AND ASKED THE SAME QUESTION.
Even the crew.
I DON'T WANT PEOPLE ASKING ANY MORE QUESTIONS...
Script
FUWA, FUWA, WHERE IS IT?
Why do you have to look it up?! It's Sho Fuwa! You must've heard of him! He's popular now! A really popular musician! He's a genius who made No.1 on the Oricon Chart with his debut single!!
bip bip bip bip
Accessing the Internet on his cell phone.
...
MAYBE...

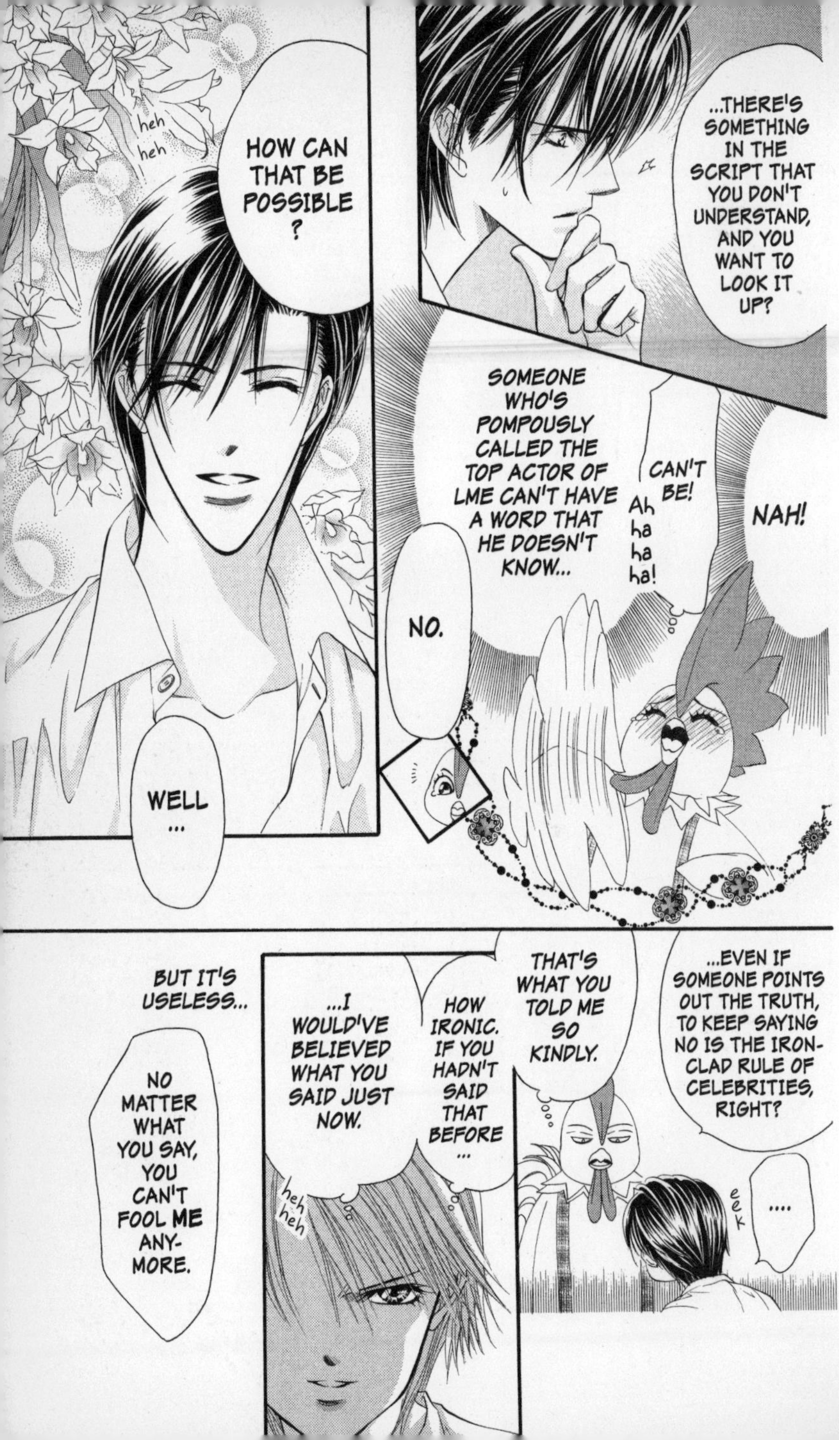

...THERE'S SOMETHING IN THE SCRIPT THAT YOU DON'T UNDERSTAND, AND YOU WANT TO LOOK IT UP?
NAH!
CAN'T BE!
Ah ha ha ha!
SOMEONE WHO'S POMPOUSLY CALLED THE TOP ACTOR OF LME CAN'T HAVE A WORD THAT HE DOESN'T KNOW...
NO.
heh heh
HOW CAN THAT BE POSSIBLE?
WELL...
...EVEN IF SOMEONE POINTS OUT THE TRUTH, TO KEEP SAYING NO IS THE IRON-CLAD RULE OF CELEBRITIES, RIGHT?
THAT'S WHAT YOU TOLD ME SO KINDLY.
eek
....
HOW IRONIC. IF YOU HADN'T SAID THAT BEFORE...
...I WOULD'VE BELIEVED WHAT YOU SAID JUST NOW.
heh heh
BUT IT'S USELESS...
NO MATTER WHAT YOU SAY, YOU CAN'T FOOL ME ANY-MORE.

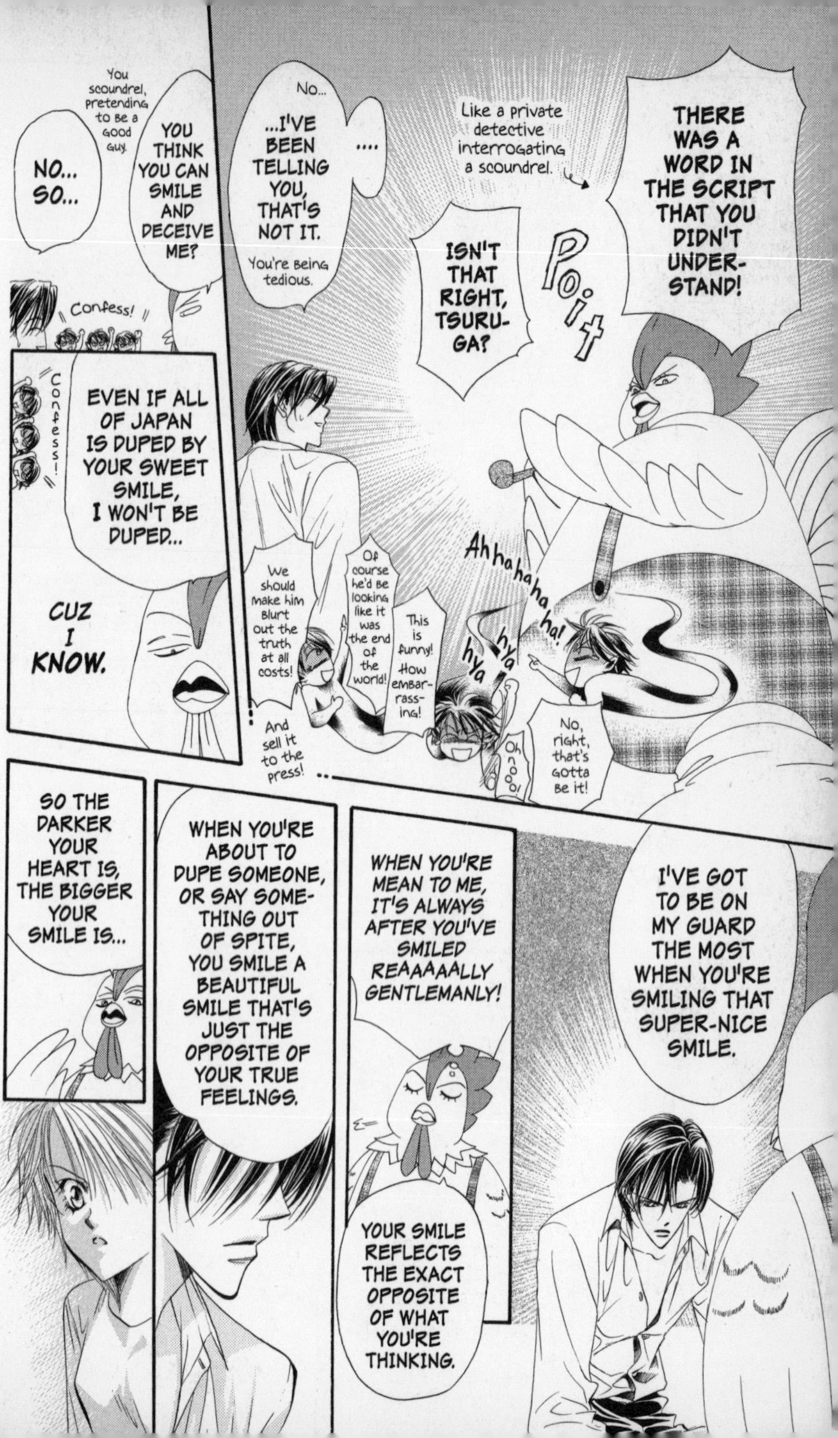
THERE WAS A WORD IN THE SCRIPT THAT YOU DIDN'T UNDER-STAND!
Like a private detective interrogating a scoundrel.
Poit
ISN'T THAT RIGHT, TSURU-GA?
No...
...I'VE BEEN TELLING YOU, THAT'S NOT IT.
You're being tedious.
....
YOU THINK YOU CAN SMILE AND DECEIVE ME?
You scoundrel, pretending to be a good guy.
NO... SO...
Confess!
Ahhahahaha!
hya hya
No, right, that's gotta be it!
Oh nooo!
This is funny! How embar-rass-ing!
Of course he'd be looking like it was the end of the world!
We should make him blurt out the truth at all costs!
And sell it to the press!
Confess!
EVEN IF ALL OF JAPAN IS DUPED BY YOUR SWEET SMILE, I WON'T BE DUPED...
CUZ I KNOW.
I'VE GOT TO BE ON MY GUARD THE MOST WHEN YOU'RE SMILING THAT SUPER-NICE SMILE.
WHEN YOU'RE MEAN TO ME, IT'S ALWAYS AFTER YOU'VE SMILED REAAAAALLY GENTLEMANLY!
YOUR SMILE REFLECTS THE EXACT OPPOSITE OF WHAT YOU'RE THINKING.
WHEN YOU'RE ABOUT TO DUPE SOMEONE, OR SAY SOME-THING OUT OF SPITE, YOU SMILE A BEAUTIFUL SMILE THAT'S JUST THE OPPOSITE OF YOUR TRUE FEELINGS.
SO THE DARKER YOUR HEART IS, THE BIGGER YOUR SMILE IS...

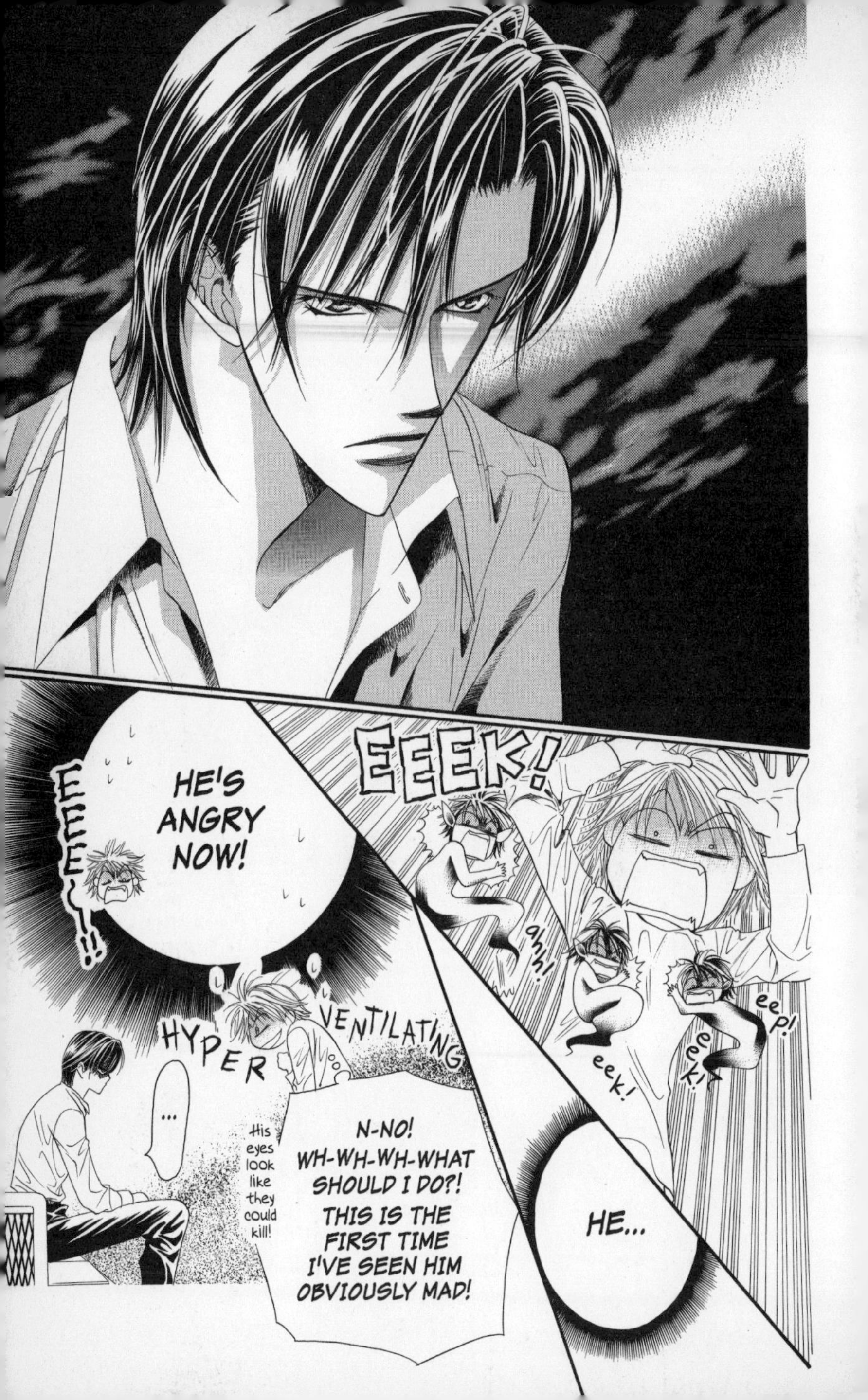
EEEK!
ahh!
eep!
eeek!
eek!
HE'S ANGRY NOW!
EEEE~~!!
HE...
HYPER VENTILATING
N-NO! WH-WH-WH-WHAT SHOULD I DO?! THIS IS THE FIRST TIME I'VE SEEN HIM OBVIOUSLY MAD!
His eyes look like they could kill!
...

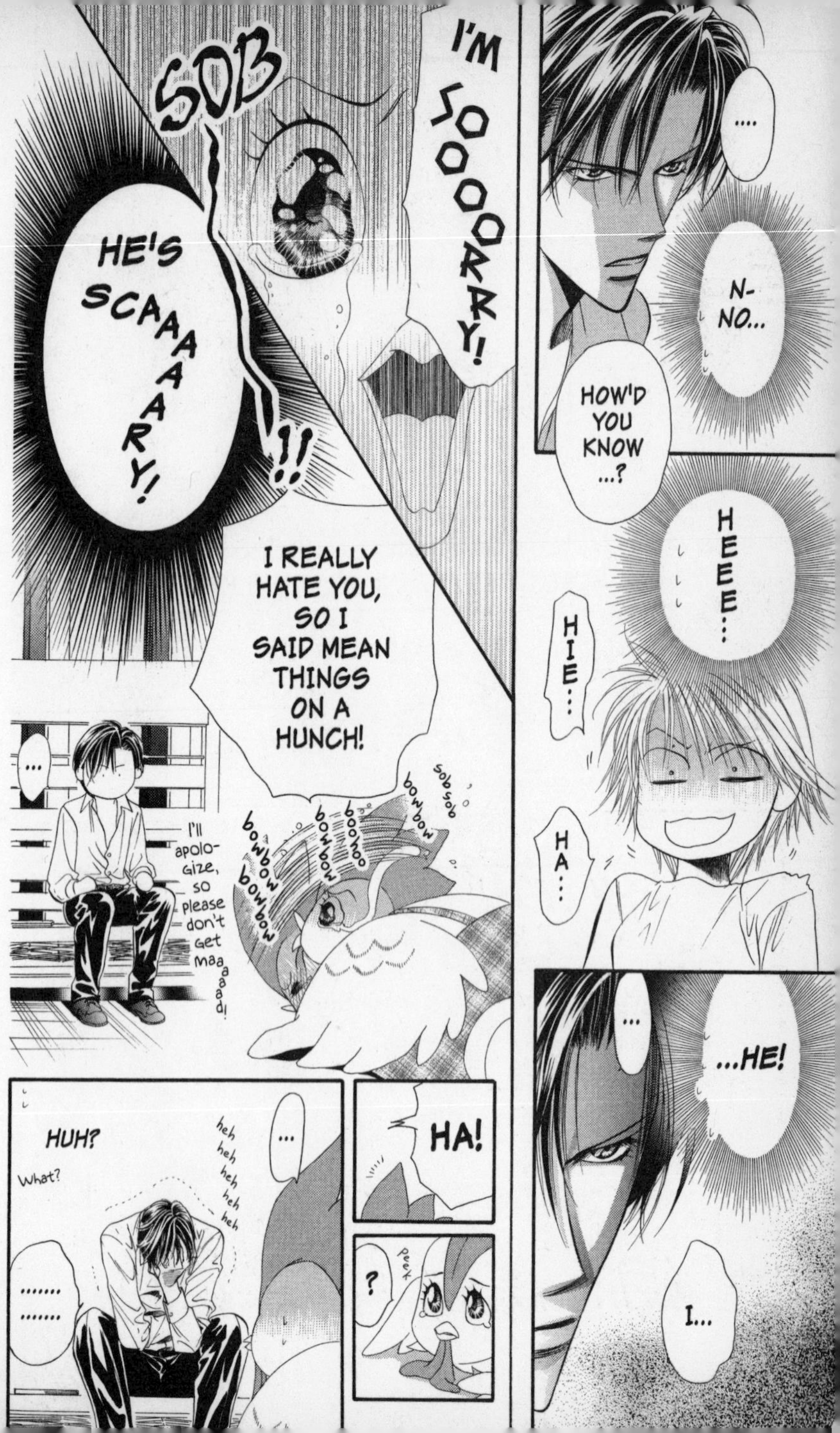
....
N-NO...
HOW'D YOU KNOW ...?
HEEE...
HIE...
HA...
...
...HE!
I...
I'M SOOOORRY!
SOB
HE'S SCAAAAARY!
!!
I REALLY HATE YOU, SO I SAID MEAN THINGS ON A HUNCH!
sob sob
bowbow
boohoo
bowbow
bowbow
bowbow
...
I'll apologize, so please don't get maaaaad!
HA!
?
peek
...
HUH?
What?
heh heh heh heh heh
....
....

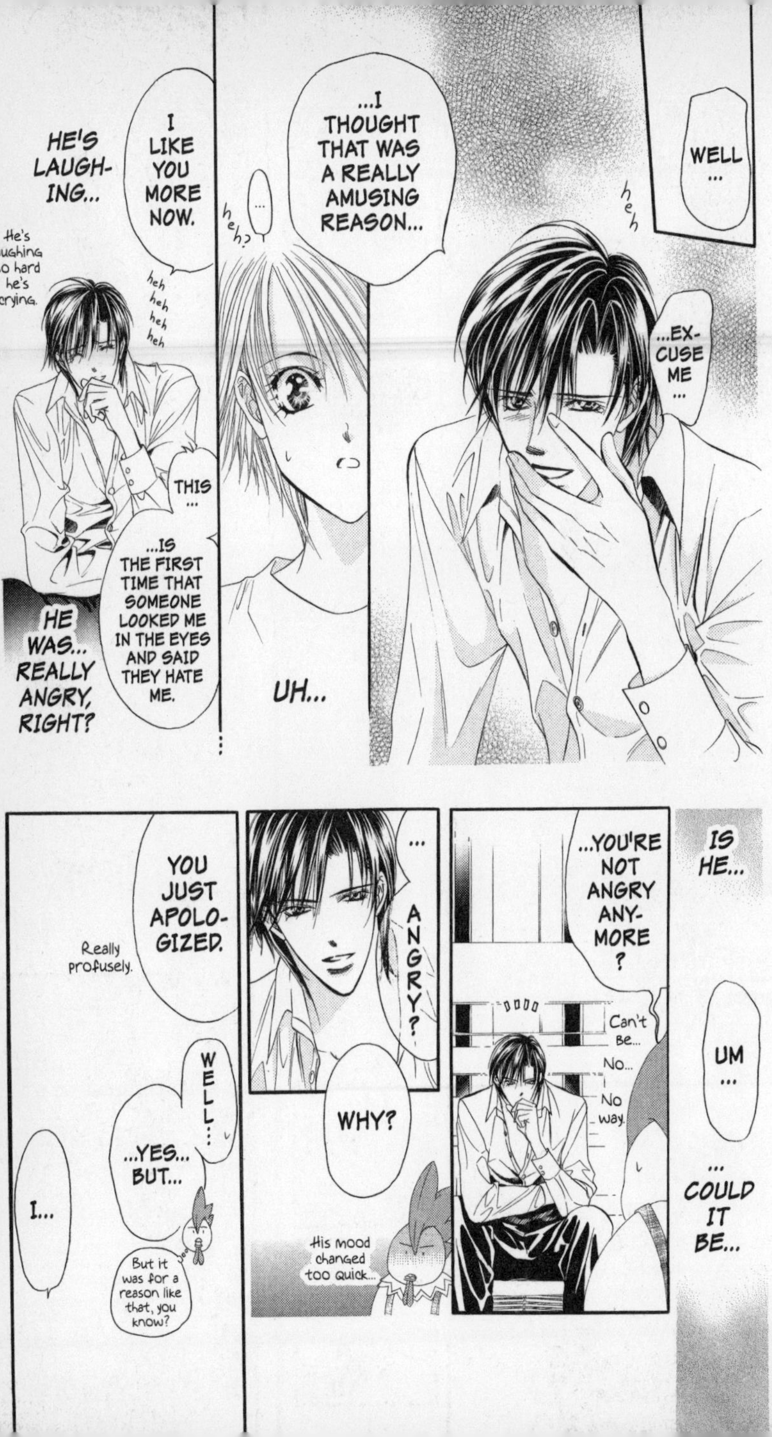
WELL...
heh heh
...EXCUSE ME...
...I THOUGHT THAT WAS A REALLY AMUSING REASON...
...
heh?
UH...
I LIKE YOU MORE NOW.
HE'S LAUGHING...
He's laughing so hard he's crying.
heh heh heh heh
THIS...
...IS THE FIRST TIME THAT SOMEONE LOOKED ME IN THE EYES AND SAID THEY HATE ME.
HE WAS... REALLY ANGRY, RIGHT?
IS HE...
UM...
...COULD IT BE...
...YOU'RE NOT ANGRY ANYMORE?
Can't be...
No...
No way.
...
ANGRY?
WHY?
His mood changed too quick...
YOU JUST APOLOGIZED.
Really profusely.
WELL...
...YES... BUT...
I...
But it was for a reason like that, you know?

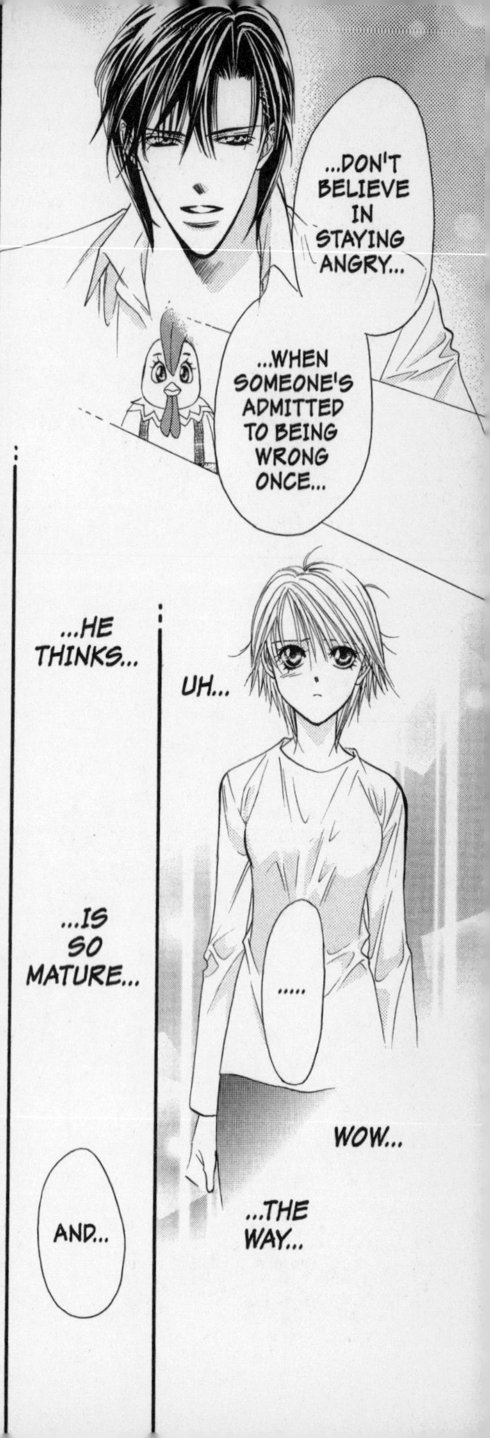
...DON'T BELIEVE IN STAYING ANGRY...
...WHEN SOMEONE'S ADMITTED TO BEING WRONG ONCE...
UH...
.....
WOW...
...THE WAY...
...HE THINKS...
...IS SO MATURE...
AND...
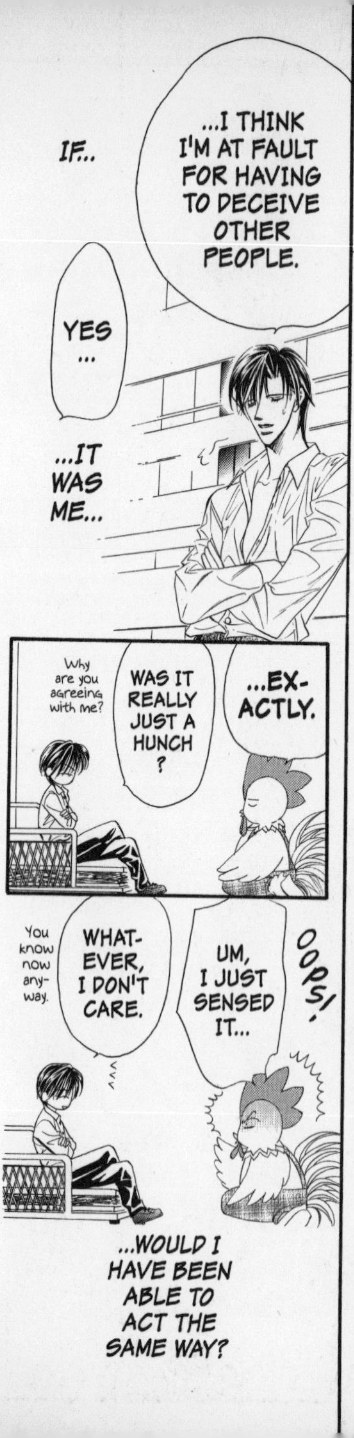
...I THINK I'M AT FAULT FOR HAVING TO DECEIVE OTHER PEOPLE.
IF...
YES...
...IT WAS ME...
...EX-ACTLY.
WAS IT REALLY JUST A HUNCH?
Why are you agreeing with me?
OOPS!
UM, I JUST SENSED IT...
WHAT-EVER, I DON'T CARE.
You know now any-way.
...WOULD I HAVE BEEN ABLE TO ACT THE SAME WAY?

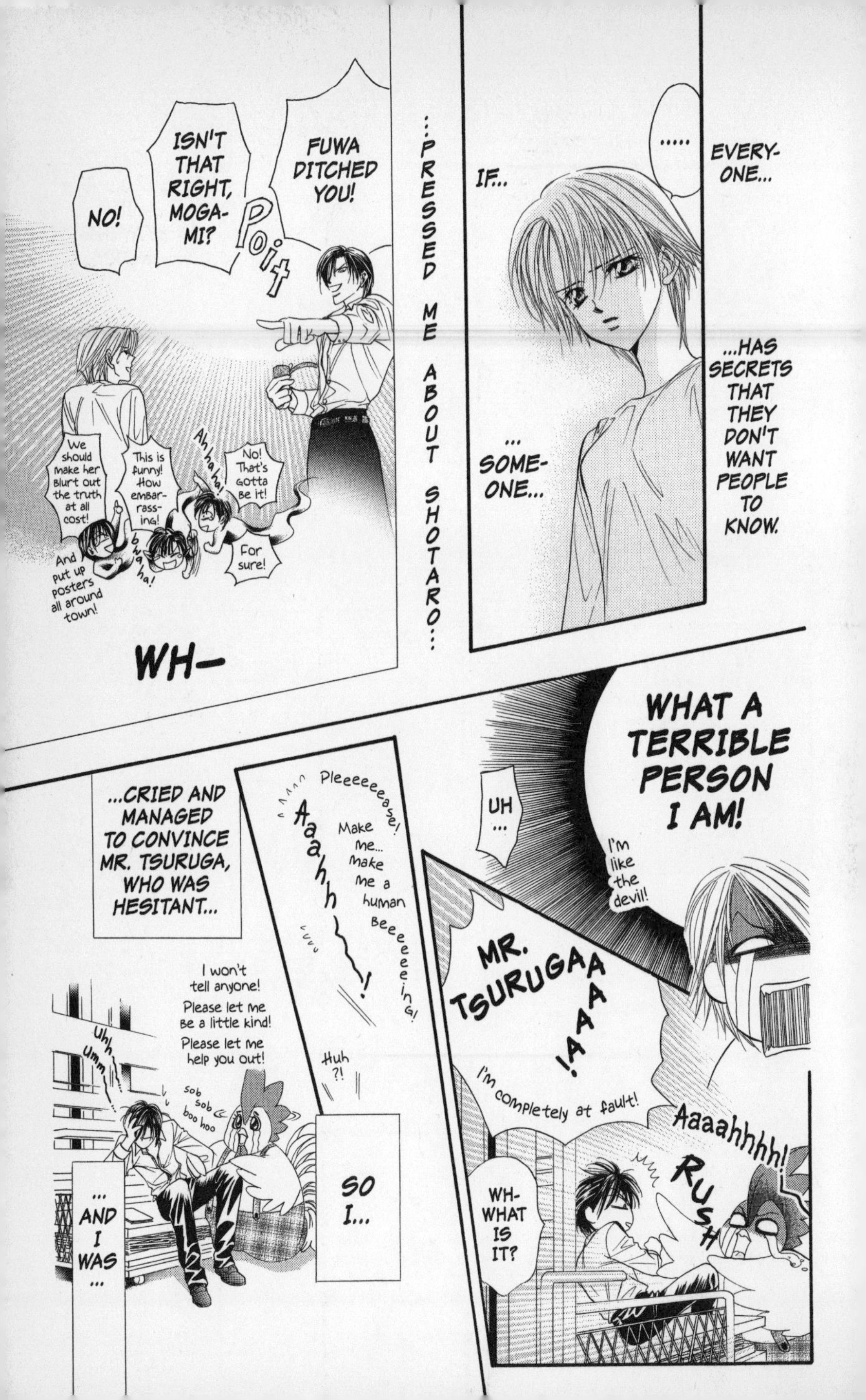
.....
EVERY-ONE...
IF...
...HAS SECRETS THAT THEY DON'T WANT PEOPLE TO KNOW.
...SOME-ONE...
...PRESSED ME ABOUT SHOTARO...
FUWA DITCHED YOU!
ISN'T THAT RIGHT, MOGA-MI?
Poit
NO!
No! That's gotta be it!
Ah ha ha!
This is funny! How embar-rass-ing!
We should make her blurt out the truth at all cost!
For sure!
bwaha!
And put up posters all around town!
WH-
WHAT A TERRIBLE PERSON I AM!
UH ...
I'm like the devil!
MR. TSURUGAAAAA!
I'm completely at fault!
Aaaahhhhh!
RUSH
WH-WHAT IS IT?
Pleeeeeeease!
Aaaahh—!
Make me... make me a human Beeeeeeeing!
Huh ?!
SO I...
...CRIED AND MANAGED TO CONVINCE MR. TSURUGA, WHO WAS HESITANT...
I won't tell anyone! Please let me be a little kind! Please let me help you out!
Uhh Umm
sob sob boo hoo
...AND I WAS ...

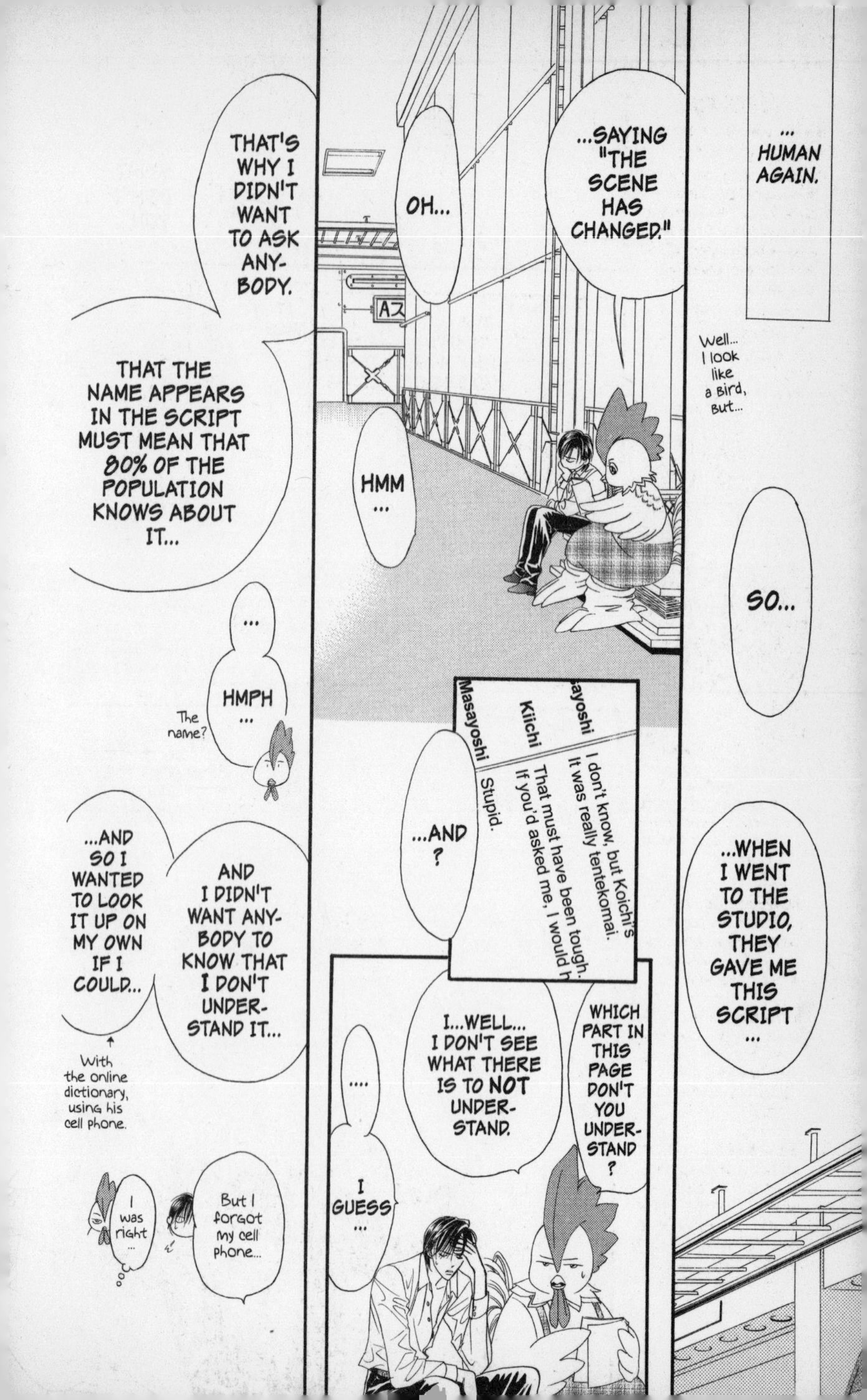

... HUMAN AGAIN.
Well... I look like a Bird, But...
SO...
...WHEN I WENT TO THE STUDIO, THEY GAVE ME THIS SCRIPT ...
...SAYING "THE SCENE HAS CHANGED."
OH...
HMM ...
ayoshi I don't know, but Koichi's
It was really tentekomai.
Kiichi That must have been tough.
If you'd asked me, I would h
Masayoshi Stupid.
...AND ?
WHICH PART IN THIS PAGE DON'T YOU UNDERSTAND?
I...WELL... I DON'T SEE WHAT THERE IS TO NOT UNDERSTAND.
....
I GUESS ...
THAT'S WHY I DIDN'T WANT TO ASK ANY-BODY.
THAT THE NAME APPEARS IN THE SCRIPT MUST MEAN THAT 80% OF THE POPULATION KNOWS ABOUT IT...
...
HMPH ...
The name?
AND I DIDN'T WANT ANY-BODY TO KNOW THAT I DON'T UNDER-STAND IT...
...AND SO I WANTED TO LOOK IT UP ON MY OWN IF I COULD...
With the online dictionary, using his cell phone.
But I forgot my cell phone...
I was right ...

History

The name is "Bo" by process of association. "Kimagure" of "Kimagure Rock" → Kimagure (Whimsical) → Free and easy → Wanderer → Bo. And for me, gives me this image...

S-Samurai?

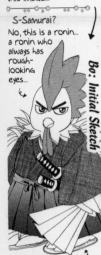

No, this is a ronin... a ronin who always has rough-looking eyes...

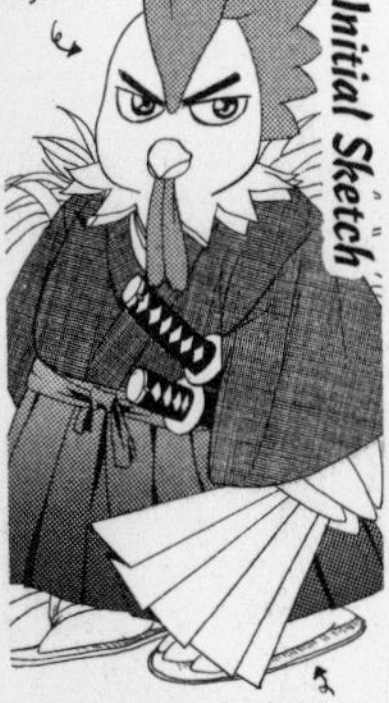

Bo: Initial Sketch

And his own harisen to put a rough punch line in no matter how famous the guest is.

However...this wasn't cute enough to be a mascot of a show, so the visuals changed to the current one...

Bo became a hen in the same way. Wanderer → Wandering in the direction the wind blows → Weathercock → Hen.

So actually, when I was working on my storyboards, the name wasn't "Bo" but "Midori" from the weathercock. But I think "Bo" suits it better now.

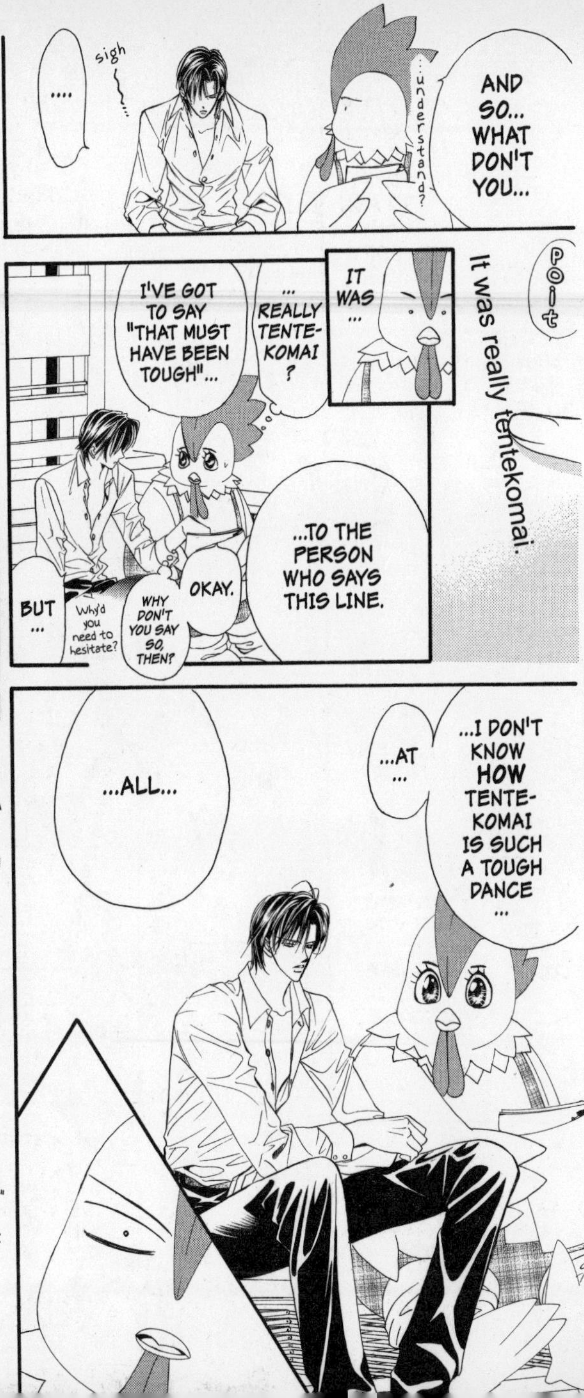

AND SO... WHAT DON'T YOU...
...understand?
sigh
....
It was really tentekomai.
Poit
IT WAS ...
... REALLY TENTE-KOMAI ?
I'VE GOT TO SAY "THAT MUST HAVE BEEN TOUGH"...
...TO THE PERSON WHO SAYS THIS LINE.
OKAY.
WHY DON'T YOU SAY SO, THEN?
Why'd you need to hesitate?
BUT ...
...I DON'T KNOW HOW TENTE-KOMAI IS SUCH A TOUGH DANCE ...
...AT ...
...ALL...

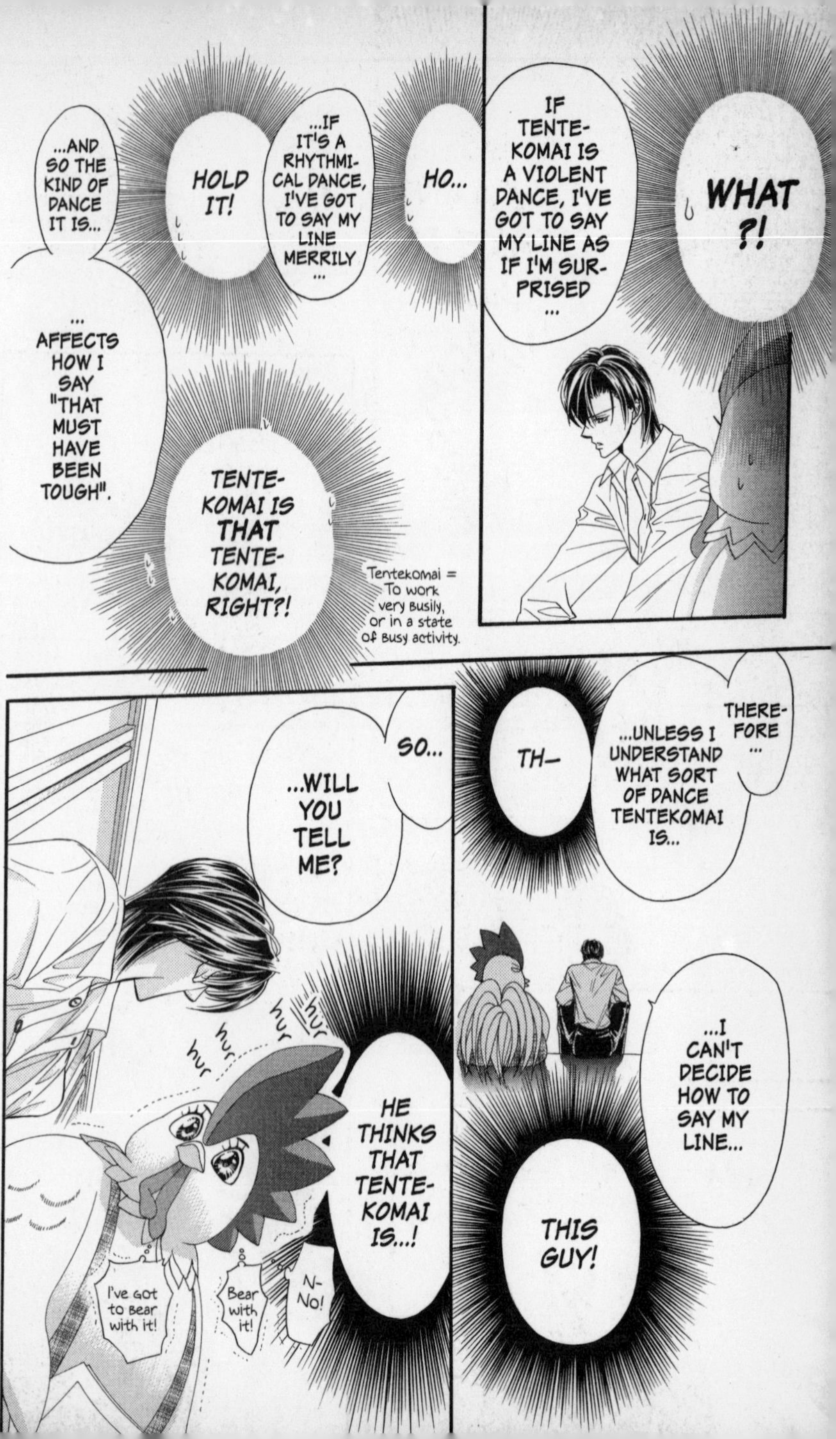
WHAT?!
IF TENTE-KOMAI IS A VIOLENT DANCE, I'VE GOT TO SAY MY LINE AS IF I'M SUR-PRISED...
HO...
...IF IT'S A RHYTHMI-CAL DANCE, I'VE GOT TO SAY MY LINE MERRILY...
HOLD IT!
...AND SO THE KIND OF DANCE IT IS...
...AFFECTS HOW I SAY "THAT MUST HAVE BEEN TOUGH".
TENTE-KOMAI IS THAT TENTE-KOMAI, RIGHT?!
Tentekomai = To work very busily, or in a state of busy activity.
THERE-FORE...
...UNLESS I UNDERSTAND WHAT SORT OF DANCE TENTEKOMAI IS...
TH—
...I CAN'T DECIDE HOW TO SAY MY LINE...
THIS GUY!
SO...
...WILL YOU TELL ME?
hur hur hur hur
HE THINKS THAT TENTE-KOMAI IS...!
N-No!
Bear with it!
I've got to bear with it!

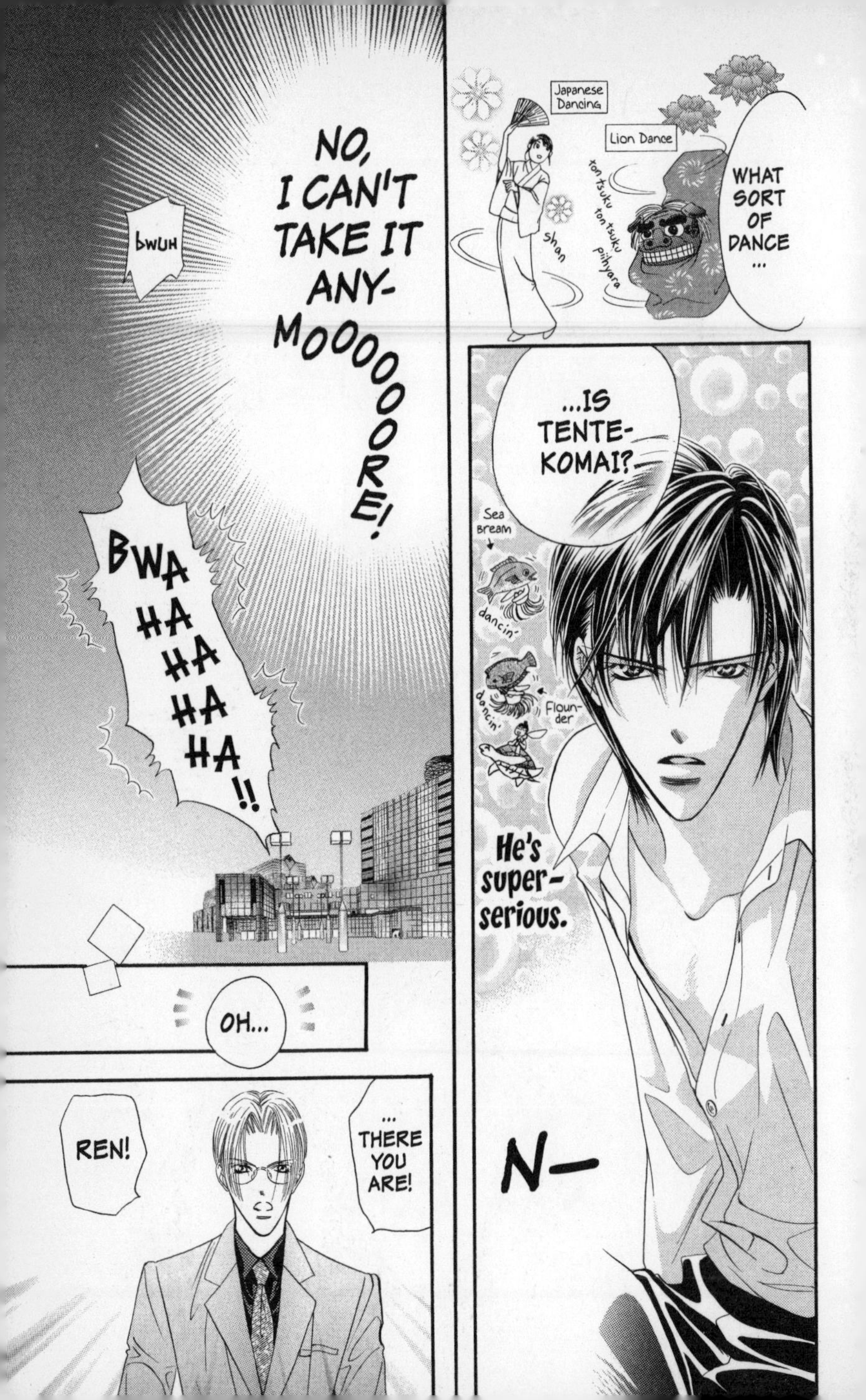
WHAT SORT OF DANCE ...
Japanese Dancing
Lion Dance
ton tsuku ton tsuku piihyara
shan
...IS TENTE-KOMAI?
Sea Bream
dancin-
Flounder
dancin-
He's super-serious.
N—
NO, I CAN'T TAKE IT ANY-MOOOOOOORE!
bwuh
BWAHAHAHAHAHA!!
OH...
...THERE YOU ARE!
REN!

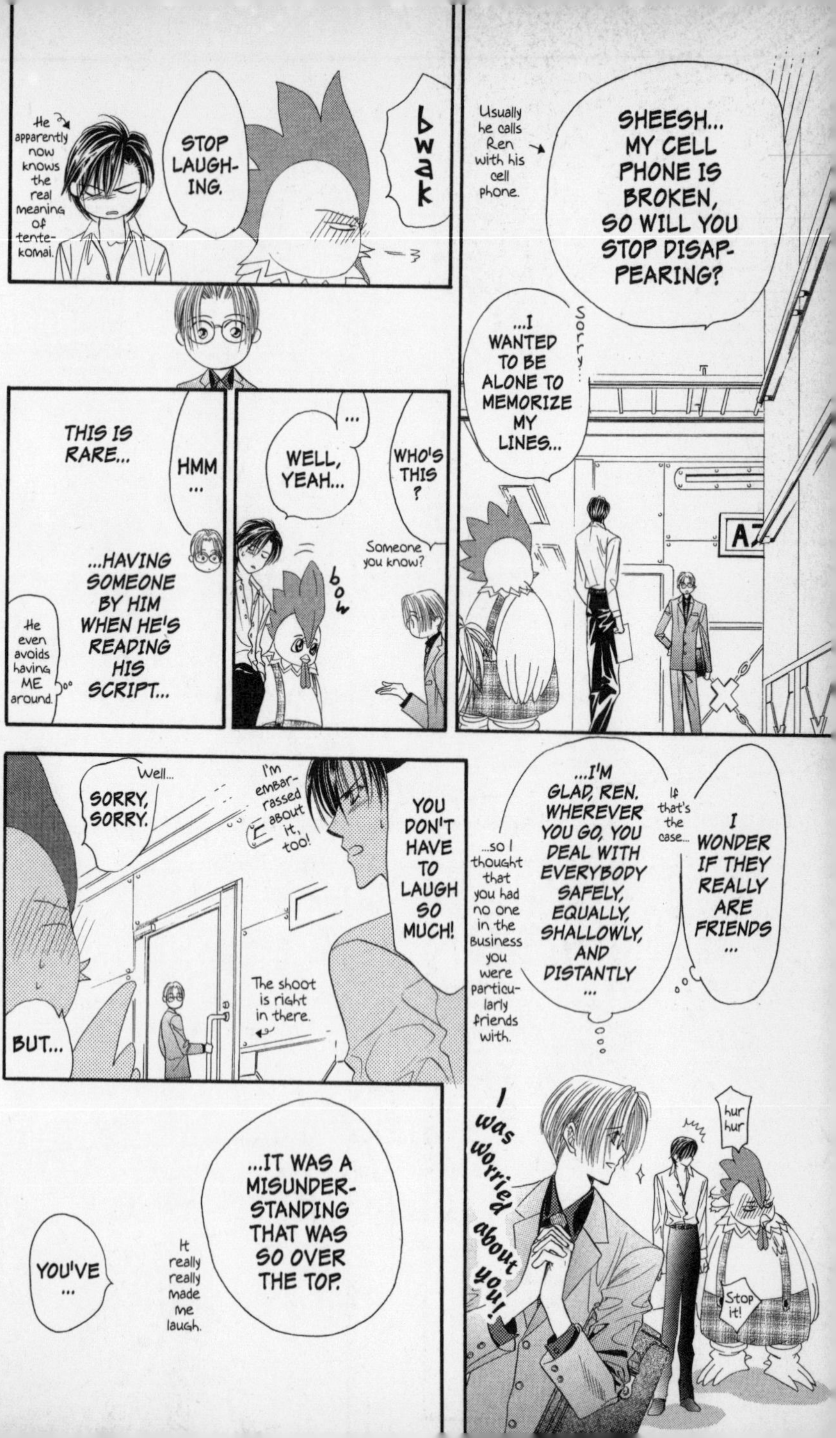
Usually he calls Ren with his cell phone.
SHEESH... MY CELL PHONE IS BROKEN, SO WILL YOU STOP DISAP-PEARING?
Sorry...
...I WANTED TO BE ALONE TO MEMORIZE MY LINES...
A7
bwak
STOP LAUGH-ING.
He apparently now knows the real meaning of tente-komai.
WHO'S THIS?
...
WELL, YEAH...
Someone you know?
bow
HMM ...
THIS IS RARE...
...HAVING SOMEONE BY HIM WHEN HE'S READING HIS SCRIPT...
He even avoids having ME around.
...I'M GLAD, REN. WHEREVER YOU GO, YOU DEAL WITH EVERYBODY SAFELY, EQUALLY, SHALLOWLY, AND DISTANTLY ...
...so I thought that you had no one in the business you were particu-larly friends with.
If that's the case...
I WONDER IF THEY REALLY ARE FRIENDS ...
YOU DON'T HAVE TO LAUGH SO MUCH!
I'm embar-rassed about it, too!
Well...
SORRY, SORRY.
The shoot is right in there.
BUT...
hur hur
I was worried about you!
Stop it!
...IT WAS A MISUNDER-STANDING THAT WAS SO OVER THE TOP.
It really really made me laugh.
YOU'VE ...

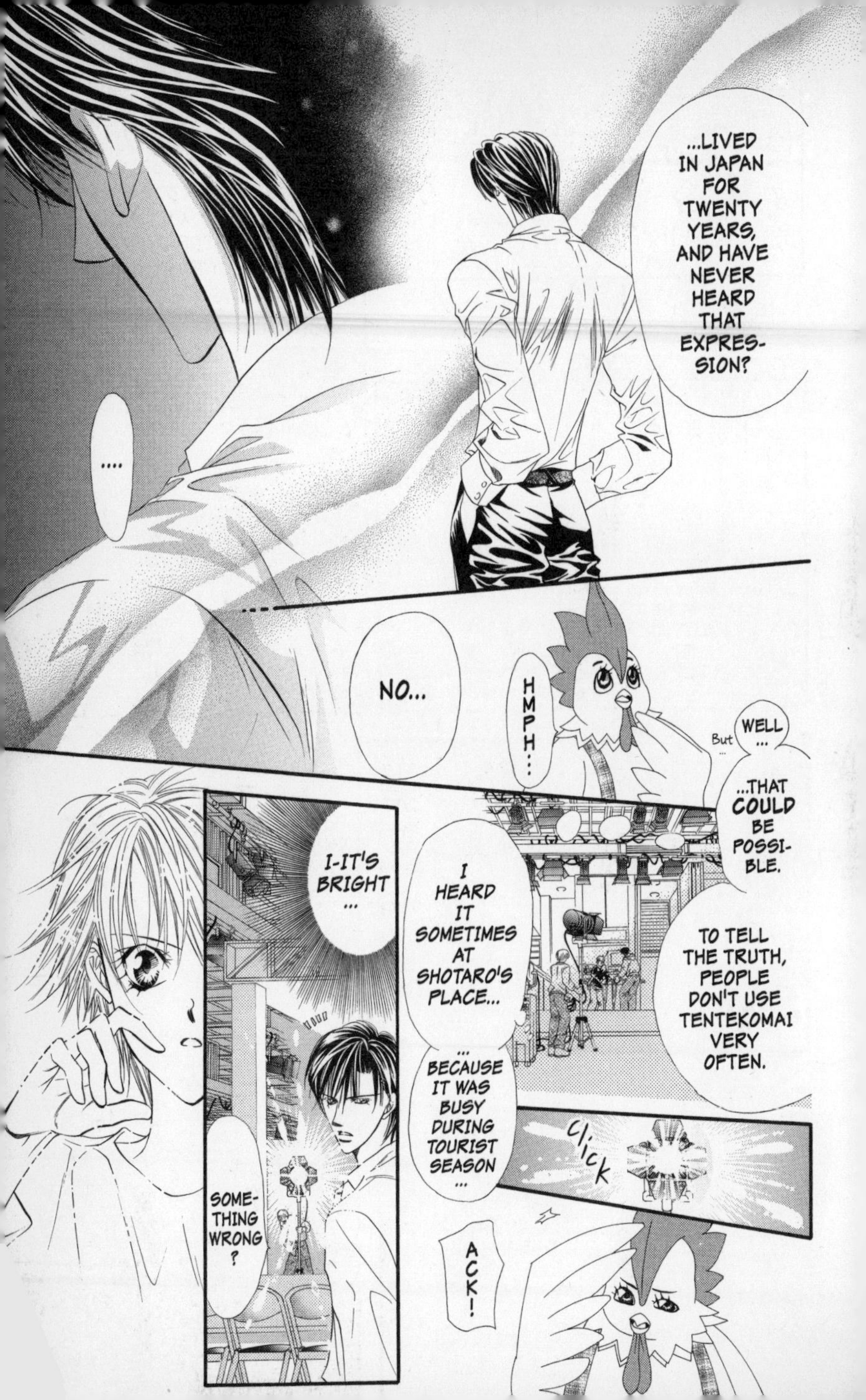

...LIVED IN JAPAN FOR TWENTY YEARS, AND HAVE NEVER HEARD THAT EXPRESSION?
....
WELL...
But...
...THAT COULD BE POSSIBLE.
HMPH...
NO...
TO TELL THE TRUTH, PEOPLE DON'T USE TENTEKOMAI VERY OFTEN.
I HEARD IT SOMETIMES AT SHOTARO'S PLACE...
...BECAUSE IT WAS BUSY DURING TOURIST SEASON...
CLICK
ACK!
I-IT'S BRIGHT...
SOME-THING WRONG?

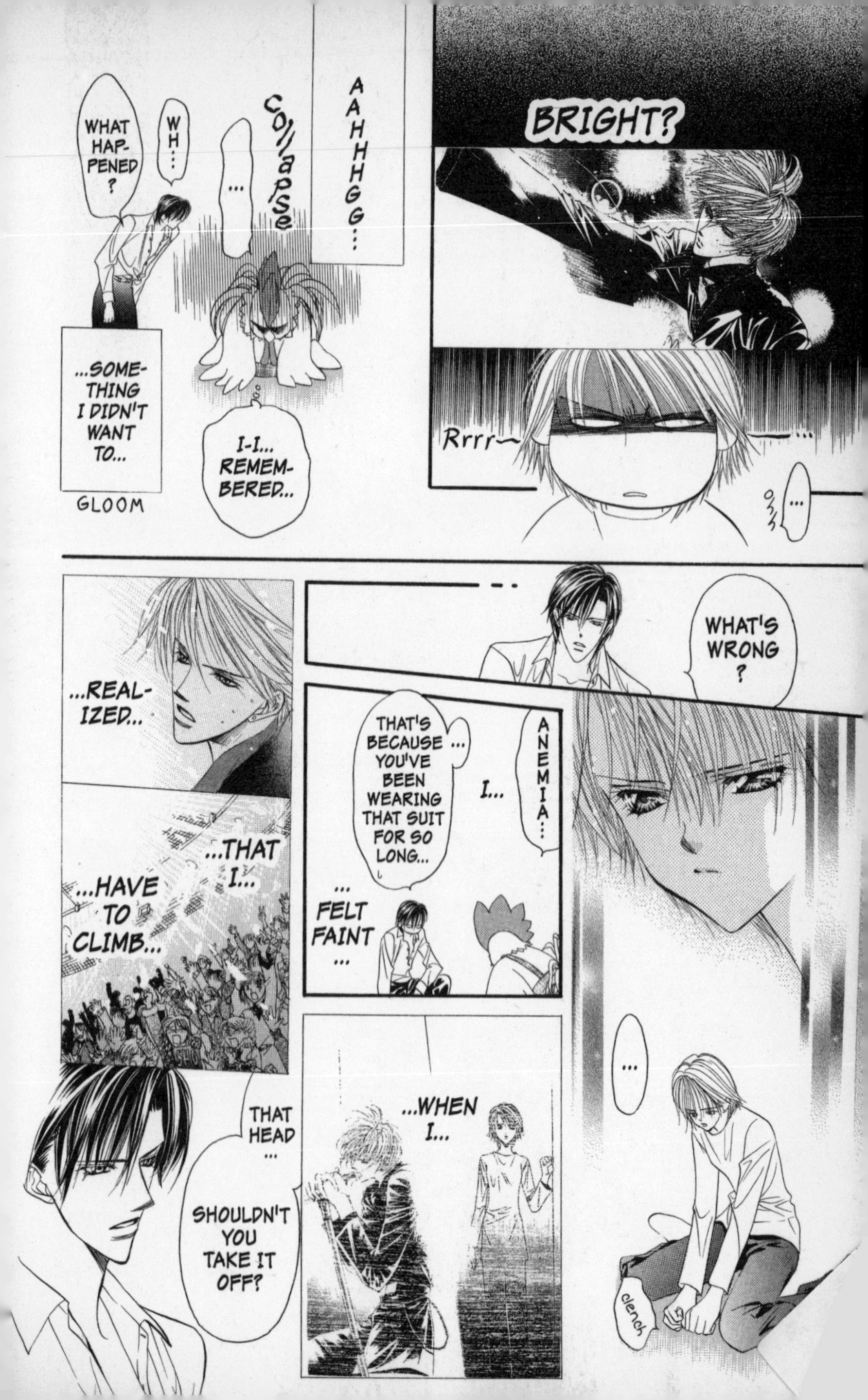
BRIGHT?
Rrrr~
...
AAHHHGG...
Collapse
...
WH...
WHAT HAPPENED?
...SOMETHING I DIDN'T WANT TO...
I-I... REMEMBERED...
GLOOM
WHAT'S WRONG?
ANEMIA...
I...
THAT'S BECAUSE YOU'VE BEEN WEARING THAT SUIT FOR SO LONG...
...FELT FAINT...
...REALIZED...
...THAT I...
...HAVE TO CLIMB...
...
clench
...WHEN I...
THAT HEAD...
SHOULDN'T YOU TAKE IT OFF?

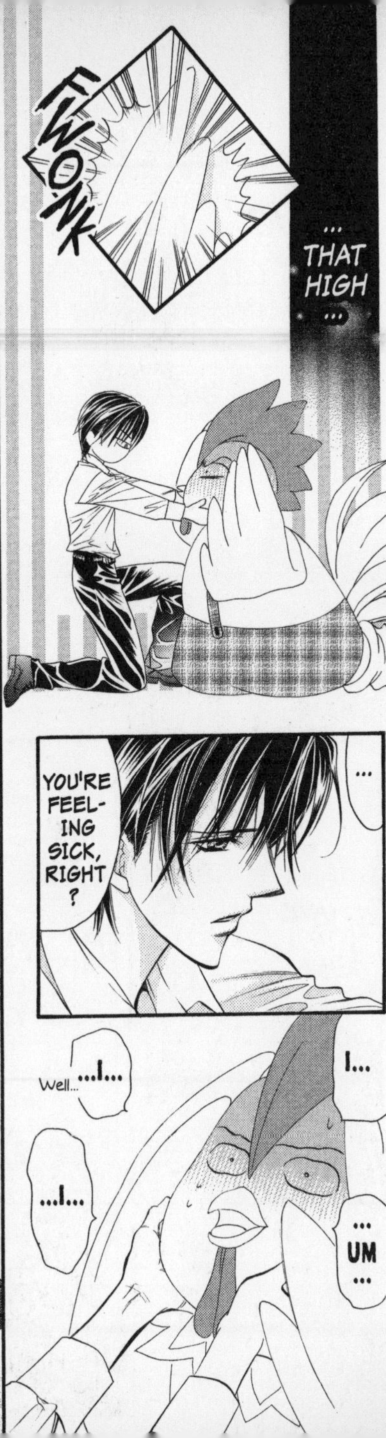
...THAT HIGH...
FWONK
...
YOU'RE FEELING SICK, RIGHT?
I...
Well...
...I...
...UM...
...I...

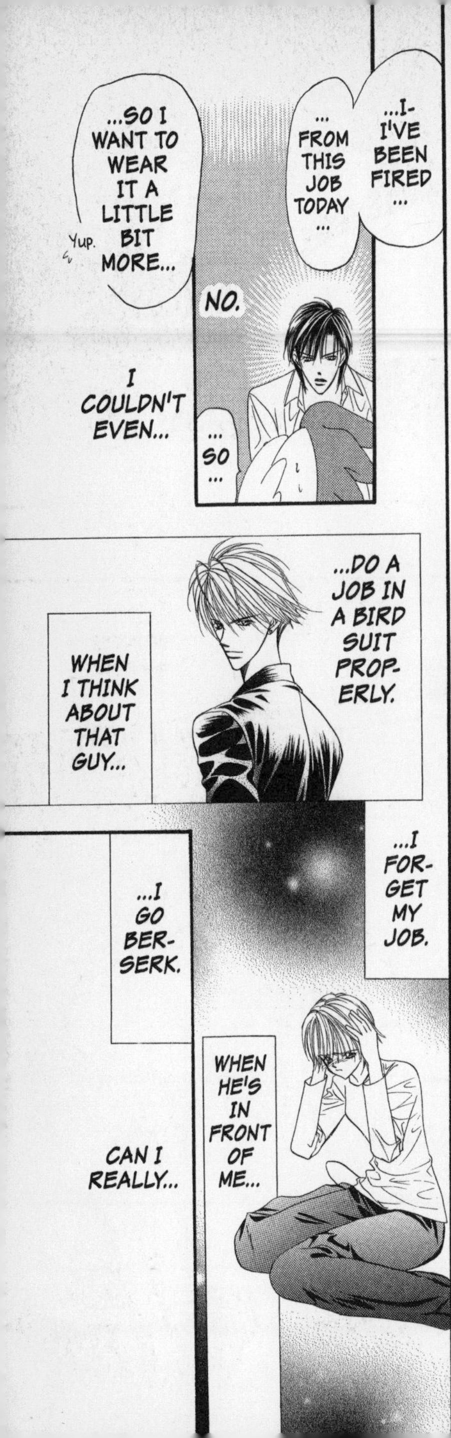
...I- I'VE BEEN FIRED...
...FROM THIS JOB TODAY...
NO.
...SO...
...SO I WANT TO WEAR IT A LITTLE BIT MORE...
Yup.
I COULDN'T EVEN...
...DO A JOB IN A BIRD SUIT PROPERLY.
WHEN I THINK ABOUT THAT GUY...
...I FORGET MY JOB.
...I GO BERSERK.
WHEN HE'S IN FRONT OF ME...
CAN I REALLY...

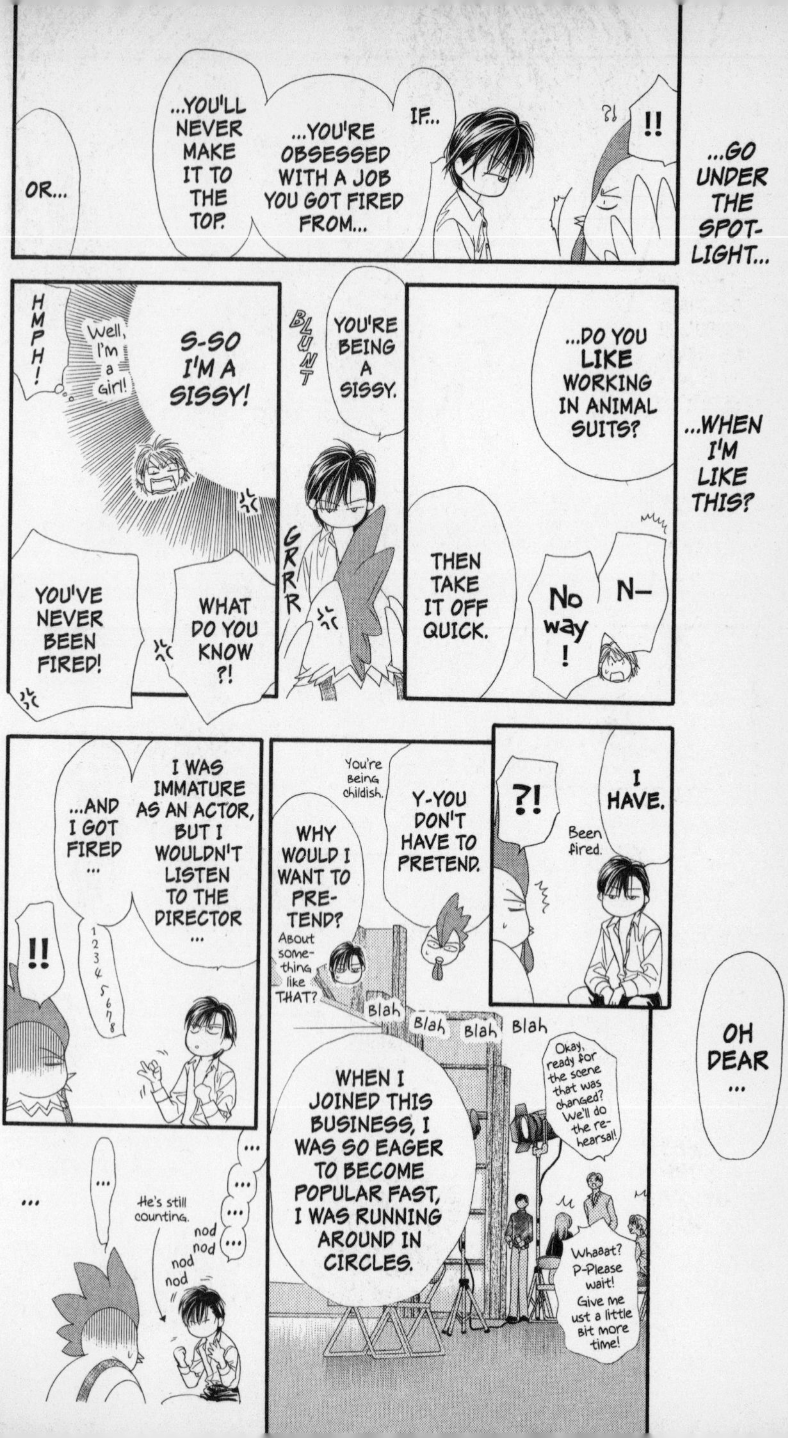
!!
?!
IF...
...YOU'RE OBSESSED WITH A JOB YOU GOT FIRED FROM...
...YOU'LL NEVER MAKE IT TO THE TOP.
OR...
...GO UNDER THE SPOTLIGHT...
...WHEN I'M LIKE THIS?
...DO YOU LIKE WORKING IN ANIMAL SUITS?
N—
No way!
THEN TAKE IT OFF QUICK.
BLUNT
YOU'RE BEING A SISSY.
S-SO I'M A SISSY!
Well, I'm a Girl!
HMPH!
GRRR
WHAT DO YOU KNOW?!
YOU'VE NEVER BEEN FIRED!
I HAVE.
?!
Been fired.
Y-YOU DON'T HAVE TO PRETEND.
You're being childish.
WHY WOULD I WANT TO PRETEND?
About something like THAT?
I WAS IMMATURE AS AN ACTOR, BUT I WOULDN'T LISTEN TO THE DIRECTOR...
...AND I GOT FIRED...
!!
1 2 3 4 5 6 7 8
OH DEAR...
Okay, ready for the scene that was changed? We'll do the rehearsal!
Whaaat? P-Please wait! Give me ust a little bit more time!
Blah Blah Blah Blah
WHEN I JOINED THIS BUSINESS, I WAS SO EAGER TO BECOME POPULAR FAST, I WAS RUNNING AROUND IN CIRCLES.
...
...
...
...
...
He's still counting.
nod nod nod nod
...

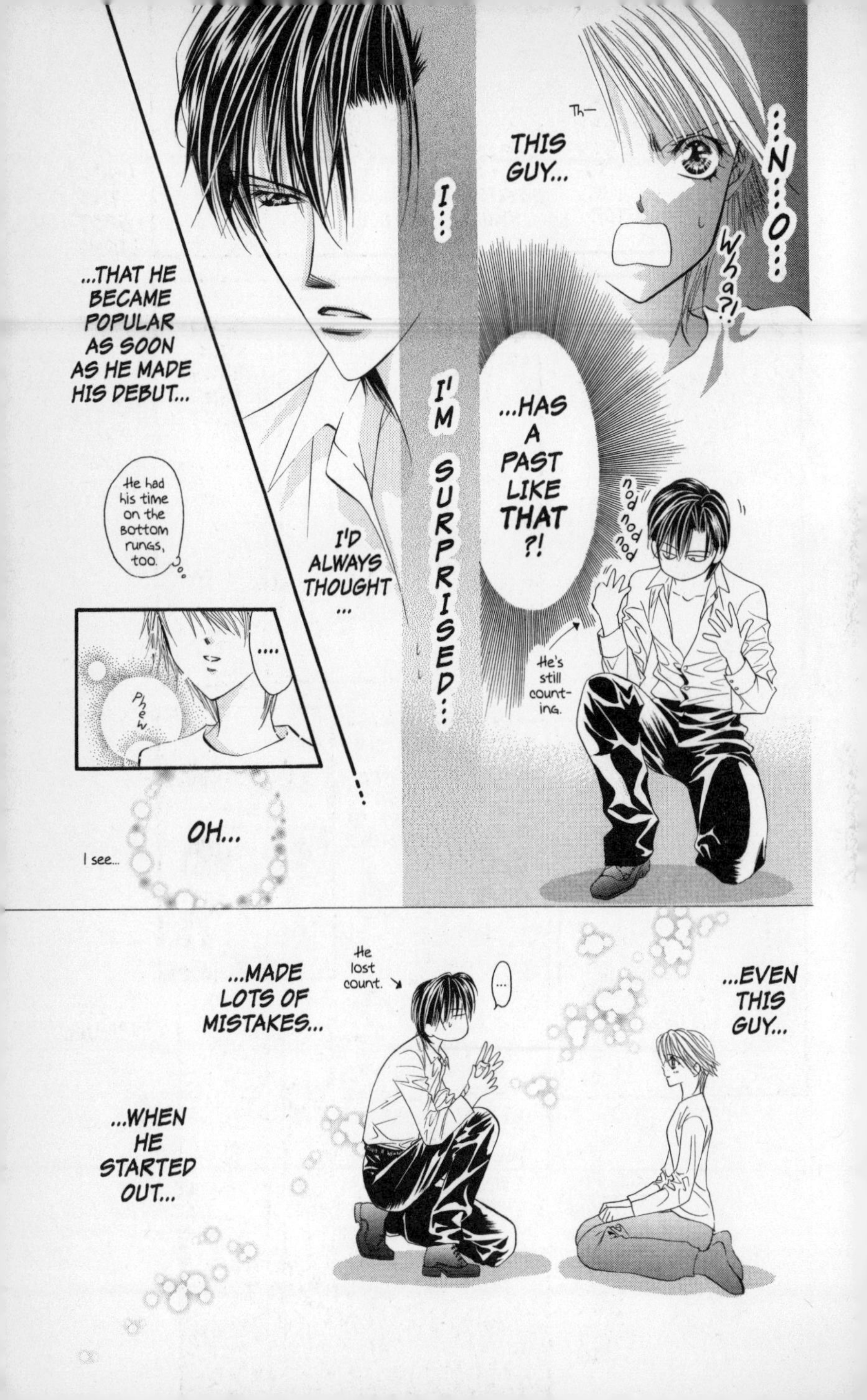
...N...O...
Wha?!
Th—
THIS GUY...
...HAS A PAST LIKE THAT?!
pon pon pon
He's still counting.
I...
I'M SURPRISED...
I'D ALWAYS THOUGHT...
...THAT HE BECAME POPULAR AS SOON AS HE MADE HIS DEBUT...
He had his time on the bottom rungs, too.
....
Phew
...
OH...
I see...
...EVEN THIS GUY...
...
He lost count.
...MADE LOTS OF MISTAKES...
...WHEN HE STARTED OUT...

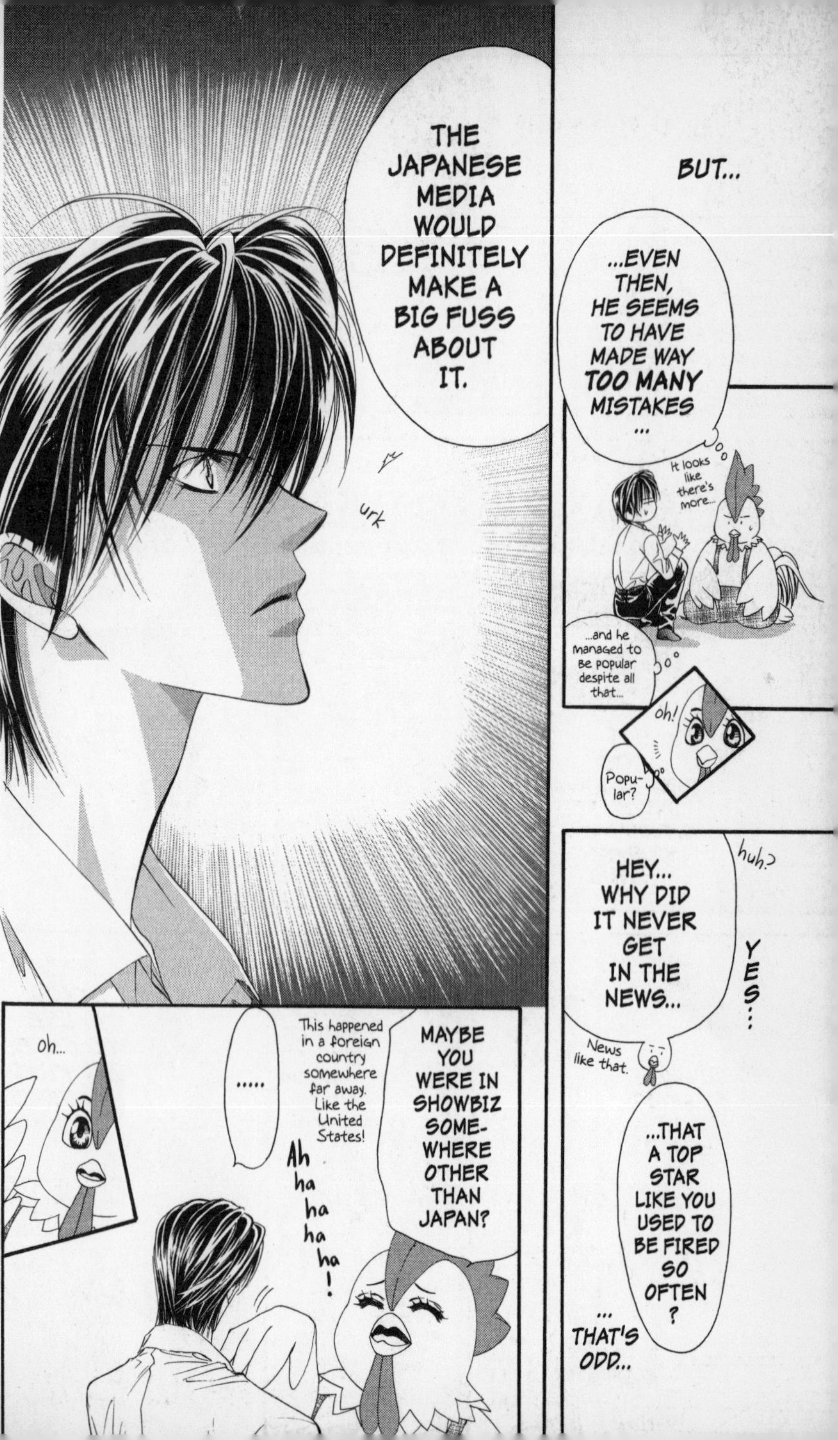
BUT...
...EVEN THEN, HE SEEMS TO HAVE MADE WAY TOO MANY MISTAKES...
It looks like there's more...
...and he managed to be popular despite all that...
oh!
Popu-lar?
HEY... WHY DID IT NEVER GET IN THE NEWS...
huh?
YES...
News like that.
...THAT A TOP STAR LIKE YOU USED TO BE FIRED SO OFTEN?
...THAT'S ODD...
THE JAPANESE MEDIA WOULD DEFINITELY MAKE A BIG FUSS ABOUT IT.
urk
MAYBE YOU WERE IN SHOWBIZ SOMEWHERE OTHER THAN JAPAN?
This happened in a foreign country somewhere far away. Like the United States!
Ah ha ha ha ha!
.....
oh...

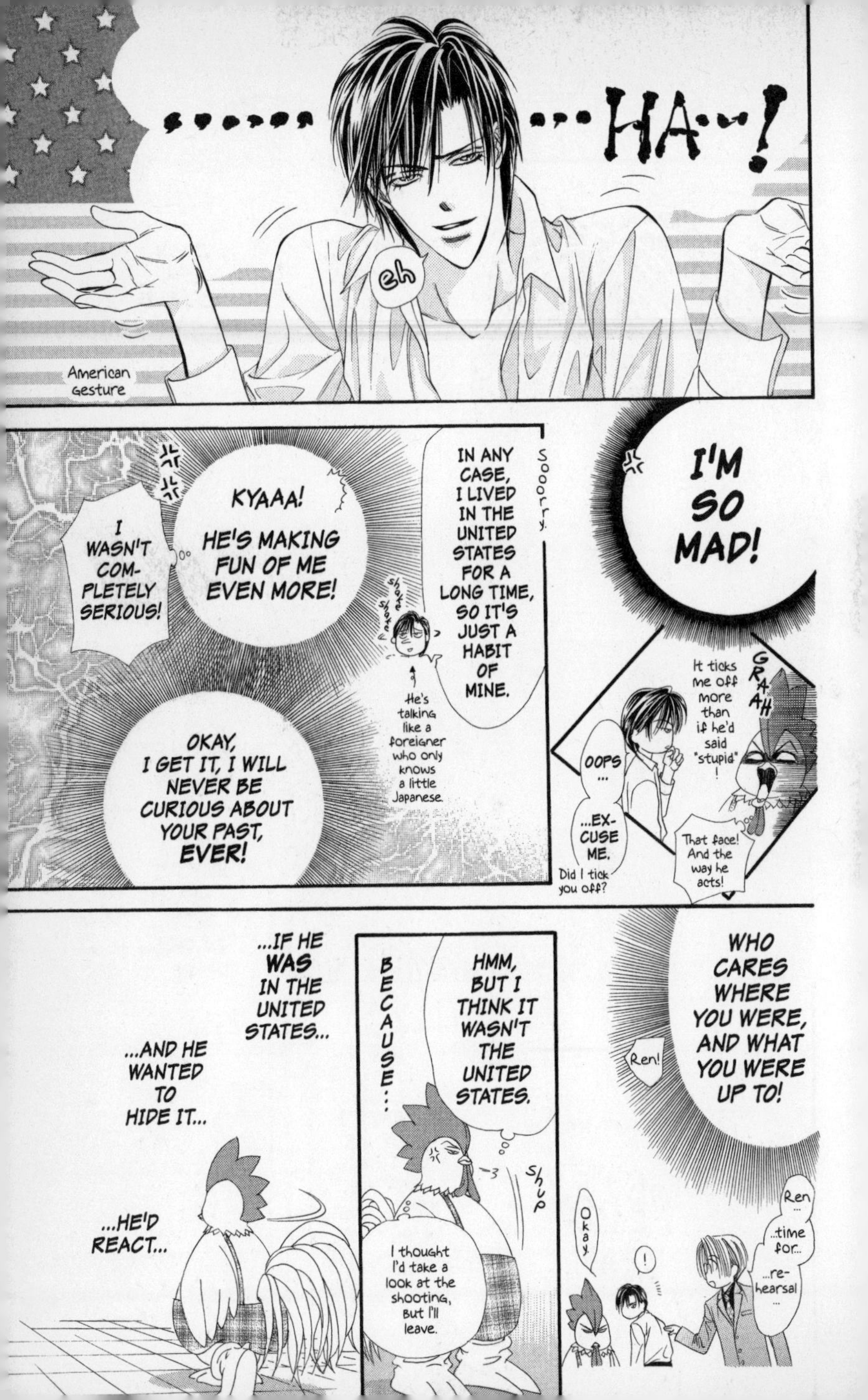
……………HA~!
eh
American Gesture
I'M SO MAD!
GRAAH
It ticks me off more than if he'd said "stupid"!
That face! And the way he acts!
OOPS…
…EXCUSE ME.
Did I tick you off?
Sooorry.
IN ANY CASE, I LIVED IN THE UNITED STATES FOR A LONG TIME, SO IT'S JUST A HABIT OF MINE.
shake shake
He's talking like a foreigner who only knows a little Japanese.
KYAAA! HE'S MAKING FUN OF ME EVEN MORE!
I WASN'T COMPLETELY SERIOUS!
OKAY, I GET IT, I WILL NEVER BE CURIOUS ABOUT YOUR PAST, EVER!
WHO CARES WHERE YOU WERE, AND WHAT YOU WERE UP TO!
Ren!
Ren… …time for… …rehearsal…
!
Okay.
BECAUSE…
HMM, BUT I THINK IT WASN'T THE UNITED STATES.
Shup
I thought I'd take a look at the shooting, but I'll leave.
…IF HE WAS IN THE UNITED STATES…
…AND HE WANTED TO HIDE IT…
…HE'D REACT…

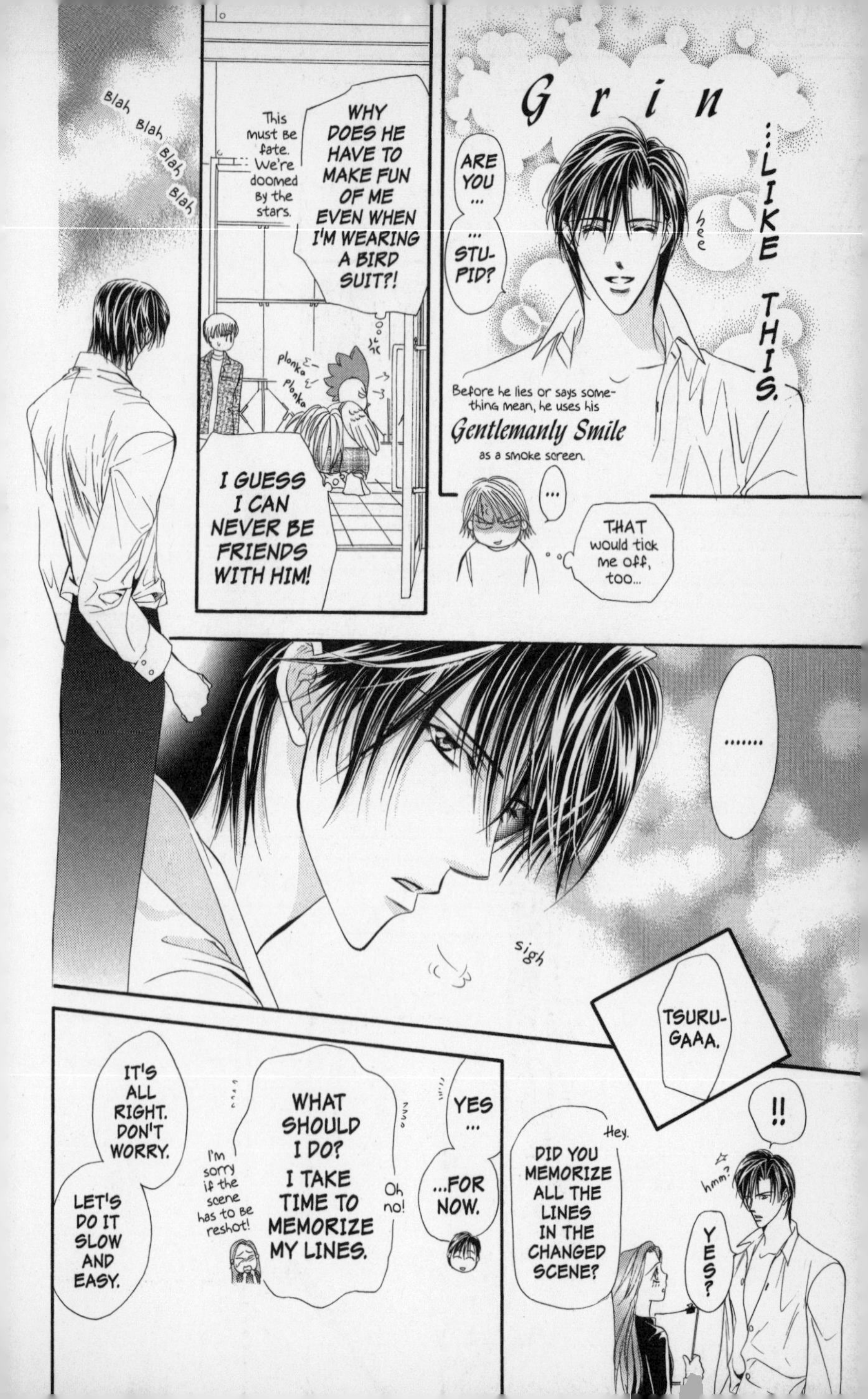
Grin
...LIKE THIS.
hee
ARE YOU...
...STUPID?
Before he lies or says something mean, he uses his Gentlemanly Smile as a smoke screen.
...
THAT would tick me off, too...
WHY DOES HE HAVE TO MAKE FUN OF ME EVEN WHEN I'M WEARING A BIRD SUIT?!
This must be fate. We're doomed by the stars.
plonka plonka
I GUESS I CAN NEVER BE FRIENDS WITH HIM!
Blah Blah Blah Blah
....
sigh
TSURU-GAAA.
!!
hmm?
YES?
Hey.
DID YOU MEMORIZE ALL THE LINES IN THE CHANGED SCENE?
YES...
...FOR NOW.
Oh no!
WHAT SHOULD I DO? I TAKE TIME TO MEMORIZE MY LINES.
I'm sorry if the scene has to be reshot!
IT'S ALL RIGHT. DON'T WORRY.
LET'S DO IT SLOW AND EASY.

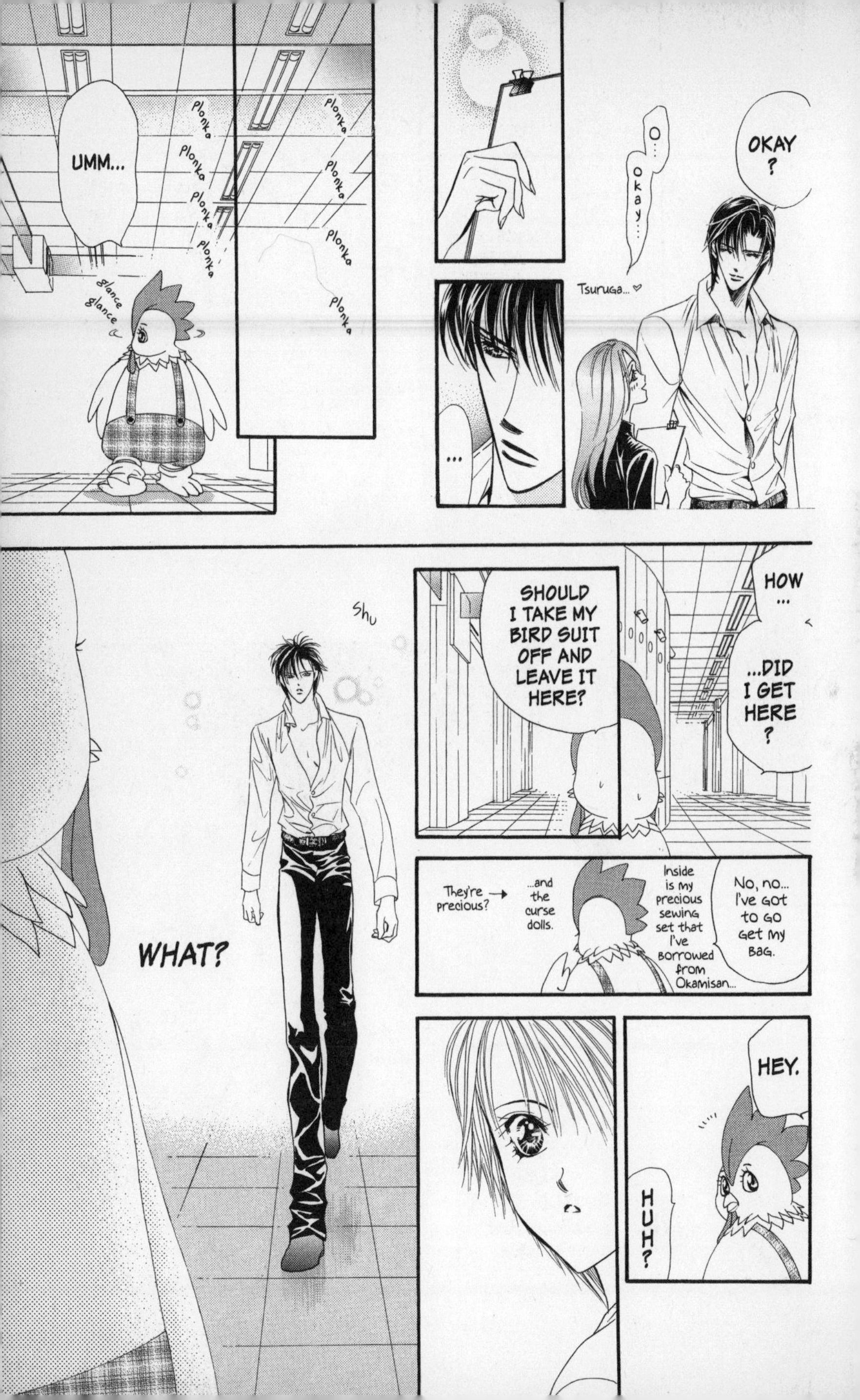
OKAY?
O... Okay...
Tsuruga...♡
...
Plonka Plonka Plonka Plonka Plonka Plonka Plonka Plonka
UMM...
glance glance
HOW...
...DID I GET HERE?
SHOULD I TAKE MY BIRD SUIT OFF AND LEAVE IT HERE?
No, no... I've got to go get my bag.
Inside is my precious sewing set that I've borrowed from Okamisan...
...and the curse dolls.
They're precious?
HEY.
HUH?
Shu
WHAT?

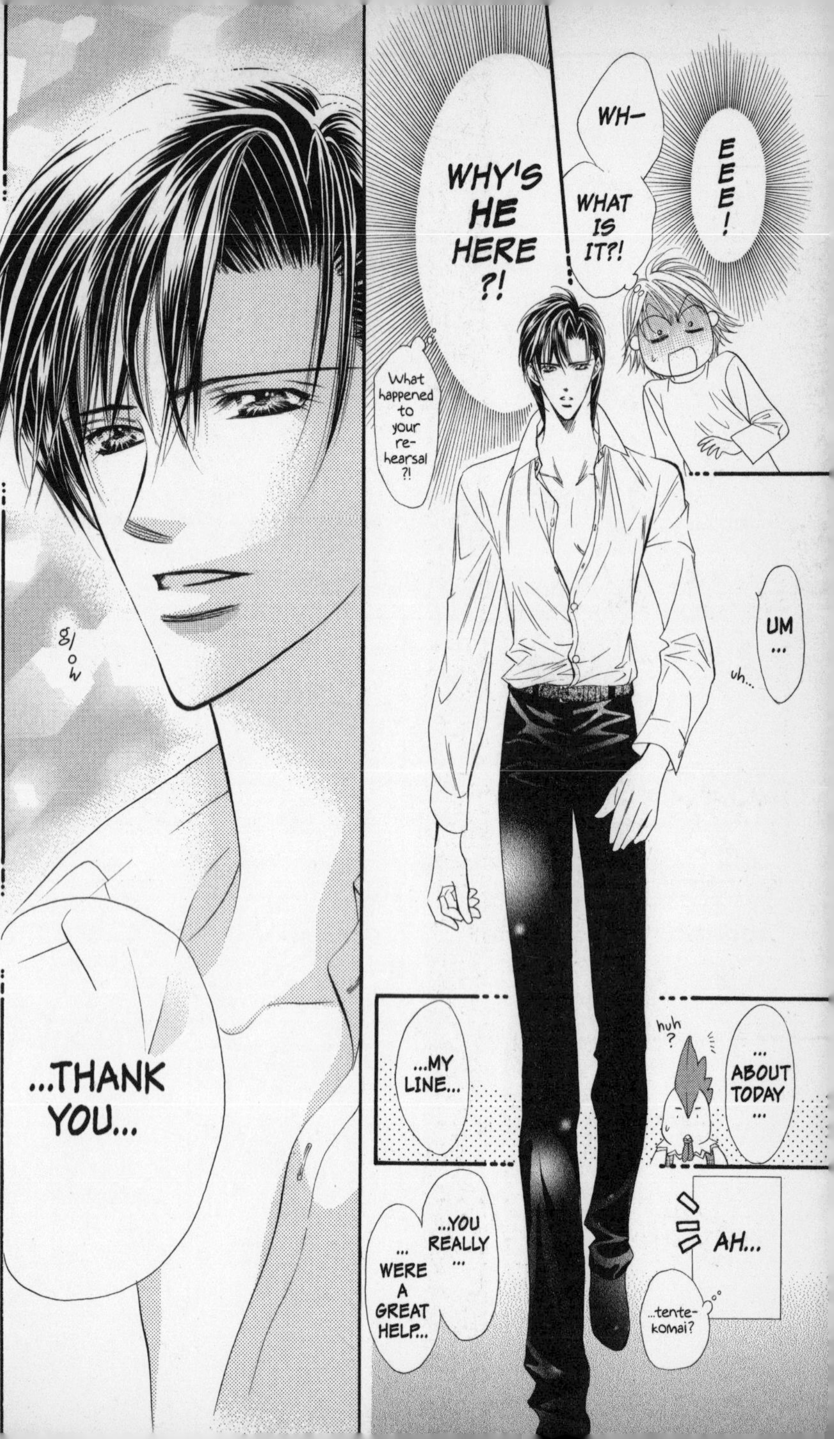
EEE!
WH—
WHAT IS IT?!
WHY'S HE HERE ?!
What happened to your re-hearsal ?!
UM ...
uh...
... ABOUT TODAY ...
huh ?
...MY LINE...
AH...
...tente-komai?
...YOU REALLY ...
... WERE A GREAT HELP...
...THANK YOU...
glow

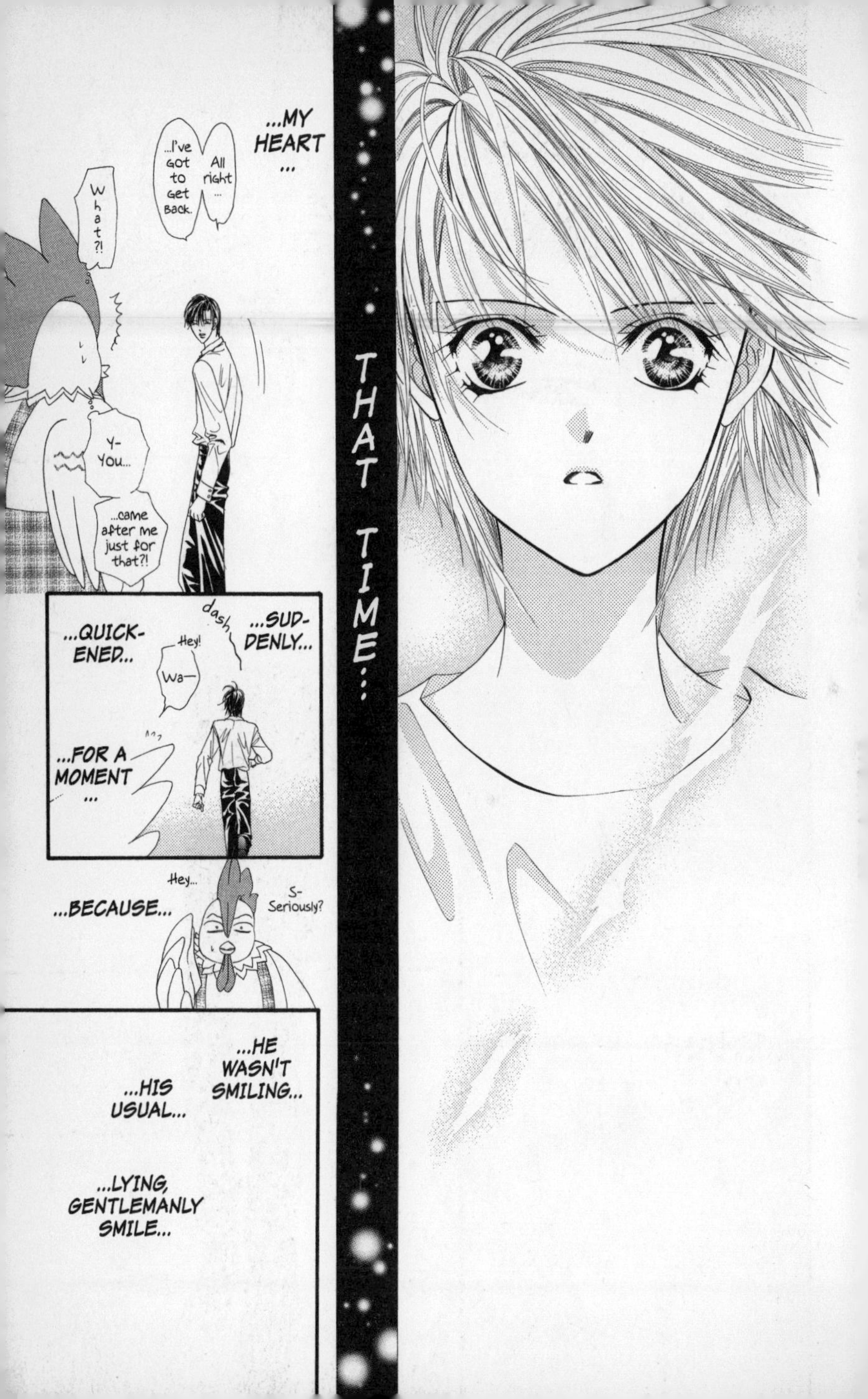
THAT TIME...
...MY HEART ...
All right ...
...I've got to get back.
What?!
Y-You...
...came after me just for that?!
...SUD-DENLY...
dash
Hey!
Wa—
...QUICK-ENED...
...FOR A MOMENT ...
S-Seriously?
Hey...
...BECAUSE...
...HE WASN'T SMILING...
...HIS USUAL...
...LYING, GENTLEMANLY SMILE...

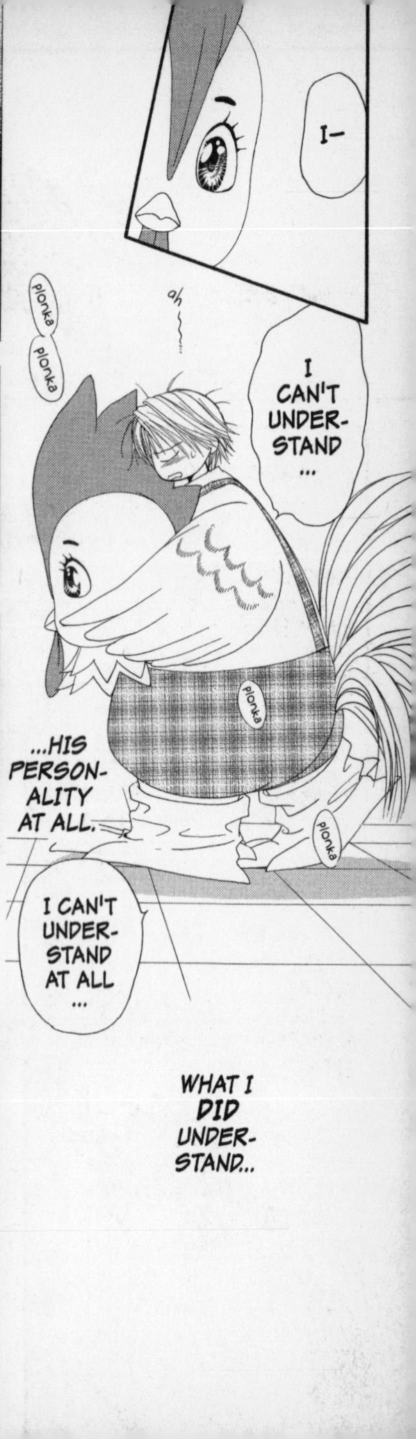
I–
ah
plonka
plonka
I CAN'T UNDERSTAND ...
plonka
...HIS PERSONALITY AT ALL.
plonka
I CAN'T UNDERSTAND AT ALL ...
WHAT I DID UNDERSTAND...

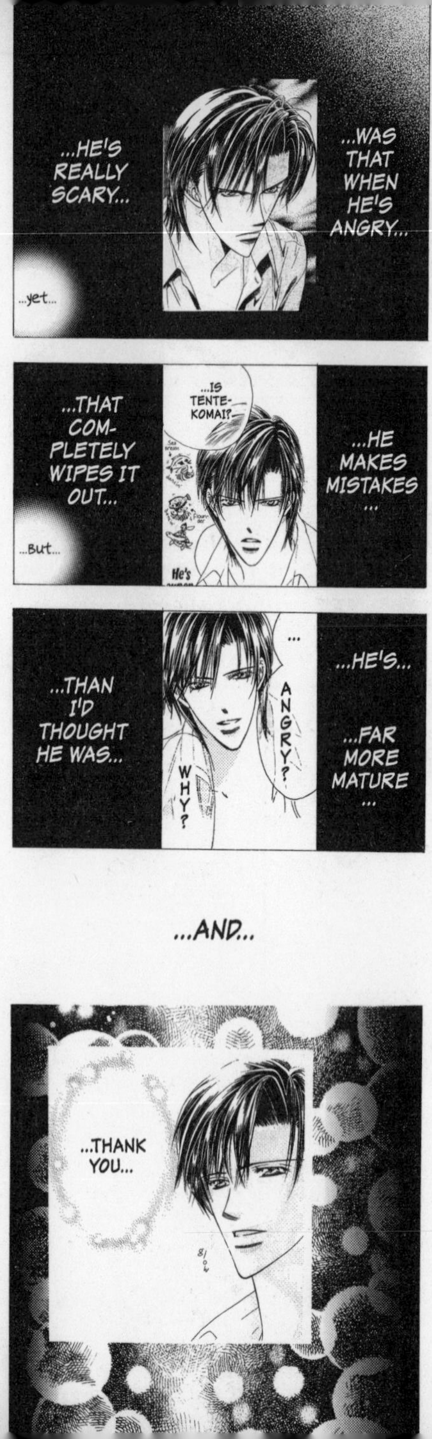
...WAS THAT WHEN HE'S ANGRY...
...HE'S REALLY SCARY...
...yet...
...HE MAKES MISTAKES ...
...IS TENTE-KOMAI?
...THAT COMPLETELY WIPES IT OUT...
...but...
...HE'S...
...FAR MORE MATURE ...
...
ANGRY? WHY?
...THAN I'D THOUGHT HE WAS...
...AND...
...THANK YOU...
glow

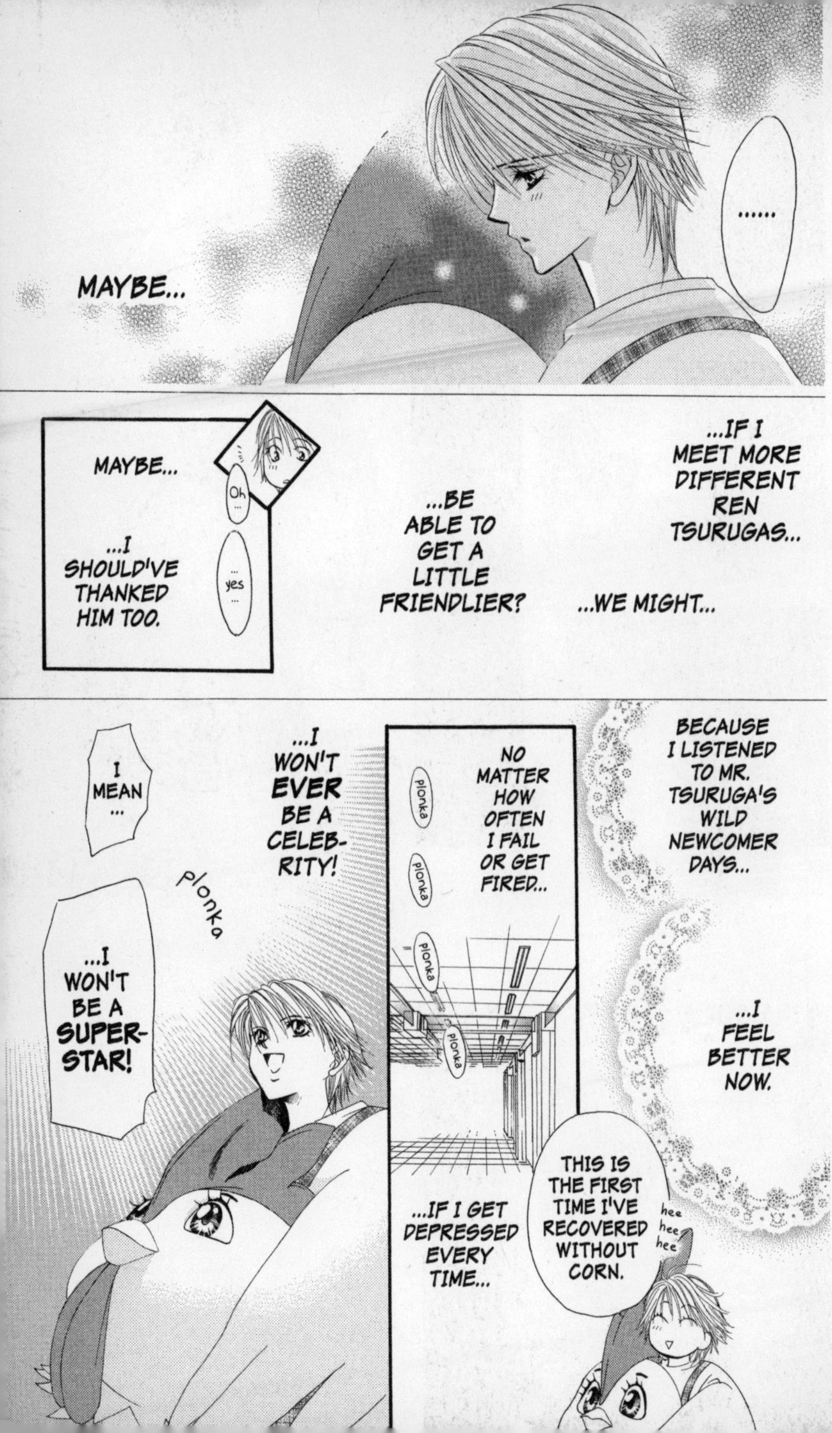
......
MAYBE...
...IF I MEET MORE DIFFERENT REN TSURUGAS...
...WE MIGHT...
...BE ABLE TO GET A LITTLE FRIENDLIER?
Oh...
...yes...
MAYBE...
...I SHOULD'VE THANKED HIM TOO.
BECAUSE I LISTENED TO MR. TSURUGA'S WILD NEWCOMER DAYS...
...I FEEL BETTER NOW.
THIS IS THE FIRST TIME I'VE RECOVERED WITHOUT CORN.
hee hee hee
NO MATTER HOW OFTEN I FAIL OR GET FIRED...
plonka
plonka
plonka
plonka
...IF I GET DEPRESSED EVERY TIME...
...I WON'T EVER BE A CELEBRITY!
I MEAN...
plonka
...I WON'T BE A SUPERSTAR!

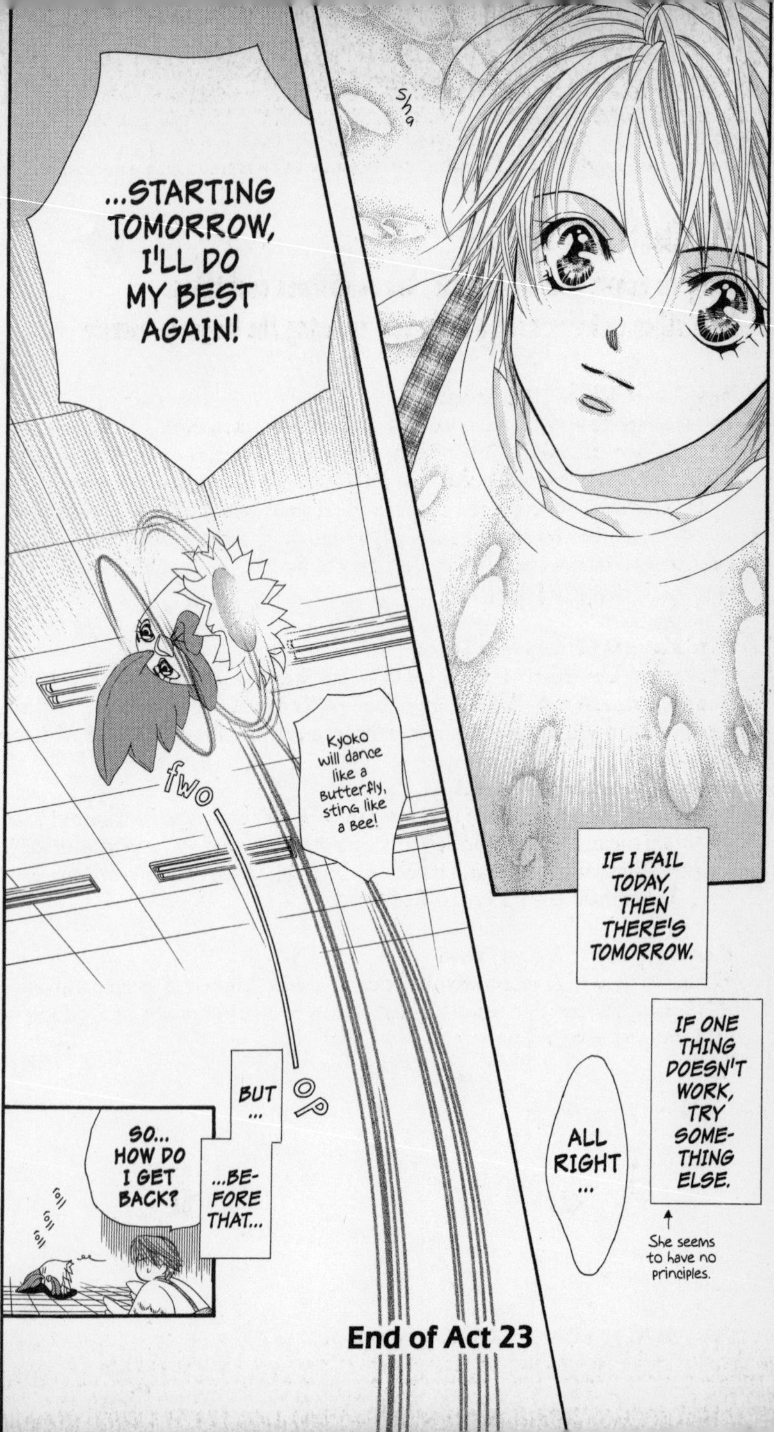
Sha
IF I FAIL TODAY, THEN THERE'S TOMORROW.
IF ONE THING DOESN'T WORK, TRY SOME-THING ELSE.
She seems to have no principles.
ALL RIGHT...
...STARTING TOMORROW, I'LL DO MY BEST AGAIN!
Kyoko will dance like a Butterfly, sting like a Bee!
fwo
op
BUT...
...BE-FORE THAT...
SO... HOW DO I GET BACK?
roll roll roll
End of Act 23

Skip-Beat! End Notes

Everyone knows how to be a fan, but sometimes cool things from other cultures need a little help crossing the language barrier.

Page 78-79: Ichiri. Niri. Shichiri...
This is a Japanese vocal exercise that stresses pronunciation. The translation is "One *ri*. Two *ri*. Seven *ri*. I barely managed to go seven *ri* in one day. You go by yourself to say all that politely. A fresh morning. It's a warm morning. A flower bloomed. A bright red rose bloomed suddenly. It is a gorgeous flower. The strange one who doesn't suspect the one he should suspect, but suspects the one who is innocent. I think I will try to figure out what he's really thinking. I'm thinking of killing that guy!"

Page 81, panel 2: Wisdom Sutras
Also called The Heart of the Great Wisdom Sutra, or *Hannya Shingyo*. It is a summary or essential distillation of the longer Great Wisdom Sutra, and explains the Buddhist concept of *ku*, or emptiness. It is the shortest of all Sutras.

Page 83, sidebar: Kinseiseki
In the Japanese spelling, the character for *Kin* means "violet" and the character for *sei* means "blue." Cordierite is a mineral popular with collectors for its unusual blue-violet color and its color-changing ability (known as *pleocroism*). The gemstone variety is called *iolite*.

Page 86, panel 3: Kanashibari
Kanae's typical response to Kyoko's demons. Also known as sleep paralysis, it is believed to happen when a ghost sits on your chest as you are waking up and tries to strangle you.

Page 95, panel 3: Yappa Kimagure Rock
The name of this variety show means "It's Gotta Be Whimsical Rock."

Page 106, panel 5: Topeggs
The original Japanese is *netamago,* or *Neta Tamago. Neta* means "topic" and *tamago* means "egg."

Page 110, panel 4: Shotaro
The kanji for *Sho* means "pine" and *taro* is a traditional name for a firstborn son. This is a very traditional, staid, uncool name. The kanji Sho uses for his stage name means "value," which better fits the way he thinks about himself.

Page 141, sidebar: Manma-chan
The dog mascot of the talk show "Sanma no Manma" by comedian Sanma Akashiya. The show is especially popular in Osaka.

Page 171, panel 5: Tentekomai
The kanji used for *mai* in this word could be interpreted as "dance," which is what has confused Ren.

Page 171, sidebar: Harisen
The big folded fan. It makes a lot of noise when you hit someone with it, but doesn't hurt much at all. It's used in Kansai comedy pair routines. The straight man (*tsukkomi*) uses it to punctuate the punch line.

Page 171, sidebar: Midori
The Japanese word for weathercock is *kazamidori.*

Yoshiki Nakamura is originally from Tokushima prefecture. She started drawing manga in elementary school, which eventually led to her 1993 debut of *Yume de Au yori Suteki* (Better than Seeing in a Dream) in *Hana to Yume* magazine. Her other works include the basketball series *Saint Love, MVP wa Yuzurenai* (Can't Give Up MVP), *Blue Wars,* and *Tokyo Crazy Paradise,* a series about a female bodyguard in 2020 Tokyo.

SKIP·BEAT!

Vol. 4

The Shojo Beat Manga Edition

STORY AND ART BY YOSHIKI NAKAMURA

English Translation & Adaptation/Tomo Kimura
Touch-up Art & Lettering/Sabrina Heep
Design/Yukiko Whitley
Editor/Pancha Diaz

VP, Production/Alvin Lu
VP, Publishing Licensing/Rika Inouye
VP, Sales & Product Marketing/Gonzalo Ferreyra
VP, Creative/Linda Espinosa
Publisher/Hyoe Narita

Printed in Canada

Published by VIZ Media, LLC
P.O. Box 77010
San Francisco, CA 94107

store.viz.com

Shojo Beat Manga Edition
10 9 8 7 6 5 4 3
First printing, January 2007
Third printing, February 2009

RATED T FOR TEEN

PARENTAL ADVISORY
SKIP·BEAT! is rated T for Teen and is recommended for ages 13 and up. This volume contains suggestive themes.

ratings.viz.com

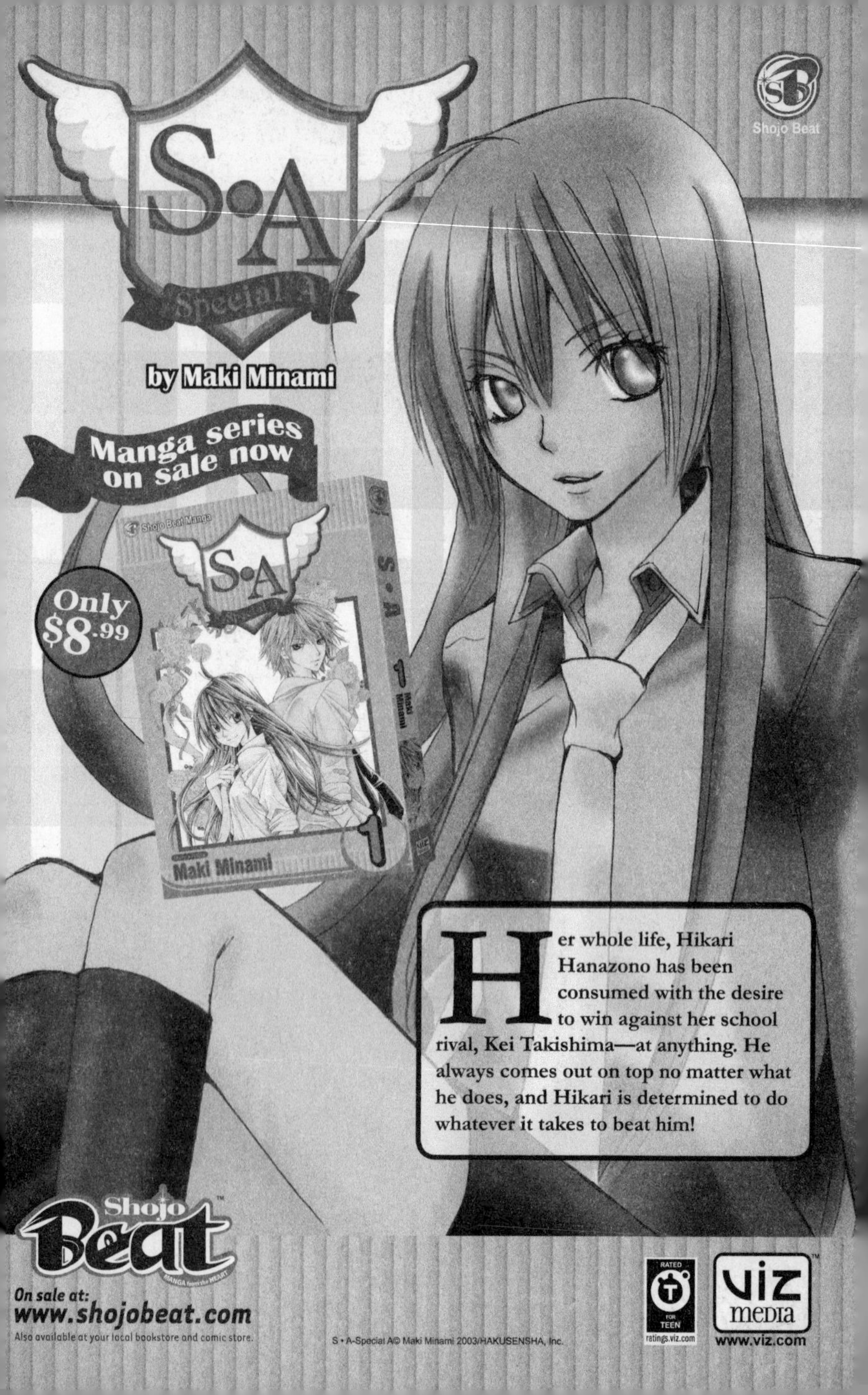
S•A
Special A
by Maki Minami
Shojo Beat
Manga series on sale now
Only $8.99
Shojo Beat Manga
S•A
Maki Minami
Her whole life, Hikari Hanazono has been consumed with the desire to win against her school rival, Kei Takishima—at anything. He always comes out on top no matter what he does, and Hikari is determined to do whatever it takes to beat him!
Shojo Beat
MANGA from the HEART
On sale at:
www.shojobeat.com
Also available at your local bookstore and comic store.
S • A-Special A© Maki Minami 2003/HAKUSENSHA, Inc.
RATED T FOR TEEN
ratings.viz.com
VIZ media
www.viz.com

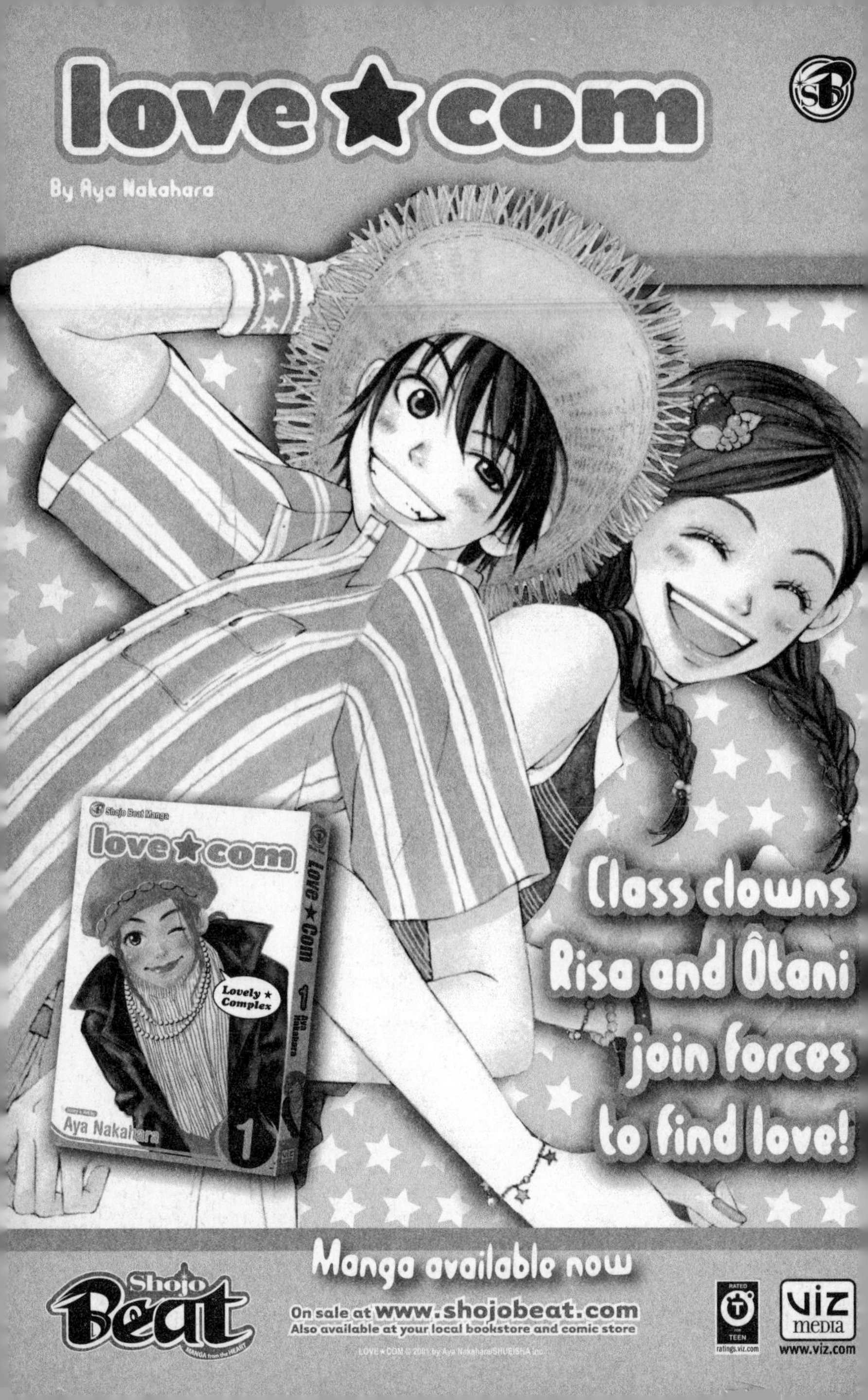

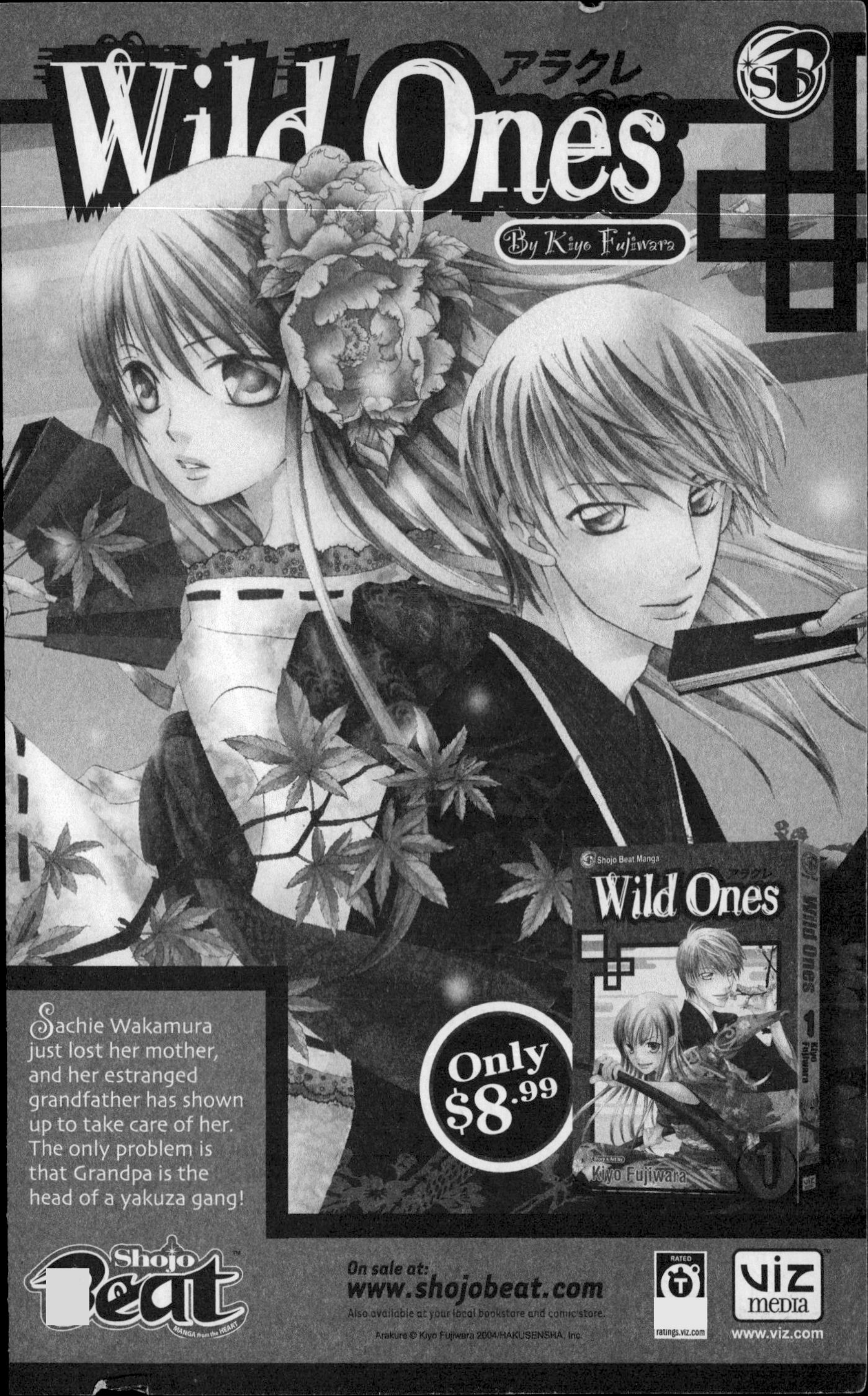

Wild Ones
アラクレ
By Kiyo Fujiwara
Shojo Beat Manga
Wild Ones
Kiyo Fujiwara
Sachie Wakamura just lost her mother, and her estranged grandfather has shown up to take care of her. The only problem is that Grandpa is the head of a yakuza gang!
Only $8.99
Shojo Beat
MANGA from the HEART
On sale at:
www.shojobeat.com
Also available at your local bookstore and comic store.
Arakure © Kiyo Fujiwara 2004/HAKUSENSHA, Inc.
RATED T
ratings.viz.com
viz media
www.viz.com

Tell us what about Shojo Beat Manga!

Our survey is now available online. Go to:

shojobeat.com/mangasurvey

Help us make our product offerings better!